Beyond Sovereignty

Issues for a Global Agenda

Fourth Edition

Maryann Cusimano Love

The Catholic University of America

WADSWORTH
CENGAGE Learning™

Australia • Brazil • Canada • Mexico • Singapore • Spain • United Kingdom • United States

WADSWORTH
CENGAGE Learning™

Beyond Sovereignty: Issues for a Global Agenda, Fourth Edition
Maryann Cusimano Love

Senior Publisher: Suzanne Jeans

Executive Editor: Carolyn Merrill

Assistant Editor: Katherine Hayes

Editorial Assistant: Angela Hodge

Senior Marketing Manager: Amy Whitaker

Marketing Coordinator: Josh Hendrick

Marketing Communications Manager: Heather Baxley

Art Director: Linda Helcher

Print Buyer: Paula Vang

Senior Rights Acquisition Account Manager, Text: Katie Huha

Production Service: Pre-PressPMG, Philominal Bosco

Text Designer: Paul Lacy

Senior Photo Editor: Jennifer Meyer Dare

Cover Designer: Grannan Graphic Design, Ltd.

Cover Image: Tonya Constantine/ Photographers Choice/©Getty Images

Compositor: Pre-PressPMG

For product information and technology assistance, contact us at **Cengage Learning Customer & Sales Support, 1-800-354-9706**

For permission to use material from this text or product, submit all requests online at **www.cengage.com/permissions.** Further permissions questions can be emailed to **permissionrequest@cengage.com.**

Library of Congress Control Number: 2009938857

ISBN-13: 978-0-495-79323-6

ISBN-10: 0-495-79323-X

Wadsworth
20 Channel Center Street
Boston, MA 02210
USA

Cengage Learning is a leading provider of customized learning solutions with office locations around the globe, including Singapore, the United Kingdom, Australia, Mexico, Brazil and Japan. Locate your local office at **international.cengage.com/region**

Cengage Learning products are represented in Canada by Nelson Education, Ltd.

For your course and learning solutions, visit **www.cengage.com.**

Purchase any of our products at your local college store or at our preferred online store **www.ichapters.com.**

Printed in the United States of America
1 2 3 4 5 6 7 13 12 11 10 09

In memory of Francis Cusimano, S.J., who taught me Africa was only as far away as your uncle's smile, and that we can imagine and create a better globalization for our future.

Contents

About the Editor and Primary Author

MARYANN CUSIMANO LOVE is an associate professor of politics at the Catholic University of America in Washington, D.C. She teaches graduate and undergraduate courses on International Relations and U.S. foreign policy at both Catholic University and the Pentagon. She serves on the U.S. Catholic Bishops' International Justice and Peace Committee, where she advises the bishops on international affairs and U.S. foreign policy, and engages in advocacy with the U.S. government. She serves on the Advisory Board of the Catholic Peacebuilding Network with Notre Dame University's Kroc Institute of Peace, a network of academics and practitioners from around the world that seeks to enhance the study and practice of peacebuilding. She serves on the board and Communications Committee of Jesuit Refugee Services, an international refugee relief and advocacy group active in over 50 countries, with a mission to accompany, serve, and defend the rights of refugees and forcibly displaced people. She is a columnist for *America* magazine, "serves as a Fellow at the U.S. Commission on International Religious Freedom," and has served as a member of the Council on Foreign Relations project on homeland security, and as a participant in the Religion and Foreign Policy Initiative. She lives on the Chesapeake Bay outside of Washington, D.C., with her husband Richard and three young children, Maria, Ricky, and Ava, who inspire her *New York Times* best-selling children's books, *You Are My I Love You, You Are My Miracle, You Are My Wish,* and *Sleep, Baby, Sleep.* She holds a B.A. degree from St. Joseph's University in Philadelphia, an M.A. degree from the University of Texas, and a Ph.D. from Johns Hopkins University.

About the Contributors

"CHRISTOPHER A. CORPORA is the President and CEO of Capitol Innovation and Strategy Solutions, LLC, serving as a Contract Senior Advisor to the Federal Bureau of Investigations. He is an Adjunct Professor at George Mason University's School of Public Policy. Dr. Corpora is a nontraditional security threats specialist with a focus on transnational organized crime and its role in the broader global security context, with nearly 20 years of military, civilian government and private sector experience. Dr. Corpora has published and presented dozens of scholarly essays, articles and book chapters and is an active Senior Fellow in several research and policy institutes, focused on international and homeland security threats. He received his Ph.D. from American University's School of International Service and is currently working on a monograph—addressing local perceptions of and attitudes toward organized crime and corruption in Bosnia and Herzegovina and Afghanistan. He and his spouse are the proud parents of three wonderfully talented daughters and live in Northern Virginia.

MARIA GREEN COWLES is an Associate Dean for Academic Affairs at the School of International Service at American University. She is coeditor of *Transforming Europe: Europeanization and Domestic Change, Developments in the European Union 2,* and *The State of the European Union,* Vol. 5. She is the author of numerous articles and book chapters on the European Union and the influence of transnational and global business organizations in global regulatory and governance matters. She is a former vice chair of the European Union Studies Association.

MARTHA CRENSHAW is a senior fellow at Stanford University's Center for International Security and Cooperation and Freeman Spogli Institute for International Studies, and a professor of political science. She was the Colin and Nancy Campbell Professor in Global Issues and Democratic Thought and Professor of Government at Wesleyan University, where she taught international politics and foreign policy, including a course on terrorism, from 1974–2007. Her research has produced many publications, beginning in 1972 with an article titled "The Concept of Revolutionary Terrorism" in the *Journal of Conflict Resolution.* She is the author of *Revolutionary Terrorism: The FLN in Algeria, 1954–1962* as well as *Terrorism and International Cooperation,* and she edited the books *Terrorism, Legitimacy, and Power* and *Terrorism in Context.* Her current research focuses on innovation in terrorist campaigns, the distinction between "old" and "new" terrorism, why the United States is the target of terrorism, and the effectiveness of counterterrorism policies.

TENG MARGARET FU serves as program associate at the Maureen and Mike Mansfield Foundation where she manages its China program development and implementation. She has worked for the International Office of AARP, Campaign Finance Institute, and Greenpeace USA in Washington, D.C. as well as the United Nations Headquarters in New York. Dr. Teng Fu has taught courses on Chinese politics, and she has also published scholarly papers and articles on globalization, environmental movements, and China's public policy issues, including pension reforms and primary education in rural and urban areas. She holds a B.A. degree in English and Diplomacy from the Foreign Affairs College (China Foreign Affairs University) in Beijing and an M.A. and Ph.D. degrees in World Politics from The Catholic University of America. Her areas of specialization include sustainable development in China, civil society, and transnational collective action on energy and environmental issues.

RICHARD A. LOVE is a Senior Research Fellow and Professor at the National Defense University (NDU), Washington, D.C. His current projects involve interdiction, foreign consequence management, international law of armed conflict, and countering WMD strategy and operations. He teaches courses on countering WMD proliferation and consequence management and incident response. He is an adjunct professor of law and politics at Catholic University and teaches Law of Armed Conflict, National Security Law, Security in the Information Age, Congress and Foreign Policy, and Law and Policy of Homeland Security to Ph.D. and M.A. candidates at the Pentagon and on Capitol Hill. Previously, he served as counsel for the Financial Crimes and Security Project at the Brookings Institution. He holds a B.A. in history and International Relations from the University of Virginia, a Juris Doctor in Law and Economics from George Mason University, an L.L.M. in international law from American University, and a Ph.D. from the Australian Defense Force Academy at the University of New South Wales in Australia.

JOHN T. PICARELLI is a Social Science Analyst at the International Center of the National Institute of Justice. He is an expert in transnational threats and international criminal justice issues, specifically international organized crime, terrorism, and trafficking in human beings. Dr. Picarelli earned his Ph.D. at American University in 2007. The opinions expressed in this chapter are Dr. Picarelli's personal views and do not represent the official views of the National Institute of Justice.

DENNIS PIRAGES is Dean's Professor of Government at the University of Nevada, Las Vegas. He previously was Harrison Professor of International Environmental Policy at the University of Maryland, College Park. He received his Ph.D. from Stanford University. He is author or editor of 13 books on global relations and environmental issues, including *Global Ecopolitics* (1978), *Global Technopolitics* (1989), *Building Sustainable Societies* (1996), *Ecological Security* (2004), and *From Resource Scarcity to Ecological Security* (2005). A lifetime fellow of the American Association for the Advancement of Science, he has been writing about the impact of deepening globalization on the spread of infectious disease for more than a decade.

PAUL RUNCI is a senior research scientist at the Joint Global Change Research Institute in College Park, MD. His research focuses on the policy dimensions of global change, and particularly on the challenges of expanding the scientific capacity of developing countries likely to be most affected by climate change. He has been an active member of the Intergovernmental Panel on Climate Change's Steering Committee on New Scenarios and is currently on assignment as an energy and climate change policy advisor to U.S. Senator Maria Cantwell. He holds a B.A. from Boston College, an M.A.L.D. from Tufts University's Fletcher School of Law and Diplomacy, and a Ph.D. from the Department of Government and Politics at the University of Maryland, College Park.

LOUISE SHELLEY is a professor and Director of the Terrorism, Transnational Crime and Corruption Center at George Mason University. Professor Shelley has written extensively on all forms of transnational crime, the links between crime and terrorism and is the author of *Policing Soviet Society*, *Lawyers in Soviet Worklife*, and *Crime and Modernization* and is presently completing a book entitled *Human Trafficking: A Global Perspective*. She is the recipient of Guggenheim, NEH, and Kennan Institute grants and received a MacArthur grant to establish the Russian Organized Crime Study Centers.

Preface

The global economic meltdown, terrorist attacks, environmental problems, disease pandemics, refugee flows, drug and human trafficking, resurgent religion, cyberattacks, weapons of mass destruction—the news headlines and policy makers are consumed with these pressing global concerns. But none of these important global issues are captured by the traditional view of International Relations (IR) as the activities of states. People are dying, but states cannot save them. The strongest states in the system cannot solve these problems alone; their institutions are not wired for it, and they are scrambling to come up with effective responses. Nearly a third of the people on the planet live in the weakest states in the system. These failed and failing states cannot provide roads and drinking water, basic law, order, and governance. Their citizens are the most vulnerable, yet these states are the least able to respond to the challenges of globalization. The worst of these states are what I call kleptocracies; their kleptomaniacal leaders treat the government as ATM machines, to be used for personal enrichment. Half the people on the planet live without basic freedoms (in both "strong" and "weak" states); their governments deny them the abilities to participate in, know of, or hold their governments accountable for the activities undertaken in their name. The worst of these states are predatory, deliberately killing the very citizens they are supposed to protect. Sovereignty—the ideas that governance aligns with territory, and that those outside the geographic boundaries have no authority to meddle in internal affairs—is not neutral or theoretical or helpful for most of the people on the planet. For example, nearly 6 million people have died in the Congo, as many Jews as died in the holocaust, in a conflict driven by failed sovereignty, the quest to control natural resources to sell to the lucrative global market that powers our cell phones, and problems spilling over central Africa's leaky borders.

Unfortunately our IR books and ideas about how the world works have not yet caught up with real-world practices. The pressing problems we face move across borders, yet our policy responses, and our textbooks, are too often state-focused. Globalization, nonstate actors, failed and failing states—policy makers are challenged in how to deal with these issues, but they are not helped much by our current treatment of these themes in IR books. Our textbooks too often "whistle past the graveyard" of states and world politics, reciting the same old categories even as they are less able to describe or guide practice in the world we live in. I struggled to find a text that would bridge the gaps between theory and practice in my first decade of teaching world politics and International Relations to undergraduate and graduate students at the Johns Hopkins University, Catholic University, and to government employees and military officers in the Pentagon in Washington, D.C. In my second decade I have tried to bridge these gaps with 4 editions of this book. In theory, the governments of countries are the primary actors in world politics. In practice, they are often unable to respond effectively to a host of problems that sweep across borders. In theory, many academics and books focus on how globalization affects global politics and state sovereignty. In practice, most of those works are not easily accessible to students, policy makers, and general readers. Many are narrowly written on one topic or theory, and do not place globalization issues in wider policy, historical, and institutional contexts. Discussion of global issues are often relegated to "readers," collections of previously published articles assembled together in an ad hoc way, without common themes and arguments uniting the pieces. These present students with a shopping bag view of world politics—"and now this!"—an unhelpful hodgepodge already prevalent in Internet and media coverage.

Ten years ago I wrote the first edition of this book. I wanted to help my students make sense of a host of global issues and nonstate actors that move across borders, in a way that connected these issues to each other, to current policy and ethical dilemmas, and to larger historical trends. Globalization is not new, but the current period of globalization is quicker, thicker, deeper, and cheaper than previous epochs, and together the trends of open economies, open technologies, and open societies present new openings and unintended consequences for global politics. Too often works on globalization become polarized and ideological—is globalization good or bad, is the state as strong as ever or withering away. Reality is not so simple, thus these works are not very helpful to students and policy makers who have to engage with a world in which globalization brings both benefits and problems, in which states are still with us but are challenged and grappling with how to respond to the unintended consequences of the globalization they helped create.

This book is a hybrid, in several ways. It is primarily a single-authored text (as I have written more than half of the text myself). But I also wanted to include other voices, subject-matter experts from a variety of national and professional backgrounds who also bridge theory and practice in their work, and who could speak pointedly to cutting-edge developments in areas as diverse as cyberspace and environmental activism in China. All the chapters were written expressly for this book, and all share a common framework. Each chapter highlights current cases, policy, and ethical dilemmas. Each chapter discusses how globalization's open technologies, open economies, and open societies affect the issue area. Each chapter discusses the roles and activities of nonstate actors (legal NGOs, MNCs, IGOs, and illicit criminal cartels and terrorist groups). Each chapter discusses policy responses to the various global issues, by states and other actors. Each chapter emphasizes that global issues are problems no one country can solve alone, yet states are still charged with responding. Globalization brings costs and benefits, and many unintended consequences, that challenge current institutions. Policy makers and citizens try to manage global issues, to garner more of the benefits for more people while limiting the costs, especially to the world's most vulnerable people. Each chapter discusses how the particular global issue and responses to it are affecting and changing ideas and practices of sovereignty. The book works well in introductory International Relations, Global Issues, Globalization, and Foreign Policy courses, presenting students with some of the basic issues, actors, and dilemmas of world politics. The book also works well in advanced and graduate classes in International Relations, Global Issues, Globalization, and Foreign Policy, as it discusses the past, present, and future of sovereignty as a theoretical and practical way to organize global politics.

Students are keenly interested in new technologies, in money, and in questions of justice, issues that are marginalized or excluded in most IR texts yet are front and center in every chapter of this book. Pedagogically, the book is written to encourage discussion over globalization's ethical, policy, and theoretical debates. The book's continued references to current cases offer natural hooks for active teaching methods, including case and classroom discussion, role playing, simulation, debates, and use of video and Internet sources, referenced on the book's Web site. Research shows that people remember information better and longer when active teaching methods are used. Students are more engaged in the material, and better able to hone critical thinking and communication skills, when they participate in the classroom. This book facilitates these teaching goals and methods.

The fourth edition includes a number of substantial changes. A new chapter on "God and Global Governance: Resurgent Religion and World Politics" discusses how resurgent religion meets challenged states the world over. Too often policy makers and academics utterly fail to understand the importance that religiously motivated actors and factors can play in world politics, in saving lives or in destroying them. From fighting terror to debt relief, from Iran to Pakistan, the world has been ill-served by this dismissal of the role of religion in world politics. Better understanding and engagement of religious factors and actors would improve progress on a host of critical global issues, from nuclear power and weapons to terrorism, disease, and the environment. This chapter discusses why and in what ways we get religion wrong in world politics. The religious dimensions of war and peace, development, and democracy are discussed, as well as the ways in which globalization, open societies, open economies, and open technologies have affected the resurgence of religion around the world. How are resurgent religions meeting challenged states around the world, and how can we "get religion right" in world politics?

Additionally each chapter has been thoroughly updated, addressing the global economic recession and cascading international financial crises, the Obama election, and current developments in global policy, issues, and institutions.

I am grateful for the patience of my family and children Maria, Ricky, and Ava Rose during the long hours I was at work on this book. I am also thankful for the vigorous discussions with my colleagues, students, and collaborators who have honed my arguments in these pages: to Dr. Richard Love, my colleague at National Defense University and my husband, for his thoughtful comments as "first reader"; to the editors at Cengage Learning /Wadsworth and the contributors whose continued commitment to this book made a fourth edition possible; to my colleagues at the U.S. Commission on International Religious Freedom; to Daniel Philpott, Scott Appleby, George Lopez, John Paul Lederach, Jerry Powers, William Headley S.C.Sp., Ferdinand Muhigirwe S.J., Archbishop Francois-Xavier Maroy from Eastern Congo, Msgr. Hector Fabio from Colombia, Myla Legura from the Philippines, and all my colleagues at Notre Dame's Kroc Institute of Peace and the Catholic Peacebuilding Network for their inspiration; to Drew Christiansen, S.J. and colleagues who let me take some of these arguments for a test run in my columns at *America* magazine; to Fred Ahearn, Karla Simons, William Barbieri, Steve Schneck, and colleagues at the Center for International Social Development and the Institute for Policy Research of Catholic University; and to colleagues whose tireless work in accompaniment of the world's most vulnerable serve as a constant inspiration—to Ken Hackett, Tom Bamat and colleagues at Catholic Relief Services, Ken Gavin, S.J., and colleagues at Jesuit Refugee Services, and Theodore Cardinal McCarrick, Bishop William Murphy, Bishop Ricardo Ramirez, Bishop John Ricard, Steve Colecchi, Major General William Burns, Ambassador Mary Ann Glendon, Dr. John Steinbruner, and the bishops and staff at the U.S. Conference of Catholic Bishops, and Michael Perry OFM, and the Franciscan Action Network. All errors of course remain entirely my own.

CHAPTER ONE

Global Problems, Global Solutions

Maryann Cusimano Love

"The challenges of our time threaten the peace and prosperity of every single nation, and no one nation can meet these challenges alone. The threat of climate change can't be contained by borders on a map, and the theft of loose nuclear materials could lead to the extermination of any city on Earth. Reckless actions by a few have fueled a recession that spans the globe, and rising food prices means that 100 million of our fellow citizens are expected to fall into desperate poverty...The only way forward is through shared and persistent effort to combat threats to our peace, our prosperity and our common humanity wherever they may exist."

—President Barack Obama

"Poverty is not natural. It is man-made and it can be overcome by human beings."

—Nelson Mandela

"Don't blow it. Put down the national flags. Look up from the numbers and look to the future."

—Bono

Every hour, 1,200 children die from disease and malnourishment—from poverty.[1] More than 10 million people a year die from poverty,[2] 30,000 each day. According to Rev. Dr. Ishmael Noko of the Consultation of International Religious Leaders on Global Poverty, "poverty is an issue that has no borders."[3]

Thirty-five thousand protestors marched in London, urging leaders at the emergency G-20 Economic Summit to "Put People First" in responding to the global economic recession. Celebrities lent their voices at news conferences during the International Monetary Fund (IMF) and World Bank meetings in Washington, DC, using the global media to spread their message that global financial institutions ought to help the world's poor who suffer most from the global economic recession. Global financial and investment companies created the worst global economic crisis since the Great Depression. When the bad investments, tricky accounting, and profiteering of these multinational corporations came to light, markets around the world fell like dominoes. Companies went bankrupt, workers lost jobs, savings and credit evaporated, and people went hungry. Nongovernmental organizations scrambled to feed more hungry people with fewer resources, as their own donations and endowments decreased. Food riots erupted from Mexico to Indonesia. Some groups profited, such as the Taliban, violent insurgents with ties to al Qaeda terrorists. Financed by the lucrative opium trade, the Taliban went on the offensive in Afghanistan and Pakistan, engaging in terrorism and threatening the survival of the nuclear-armed Pakistani government.[4]

The pattern was similar to the attacks of September 11, 2001, when the world witnessed another demonstration of global issues that move beyond sovereignty. Nonstate actors used nonmilitary means to attack primarily nongovernmental targets. Nineteen terrorists who represented no state inflicted massive casualties and approximately 3,000 deaths against citizens from the most powerful state in the international system as well as from 80 other countries. They used commercial airlines, the tools of transportation and commerce, to attack, and chose as their primary targets the twin towers of the World Trade Center, symbols of global capitalism. Members of the al Qaeda terrorist network operate across sovereign borders through cells in an estimated 65 countries. The suicide bombers were Saudis and Egyptians who had been living in the United States, trained in Afghanistan, and organized and financed in Germany, England, and Spain with information and money sent to them from companies, nongovernmental organizations (NGOs), and individuals around the world. The al Qaeda financial network drew from the diamond trade in Sierra Leone and the heroin trade in Afghanistan, effectively linking the terrorist network with global crime and drug trafficking networks. The hijackers exploited the very global transportation, communication, and economic systems they protested—and which they believed carry undue and unwanted U.S. and Western influence around the world. Their high-visibility attacks were planned to maximize global media exposure.

None of these important global actions is captured by the traditional view of International Relations as the activities of states.

This book investigates global issues that move beyond sovereignty in both the nature of problems and solutions. As one UN official observed, "Disease and pollution cross borders without passports."[5] Borders are more permeable, and threats are fast, fungible, fluid, and decentralized. How can global or transsovereign issues be tackled in a system that is based on sovereignty?

How does globalization facilitate both global problems and attempts to manage them? How do the debates over globalization frame our understanding of these issues? I describe the rising importance of nonstate actors and global issues, and the challenges to changing institutions. Finally, I review the various theories on the status and future of sovereignty and assess where sovereignty is heading.

Transsovereign problems represent the downside of globalization. Globalization is the fast, interdependent spread of open society, open economy, and open technology infrastructures. Globalization is not new, but the speed, reach, intensity, cost, and impacts of the current period of globalization are. Earlier periods of globalization moved trade, missionaries, and colonizers far more slowly, with the speed of frigates. Now people and products cross borders in hours. Ideas and capital move around the globe at the touch of a keystroke. Global or transsovereign problems move across borders, and cannot be solved by any one country alone. Nonstate actors are important players both in creating and managing global issues—from legal groups such as NGOs, intergovernmental organizations (IGOs), and multinational corporations (MNCs) to illicit groups such as international crime cartels and terrorist organizations. The rise of transsovereign problems is made possible by the very changes that have been facilitated and celebrated by many policy makers: the rise of democracies and liberal; capitalist economies; and advances in technology, transportation, and communication. The rise of global problems is full of irony. It is physically difficult to limit the flow of particular people and goods at a time when technological, market, and societal forces make such movements easier than ever before.

Although globalization did not create transsovereign problems, it has facilitated and intensified them. For example, although terrorism existed long before, the modern period of globalization certainly facilitates the work of terrorist groups such as al Qaeda.[6] Open economies, societies, and technologies gave al Qaeda the opportunity to take its complaints to a global stage, to act at a distance cheaply, to perpetrate greater casualties using global technologies, and to elicit greater fear by playing in front of cameras and satellites that broadcast its members' actions instantly and globally. Globalization gives breakdowns in state authority and capacity and transsovereign problems greater reach, speed, intensity, and impact.

Sovereignty is the form of political organization that has dominated the international system since the Treaty of Westphalia in 1648. Sovereign states have exclusive and final jurisdiction over territory, as well as the resources and populations that lie within such territory. A system based on sovereignty is one that acknowledges only one political authority over a particular territory and looks to that authority as the final arbiter to solve problems that occur within its borders. Sovereign states have four characteristics, three of which are negotiable: territory, population, a government with control over the territory and population, and international recognition. In practice, only international recognition is nonnegotiable. If a political entity has territory, population, and a government but lacks international recognition, such as the Palestinian Authority, then it is not considered a sovereign state. Once a state is internationally recognized, such as Somalia, it does not matter if it lacks a government with the ability to control the territory and population, if territory is contested, or if population varies widely (because of large refugee flows, for example).

The term *nation* is not synonymous with the term *sovereign state*. The distinction is not just academic. Each year, tens of thousands of people die trying to make their nations into states. A nation is a group with a common cultural, linguistic, ethnic, racial, or religious identity—such as the Sioux nation of the U.S. plains or the Moluccans in Northern Europe. A sovereign state or country, however, is an internationally recognized unit of political authority over a given territory, such as the United States of America or the Netherlands. National boundaries—where various ethnic or linguistic groups are located—often do not coincide with sovereign state boundaries. For example, the Basques live on either side of the border between Spain and France, and the Kurds live in the region straddling Iraq and Turkey. By some counts, more than 8,000 national groups exist—but only 192 sovereign states exist.[7] This volume uses the terms *transsovereign* or *global* to keep clear the distinction between sovereign states and national groups.

Twentieth-century international relations were epic battles of behemoth states, a century of "heroic warfare" among strong, competing states—for example, World Wars I and II and the Cold War. In contrast, the twenty-first century is marked by "postheroic warfare."[8] Conflicts now come not from battles among strong states but from the problems posed by nonstate actors and weak or disintegrating states ("Humpty Dumpty wars" in which all the king's forces and men may not be able to put fractured states back together again). Although global issues move beyond sovereignty, the machinery we have to manage these problems is still wired for the sovereign, often state-to-state, military confrontations of a bygone era. For example, the U.S. government responded to the September 11 terrorist attacks with a military attack on the Taliban government in Afghanistan not only because it was sheltering Osama bin Laden but also because this is what the U.S. government knows how to do: fight other states. It is difficult to attack an unknown, moving target, a nonstate actor with no known address.

The twenty-first century is witness to the collapse of many weak states that had previously been kept afloat by Cold War aid and alliances.[9] The same trends of open societies, open economies, and open technologies can further erode already weak state institutions in many quasi-states, pushing them closer to collapse. Failed states provide a natural breeding ground for global problems such as terrorism, international criminal activity, flows of refugees, the spread of contagious disease, and trafficking in drugs and nuclear materials. Failed states also attract the relief and development efforts of NGOs and IGOs. In a world primarily organized around state sovereignty, world politics practitioners are challenged by a double bind.

How can transsovereign issues be dealt with effectively in a world of sovereign states? Simultaneously, how can democratization and economic liberalization be promoted in ways that do not undermine already fragile state institutions to the point of collapse, thus increasing the spread and intensity of global problems?

GLOBAL PROBLEMS AND THE GLOBALIZATION DEBATES

Globalization creates a world of paradox. Global transportation, communication, and economic interdependence make the vision of a closer human family possible. Two million people cross an international border every day. Terrorists and dangerous microbes, however, use the same global infrastructure that tourists do. Although capital flows of $2 trillion cross borders each day, most poor people and poor countries see little of it. Building the global infrastructure of open economies, open technologies, and open societies creates great benefits, but globalization also carries significant costs that are often not equitably dispersed, especially to the world's poor.

Some scholars[10] and advocates argue that globalization is a means to bring people and cultures together; rout tyrannical governments; easily and cheaply spread information, ideas, capital, and commerce; and transfer more power than ever before to civil society and networked individuals.[11] For advocates, curtailing globalization would be immoral. Global poverty is a problem—and globalization is the key to solving it. The world's most impoverished countries are those that are least globalized.

Other scholars and critics, however, see globalization as neoimperialism wearing Bill Gates's face and Mickey Mouse's ears, extending the web of global capitalism's exploitation of women, minorities, the poor, and developing regions. It fouls ecosystems, displaces local cultures and traditions, mandates worship at the altar of rampant consumer capitalism, and deepens the divide (digital and otherwise) between the global haves and have-nots.[12]

Opposition to globalization comes from many different camps, but critics share a common view that globalization puts profits before people. Globalization benefits a few at the top, and in the West at the expense of the rest. Environmental, human rights, and labor advocates charge that globalization brings a race to the bottom in human rights and environmental standards as businesses extend their reach to benefit the corporate bottom line. Local laws and control may be sacrificed to international regimes that are controlled by a few powerful states or corporations. These regimes are not democratic, representative, or transparent. Critics see globalization as a new form of imperialism—whether corporate, cultural, or Western—that is immoral and unjust. Liberal consumer advocates such as Ralph Nader in the United States, conservative protectionists such as the Peronistas in Argentina and Patrick Buchanan in the United States, radicals such as Osama bin Laden and al Qaeda, and anticorporate activists such as anti-McDonald's farmer José Bové in France have little in common other than their opposition to globalization. For these opponents, the biggest question is how to stop globalization and the harms that come from it.

Opponents and advocates see globalization differently in part because the costs and benefits of globalization are asymmetrically distributed rather than shared equally. Capitalism is criticized for disparities between rich and poor in terms of income, political power, participation, and opportunities. In parallel, the worldwide spread and intensification of capitalism that globalization represents is criticized for exacerbating capitalism's excesses and exporting the resulting problems to the entire world, as in the global economic recession. For example, global income inequality is increasing in the latest phase of globalization, both within and across countries. The wealth of the world's three richest individuals surpasses the combined gross domestic product (GDP) of all the world's underdeveloped countries. The world's richest 20 percent consume over 76.6 percent of global resources, whereas the world's poorest 20 percent consume only 1.5 percent of world resources.[13] Of the 6.6 billion people now on the planet, half live on less than $2.50 per day, and 1.4 billion live on less than $1.25 per day. As bad as these poverty statistics are, they understate the problem in many ways, including that these numbers do not include the increases in poor people from the global economic recession or from rising food prices. Half of all children live in poverty. Half of all Africans live in poverty.[14] Sixty countries are poorer than they were in the early 1980s, and 18 countries (460 million people) are poorer than they were in the early 1990s.[15] Critics say globalization widens the gap between rich and poor. Advocates say the lack of globalization causes such poverty.

Does globalization increase income inequality, making the rich richer and the poor poorer? Debates rage over this question, and there is some evidence on each side. On the one hand, China and India have moved their economies toward more industrial and high-tech sectors, and so have been able to benefit from foreign direct investment (FDI), and incomes have improved.[16] Plenty of poverty remains in these countries, especially among women and people in rural areas, but because of the large populations in China and India, growth in income, life expectancy, and education there allows advocates for globalization to claim that globalization is decreasing global poverty (even though almost all of the poverty reduction has occurred in China, which has not followed the Western consensus for globalization). Even in China and India, poverty reduction has been overstated due to problems with economic measurements, and lack of accurate and transparent figures from the Chinese communist government. Poverty is much worse in sub-Saharan Africa and economies in transition, such as those in Eastern Europe. The world's poorest countries have experienced declining income rather than economic growth, and advances in life expectancy and education made immediately after decolonization have been reversed in the last decade due to the HIV/AIDS pandemic. African countries find their agricultural products shut out of global markets due to protectionist agriculture policies. Their cheaper labor is excluded from developed country markets due to restrictive immigration policies. These countries do not benefit from FDI, which goes to more developed economies rather than to the poorest economies. Income inequality has increased within countries as well as among countries. If death rates increase among the world's poorest people, does that count as "globalization decreasing poverty"?[17]

Wealth is only one indicator of global asymmetries. Decisions about globalization are made in corporate boardrooms and state capitals generally in economically developed states. Toxic waste from developed countries, however, is shipped to the world's poorest communities as some corporations exploit regions where environmental legislation or enforcement is weak. Most foreign direct investment and corporate shareholder profits go to developed states. All developing countries combined together received only 16 percent of FDI in 2000, whereas the United States alone received 26 percent of FDI.[18] Globalization's costs and benefits are unequally distributed, with poor people and poor countries too often not participating in the full benefits that globalization may bring. Maximizing the benefits of globalization while minimizing or managing the challenges is difficult because the institution we generally task with managing global problems—the sovereign state—cannot do the job alone.

Most of the clashes between globalization's proponents and skeptics are peaceful, carried out in op-ed pages, in consumer boycotts, and on the floors of parliaments. But as globalization is embraced by more governments around the world, and as global economic busts show the volatility of integrated global financial markets, frustrations are also rising. Tensions rise as opponents are shut out of the boardrooms in businesses, international organizations, and governments where crucial decisions are made about the pace and nature of globalization.

This book takes a third way in this debate: Globalization is neither inherently good nor evil—but both. Terrorists and tourists alike use the same global infrastructure. Transsovereign problems are the unintended side effects of globalization. As globalization advances, so will both opposition to globalization and its unintended adverse effects. To better harness and spread the benefits of globalization, we must take these adverse effects and the ethics of globalization seriously and work to better contain globalization's challenges. As the sides become polarized, this third way is often overlooked. Proponents do not adequately recognize globalization's failures, while opponents do not fully recognize its benefits. Some proponents argue that the way to address global inequities and poverty is more globalization more quickly— and full speed ahead. Some opponents argue that attempts to lessen globalization's downsides are misplaced. Creating a kinder, gentler "globalization with a human face"[19] allows unjust systems to persist longer rather than allowing them to fall from the weight of their problems. Ironically, opponents to globalization use the tools of globalization (global media and the Internet, for example) to organize, mobilize, and publicize their opposition to globalization. Also, proponents of globalization use the arguments of opponents who are concerned with serious poverty and environmental problems to justify more globalization, arguing that only greater globalization will increase living standards and eventually leave more disposable income to address environmental problems. Too often both sides talk past each other.

The same is true in the sovereignty debates. Some argue sovereignty is dead, while others argue it remains unchanged. This book takes the third approach: Sovereignty remains but is changing in important ways.

Understanding pressing global issues means understanding that globalization creates both benefits and challenges that states cannot control or solve alone. Because the problems go beyond sovereignty, so must the solutions. But going beyond sovereignty to manage global problems also carries unintended consequences for the state. The growth of the private sector, often with the aid of deliberate policy choices by states (political, economic, and technological liberalization) now often dwarfs the capacity of the public sector, even in the strongest states. In their attempts to manage pressing global problems, states contract out and form networks and alliances with the private sector (NGOs and MNCs) and with other states and multilateral organizations (IGOs). States enter into these partnerships voluntarily, expecting help in managing global problems. Yet in doing so, states unintentionally lose some autonomy, authority, and legitimacy as they acknowledge their incapacity to solve problems alone and the rising capacity of other actors.

THE DIFFICULTIES IN ADDRESSING TRANSSOVEREIGN PROBLEMS

Transsovereign problems are difficult to solve for many reasons. First, states and the private sector have to figure out how to control or contain these problems without moving to close off economies, societies, or technologies. Second, because their very nature precludes unilateral solutions, global problems are harder to tackle because they require the cooperation of a greater number of actors. Third, they are complex because they entail both state and nonstate actors, which creates coordination problems. Effective action requires complex coordination among states, NGOs, IGOs, MNCs, and other nonstate actors. These groups have different interests, capabilities, and constituencies. As more groups attempt to coordinate action, more opportunities are created for policy to go awry. As a British minister for the environment explained:

> We face new dilemmas—of problems that cross boundaries, of issues that no single government can control, of shared risk. Nowhere is this collectivity more true than with the environment. Pollution, global warming, ozone depletion, and loss of species do not respect borders. . . . Globalization—in the form of increasing trade, the communications revolution, and increasing cultural exchanges—means that . . . governments have less influence over activities and economic sectors that were formerly under their control. . . . Some people refer to the effect this has on governments as "loss of agency." But the need for intervention in the public interest has not diminished—it is just that the locus has changed. Activities that were formerly national are now international, but the institutional capacity to deal with them has yet to evolve. . . we must manage the changing responsibilities of governments, business and civil society, forming new partnerships, learning from each other, finding new ways of harnessing the expertise and legitimate concerns and aspirations of each.[20]

Fourth, global problems are challenging because they often take place in the economic and social spheres, where the arm of liberal capitalist states has the shortest reach. Fifth, addressing global issues is difficult because these problems blur the borders between domestic and foreign policy. As domestic constituencies become mobilized over global issues, policy makers find their tasks complicated because they must address and coordinate the interests of additional groups. Domestic labor, environmental, and industry groups mobilize for international discussions of acid rain, for example. Politics does not stop at the water's edge. Efforts to manage global issues may stumble over contentious and unsettled domestic policy debates. For example, Brazilian government policies toward global warming involve discussions of the rights of indigenous people and the private industries that cut, burn, and develop the rain forests.

As a U.S. Department of State official described it, transsovereign issues signal a fundamental change in foreign policy:

> Foreign policy as we have known it is dead . . . because it is no longer foreign. . . . The distinctions between domestic and foreign are gone. Look at the issues: The . . . fight against drugs and crime has major international components. Our stolen cars end up in El Salvador or Guatemala or Poland.
>
> Our drugs come from Peru or Pakistan or Burma or elsewhere and transit almost anywhere. Crime cartels spread tentacles from Nigeria or Russia or Colombia. Today it is inconceivable to consider a coordinated attack on crime without working a part of the strategy in the international arena. . . . International terrorism has reached our shores. . . . We cannot deal with the threats to our environment, to assaults on biodiversity with domestic policy. Ozone layer depletion and global warming cannot be addressed by domestic environmental regulations alone. Over and over again we find issues that are domestic in consequence but international in scope. These are the consuming issues of the twenty-first century.[21]

Global problems also can be difficult for states to address because of institutional gaps (these are discussed more fully in Chapter 13). Existing institutions were not created to handle these problems, and they may be slow to change, resist taking on new functions that may divert resources from their traditional missions, and have difficulties coordinating with other institutions. Finally, contracting out or cooperating with the private sector and multilateral organizations to combat or contain global problems may unintentionally further undermine sovereignty.

YESTERDAY: WHERE SOVEREIGNTY CAME FROM

The international system has not always been organized around sovereignty. Prior to the Treaty of Westphalia in 1648, there were overlapping jurisdictions of political authority with no clear hierarchy or pecking order among them. In this feudal system, claims to authority were diffuse, decentralized, and based on personal ties rather than territory. Medieval subjects faced simultaneous and competing claims for allegiance to the pope, the king or emperor, the bishop, and local feudal princes, dukes, counts, lords, and so on.[22] Taxes and military service could be required of a person from several different authorities within the same territory. A person's bonds to an authority figure were based on personal ties and agreements, and "political authority was treated as a private possession."[23] This made secession problematic because contractual obligations might not survive a person's death.

Rather than land, authority claims were based on the divine—on spiritual connections or on the legitimacy of lineage to the Church (and in the days before the Reformation, that meant the Roman Catholic Church). Secular and spiritual authority were intertwined. Kings were anointed with holy insignia (for example, British monarchs took the title "Defender of the Faith"), emperors were crowned as "servants of the apostles," and popes and bishops needed the support of nonclerical leaders to gain and retain power. Both the Church and the Holy Roman Empire sought to fill the vacuum left by the fall of the Roman Empire and made universal claims of authority.

People, not territory, were the primary objects of rule, and "rule was per definition spiritual" rather than spatial.[24] In the struggle between the papacy and the Holy Roman Empire for control, both institutions were weakened in ways that helped new forms of political organization to emerge.

There were many reasons why the feudal system declined and the sovereign state emerged. According to scholar Hendrik Spruyt, the rise of long-distance trade in the late Middle Ages created both a new merchant class of elites and the need for a new political system that could better accommodate the mercantilist economic system. The Church was against the exchange and loan of money and the taking of oaths, but currency and contracts were crucial to long-distance trade. Trade also required more precise and consistent measurements of time, weights, jurisdiction, and private property. As Spruyt notes,

> [t]he result of this economic dynamism was that a social group, the town dwellers, came into existence with new sources of revenue and power, which did not fit the old feudal order. This new social group had various incentives to search for political allies who were willing

to change the existing order. The new trading and commercial classes of the towns could not settle into the straitjacket of the feudal order, and the towns became a chief agent in its final disruption.... Business activity could not be organized according to the.... system of personal bonds.... Contracts could not depend on the initiating actors.

Sometimes these contracts might have to carry through beyond the death of the original contractors.[25]

The rise of a new economic system with its own needs, however, was not enough to bring about the rise of the sovereign state. The currency of other ideas aided the development of the concept of sovereignty. Martin Luther and the Protestant Reformation, Henry VIII and his Anglican separatists, the rise of scientific knowledge and explorations of the non-European world, along with the new merchant elites, challenged the authority and legitimacy of the Church in Rome. Roman ideas of property rights—which stressed exclusive control over territory—also were on the rise.[26] Ideas of individual autonomy and freedom from outside interference, later captured by Immanuel Kant, were important in the development of sovereignty.[27] According to Daniel Philpott, these religious ideas that gave rise to today's modern conceptions of human rights played a vital part.[28] Nicholas Onuf cites three conceptual crucial antecedents to the genesis of sovereignty: *majestas*, or the idea that institutions inspire respect; *potestas imperiandi*, or the ability to coerce and enforce rules; and the *Protestant idea of stewardship*, or rule on behalf of the citizens of the body politic, not the personal rule of the Middle Ages.[29]

Besides conceptual changes, sovereignty also emerged because of changes in practical political balances. Sovereign states were more effective and efficient at waging war and conducting trade than were competing political organizations.[30] Elites who benefited from the new form of organization sought to delegitimize actors who were not like them (who were not organized as sovereign states) by excluding them from the international system.

Other forms of political organization competed with the sovereign state to succeed the feudal system: the city-state, the urban league, and the empire. Hendrik Spruyt believes that the sovereign state eventually won out for three main reasons. First, states were better able to extract resources and rationalize their economies than were other forms of political organization.

Second, states were more efficient and effective than were medieval forms of organization, especially at being able to "speak with one voice" and make the external commitments necessary to the new trading system. And third, social choice and institutional mimicry meant that sovereign states selected out and delegitimized other actors who were not sovereign states.[31]

Out of these changes in ideas, economics, and political balances, came the eventual acceptance of the sovereign state. Authority was now based on exclusive jurisdiction over territory. Identity became based on geography: You were where you lived—a citizen of French territory, not primarily a member of the Holy Roman Empire or the community of Christians or the Celtic or Norman clans.

In theory, the sovereign state had a monopoly on the legitimate use of force within a territory. Sovereignty was reciprocal. One state recognized the others' exclusive jurisdictions over their territories and the populations and resources that resided on their lands; in return, they recognized that state's exclusive jurisdiction over its territory and everything on its land.[32] From the beginning, sovereignty was based on a social compact. Sovereignty never meant that all states had equal power or resources— some had vast lands, populations, and resources, while the capabilities of other states were meager. But sovereignty meant that only other sovereigns had legal standing in international agreements. States were the main unit of the international system.

From its origins in Europe, the idea and practice of sovereignty spread around the globe as Europeans conquered and carved up the planet into colonial territories. Sovereignty (with its territorial limits) came into conflict with the unlimited, universal Chinese, Japanese, and Ottoman empires, but eventually sovereignty came to dominate worldwide, whether by force or accession. When European colonies became independent after World War II and later when the Soviet bloc disintegrated between 1989 and 1991, the political units that emerged sought sovereign statehood, not recognition of other forms of political organization.

Sovereignty is an equalizing concept. Internally, governments organize themselves in whatever fashion they choose: monarchy, republican constitutional parliamentary system, autocracy, theocracy, and so on. Externally, however, all a state needs is international recognition as a sovereign state.

TODAY: SOVEREIGNTY CHALLENGED

The modern international system is built on the foundation of sovereignty. Today, sovereignty is under siege. There have always been weak states, and distinctions between the theory and the practice of sovereignty, yet both de jure and de facto sovereignty are now under assault more than ever. The sovereign state will likely continue to be the main unit in the international system for some time, but the operation and legitimacy of sovereignty are being undermined by both external and internal dynamics.

The principle of sovereignty is under siege by those who contend that in grave humanitarian crises the international community (of NGOs, IGOs, and states) has a right to intervene to aid citizens who are not being protected by the state. In Somalia, Bosnia, and Rwanda, the international community intervened in the internal affairs of states to distribute aid directly to individuals in times of grave humanitarian crisis without either the invitation or consent of the sovereignties involved. In the past, only sovereign states, not individuals, had standing in international law; within sovereign borders, a polity could do whatever it pleased with its citizens, even if that meant abusing their human rights or neglecting basic human needs.

Now such thinking is changing among some observers. In his speech accepting the Nobel Prize, then UN Secretary General Kofi Annan said, "In the twenty-first century I believe the mission of the United Nations will be defined by a new, more profound awareness of the sanctity and dignity of every human life. . . . This will require us to look beyond the framework of sovereign states. . . . The sovereignty of States must no longer be used as a shield for gross violations of human rights."[33] These are strong words from the director of an organization founded on the principle of sovereign states and constituted solely of sovereign states as voting members.

The Wall Street Journal editorialized in a similar vein, saying that sovereignty is not an absolute right because starvation and wanton killing are "everybody's business," and that in cases such as Somalia or Rwanda, "any absolute principle of nonintervention becomes a cruel abstraction indeed."[34] Editorial writers at *The Economist* agreed, noting that we are

> increasingly concerned not just to see countries well governed but also to ensure that the world is not irreparably damaged—whether by global warming, by the loss of species, by famine or by war. . . .
>
> Increasingly, world opinion, when confronted by television pictures of genocide or starvation, is unimpressed by those who say "We cannot get involved. National sovereignty must be respected.". . . National sovereignty be damned.[35]

A "responsibility to protect" norm is emerging at the United Nations to justify humanitarian response in cases of genocide, war crimes, ethnic cleansing, and crimes against humanity.[36] Principles of sovereignty took centuries to become established and are not in danger of dissolving any time soon. However, perhaps we ought to take notice anytime voices across the ideological spectrum agree that the principle of sovereignty is challenged, and that individuals in need should receive international redress if states are unable or unwilling to carry out basic duties to their citizens.

Sovereignty is being challenged not only in theory, but also is under siege in practice. Sovereignty is challenged externally by the globalizing dynamics of open markets, open societies, and open technologies, which make the borders of even strong states permeable by outside forces. Sovereignty is also under siege internally from the rise of internal conflicts and subnational movements, as well as from the reinforcing crises of economic development (resource scarcity, environmental degradation, population growth) that undermine the international and internal legitimacy on which sovereignty stands. Both of these dynamics have led to a growing number of collapsed and collapsing states. But even the strongest states in the system cannot effectively manage global issues alone.

Nearly one third of the people on the planet, more than 2 billion people, live in failed or failing states. Seven of the top 10 failed states are in Africa.[37] In his book *Collapsed States*, I. William Zartman notes that half the states in Africa may be in serious or maximum "danger of collapse, if not already gone."[38] Not coincidentally, all major armed conflicts are internal conflicts,[39] showing that sovereign states beyond Africa are feeling the effects of substate challenges.

When sovereign states collapse, the international system feels the shock waves. A state is in a process of collapse when its institutions and leaders lose control of political and economic space. When state authorities can no longer provide security, law and order, an economic infrastructure, or other services for citizens, then government retracts and the countryside is left on its own. Political space broadens as outside actors usurp (as in Lebanon) and intervene (as IGOs and NGOs enter to provide relief services necessitated by state breakdown). Economic space contracts as the informal economy takes over beyond state control, and as localities resort to barter, as occurred in Somalia.[40] In the power vacuum left by state collapse, global problems thrive. For example, as al Qaeda fighters were pushed out of Afghanistan, they moved to Sudan, Somalia, and Yemen—other areas where state control is weak.

When states implode, more than the residents are affected. In an interdependent world, the event can hurt distant international actors. Refugee flows, disease, terrorism, crime, drug smuggling, ethnic conflict, and civil war all thrive as the states recede and often spread beyond borders. NGOs, IGOs, and criminal organizations are all drawn to collapsed states, whether to help restore law and order or to exploit its absence.

Robert Jackson, in his book *Quasi-States*, notes that the international system used to be based primarily on "positive sovereignty," the actual, empirical ability of a state to control its political and economic space, to

15

"provide political goods for its citizens... the sociological, economic, technological, psychological, and similar wherewithal to declare, implement, and enforce public policy both domestically and internationally."[41] Weak states existed, but not for long, as it was considered perfectly legitimate for an outside power to conquer and absorb a weak state. The "old sovereignty game" recognized but did not protect weak sovereignties. They were vulnerable links in the international system's food chain. Their digestion by more powerful states was internationally sanctioned behavior.

This changed with the rise of Woodrow Wilson's idea of self-determination, with the discrediting of the concept of "salt-water colonialism"[42] and the end of colonial empires, and with the rise of democracy. The "new sovereignty game," Jackson contends, is increasingly based on "negative sovereignty," the formal legal entitlement to freedom from outside interference and the de jure norm of nonintervention.[43] Thus, the current norms and practices of the international system create conditions that allow weak, ineffectual quasi-states to exist.

Sovereignty is under siege from internal pressures and conflicts that weaken state institutions. Many states in the developing world are undergoing related crises of poverty, disease, environmental degradation, and internal conflict. According to the United Nations, the top 25 worst places to live in the world are all African countries. Life expectancy is dropping precipitously in Africa as HIV/AIDS ravages the continent.[44] High external debt diverts government budgets from critical public health, education, and social welfare investments to making interest payments that further profit Western banks. Corruption flourishes as survival is endangered, a "get mine" mentality permeates public life, and people don't expect to live long enough to face consequences for their actions. Where political institutions are seen as weak and ineffective to meet public needs, cynicism, hostility, and armed conflicts multiply. Most African countries now struggle to respond to this "perfect storm" of poverty, disease, and political instability. The opportunity for conflict among societal groups increases as resources shrink.

Reinforcing economic and political crises are not restricted to Africa. GNP in the former Soviet states fell by as much as 30 percent after the Cold War, while major armed conflicts in the region quadrupled.[45] Pressure on (and disillusionment with) fragile state institutions grows as the state fails to break (or contributes to) the scarcity cycle and as the chasm grows between the less-developed and the developed states. States that are confronted with reinforcing crises can "harden," resorting to increased repression in an attempt to establish control.[46] Repressive tactics are costly, however. Civil institutions of the state atrophy (and economic and social performance often suffer) as power and resources concentrate in the military and police. State legitimacy and authority are further undermined, and opposition grows with the increase in repressive tactics.

The result is not just a crisis of a particular regime but of the sovereign state itself. Any regime that wins power will face extremely denigrated (to nonexistent) state institutions and societal bases of state power. Thus, the related crises of poverty and internal conflicts undermine the foundations of sovereign power. Many areas of Afghanistan respond entirely to tribal and local authorities, not the sovereign state. After decades of warfare, arms are readily available, leaving the state with nothing close to a monopoly on the use of force. As NGOs, IGOs, and states aid Afghanistan's post–Taliban transition, many worry not only about the capacity of any new government but also whether the area is governable.

Sovereignty also is undermined by external trends that have been heralded since the end of the Cold War: the opening of societies, economies, and technologies. Strong states are not immune to the problems of globalization, as shown by the London bombings, the Madrid bombings, and the September 11 attacks. Developing states are also caught in a bind. Leaders are attracted to the prospect of wealth promised by democracy, capitalism, and technology (which can strengthen the state), yet they fear the loss of control and the decentralization of power that these processes entail (which can weaken the state). Capitalism, democracy, and technology can devolve power away from central state institutions and undermine the state's ability to control its borders.[47] Many developing states desire international capital and jobs, but the process of liberalizing economic and political systems can be quite destabilizing. Citizen demands on government cannot wait until new institutions are built and put into place, so developing states are in the challenging position of trying to modernize and democratize their institutions as these same institutions try to solve critical problems. As Jack Snyder and Edward Mansfield describe the dangers of democratization, it is like changing the steering wheel while driving the car.[48]

The end of the superpower conflict has also increased the pressure on many weak states. More states compete for overseas development assistance. The standard of living has dropped precipitously in many states that had received Cold War assistance, such as Cuba and North Korea (where famine has been a problem in recent years). The underlying ineffectiveness of state political and economic institutions becomes clear without the mask of Cold War aid and alliances. The authority and legitimacy of the state suffer because the state cannot meet citizen expectations, and living standards decline.

It is not just the case, as Max Singer and Aaron Wildavsky argued, that the twenty-first century world is increasingly segregated into two zones—peace and turmoil—with a widening gap between the advanced capitalist democracies and the underdeveloped nondemocratic states. According to Singer and Wildavsky, the stabilizing solution to this dilemma was the advancement of democratization, economic liberalization, and development so that more states would move from the "zone of turmoil" to the "zone of peace."[49]

It is not that simple. Democratization and economic liberalization can undermine already fragile state institutions. During the transition period, attempts to establish open societies and open markets can further move a weak state into the zone of turmoil. Even in peaceful and prosperous open-market democracies, terrorists blow up trains and fly planes into buildings. Singer and Wildavsky might have argued that the zone of peace (even with its problems of drugs and crime) is preferable to the zone of turmoil (with its starvation and war), but surely their argument needs qualification—at least to check the expectations of fledgling democracies. Singer and Wildavsky's zone of peace is not the Promised Land. Democratization and economic liberalization carry their own costs in terms of transsovereign problems. Even strong, wealthy states with healthy internal institutions cannot unilaterally defeat global problems.

Open Economies

Developed countries have long histories of promoting international trade and global capitalist economic systems, sometimes even through force, while also trying to protect some domestic markets from international competition. Squabbles with the Barbary pirates, who were supported by the pasha of Tripoli (present-day Libya—even in the 1790s, the United States had poor relations with Libya because of a form of state-sponsored terrorism), led to the formation of the U.S. Navy and the beginning of the president's ability to commit troops abroad without a formal declaration of war by Congress, in this case in order to protect commercial shipping engaged in trade. U.S. tensions with China and Japan in the nineteenth and twentieth centuries concerned the opening of Asian markets to U.S. goods.

European imperialism in Asia, Africa, and the Americas also served commercial interests. From the trade in spices, slaves, and rum to the extraction of precious metals, foreign commerce drove earlier periods of globalization. U.S. imperialism in Latin America and the Pacific was also conducted in the name of promoting trade and opening commerce. The American empire—in the form of U.S. protectorates in Puerto Rico, Guam, Samoa, and Hawaii, among others—was acquired largely to assist U.S. commercial interests in their efforts to expand foreign trade. The United States forcibly created the country of Panama (by seizing territory from Colombia) in order to build the Panama Canal to facilitate trade. Military intervention in Guatemala in 1954 was done largely to protect the interests of the United Fruit Company. As one U.S. trade official argued, "For most of America's history, foreign policy has reflected an obsession with open markets for American business. . . . Business expansion abroad was often seen as an extension of the American frontier, part of the nation's manifest destiny."[50]

Given these ties between colonialism and free-market economics, it is no wonder that many citizens in developing countries are suspicious of globalization and the spread of international trade and capitalist systems. Many question just how "free" trade is among unequal trading partners and how "open" developed economies are to the goods (especially agricultural products) of less-developed countries. Developed countries retain protectionist obstacles to the products in which developing countries enjoy comparative advantage. Some see free trade and monetary policies as neoimperialism, with multinational corporations and international economic organizations such as the IMF and World Trade Organization (WTO) now infringing on the sovereignty of developing states in place of the colonial armies of a previous era. Trade ministers in developed countries counter that open markets, for all their imperfections, perform better than do state-controlled markets.

The Cold War was caused in part by this clash between state and market economies, with the United States opposed to the Soviet Union closing Eastern European markets to Western goods and trade. During the Cold War, many in the West believed that the superior economic performance of capitalist, free-market systems would eventually bring state-controlled, communist economic systems to their knees. George Kennan presciently predicted that the demise of the Soviet sphere would come about not through the external military confrontation of a globalized and militarized U.S. containment policy, which the United States could not afford, but through the West's building of strong, internal open societies and open markets. Eventually, the Soviet bloc would be "unable to stand the comparison."[51]

> If economic recovery could be brought about and public confidence restored in Western Europe—if Western Europe, in other words, could be made the home of a vigorous, prosperous and forward-looking civilization—the communist regime in Eastern Europe . . . would never be able to stand the comparison, and the spectacle of a happier and

more successful life just across the fence . . . would be bound in the end to have a disintegrating and eroding effect on the communist world.[52]

His prediction was confirmed at the Cold War's end. The Marshall Plan and 45 years of a concerted policy of building open economic and political institutions in Western Europe succeeded in rebuilding a continent destroyed by war. Such rebuilding never took place in much of Eastern Europe. Eventually, even the top leaders of the Soviet Union were forced to admit that their economic system was in need of reform when Gorbachev came to power in the 1980s.

Gorbachev's reforms began as attempts to improve the productivity and efficiency of the state-controlled economy: cutting down on vodka abuse on the job, decreasing bureaucratic red tape, and increasing worker and industry accountability. Quickly, these internal attempts to reform and strengthen the communist system unleashed massive dissatisfaction with the existing system. Gorbachev's reforms tapped into consumer and social unrest over shortages and poor economic performance (for example, exploding television sets in Moscow were a common cause of hospital emergency room visits), including the Chernobyl nuclear disaster. The legitimacy of the communist model was undermined, accelerating the pace of Gorbachev's initially modest reforms into the eventual overthrow of the entire system.[53] Gorbachev soon learned what the Chinese are now grappling with: that it is difficult to uncork just a little economic freedom.

With the demise of communist regimes in Eastern Europe and the former Soviet Union, and with the demise of state-controlled economies and authoritarian regimes in Latin America, many in the West assumed that it had won the Cold War's economic battle. As Paul Krugman put it, "Governments that had spent half a century pursuing statist, protectionist policies suddenly got free market religion. It was the dawn of a new golden age for global capitalism." In addition, there

> was a sea change in the intellectual Zeitgeist: the almost universal acceptance, by governments and markets alike, of a new view about what it takes to develop. This view has come to be widely known as the "Washington Consensus.". . . It is the belief that . . . free markets and sound money [are] the key to economic development. Liberalize trade, privatize state enterprises, balance the budget, peg the exchange rate, and one will have laid the foundations for an economic takeoff.[54]

That view is changing. Many in the developing world have long criticized the "Washington Consensus" as adverse to the poor, and question the desirability of interconnected economies built on a "one-size-fits-all" Western model. They also point out that Washington rarely followed its own advice, as the United States routinely ran large budget deficits. The global economic meltdown has given credence to this view. The worst global economic crisis since the Great Depression began with a bad idea: Why not give home loans to people for houses they couldn't really afford, at interest rates that start low but which ratchet up over time? As long as housing demand continued and prices continued to rise, buyers could quickly sell or "flip" their properties for a higher price, and the lenders and buyers would profit before the higher rates ever kicked in. If buyers did not "flip" but stayed in the home, incomes could rise over time to afford the purchase. If not, lenders reasoned that the bad loans would not cause trouble for the companies that originated them because they would sell the loans to other financial institutions. Riskier loans were mixed in with good loans, in complex, little-regulated and little-understood investment bundles called "derivatives." Bankers and investors believed this made sense because risk was widely divided among financial institutions across the globe, and in any case they had purchased insurance from highly rated global insurance companies like American International Group, Inc (AIG), which would insulate them from losses if the investments went bad. They thought that widely dividing the risk lessened it. But instead it put contaminated or "toxic" assets on the books of so many financial institutions, that all were vulnerable when the housing bubble burst. Rising foreclosures and investors pulling their money out of the market sent financial institutions falling like a line of dominoes; banks and insurance companies did not have the capital on hand to cover all the losses. Stock markets crashed and credit markets froze, hurting all, not only the people who had profited in the "subprime mortgage" fiasco. The cascading financial crises revealed many underlying structural problems as well, such as excess capital in some economies (e.g., China, oil-rich states) financing excessive debt in other countries (e.g., the United States). U.S. households and companies engaged in excessive spending on credit, while the Chinese paid the bill, to a degree not fully appreciated. Markets operate best when they operate under law and transparency, but regulations and transparency were weak or nonexistent in this case. Global capitalism is prone to market booms, busts, and financial flues, but many leaders believed markets would regulate themselves, and market problems would come from developing countries in a "it can't happen here" mentality. More than 20 years earlier, Susan Strange predicted this type of "Casino Capitalism" where extreme market volatility destroys lives due to: innovations in financial markets, the sheer size of markets, commercial banks turning into investment banks, the rise of Asian economies, and the shift to corporate self-regulation.[55]

Many countries are now less inclined to accept economic advice from the United States and Britain, since the economic crisis began in those countries' markets. Even British Prime Minister Gordon Brown concludes, "The old Washington consensus is over" and a "new world order" is emerging. He seems to mean by this, however, not a reduction in globalization's free trade or markets, but rather reform of global markets and institutions, moving toward more effective transparency and regulation of global financial markets.[56]

Of course, even before the Great Recession, "free-market religion" was never established universally. While many states "talk the talk" of capitalism, developed countries retain popular, protectionist, agriculture subsidies and restrictions on certain foreign products. Corruption is a huge obstacle to economic development around the world. Property rights remain poorly defined and protected in many parts of the world.[57] Many countries, such as Mexico, are privatizing state-owned industries, but the process is vulnerable to distortion by corruption as the transition to free-market economies is ongoing. There are still some states, such as North Korea, with closed economies. Others, such as China, Vietnam, and Cuba, are trying to attract foreign capital and investment and encourage some privatization of the economy, but the central government still owns and plays a key role in many industries. Yet the spread of capitalism, some contend, helps to spread peace and democracy as well. People with economic rights tend to demand political rights. There is some evidence of this today in China, where a growing middle class increasingly demands an end to political corruption, and where there are now contested local elections. Thomas Friedman argues that capitalism and economic interdependence bring peace; no two countries with a McDonald's have ever gone to war with one another. The economic price of war is too heavy for countries whose economies are deeply intertwined, both supplying Dell computers for example. "The Dell Theory stipulates: No two countries that are both part of a major global supply chain, like Dell's, will ever fight a war against each other as long as they are both part of the same global supply chain."[58]

U.S. and Western dominance of international economic regimes is precisely the point that draws concern from many people around the world. The European Union (EU), WTO, IMF, and World Bank were all created by the United States and its developed allies. Developing countries often have little say in the rules and regimes that govern the global economy. Many poor countries cannot even afford to send delegates to the WTO meetings. For example, for many years the WTO's rules favored Western pharmaceutical companies that were interested in protecting their patents and profits over developing countries that were interested in producing cheaper generic AIDS drugs to fight a pressing public health crisis.[59]

However, even though open economies often perform better than their state-run counterparts, they also carry costs, as the cascading financial crisis and global economic meltdown show.[60] Resentment over a widening gulf between rich and poor states and developed countries' dominance of the global economy leads to increasingly violent protests of globalization. The transition to capitalist economic structures also can destabilize states. Amy Chua disputes that "markets and democracy go hand in hand," and instead argues that "Exporting free market democracy breeds ethnic hatred and global instability." When market liberalization helps "foreign minorities" earn disproportionate wealth while the local majority suffers economically, this lights the match to violence. Wealthy ethnic minorities, from Chinese in Southeast Asia to Croatians in the former Yugoslavia, become violently hated, at the same time as emerging democracy "empowers the impoverished majority, unleashing ethnic demagoguery, confiscation, and sometimes genocidal revenge."[61]

Instability provides openings for organized crime to step into the vacuum, as has occurred in Russia. The old order has been pulled down, but new laws and institutions that support free-market economies are still being built, and much turmoil can arise in the interim.

Decreased regulation and increased transborder trade decreases the opportunities for shipments to be searched or monitored. Thus, states lose significant control over their borders, one of the hallmarks of sovereignty.

"Dirty money" follows many of the same paths as "clean money." The same emerging global financial infrastructure useful to legal businesses also increases the opportunity and ease of conducting and covering illicit economic activities, such as the smuggling of narcotics and nuclear materials. Profits from illicit activities can be hidden in legal investments, sprinkled into front companies, bank accounts, and small investments across a range of industries and states. With the Internet and e-cash, the money trail can move quickly and be erased as investments can be changed and moved with a keystroke. Attempts to freeze and seize the monies of terrorist organizations show how difficult it can be to track and stop illicit cash in interdependent economies.

Open economies also decentralize power as more and more actors have autonomous economic power, and the central government loses its ability to control economic activities in a global marketplace. Microsoft

Corporation's founder Bill Gates's annual income is more than the annual GNP of many states. The income of prominent drug lords often overwhelms and distorts the legal economy in a state because it is difficult to control or regulate.

Open Societies

Francis Fukuyama argues that the end of the Cold War also signaled the end of history, by which he means that "a remarkable consensus concerning the legitimacy of liberal democracy as a system of government has emerged throughout the world, as it conquered rival ideologies like hereditary monarchy, fascism, and most recently communism."[62] Although liberal democracy has not triumphed and may never prevail in all areas of the globe, Fukuyama contends that the twentieth century was marked by great battles of competing ideologies, and that now no alternative universal ideology of consequence exists to challenge liberal democracy. According to Fukuyama, liberal democracy "gives fullest scope" to satisfying "all three parts of the soul [desire, reason, and spirit] simultaneously."[63]

Fukuyama's thesis may be increasingly challenged by the ideas of some Islamic extremist groups that are intent on challenging Western government forms and promoting fundamentalist Islamic rule. Yet even analysts less optimistic about the liberal democratic form agree that we "are currently witnessing the fourth historical wave of democratization . . . more global in its reach . . . affecting far more countries and more thorough than its predecessors."[64] Democracy is not new and has been around in one form or another since the ancient Greeks. What is new, however, is the number of states that are turning to representative government forms with free multiparty elections and the protection of individual and minority rights including free speech and free press, freedom of association, freedom of movement, and freedom of religion. For the first time in history, a majority of states are either democracies or in transition to democracy.

In the first wave of democratization in the 1800s, universal suffrage was extended in states that were committed to democratic principles so that more than white male property owners could vote. This movement toward democracy ended as monarchies and authoritarian rulers sought to reestablish control in many states after the "springtime of freedom" in Europe in 1848–1849. Although the first wave expanded democracy within societies and sought to spread democracy in Western Europe and North America, these same states were involved simultaneously in carving up the non-Western world into colonial empires in profoundly nondemocratic ways.

The second wave of democratization occurred during and after World War I as many states believed that autocracies were more to blame for starting the war than were democratic states. However, many of the democracies established after World War I were weak, such as the Weimar Republic, and many of these states reverted to authoritarianism as fascism swept the globe.

The third wave of democratization occurred with World War II as colonial powers were no longer able or willing to hold onto their overseas possessions, and a tidal wave of decolonization swept the globe. The number of independent states tripled from 1945 to 1979, and many of these former colonies turned to democratic government forms. Once again, however, this wave of democratization was followed by reversals. After historic initial democratic elections, many leaders would not hand over power to others, barring further elections. This pattern was pernicious in Africa. Ironically, the Cold War also caused some democratic backsliding, as the United States and the West supported noncommunist but nondemocratic regimes. "By some counts, one-third of the globe's democracies had fallen under authoritarian rule by the late 1970s,"[65] as personal rule, military rule, or single-party autocracy replaced democratic political participation and institutions in developing states. Even though there were reverses, with each wave the number of democracies overall increased, as states, such as India, joined and stayed in the community of democracies.

The fourth wave of democratization differs from previous eras in three important respects. First, it was not the result of a single external event such as World War I or II. Although the end of the Soviet empire led many Eastern European states into the democratic experiment, other states such as Portugal, Spain, and South Africa turned to democracy for reasons other than (and prior to) the end of the Cold War.

Second, the most recent wave of democratization differs from its predecessors in scope and intensity. More states on more continents are becoming more democratic than ever before. This wave is not restricted to Europe or to former colonial empires, and this wave is more intensive, entailing a restructuring of political and economic institutions.

Third, democratization in this wave occurred overwhelmingly in Catholic countries, as discussed in Chapter 7. While democratization is by no means secure, this wave has advantages. Open markets and technologies support and facilitate political openings. An international audience watches via the Internet and real-time media, and can offer real time support. Liberalizing political institutions sometimes can be a prerequisite to receiving international capital investments. The growth of civil society internationally may also help solidify the current wave of democratization.

Two decades ago, policy makers and scholars thought such extensive opportunities for democratization were unlikely. The opening of societies may lend itself to more open economic systems, as people with some say in their political futures tend to desire openness in their economic futures as well.[66] Of course, movement toward open societies is not complete.

Some states, such as China, are trying to open their economic systems to achieve prosperity and development without allowing significant political freedoms. Many states, particularly in Africa and the Middle East, retain authoritarian political systems.

Democracy is spreading for several reasons (of course, there are significant disagreements over how best to promote democracy in practice). Global media and cheap and ready access to information technology can help democratization. Democracies are more likely to have free-market and free-trade capitalist economies (encouraged by international financial institutions) and to have more prosperity and better records of economic development. Democratic protections of property rights and individual liberties provide a rule of law that fosters a more stable investment and business climate and better protects the larger number of citizens now traveling abroad and taking advantage of more advanced transportation and communication links. Perhaps most important, developed democracies tend not to go to war with one another.[67] Democracies are not more peaceful overall. They tend to go to war with nondemocracies, and the transition period of democratization can be fraught with conflict. But the empirical record of democracies not warring with other democracies is strong.

However, democratization carries costs. Transitions to democracy can be destabilizing in the short run, as "[d]emocratization typically creates a syndrome of weak central authority, unstable domestic coalitions, and high-energy mass politics."[68] Democratic elections and liberal protections—of human rights, rule of law, and separation of powers—may not coincide.[69] If privatization and liberalization of the economy are occurring simultaneously with democratization efforts (as is often the case), then corrupt, powerful corporate or criminal organizations may gain assets and influence before the civic institutions of public control and accountability are established (many observers argue that this has occurred in Nigeria, Russia, Ukraine, Tajikistan, Uzbekistan, Kazakhstan, etc.). Any one of these transitions would be highly complex and destabilizing for a society. The simultaneous and often sudden overlapping of these transitions only increases the level of difficulty for polities and increases the pressures for fragmentation that can undermine states.

Open Technologies

Developed countries tend to be enamored with technological advances, and it is easy to understand why. Cellular phones connect areas that are difficult to link by landlines in places such as Hong Kong and Israel. Technology made possible the settlement of the American continent and still undergirds the U.S. military's preeminent position in the world today.

Americans own more computers and televisions than the citizens of any other country.[70] China and the United States have the most Internet users by far (although some countries, such as Iceland, the Netherlands, and Norway, have over 85% of their smaller populations online).[71] U.S. scientists, industry, and government invented the computer and developed the Internet.

The "information revolution" is profoundly changing the way all states do their business: "Today all of humankind is linked by almost instantaneous communications. There is no corner of the globe that is not accessible to us, or us to them. Marshall McLuhan's global village is upon us with profound consequences . . . a market crash in Hong Kong is felt immediately by pensioners in Dubuque (Iowa)."[72]

Technological advances have been dramatically spurred by advances in computers. The first modern computer, developed in 1946 to calculate firing trajectories for artillery shells, "could execute the then-astonishing number of 5,000 arithmetic operations per second . . . weighed 30 tons, filled an enormous room at the University of Pennsylvania, consumed 150,000 watts of power, and used 18,000 vacuum tubes."[73] (The term "*bugs in the system*" literally referred to insects in these huge machines that interfered with operations.) Today, a Pentium chip is built on a thumbnail-sized piece of silicon, and laptop computers are smaller than briefcases, weighing less than 4 pounds.[74]

Many theorists argue that technology drives globalization and that the digital divide between rich and poor countries has kept the world's poor from enjoying the benefits of globalization. Computers, faxes, cell phones, and air travel have shrunk the planet and made sovereign borders less important for economic transactions. Television, radio, cell phones, video cameras, and computers have made sovereign authorities less able to control the flow of information and ideas and thus made authoritarian control more expensive and difficult to maintain. Anyone with a cell phone camera can record government abuses and instantly transmit these images via the Internet to place international pressure on the offending regime.

Technology, in essence, has undermined sovereign authority, decentralized power, and opened markets and societies.[75] To some extent, this presents a "chicken-or-egg" question. Although technology may in some sense "drive" the process of globalization, technological advances do not occur in an economic or political vacuum. Sustained political and investment decisions drive technological advances. Scientists did not suddenly develop powerful supercomputers, tiny microchips, and fiber optic telecommunications links by accident. These advancements came about through sustained investment, supported by political and social policies that harnessed resources in pursuit of technological progress and innovation as tools to advance economic and political goals. The first mainframe computer and the Internet were developed by the U.S. Department of Defense working in close connection with universities.

Causality flows in all directions, but together the trends of open economies, open societies, and open markets substantially reinforce each other. When combined, they equal more than the sum of their parts. Technological advances facilitate the opening of markets and societies, and vice versa.

However, like their counterparts, open technologies also undermine sovereignty and make transsovereign challenges possible. Technology moves legal and illegal information, people, and goods more quickly and efficiently than ever before across borders without the consent or even knowledge of sovereign authorities. Human smugglers use cell phones, e-cash, laptops, the Internet, and encryption software to track and direct their "product" flow.

Noting that globalization has downsides does not mean that sovereignty is dead or that state-controlled economies and authoritarian societies free of advanced technologies would be beneficial. Human history is the unfolding story of numerous and varying social organizing frameworks. The sovereign state has had a good, 360-year run as an organizing unit. Although it is in no imminent danger of disappearing, we cannot expect that the sovereign state will be in the form we know it 360 years from now. For globalization to be both sustainable and just, its costs must be clearly understood and addressed. Sovereignty and globalization carry many benefits, but there is nothing sacrosanct about either.

TOMORROW: DEBATES ABOUT THE FUTURE OF SOVEREIGNTY

There are three main views about the future of sovereignty. According to the first view, we are witnessing the end of the state. The second view argues that the sovereign state continues to be an important actor on the world scene, especially in the military security realm, but that sovereignty is changing, especially as the state increasingly loses power to markets and nonstate actors. The third view argues that states are still the primary actors in international politics, and other actors (NGOs, IGOs, MNCs) exist and operate only as much as allowed by states.

The first view contends that sovereign states are a "nostalgic fiction" in the global economy. According to Kenichi Ohmae, states "are little more than bit actors." Decisions over investments, production, and exchange rates "are made elsewhere by individuals and institutions over which they have little practical control." National labels are becoming meaningless. Is a Toyota made in Mississippi a Japanese car? This does not mean that international politics will now be marked by the "clash of civilizations" or cultures, as Samuel Huntington contends. "There are now tens of millions of teenagers around the world who, having been raised in a multimedia-rich environment, have a lot more in common with each other than they do with members of older generations in their own cultures." States are losing their capacity to respond to economic bumps in the road, and so regions are becoming more important. Although it may still be politically correct to talk about states as the important actors, "it is a bald-faced economic lie."[76]

The second view sees the state retreating as its functions change.[77] Today, either other actors are increasingly filling these functions or no one fills them. For example, Susan Strange discusses 10 important functions or authorities claimed by states that are on the decline. First, the state is responsible for defending national territory against foreign invasion, but in developed countries the threat of foreign invasion is declining or minimal, thereby eroding this source of state authority. Second, the state is responsible for maintaining the value of its currency, but inflation in one country can spread to others, revealing that this responsibility is now a more collective one. Third, the state used to choose the appropriate form of economic development, but open economies now allow market pressures from the IMF, World Bank, and private investors to limit state choice and force convergence on a narrow range of development models. Fourth, the state used to be responsible for correcting the booms and busts of market economies through state spending to infuse money into public works or other state enterprises. Franklin Delano Roosevelt fought the Great Depression in the 1930s in the United States by initiating large public works projects, building national parks, the Tennessee Valley Authority dams, and highways and bridges to put people back to work and get the economy moving again. But this option is more difficult for governments now, given the market pressures to keep government spending at a minimum. Fifth, states used to provide a social safety net for those who were least able to survive in a market economy by providing assistance to the very old and young, sick, disabled, and unemployed. Today, market pressures are leading states to cut back on their social welfare benefits and protective regulations. Sixth, states used to have the ability to set appropriate tax rates to pay for government public works or social benefits spending. Today, all states are pressured by international market forces to keep tax rates to a minimum, thereby limiting their autonomy and authority to raise funds. Seventh, states used to have great autonomy in control over foreign trade, especially imports. Today, government intervention can only affect the margins because most of the decisions that concern trade flows are the "aggregate result of multiple corporate decisions."[78] Strong international market forces pressure governments to reduce obstacles to cross-border trade.

Eighth, governments used to take responsibility for building the economic infrastructure of the state "from ports and roads to posts and telegraphs. . . . Even where governments, as in the United States, looked to private enterprise to find the necessary capital, they never hesitated in revising the laws on landed property so that landowners could not easily obstruct the infrastructural investment."[79] Today, public utilities are being privatized, and the key infrastructure needed in modern economies are communications technologies, most of which do not depend on government's control over territory. Infrastructure development decisions are being made in corporate boardrooms, not state offices. Eastern European states are being integrated into the modern telecommunications grid not by governments primarily, but by private corporations that recognize the profit margins that are available to the corporation that gets there first. States may have built the infrastructure of highways, but firms and private actors are building and extending the information superhighways.

Ninth, states used to be able to create or allow public or private monopolies to dominate the local market, but today international market pressures impose greater costs on state governments that try to maintain monopolies. Finally, states used to entertain one "special kind of monopoly—that of the legitimate use of violence against the citizen or any group of citizens."[80] Now, the globalization of the arms trade and easy access to technology make the means of violence more readily available to nonstate actors. Strong and weak states alike are losing their monopolies on force, as evidenced by the chemical attack on the Japanese subway and the destruction of the World Trade Center in the United States.

In essence, we are witnessing the incredibly shrinking state. States continue to exist, but their powers are not as extensive as they used to be, and other actors take or share power with states over key functions or sectors. The result is "a ramshackle assembly of conflicting sources of authority" in which individuals' loyalties and identities will not necessarily lie with the sovereign state but are spread among professions, civic groups, ethnic ties, firms, etc., just as state power is becoming diffused.[81] As more power shifts away from states and toward markets, accountability and democracy may decrease because corporate leaders are not subject to democratic accountability and market forces cannot be voted upon.

Other theorists agree that we are in a period of transition or turbulence[82] in which the sovereign state is increasingly under challenge but not obsolete yet because alternatives to sovereignty have not established themselves. James Rosenau argues that not only markets but also increasingly skilled individuals are driving the changes. He believes that access to the Internet, personal computers, faxes, jet planes, and so on, have led to a "skills revolution." People who are plugged in have become better able to assess, compare, and contrast large amounts of data; are more sophisticated in critiquing the information provided to them by states and in seeking alternative information; and are better able to articulate and mobilize around goals. "It is unimaginable that people have not learned and become more complex in order to adapt to an increasingly complicated world."[83] In an evolutionary way, people are adapting to changes in their environment. "People have become increasingly competent in assessing where they fit in international affairs and how their behavior can be aggregated into significant outcomes."[84] Thus, the globalization of democratization is no accident, because the telecommunications revolution that is fueling the skills revolution is global. A people plugged in is a people empowered to bring about change, to end apartheid in South Africa, to tear down the Berlin Wall and the communist empire, and to challenge the dictatorship in Tiananmen Square. Rosenau believes the skills revolution makes governments more responsive to citizens' needs and more democratic, whereas Strange and others believe that increased market and corporate power reduces democracy and accountability.

Because of the digital divide, the rate of change is not uniform. But even though "the information-rich are getting richer at a quicker rate than the information-poor, the trend line is conceived to slope in the same upward direction for both groups."[85] Even citizens in less-developed countries (where poverty and repressive regimes may limit access to technology) are becoming more skillful. For example, Haitians demonstrating in 1994 to turn back the USS Harlan County from intervening and Iranians denouncing U.S. support of the shah of Iran in 1979 carried signs in English and timed their protests to appear on the U.S. evening news broadcasts. South African child AIDS activist Nkosi Johnson successfully used the media to draw attention to the plight of African AIDS victims and to change policy. As people become more skillful, they also become less deferential. Traditionally, state legitimacy and compliance

> derived from constitutional and legal sources. Under these circumstances individuals were habituated to compliance with the directives issued by higher authorities. They did what they were told to do because . . . that is what one did. As a consequence, authority structures remained in place for decades, even centuries, as people unquestioningly yielded to the dictates of governments.[86]

Today, because of the skills revolution, a pervasive "authority crisis" exists as people are increasingly inclined to question authority and have the means to do so. Legitimacy now derives not from tradition but from performance. States are no longer the only key actors, and they must manage and compete with a variety of organizations. Sovereignty continues to limp along—not because of its strength, but more by default because none of these new organizations has yet delivered a knockout blow.

Another cut at this second view is that sovereignty is losing its identification with territory. Richard Rosecrance argues, "In economies where capital, labor, and information are mobile and have risen to predominance, no land fetish remains. Developed countries would rather plumb the world market than acquire territory. The virtual state—a state that has downsized its territorially based production capability—is the logical consequence of this emancipation from the land."[87] By shedding outmoded functions to nonstate actors and by downsizing territory, states are adapting their logic to market forces. When the Treaty of Westphalia was signed, the economic system was mercantilist and land-based. Wealth and power depended on the control of land, access to raw materials, and control of the means of production. In a world of slow-moving ships and horseback messengers, capital and labor were fixed in place, not mobile. Increasing power meant increasing land, and thus the European colonial empires were born. It is no accident that under this economic system, the political organization that developed—sovereignty—directly correlated authority to territory. But now the economy has changed, and states are changing to reflect the new reality. The new economic system is based on information, technology, and services—none of which depends on the control of land. In a world of open borders and economic flows—and people who have access to computers, faxes, phones, the Internet, e-cash, and other advanced technologies—the means of production, capital, and labor are mobile. States have access to raw materials through trade, not conquest. Thus, for states with modern, information-based economies such as Japan, territory is not the source of their power, so conflict over territory becomes passé. For states with less-developed economies that are still land-based (and primarily dependent on natural resource extraction or agricultural exports), territory will not become passé and may still be a source of conflict. A population explosion might make land important again. But these trends are not sustainable in the long term because land does not produce a better return than knowledge, so states with lots of land (such as Russia) may not be especially powerful in the new economy. Knowledge allows more extraction and more efficient and effective utilization of resources. States recognize the success of "virtual" states such as Japan and will try to emulate them and thus develop modern economies that are less shackled to land.

The virtual state no longer commands resources as states did in the mercantilist yesteryear. It negotiates, deriving its power from direct foreign investment, an educated workforce, and market savvy, not from military superiority or control over territory. This brings a crisis for democratic politics as states lose some of their autonomy over electing and enforcing policy to unelected, nonstate actors. Citizens can, however, vote with their feet if they are unimpressed by their state's performance.[88]

The final view argues that nothing fundamental has changed. Stephen Krasner argues that weak states have always existed, and that sovereignty has always been "organized hypocrisy," challenged in theory and practice.[89] But even examples of problematic sovereignty only show how embedded the concept of sovereignty is.[90] It continues to be our default assumption. Changes in the environment do not readily or easily translate into institutional changes. Sovereign states persist over time, even when their functions are not in sync with a changed international environment because of vertical and horizontal linkages:

> Vertical depth refers to the extent to which the institutional structure defines the individual actors. Breadth refers to the number of links that a particular activity has with other activities, to the number of changes that would have to be made if a particular form of activity were altered. . . . With regard to both breadth and depth, sovereign states have become increasingly formidable institutions. They influence the self-image of those individuals within their territory through the concept of citizenship, as well as by exercising control, to one degree or another, over powerful instruments of socialization. With regard to breadth, states are the most densely linked institutions

in the contemporary world. Change the nature of states and virtually everything else in human society would also have to be changed.
Hence, even though environmental incentives have dramatically
changed since the establishment of the state system in the seven-
teenth century, there is little reason to believe that it will be easy to
replace sovereign states with some alternative structure for organizing
human political life.[91]

Despite interdependence, weak states, and compromised or problematic sovereignty, the sovereign state is not retreating. The costs of changing
to an alternative system would be prohibitive, and people cannot conceive
of a plausible alternative to sovereignty.

Others in this school of thought argue that no such fundamental
change away from sovereignty is imminent because existing states have
little incentive to alter the system. States are the gatekeepers to the international system, so it is difficult for actors other than states to be accorded
equal participation in that system. The growth of the European Union(EU)
is providing an alternative model to traditional sovereignty, but there are
few other serious challengers to sovereign arrangements. Hendrik Spruyt
argues that, for sovereignty to be replaced, there must be competition
among alternative models of organization—as there was at sovereignty's
initiation after competition with the urban league and city-state. If anything, sovereignty is becoming more entrenched because ethnic, religious,
and nationalist challenges to sovereignty reinforce the state as a prize worth
fighting for. Although sovereignty is not the optimal institutional arrange-
ment, new institutional challengers have not yet arisen. Sovereignty took
centuries to emerge, Spruyt argues. It is too early to declare its demise, and
many countries (although not all) tried to reinvigorate state institutions
and state spending to respond to the global economic crisis.

Another perspective argues there is no such thing as globalization, only
Americanization. Kenneth Waltz argued that we are witnessing the advance
of one incredibly powerful state—the United States—rather than the retreat of the state.[92] This third viewpoint paraphrases Mark Twain's famous
observation by noting that the territorial state is being "buried too soon."
William McNeill believes that challenges to the existing sovereign state do
not mean its death but that "pride of place [will go] to whatever authorities
are able to organize and maintain superior armed force. This implies that
their requiem for the Westphalian state is premature. So far, no promising
alternative to the territorial organization of armed force has even begun to
emerge."[93] To this assertion, the other schools of thought argue "Yes, but so

what?" If state military power is less able to prevail against nonstate threats in an interdependent world, then the state may retain coercive powers that are less and less useful. The state still exists but is more compromised in its ability to act effectively in the economic and social spheres that increasingly affect citizens' everyday lives. Too often these views are considered as zero-sum, either/or, and thus talk past one another. One can track changes or adaptations in the sovereign state without signing its death certificate.

Mapping out these debates in the scholarly literature helps establish questions to consider in reading the chapters of this book.

- ❏ Do global problems challenge not only the interests of states (as the traditional realist International Relations theory stipulates) but also the very architecture of states?
- ❏ How can transsovereign problems be dealt with in a system of sovereign states?
- ❏ Do the responses to global problems (greater reliance on NGOs or IGOs, for example) change or undermine sovereignty?
- ❏ Are alternatives to sovereignty evolving as people struggle to respond to global problems? Or is the state becoming more entrenched as people rely on old responses to combat new threats?

THE NEW SECURITY DILEMMA

Security has been the dominant realm of sovereign states, but even this is changing. Weakened sovereignty and transsovereign challenges create a new security dilemma. In previous eras, threats came from strong states. The "old security dilemma" was how one state could contain another strong state without provoking counteractions on the other side that would make the state stronger. This spiral of insecurity was often cited in arms races, the outbreak of World War I, and the Cold War. The temptation was to overrespond and appear offensive, thus triggering a heightened response from opponents that further decreased one's own security. In a self-help international system of strong sovereign states, how could a state provide for its own military security against another state without setting off a self-defeating spiral of counteractions by other states?

But if the old security dilemma was how states could protect against strong states without making them stronger, then the new security dilemma is how to protect against global challenges and the implosion of weak states without taking actions that make weak states weaker and transsovereign problems more severe. Globalization plus weak states and transsovereign problems equals the new security dilemma. Globalization gives breakdowns in state authority and capacity and transsovereign problems greater reach, speed, intensity, and impact. Borders are more permeable, and threats are decentralized, fast, fungible, and fluid. The twenty-first century security dilemma is how to respond to the problems of weak states and nonstate threats without making these problems worse. Responding with the predominant tool of the old security dilemma—military force—may not be effective. For example, using force may make terrorist organizations stronger because they can appeal to messianic visions and have heightened international importance. Failure to respond to nonmilitary threats, however, allows these problems to grow until they present a threat of violence and instability that cannot easily be met by force. As HIV and AIDS spread throughout sub-Saharan Africa, millions of orphans (especially boys) live in gangs on the streets, supported by begging and crime and without socialization into families or community values. Although these growing numbers of hardened throwaway children pose real threats to security, military forces can do little to prevent the spread of HIV and AIDS or care for orphans.

The new security dilemma requires both creation of more powerful nonmilitary tools (including more effective involvement of the private sector), and the retooling of military forces to meet nonstate threats. This presents a challenge even for the world's most powerful military. But even if doctrine, organization, training, and equipment priorities are changed to better prepare for the type of conflict that now predominates, military force is just not sufficient to combat global problems, which often stem from economic or other causes. Threats are decentralized, as are the resources needed for the fight, which are not primarily military. We must go beyond the military tools of sovereignty to contain security dilemmas that go beyond sovereignty.

Realizing this, militaries are increasingly reaching out to the private sector to help manage pressing security problems. The British government debates hiring mercenaries. The U.S. government enlists the private sector in the war on terrorism, and in curtailing the proliferation of weapons of mass destruction. When the strongest military in the strongest state needs the private sector to help manage security problems (traditionally, the state's strong suit), then sovereignty is changing.

ENDNOTES

1. UNICEF, "State of the World's Children 2009," http://www.unicef.org/sowc09/docs/SOWC09-FullReport-EN.pdf.
2. World Bank, "The Developing World Is Poorer than We Thought," August 1, 2008, <http://econ.worldbank.org/external/default/main?pagePK=6416

5259&piPK=64165421&theSitePK=469372&menuPK=64166093&entity ID=000158349_20080826113239>; Jeffrey D. Sachs, *The End of Poverty: Economic Possibilities for Our Time* (New York: Penguin Press, 2005); Jeffrey D. Sachs, *Investing in Development: A Practical Plan to Achieve the Millennium Development Goals* (UN Millennium Project), (London: Earthscan Publications, 2005).

3. "Religious Leaders Say Global Poverty Has No Borders," The Christian Post, September 13, 2005, <

4. ONE Campaign, "ONE Hosts Press Conference at IMF Headquarters," April 23, 2009, <http://www.one.org/blog/?p=5100>; Associated Press, "Tens of Thousands Protest G-20 Summit," March 28, 2009 http://www.msnbc.msn.com/id/29916843/; Pamela Constable, "Taliban Tightens Hold in Pakistan," *The Washington Post*, May 6, 2009, <http://www.washingtonpost.com/wp-dyn/content/article/2009/05/04/AR2009050400189.html>.

5. Gillian Sorensen, *The United Nations and Civil Societies: Redefining the Partnership for the 21st Century.* Keynote address to Women in International Security summer symposium, Washington, DC, June 15, 1998.

6. Maryann Cusimano Love, "Globalization, Ethics, and the War on Terrorism," *Notre Dame Journal of Ethics, Law, and Public Policy* (special "Violence in America" edition, 2002): 65–80; Maryann Cusimano Love, "Morality Matters: Ethics and Power Politics in the War on Terrorism," *Georgetown Journal of International Affairs* (Summer–Fall 2002): 7–16.

7. United Nations, "Member States," <http://www.un.org/en/members/index.shtml>; Ernest Gellner, "Nations and Nationalism," in Richard Betts (Ed.), *Conflict after the Cold War: Arguments on the Causes of War and Peace* (New York: Macmillan, 1994), 286.

8. Edward Luttwak, "Toward Post-Heroic Warfare," *Foreign Affairs* 74 (May–June 1995): 109–122; Francis Fukuyama, *The End of History and the Last Man* (New York: Free Press, 1992).

9. Foreign Policy and the Fund for Peace, "The Failed State Index 2009," *Foreign Policy* (July/August 2009), <http://www.fundforpeace.org/web/index.php?option=com_content&task=view&id=99&Itemid=140>; I. William Zartman, *Collapsed States* (Boulder, CO: Lynne Rienner, 1995); Robert Jackson, *Quasi-States: Sovereignty, International Relations, and the Third World* (New York: Cambridge University Press, 1990); Ted Robert Gurr, "The State Failure Project," now the Political Instability Task Force <http://globalpolicy.gmu.edu/pitf/>; Michael Brown, "Introduction," in *The International Dimensions of Internal Conflict* (Cambridge: MIT Press, 1996); Pauline H. Baker and John A. Ausink, "State Collapse and Ethnic Violence: Toward a Predictive Model," *Parameters* (Spring 1996): 19–31.

10. The following remarks are taken from Maryann Cusimano Love, "Globalization: A Virtue or a Vice," Chapter 5 in Siamack Shojai (Ed.), *Globalization: A Virtue or a Vice?* (New York: Praeger, 2002).

11. Jagdish N. Bhagwati, *In Defense of Globalization* (New York: Oxford University Press, 2004); Martin Wolf, *Why Globalization Works* (New Haven, CT: Yale University Press, 2004); John Micklethwait and Adrian Wooldridge, *A Future Perfect: The Challenge and Hidden Promise of Globalization* (New York: Random House, 2000); Thomas Friedman, *The Lexus and the Olive Tree* (New York: Farrar, Straus, & Giroux, 1999).

12. Robin Broad (Ed.), *Global Backlash* (Lanham, MD: Rowman & Littlefield, 2002); Joseph E. Stiglitz, *Globalization and Its Discontents* (New York: Norton, 2003); Lester R. Brown, *Outgrowing the Earth: The Food Security Challenge in an Age of Falling Water Tables and Rising Temperatures* (New York: Norton, 2005); William Easterly, *The Elusive Quest for Growth: Economists' Adventures and Misadventures in the Tropics* (Cambridge, MA: MIT Press, 2002); John Cavanagh, *Alternatives to Economic Globalization: A Better World Is Possible*, 2nd ed. (San Francisco: Berrett-Koehler Publishers, 2004); Noreena Hertz, *The Silent Takeover: Global Capitalism and the Death of Democracy* (New York: Simon & Schuster, 2002); James

H. Mittelman, *The Globalization Syndrome: Transformation and Resistance* (Princeton, NJ: Princeton University Press, 2000); Dani Rodrik, *Has Globalization Gone Too Far?* (Washington, DC: Institute for International Economics, 1997); Benjamin R. Barber, *Jihad vs. McWorld: How Globalism and Tribalism Are Reshaping the World* (New York: Ballantine Books, 1995); Hans-Henrik Holm and Georg Sorensen, *Whose World Order?* (Boulder, CO: Westview Press, 1995).

13. World Bank, "World Bank Development Indicators 2009," World Bank, Washington, DC, April 2009; *Forbes*, "The World's Billionaires," March 2008, <http://www.forbes.com/2008/03/05/richest-people-billionaires-billionaires08-cx_lk_0305billie_land.html>; International Labor Organization, "The World of Work 2008: Income Inequality Is Growing," Geneva, October 16, 2008, <http://www.ilo.org/public/english/region/ampro/cinterfor/news/world_r.htm>; "In the United States in 2007, the chief executive officers (CEOs) of the 15 largest companies earned 520 times more than the average worker. This is up from 360 times more in 2003. Similar patterns, though from lower levels of executive pay, have been registered" in 70% of other countries. According to the World Bank, "Global inequities are massive!" World Bank, World Development Report 2006, <http://siteresources.worldbank.org/INTWDR2006/Resources/477383-1127230817535/WDR2006overview.pdf>, 6.

14. World Bank, "The Developing World Is Poorer than We Thought," August 1, 2008, <http://econ.worldbank.org/external/default/main?pagePK=6416 5259&piPK=64165421&theSitePK=469372&menuPK=64166093&entity ID=000158349_20080826113239>; United Nations, Human Development Report 2005, Overview, < http://hdr.undp.org/en/media/HDR05_complete.pdf >, 4; World Bank "Food Price Crisis Imperils 100 Million in Poor Countries, Zoellick Says," April 14, 2008, http://web.worldbank.org/WBSITE/EXTERNAL/NEWS/0, contentM DK:21729143~pagePK:64257043~piPK:437376~theSitePK:4607,00.html; Sanjay G. Reddy and Thomas W. Pogge, "How Not to Count the Poor," Colombia University, October 29, 2005, http://www.columbia.edu/~sr793/count.pdf; Adam Parsons, "World Bank Poverty Statistics: What Do They Mean?" September 15, 2008, http://www.stwr.org/globalization/world-bank-poverty-figures-what-do-they-mean.html; Nicolo Tomaselli, "World Bank Poverty Estimates: More Confusing than Ever," September 29, 2008, http://www.brettonwoodsproject.org/art-562473.

15. Ibid., 3 The IBID was from the previous edition, refering to United Nations, Human Development Report 2005, Overview, <http://hdr.undp.org/en/media/HDR05_complete.pdf.

16. World Bank, "The Developing World Is Poorer than We Thought," August 1, 2008, <http://econ.worldbank.org/external/default/main?pagePK= 6416 5259&piPK=64165421&theSitePK=469372&menuPK=64166093&entity ID=000158349_20080826113239>; Clyde Prestowitz, *Three Billion New Capitalists: The Great Shift of Wealth and Power to the East* (New York: Basic Books, 2005); Asian Development Bank, "ADB Study Offers New Way to Measure Poverty in Asia," August 27, 2008, http://www.adb.org/media/Articles/2008/12586-asian-poverties-indicators/.

17. World Bank, World Development Report 2006, Chapter 3, <http://wdsbeta.world-bank.org/external/default/WDSContentServer/IW3P/IB/2005/09/20/000112742_20050920110826/additional/841401968_200508263001617.pdf>.

18. World Bank, World Bank Global Development Finance Report, 2000. http://siteresources.worldbank.org/INTGDF2000/Resources/gdf2000fulltext.pdf

19. United Nations Development Program, *Globalization with a Human Face* (New York: United Nations, 1999).

20. Michael Meacher (UK minister for the environment), Speech at the Royal Society of Arts, April 1998.

21. L. Craig Johnstone, *Strategic Planning and International Affairs in the 21st Century*. Address to the Conference Series on International Affairs in the 21st Century, U.S. Department of State, Washington, DC, November 18, 1997.

22. F. H. Hinsley, *Sovereignty* (London: C. A. Watts, 1966); The Treaty of Westphalia is a commonly used if somewhat controversial marker for a historical process that took centuries. Scholars such as Bruce Bueno de Mesquita claim that the move toward sovereignty actually came much earlier, whereas others such as Stephen Krasner point out that even after Westphalia there were struggles between religious and secular leaders and contested and overlapping authority claims.

23. Hendrik Spruyt, *The Sovereign State and Its Competitors* (Princeton, NJ: Princeton University Press, 1996), 40.

24. Ibid., 47.

25. Ibid., 62, 75.

26. Friedrich Kratochwil, "Sovereignty as Dominium: Is There a Right of Humanitarian Intervention?" in Gene M. Lyons and Michael Mastanduno (Eds.), *Beyond Westphalia: State Sovereignty and International Intervention* (Baltimore: Johns Hopkins University Press, 1995), 21–42.

27. Nicholas Onuf, "Intervention for the Common Good," in *Beyond Westphalia*, (Baltimore, MD: The Johns Hopkins University Press, 1995), 43–58.

28. Daniel Philpott, *Revolutions in Sovereignty: How Ideas Shaped Modern International Relations*. (Princeton, NJ: Princeton University Press, 2001).

29. Ibid.; Nicholas Onuf, "Sovereignty: Outline of a Conceptual History," *Alternatives* 16 (1991): 425–446.

30. Charles Tilly, *The Formation of National States in Western Europe* (Princeton, NJ: Princeton University Press, 1975).

31. Spruyt, *The Sovereign State and Its Competitors*.

32. Michael Ross Fowler and Julie Marie Bunck, *Law, Power, and the Sovereign State: The Evolution and Application of the Concept of Sovereignty* (University Park: Pennsylvania State University Press, 1995), 5–6.

33. UN Secretary General Kofi Annan, Nobel Prize for Peace acceptance speech, December 10, 2001; International Commission on Intervention and State Sovereignty, *The Responsibility to Protect* (Ottawa, Canada: International Development Research Centre, 2001), <http://www.iciss-ciise.gc.ca/pdfs/Commission-Report.pdf>.

34. "Everybody's Business," *The Wall Street Journal* (August 24, 1992): A8.

35. "New Ways to Run the World," *The Economist* (November 5, 1991): 11.

36. This principle was established in UN Security Council Resolution 1674, adopted April 28, 2006, accepting "the responsibility to protect populations from genocide, war crimes, ethnic cleansing, and crimes against humanity." <http://daccessdds.un.org/doc/UNDOC/GEN/N06/331/99/PDF/N0633199.pdf>.

37. Foreign Policy and the Fund for Peace, "The Failed State Index," *Foreign Policy* (July/August 2008), <http://www.foreignpolicy.com/story/cms.php?story_id=3098. This is the same cite and same url as endnote 9>.

38. Zartman, *Collapsed States*, 3.

39. Stockholm International Peace Research Institute (SIPRI), "Major Armed Conflict," SIPRI Yearbook 2009, <http://yearbook2009.sipri.org/ch2/ch2>. The report notes, however, that the wars in Iraq, Rwanda, and the war on terrorism had significant international components. See also, Project Ploughshares, "2009 Armed Conflict Report," http://www.ploughshares.ca/libraries/monitor/monj09h.pdf

40. Zartman, *Collapsed States*, 1–11. State collapse is more than a succession struggle over which group will control the levers of state—it is the failure of function of those very state institutions. Although groups may be involved in leadership contests, state collapse continues no matter who wins the helm, because state authority, legitimacy, and competence have badly disintegrated. States that have protracted or persistent leadership battles are vulnerable to collapse as state institutions atrophy during continued warfare and as the legitimacy and authority enjoyed by these institutions are undermined by the conflict. *Civil war* and *state collapse* are not synonymous terms. Internal war can occur in states that are not in the process or in danger of collapse—as in Britain and Israel. More rarely, states can collapse without violence—as in the breakup of Czechoslovakia. Not surprisingly, however, state collapse is highly correlated with internal violence, which can weaken state institutions and precede and contribute to state collapse. Alternatively, state collapse can provide the opportunity for groups to use violence as they try to assert authority in the power vacuum left by state failure. See also Foreign Policy and the Fund for Peace, "The Failed State Index," *Foreign Policy* (July/August 2009), <http://www.foreignpolicy.com/story/cms.php?story_id=3098>; Gurr, "The State Failure Project"; and Jackson, *Quasi-States*.

41. Jackson, *Quasi-States*, 29.

42. Morton Halperin, *Self-Determination in the New World Order* (Washington, DC: Carnegie Endowment for International Peace, 1992).

43. Jackson, *Quasi-States*, 27.

44. United Nations, UN Human Development Report 2008, <http://hdr.undp.org/reports/global/2008/pdf/>.

45. SIPRI, *SIPRI Yearbook 1995* (New York: Oxford University Press, 1995), 23–24.

46. Zartman, *Collapsed States*, 7–10.

47. Terry Lynn Karl and Philippe C. Schmitter, "Democratization around the Globe: Opportunities and Risks," in Michael Klare (Ed.), *World Security: Challenges for a New Century* (New York: Palgrave McMillan, 1998).

48. Edward D. Mansfield and Jack Snyder, "Democratization and War," *Foreign Affairs* (May–June 1995): 79–97.

49. Max Singer and Aaron Wildavsky, *The Real World Order: Zones of Peace and Zones of Turmoil* (Chatham, NJ: Chatham House, 1993).

50. Jeffrey E. Garten, "Business and Foreign Policy," *Foreign Affairs* (May–June 1997): 68.

51. George Kennan, "Moscow Embassy Telegram #511: 'The Long Telegram,' February 22, 1946," *Foreign Relations of the United States: 1946*, vol. I, 696–709.

52. George Kennan, 1948, as quoted in John Lewis Gaddis, *Strategies of Containment* (New York: Oxford, 1982), 45.

53. Jessica Tuchman Matthews, "Lessons of Chernobyl," *Washington Post* (April 1996); "Sunshine and Shadow: The CIA and the Soviet Economy," John F. Kennedy School of Government case program.

54. Paul Krugman, "Dutch Tulips and Emerging Markets," *Foreign Affairs* (July–August 1995): 28–43.

55. World Bank, "World Bank Development Indicators 2009," Chapter One: World View, <http://siteresources.worldbank.org/DATASTATISTICS/Resources/wdi09introch1.pdf>; Susan Strange, *Casino Capitalism*. New York: Blackwell, 1986.

56. Gordon Brown, "Remarks at G-20 Summit," April 2, 2009.

57. World Bank, World Development Report, 2006, Equity and Development, <http://wdsbeta.worldbank.org>, 162.

58. Friedman revised his "Golden Arches Theory of Conflict Prevention" to the "Dell Theory of Conflict Prevention" in light of conflicts between countries with McDonald's franchises

(for example, Russia and Georgia in 2008), however these conflicts never rose to the level of a war or major armed conflict with 1000 dead. Thomas Friedman, *The World Is Flat: A Brief History of the Twenty-First Century* (New York: Farrar, Straus and Giroux, 2005), 421; Thomas Friedman, *The Lexus and the Olive Tree* (New York: Anchor, 2000).

59. Jeffrey Sachs, *The End of Poverty: Economic Possibilities for Our Time* (New York: Penguin Press, 2005); Michael Barnett and Martha Finnemore, *Rules for the World: International Organizations in Global Politics* (Ithaca, NY: Cornell University Press, 2004).

60. Clearly, many more costs have been attributed to global economies than those discussed here. These include exploitation of labor; the exploitation (even the apartheid) of the developing South by the developed North (Richard Falk, "Democratizing, Internationalizing, and Globalizing," in Yoshikazu Sakamoto [Ed.], *Global Transformation: Challenges to the State System* [Tokyo: United Nations University Press, 1994], 475–502); and environmental degradation and endangerment of indigenous peoples and their civilizations (Falk, "Democratizing, Internationalizing, and Globalizing," 475–502).

61. Amy Chua, *World On Fire: How Exporting Free Market Democracy Breeds Ethnic Hatred and Global Instability* (New York: Anchor, 2004).

62. Francis Fukuyama, *The End of History and the Last Man* (New York: Free Press, 1992), xi.

63. Ibid., 337; see also Michael Mandelbaum, *The Ideas That Conquered the World: Peace, Democracy, and Free Markets in the Twenty-First Century* (New York: Public Affairs, 2003).

64. Terry Lynn Karl and Philippe C. Schmitter, "Democratization around the Globe: Opportunities and Risks," in *World Security: Challenges for a New Century*, 43–44. This description of the four waves of democratization is based on Karl and Schmitter's work. It should be noted that some theorists, such as Samuel Huntington, merge waves one and two into an overly long and undifferentiated category and thus count only three waves of democratization.

65. Ibid., 60.

66. This has been a problematic point for states such as Singapore, which have tried to open up free-market, capitalist economic systems while restricting political participation and democratic political reforms.

67. Michael Doyle, "Liberalism and World Politics," in *Conflict after the Cold War*, 263–279 Longman 2007.

68. Mansfield and Snyder, "Democratization and War," 88.

69. Fareed Zakaria, *The Future of Freedom: Illiberal Democracy at Home and Abroad* (New York: Norton, 2004), <www.freedomhouse.org>.

70. Daniel F. Burton, Jr., "The Brave New Wired World," *Foreign Policy* (Spring 1997): 32.

71. Internet World Usage Stats, May 2009, <http://www.internetworldstats.com/stats>.

72. Johnstone, *Strategic Planning and International Affairs in the 21st Century*.

73. Burton, "The Brave New Wired World," 26.

74. Ibid.

75. Gaddis, "Toward the Post Cold War World," 27–42.

76. Kenichi Ohmae, *The End of the Nation State: The Rise of Regional Economies* (New York: Free Press, 1995).

77. Susan Strange, The *Retreat of the State: The Diffusion of Power in the World Economy* (Cambridge, UK: Cambridge University Press, 1996), 189.

78. Ibid., 78.

79. Ibid., 79.

80. Ibid., 81.

81. Ibid., 77, 199.

82. James N. Rosenau, "Sovereignty in a Turbulent World," in Gene M. Lyons and Michael Mastanduno (Eds.), *Beyond Westphalia? State Sovereignty and International Intervention*

(Baltimore: Johns Hopkins University Press, 1995), 193; James N. Rosenau, *Turbulence in World Politics* (Princeton, NJ: Princeton University Press, 1990).

83. James N. Rosenau and W. Michael Fagen, "A New Dynamism in World Politics: Increasingly Skillful Individuals?" *International Studies Quarterly* 41 (December 1997): 660. Although he does not draw this comparison, Rosenau's arguments dovetail those of Neil Postman in *Amusing Ourselves to Death*, in which he maintains that the media technologies available to a generation affect not only the mode of their public discourse but also its content, as well as the way they think about and interact with the world. Postman sees the move to a visual era as negative, reducing public discourse to sound bites, whereas Rosenau points up the positive effects that a skills revolution can have on political outcomes and dismembering repressive regimes.

84. Rosenau, "Sovereignty in a Turbulent World," 204.

85. Ibid., 206–207; Rosenau, *Turbulence in World Politics*, 90–113.

86. Rosenau, "Sovereignty in a Turbulent World," 206–207; Rosenau, *Turbulence in World Politics*, 90–113.

87. Richard Rosecrance, *The Rise of the Virtual State: Wealth and Power in the Coming Century* (New York: Basic Books, 2000); and "The Rise of the Virtual State," Foreign Affairs (July–August 1996): 59–60.

88. Ibid., 59–61.

89. Stephen D. Krasner, Sovereignty: Organized Hypocrisy (Princeton, NJ: Princeton University Press, 1999).

90. Robert Jackson, *Sovereignty*. Cambridge: Polity Press, 2007; Stephen D. Krasner, *Problematic Sovereignty: Contested Rules and Political Possibilities* (New York: Columbia University Press, 2001); K. J. Holsti, *Taming the Sovereigns*. Cambridge: Cambridge University Press, 2004; Samy Cohen, *The Resilience of the State*. Boulder, CO: Lynne-Reinner, 2006; Beatrice Hibou (Ed.), *Privatizing the State*. New York: Colombia University Press, 2004.

91. Stephen D. Krasner, "Sovereignty: An Institutional Perspective," *Comparative Political Studies* 21 (April 1988): 74.

92. Kenneth Waltz, "Globalization and Governance," *PS: Political Science & Politics* (December 1999): 693–700.

93. William H. McNeill, "Territorial States Buried Too Soon," *Mershon International Studies Review* 41 (1997): 269.

CHAPTER TWO

Intergovernmental Organizations

Global Governance and Transsovereign Problems*

Maria Green Cowles

"We need to reform and strengthen international institutions, giving them power and resources to invest at a global level. ... This is a time not just for individual, national measures to deal with the global financial crisis. This is the time ... for the world to come together as one."

—Gordon Brown, Prime Minister of the United Kingdom[1]

Intergovernmental organizations (IGOs) are increasingly in the global spotlight, but their precise role in global governance is not easy to define. Some scholars recognize IGOs such as the United Nations as vestiges of the nation-state system.[2] Others view the same IGOs as actors who increasingly operate independent of their member states.[3] Some policy makers identify IGOs such as the World Bank, International Monetary Fund (IMF), and World Trade Organization (WTO) as important forces in promoting economic development throughout the world. Many nongovernmental organizations (NGOs), however, regard these organizations as a means for the wealthy North to continue to dominate the economies, despoil the environment, and denigrate the cultures of the Global South. Some U.S. policy makers have expressed concern that IGOs have become hostile entities designed to constrain American power and delimit U.S. sovereignty.[4] Others argue that the principles that emerge from these supranational bodies reflect compromises among member states, and not campaigns to thwart U.S. hegemony.

There is much on which to disagree when defining and analyzing IGOs. They have been called the "ugly ducklings" of International

*Special thanks go to Stephanie Curtis and Martin Hermida for their research support. I also thank Tammi Gutner and Maryann Cusimano Love for their comments and suggestions.

Relations studies because they are often misconstrued and do not fit easily into our understanding of how the international system of states functions.[5] But supporters and detractors of IGOs may agree on one point: It is increasingly difficult to discuss transsovereign problems today without any mention of IGOs. It is inconceivable, for example, to address the refugee situation in collapsed states such as Sudan without reference to the UN High Commissioner for Refugees (UNHCR). It would be shortsighted to combat the Swine Flu outbreak without involving the World Health Organization (WHO). It is rather difficult to understand the history of the Asian financial crisis without citing the policies of the IMF. Ugly ducklings or not, IGOs serve and will continue to serve an important function in a world where problems can no longer be addressed by individual member states. They have also become a focal point for competing views on how these transsovereign problems should be addressed.

This chapter explores the changing nature of IGOs and their role in the international system. The first two sections define IGOs, examine their rise in the twentieth century, and then highlight some of the key challenges they face in this increasingly interdependent world. The chapter then examines the global governance of—as well as the reform efforts aimed at—four key IGOs: the United Nations, the IMF, the WTO, and the European Union (EU). The chapter concludes with prescriptions for and reflections on the future of IGOs.

INTERGOVERNMENTAL ORGANIZATIONS: AN INTRODUCTION

Intergovernmental organizations are organizations whose members are state governments. In many respects, IGOs are creatures of the twentieth century. Their roots, however, can be traced back to basic ideas and practices that promote international cooperation and stem from diplomacy, rules of warfare, and international law in preceding centuries.

Today, there are more than 300 formal IGOs—that is, organizations that are permanent and have a secretariat to carry out functions, a voluntary membership, and a specific structure.[6] Many of the "classic" institutions are formal intergovernmental institutions: the United Nations, the IMF, the Organization for Economic Cooperation and Development (OECD), the WTO, and the WHO. Another 200 to 1500 informal IGOs lack permanent bureaucracy and structure but function nonetheless to promote cooperation among governments.[7] An example of an informal IGO would be the Group of Eight (G-8). Its members—the large industrialized states of Canada, France, Germany, Italy, Japan, Russia, the United Kingdom, and the United States—regularly meet in an attempt to coordinate economic policies.

IGOs also differ significantly in terms of their scope and purpose. IGOs can be global, regional, and even bilateral in scope. At the same time, the organizations may hold broad, overarching purposes or more specific technical ones. The United Nations is an example of a global organization with a broad mandate. By contrast, the Universal Postal Union (UPU)—the world's second oldest international organization (established in 1874)—is a global organization (191 member countries) with a technical focus. The UPU sets the rules for international mail exchange and makes recommendations for improving the quality of mail services around the world.

The EU, comprising 27 European countries, is arguably the most important regional IGO. The EU covers a broad range of activities, including agricultural policy, commercial policy, competition policy, currency, customs union, and an embryonic foreign and security policy. Some scholars argue that the EU, with its strong supranational bureaucracy and multilevel system of governance, should no longer be classified as a traditional international organization. Other regional organizations include the Association of Southeast Asian Nations (ASEAN), Mercosur, and the African Union (AU).

There are differing views of the relationship between states and IGOs in the international system. Some scholars believe that IGOs are created to serve the interests of states and to encourage cooperation among states by reducing transaction costs—the costs of making and enforcing agreements.[8] As such, IGOs are designed to reflect the wishes of the most powerful states. If an IGO does not effectively champion the interests of these countries, then the countries can pick and choose other IGOs to suit their purposes. Thus, IGOs themselves have minimal influence on—and do not challenge the sovereignty of—the member states that formed them.[9]

Other scholars disagree. They point out that the purpose of IGOs is not merely to represent states' interests or reduce transaction costs. IGOs "may be created not for what they do but for what they are for, what they represent symbolically and the values they embody."[10] Although states may still be the dominant actors within IGOs, they do not dictate the behavior of the organization. Many IGOs can and do exercise power autonomously, notably in the areas of human rights and refugees. They are purposive actors that can develop their own agendas, rules, and norms. Thus, states may choose one IGO over another not because one organization serves its interests better than another, but because the organization is more adept at creating, developing, and implementing broader policies and norms that are important in the international system.[11]

Globalization processes, it is argued, bring greater autonomy to IGOs because they place more tools at their disposal.[12] IGOs may be better positioned than states to respond to the challenges of open societies, open economies, and open technologies and the resulting call for greater international cooperation. Understanding the effects of globalization on the rise and development of IGOs is the point to which we turn next.

THE RISE OF IGOs: THE RESPONSE TO GLOBALIZATION

IGOs increasingly became visible and important global actors in the twentieth century, particularly after World War II. Since 1945, the number of IGOs has increased fivefold. The creation of several institutions in the 1943–1945 period—the IMF, World Bank, and United Nations—promised to usher in a new era of international cooperation and dialogue in the aftermath of World War II. However, the advent of the Cold War and the growing geopolitical concerns of the United States and the Soviet Union dampened any expectations that these organizations would rival powerful states for global leadership. IGOs often found themselves part of the Cold War battlefield—with the United States and Soviet Union opposing each others' positions in the WHO, the Universal Telecommunications Union (UTU), and the International Atomic Energy Agency (IAEA).[13] Even UNICEF, the UN International Children's Education Fund, was tainted by superpower conflicts during this era.

At the same time, decolonization in the 1960s and 1970s produced new tensions within IGOs as the number of newly independent states increased. Many of these new countries did not cast their votes along the lines of their Western counterparts. Soon, certain organizations became forums for highlighting North–South conflicts—the differences between the wealthier countries of the North and the poorer countries of the South. The Group of Seventy-Seven (G-77), for example, was established in 1964 at the end of the first session of the UN Conference on Trade and Development (or UNCTAD, as it is more commonly known). As part of its mandate, the G-77 sought to improve the terms of trade between industrialized northern and poorer southern countries. Because of these Cold War and North–South tensions, countries such as the United States grew increasingly distrustful of key IGOs that were purportedly designed to promote international cooperation.[14]

IGOs created during this period, however, were still relevant. The North Atlantic Treaty Organization (NATO) and its Eastern bloc counterpart, the Warsaw Pact, proved to be powerful organizations. The creation of the Organization of Petroleum Exporting Countries (OPEC) in 1960 also demonstrated how an IGO could influence international economic and political relations. If anything, the oil crisis and growing environmental awareness in the 1970s brought home all too clearly to some countries the need to cooperate in international forums.[15]

The fall of the Berlin Wall in 1989 signaled the end of paralysis within many IGOs. When former President George H. W. Bush called for a "new world order" that emphasized multilateral cooperation in solving global issues, institutions such as the United Nations stood poised to gain further prominence in international affairs. The initial euphoria over this new world order was short-lived, however, with failed UN peacekeeping missions in Bosnia, Rwanda, and Somalia.[16] Although the new world order held promise for some IGOs, it threatened the existence of others. NATO, for example, found itself lacking a central mandate and having to reinvent itself. The Warsaw Pact, on the other hand, lost its overarching purpose and collapsed with the fall of the Berlin Wall.

The end of the Cold War and the emergence of what Thomas Friedman called the "turbo-charged" era of globalization[17] infused many IGOs with new life, new roles, and newfound influence. The opening of societies, for example, led to greater roles for IGOs. The breakup of the Soviet Union and the democratic developments in Central and Eastern European states provided new members and new agendas for organizations such as the Council of Europe and the Organization for Security and Cooperation in Europe. The new wave of democratization also meant a growing role for IGOs in election monitoring around the world.

The opening of economies also empowered IGOs to play a greater role in the global economic arena. The IMF's "seal of approval," for example, became vital for governments that wished to attract greater foreign investment.[18] The IMF set down rules and conditions that governments were required to meet to receive the organization's blessing and funding. Although no sovereign government was forced to accede to these conditions, many accepted IMF recommendations that called for restructured and downsized government agencies, reprioritized government programs, and restricted government practices.

Globalization and changing technology also increased the number and types of parties who were interested in international policy making—which, in turn, impacted international organizations. For example, people can now follow international political activities on a real-time basis over the Internet and buy and sell foreign countries' bonds in online trading. They are thus given greater incentive to follow and affect international policy making by working alone or within NGOs to make their interests known and heard. Moreover, states must now consider these domestic political actors in their foreign policy calculus.[19] In this respect, globalization empowers more actors who, in turn, limit the policy choices of individual states and encourage them to cooperate in international policy making.

Many IGOs sought to take advantage of these globalization trends to attain greater autonomy and influence in global affairs. They reached out to domestic organizations while building their own transnational coalitions with NGOs to promote agendas that, at times, contradict those of key member states. In the late 1990s, the United Nations, for example, allied itself with the International Campaign to Ban Landmines (ICBL) despite the U.S. government's position against the ban.

And while the so-called era of globalization helped strengthen some IGOs, it also empowered other international organizations to serve as bulwarks against globalization—or at least an American style of globalization. On the one hand, the EU advocates the opening of economies through its single market program, which was designed to remove barriers to trade among its member states. At the same time, however, the EU espouses policies that effectively seek to limit or counter globalization forces. The creation of the European currency, the euro, was not merely designed to integrate European economies more effectively. It was also promoted as a means to challenge the U.S. dollar in global finance. The rise of Mercosur, the "Common Market of the South," is another example of a regional IGO that both welcomed the opening of economies while seeking to contain them. While Mercosur countries have opened their economies through the gradual elimination of tariffs, many also considered creating their own currency that could impede the U.S. dollar's global reach.

While the near meltdown of global financial markets in 2008–2009 soon quieted the most vociferous enthusiasts of the "turbo-charged" era of globalization, it did not diminish the importance of IGOs. Indeed, many government leaders cited the lack of coordination in the global financial system as a contributing factor to the near-collapse. In 2009, the German chancellor and French prime minister called for the creation of a new economic regulatory body similar to the UN Security Council.[20] On the eve of the G-20 meeting in March 2009, UK Prime Minister Gordon Brown promoted the IMF to serve as global regulator of the global financial system.[21]

As discussed below, IGOs have emerged as participants in, bulwarks against, and regulators of globalization. Globalization, in turn, has prompted many new challenges to the roles, effectiveness, and legitimacy of IGOs in the world today.

CHALLENGES TO INTERGOVERNMENTAL ORGANIZATIONS: PROBLEMS, PERFORMANCE, AND PERCEPTIONS

The challenges faced by IGOs can be placed in three broad yet interrelated categories: the number and nature of today's problems; the emphasis on IGO performance; and the perceptions of IGO legitimacy, transparency, and fairness.

The Number and Nature of Problems

The past four decades have seen an explosion both in the number of transsovereign issues and in the demands for international policy coordination. According to some observers, the opening of societies and economies, coupled with advancements in technology have created a more informed population that calls on states to undertake greater international problem solving and global public policy making.[22] When then President George H. W. Bush appealed for a new world order, there was the expectation that transsovereign issues would increasingly be addressed in the multilateral forums of IGOs.

Flying in the face of these expectations, however, is the problem of "mandate congestion" and what Oran Young calls the growing "gap between the demand for governance and the supply of governance at the international level."[23] For example, many countries now demand that the United Nations assume more peacekeeping operations—without any significant increase in funding or meaningful revisions of the rules of engagement. Simply put, IGOs are asked to put more and more on their agendas without necessarily having the proper means to address these expanding issues.

It is not only the demand that has changed, but also the nature of the problems themselves. While the United Nations' founders assumed that it would address interstate disputes, most wars today are the result of intrastate conflict. Twenty-first century wars in Rwanda, Bosnia, Kosovo, and Sudan, for example, have intrastate conflict roots, although outside groups figured in the conflicts. Today, the United Nations finds itself addressing not only refugee, human rights, health, and environmental matters in the aftermath of intrastate conflict but also the prospects of "state building."[24] Often, the United Nations is charged with rebuilding the administrative, political, judicial, and economic structure of these collapsed states.[25] Failed states form the core of today's security dilemma and now dominate the agendas of many IGOs.

Performance

Of course, it is difficult for IGOs to perform and address these new and varied problems without the necessary financial and leadership support. This point was made to the United States more than once after it fell more than $1.5 billion behind in dues to the United Nations. Critics of U.S. foreign policy charged that by withholding funds and refusing to support specific programs, the United States set up IGOs for failure.

Some critics of international institutions maintain that long-established IGOs have not adequately responded internally to the changed international agenda, or have been hostile to U.S. efforts to address this agenda. They reason that just as the private sector needs to restructure itself in light of economic trends, so too must IGO bureaucracies reform and transform themselves to better address today's political and economic environment. The United Nations in particular has come under criticism for its bloated bureaucracy.

Others argue that the problem is not how these institutions perform, but for whom. Critics of the original G-7 meetings maintained that the organization was designed for the wealthiest countries to create a united front on issues that would later be discussed in other organizations. They charge that these same countries move important issues, such as the Code of Conduct for Multinationals and the Multilateral Agreement on Investment (MAI), to rich countries' "clubs," such as the Organization for Economic Cooperation and Development, instead of addressing them solely in the United Nations.[26] The result, according to some critics, is a "crisis of multilateralism"[27] in which international institutions are sustained to reinforce the hegemony of the wealthiest countries.

IGOs have succeeded in "reinventing" themselves and their purposes in the post–Cold War, globalizing world. For example, although still not "lean and mean" as bureaucracies go, NATO has been successful in redefining its mission. Similarly, the International Telecommunications Union (ITU)—the oldest IGO (created in 1865)—has developed into a significantly streamlined organization by ridding itself of obsolete departments.

Pressure from NGOs and other governments have also led to the restructuring of IGOs or the creation of new ones. In 1999, the G-7 launched the G-20—more formally known as the Group of Finance Ministers and Central Bankers, although heads of government met in special summits twice a year. Instead of representing only seven large countries, the G-20 comprises nineteen of the world's largest economies, as well as the EU. Of course, the G-20 means that traditional world powers like the

United States must now share the international economic policy stage with important emerging economies like China, India, and Brazil.

Still other IGOs have sought to reinvent themselves and/or strengthen their performance by developing NGO partnerships and building transnational coalitions around key agenda items. These "born-again institutions" are often infused with new life and influence as a result.[28] Yet the coalitions themselves can hinder an IGO's performance if it is "captured" by an NGO, a common phenomenon in domestic policy making of member states. Indeed, the participation of NGOs can lead to problems of perception for the organization.

Perception

Perceptions—whether based on truth or fiction—can have considerable consequences for IGOs. As noted earlier, critics—including many NGOs and developing countries—view the OECD as a tool of rich countries and big businesses setting their international agendas. The OECD's failed behind-the-scenes meetings to develop an MAI with representatives of multinational corporations (MNCs) are cited as a classic case of this collusion. Other critics, however, charge that certain organizations, including programs within the United Nations, are being run by zealous NGOs that have developed their own global public policy fiefdoms. Government officials at the 1992 UN Conference on the Environment and Development in Rio de Janeiro, for example, found themselves surrounded by 1,500 NGOs accredited to the conference. In the conference's final days, officials opted to work behind closed doors to escape the NGOs and complete the work at hand.[29]

Even well-respected IGOs can suffer perception problems. For example, the WHO has been hailed in recent years for its progressive approach to eradicating disease. According to former WHO Secretary General Gro Bruntland, the WHO's forging of partnerships with both NGOs and MNCs to carry out these global public policies has been key to its success. Nonetheless, certain NGOs have argued that the WHO's reputation and prestige will forever be tainted because of its working relationships with the multinational firms.[30]

Arguably the most important challenge to IGOs today involves the perception of legitimacy. For too many IGOs, the lack of transparency and meaningful participation in IGO policy making are at the core of this perception problem. As IGOs address more and more transsovereign issues, they are taking actions that have far-reaching implications for millions of people. The role of the IMF in the Asian financial crisis in the late 1990s prompted Asian governments to make important policy changes in employment, taxation, environmental, and even health policies. These changes in turn led to massive protests in the streets of South Korea and the downfall of the political leadership in Indonesia. The IMF was criticized for both the policies undertaken and how these issues were decided in the first place. Managing the IMF is a technocratic elite that meets and consults with high-ranking government officials from its membership. Members of civil society are rarely involved in these discussions. Little, if any, democratic accountability or control is exercised over the IMF. This democratic deficit is compounded by the lack of transparency. More often than not, key IMF negotiations are made behind closed doors. How decisions are made, who makes them, and for what reasons are rarely disclosed—much to the dissatisfaction of many citizens, NGOs, and even MNCs.

Thus, whether IGOs like the IMF have or should have this influence in other states' public policy making is controversial. Whether these IGOs are the legitimate decision makers in sovereign states is contested. It matters not whether the alleged crisis of legitimacy is valid—the perception is real.

THE IGOs: GLOBAL GOVERNANCE AND CALLS FOR REFORM

Four key IGOs will now be examined in greater detail: the United Nations, the IMF, the WTO, and the EU.

The United Nations

Established by 51 countries in 1945, the United Nations boasts a membership of 192 countries over sixty-five years later. The organization has six main bodies: the General Assembly, the Security Council, the Economic and Social Council, the Trusteeship Council, the Secretariat, and the International Court of Justice. The UN Charter identifies four main purposes for the organization: "to maintain international peace and security, to develop friendly relations among nations, to cooperate in solving international problems and in promoting respect for human rights, and to be a centre for harmonizing the actions of nations." These objectives result in a rather broad mandate that has been expanded upon over the years. In September 2000, UN members approved the Millennium Declaration, identifying a global agenda for the new century that addresses seven key areas: peace, security, and disarmament; development and poverty eradication; protecting our common environment; human rights, democracy, and good governance; protecting the vulnerable; meeting the special needs of Africa; and strengthening the United Nations.[31]

The United Nations also has several independent organizations, special programs, and funds that make up what is known as the UN family or UN system. For example, the Office of the UN High Commissioner for Refugees (UNHCR) and United Nations Children's Fund (UNICEF) are UN programs with separate government bodies, budgets, and secretariats that also are linked to the UN system.[32] The IMF, the World Bank Group, and specialized agencies such as the WHO and Universal Postal Union are all linked to the United Nations through cooperative technical agreements but are autonomous organizations in practice.

The United Nations is recognized as a provider of "international public goods," including international air traffic control, telecommunications and posts, humanitarian relief for refugees and victims of natural disasters, and protection of the environmental commons.[33] In recent years, it has been heralded as a promoter of "human security"—protecting states and individuals from danger and promoting individuals' political, social, and economic human rights.[34] Since they were first deployed in 1948, UN peacekeepers have taken part in sixty-three operations (including seventeen underway in 2008) and were awarded the 1988 Nobel Prize for Peace.[35] Moreover, the United Nations has established international tribunals to prosecute individuals accused of war crimes and genocide in Rwanda and the former Yugoslavia. The United Nations protects more than 34.4 million refugees each year, buys vaccines for half of the world's children, and champions human rights around the globe.[36]

Despite these UN successes, critics charge that the United Nations is in need of serious reform. While the demand for UN reform is not novel—various groups have called for significant changes to the organization since its inception—the intensity of this call is new.[37] In recent years, UN reform has become a regular feature on news stories and a source of constant discussion within think tanks. Reform efforts have also captured news headlines. In June 2005, the U.S. House of Representatives passed the "Henry J. Hyde United Nations Reform Act" that threatened to cut U.S. monetary contributions to the UN in half if major reforms were not undertaken.

UN critics charge that the IGO is a bloated, unruly bureaucracy prone to fraud and abuse. The "Oil for Food" scandal highlighted the "serious mismanagement and outright corruption" of this major UN program.[38] The "Oil for Food" program—initially designed to safeguard Iraqi citizens from starvation in light of economic sanctions—allowed then-Iraqi President Saddam Hussein's government to garner over $1.7 billion in illicit oil revenues. Moreover, million-dollar kickbacks to certain UN officials and contracting companies were discovered.[39] To prevent another Oil-for-Food scandal in the future, U.S. critics advocate for "results-oriented" changes to the organization. Their solution is a fundamental overhaul that would include cutting unneeded or unnecessary programs and trimming the ranks of bureaucrats. Critics point out, for example, that although the United Nations devotes most of its time to development issues, it provides only 5 percent of the development aid to poorer regions of the world. The rest of this aid comes from private corporations, states, and NGOs.[40] Critics maintain that instead of being an organization that tries to cover everything under its broad mandate, the United Nations should focus on "global problems that nobody else can tackle" such as refugees and peacekeeping.[41]

While acknowledging the need for reform, UN supporters charge that a "results-oriented" reform campaign based on cost cutting alone is misguided. They point out that the UN's inability to carry out certain missions effectively may in fact be due to member states' weak UN support and lackluster funding. Peacekeeping efforts are a prime example. Creating a small standing army to bring peacekeepers to trouble spots immediately instead of wrangling with member states over troop numbers, contributions, and commands would render the UN more effective in this core function. Yet it is unlikely that certain countries would give the United Nations the funding to do so. Nor would countries like the United States support giving the UN something as symbolic of sovereignty as an army—or allow any of their own troops to operate under a UN commander. Thus, few foreign observers trust the intentions of U.S. congressional leaders in UN reform efforts. They view American actions as an excuse for not paying U.S. dues in the past and "doubt that America really wants to see a more efficient [United Nations]—just a smaller one."[42]

Another area for UN reform focuses on the expansion of the UN Security Council to better reflect the current configuration of power in the world by including countries such as Japan and Germany. Both countries are key contributors to the regular UN budget and the largest contributors to UN special programs.[43] Many UN member countries also believe that the Security Council should be more representative of other regions and populations of the world by permanently including countries such as Brazil, India, Egypt, and Nigeria. The current permanent members, however, are reluctant to revamp the body out of concern that such revisions would reduce their own powers.

Not surprisingly, countries' concern over their power in the UN features prominently in reform debates. While everyone agrees the United

Nations needs reform, there is little consensus over the shape and purpose of the reform. U.S. efforts to bring "results-driven" reform are eyed warily by countries in the Global South that do not want to see development programs cut, and are reluctant to support any efficiency reforms that might undercut their own voices in the UN system.

Similarly, the United States has often looked warily at the United Nations' own reform efforts. In the late 1990s, when U.S. congressional leaders called on then UN Secretary General Kofi Annan to reduce bureaucratic bloat and run the IGO more like a private company, they and other government leaders were unwilling to grant him the administrative powers to hire and fire at will. As the *Economist* noted,

> [t]he job of secretary-general at the United Nations is not unlike that of a medieval pope. In one sense, you are the leader of Christendom. Yet, at the same time, your power is limited: you have no battalions of your own (all those peacekeeping troops are only on loan); your own organisation is a hotchpotch of feuding bishoprics, most of whom feel more loyalty to temporal rules than to you; and you are normally broke.[44]

Nonetheless, the UN Secretary General proposed a major reform program, the Millennium+5 reforms, in March 2005. Designed, according to some observers, to placate the United States, the reforms focused on accountability measures but failed to address the United Nations' more fundamental financial woes or the final structure in the UN Security Council. Perhaps as a consequence, the UN summit on institutional reform in September 2005 produced "watered-down results."[45]

How the United Nations develops and its reform efforts unfold over the next decade remains to be seen. Some critics suggest the United Nations will simply "fade into irrelevance."[46] Others charge that the UN—including the Security Council—will continue to play an important role in global governance. While recognizing the Security Council's unattained lofty goals and many failures, David Bosco argues that the five permanent members have succeeded in preventing conflict between the world's most powerful countries.[47]

Former UN Secretary General Annan points out that while the United States led initial relief efforts to tsunami-ravaged countries in 2005, countries readily agreed that the United Nations and its Office for the Coordination of Humanitarian Affairs should take over as the lead relief coordinating agency. While the UN office's "light structure" and long track record in coordinating relief efforts are well recognized, Annan maintains that the positive perception of the United Nations was the underlying reason why it assumed the leadership role:

> ... everyone was willing to work with the U.N.: the governments and people of the affected countries, the donors, and the nonprofit organizations whose role is so essential in all emergencies, great and small. All of them recognize that the U.N. is the right body to lead, because it is in no one's pocket. It belongs to the world.[48]

The International Monetary Fund

Since its conception in 1944, the IMF has lent hundreds of billions of dollars to countries in need of economic assistance. The IMF charter, and that of its sister IGO, the World Bank, was formulated during a three-week conference held in Bretton Woods, New Hampshire. Both organizations and their respective organs are commonly referred to as the *Bretton Woods system*. The World Bank was tasked with postwar reconstruction. The IMF's mandate was to promote international monetary cooperation through exchange rate stability and to facilitate the expansion of international trade by addressing balance of payment problems among the initial twenty-nine member countries.

In recent decades, IMF members significantly expanded the IGO's mandate. As national economies have grown increasingly integrated, the global economy has become considerably more complex. The introduction of new technologies, coupled with a staggering increase in private capital flows and international transactions, has required organizations such as the IMF to broaden their functions.

The collapse of the gold standard in 1971, and the subsequent switch to floating exchange rates, for example, forced the organization to seek out a new raison d'être. Beginning with the debt crisis in Mexico and other Latin American countries in the 1980s, IMF members discovered a new and important role for the IGO in the international system. In addition to offering financial support and credit, the IMF began providing fiscal and monetary advice to governments and local economists. The organization increased its monitoring activities and vastly expanded the scope of conditions attached to the aid packages. For instance, the fund demanded that politicians make specific macroeconomic policy changes to improve the economic health of their countries in exchange for IMF loans.

Later economic crises in the former Soviet bloc countries and in Southeast Asia triggered an even greater expansion in the functions and monetary support of the IMF. For example, in 1997 the fund was called upon to aid the struggling economies of South Korea, Thailand, and Indonesia. The South Korean package alone amounted to $57 billion. The IMF "bailouts"—as some have termed the action—"provided enough credit to prevent formal government defaults and maintain future access to capital markets."[49] Had the IMF not intervened, the future of the Asian economies could have been even more precarious.

In addition to constructing aid packages intended to avoid liquidity crunches, the IMF began providing loans to developing countries to assist with poverty alleviation and good governance programs. With its Multilateral Debt Relief Initiative launched in 2005, the IMF became the first major international organization to offer extensive debt relief to the world's poorest countries. By 2009, the IMF emerged as an important player for countries suffering from the global economic crisis and announced a strengthening of its partnership with African countries.[50] Some government leaders such as the UK's Prime Minister Gordon Brown even looked to the IMF to serve as the global regulator in addressing the global crisis.

Despite continual requests for its assistance, the IMF has received its share of criticisms.[51] Critics, for example, have found fault with the clandestine workings of the organization. According to these critics, most of the fund's activities "are shrouded in secrecy, and even when it releases statements or documents to the public, it tends to hide behind a smoke screen of technical jargon."[52] The secrecy surrounding the organization translates into a lack of transparency and accountability. IMF country documents and annual economic surveys remain private. As a consequence, its warnings and speculations about weak economies fail to reach the same international bankers and investors that the organization later bails out. Various reform agendas have sought to redress the problem of transparency through requests for increased public input and scrutiny, an independent evaluation board, and an overall demystifying of the fund.[53]

A second set of IMF criticisms is directed at the Fund's prescriptions for economic recovery of troubled countries. According to Joseph Stiglitz, a former chief economist and vice president of the World Bank, during the Asian crisis the IMF delivered the "same medication for each ailing nation that showed up on its doorstep. . . . even as evidence of the policy's failure mounted."[54] Moreover, the IMF attempted to temper the Asian financial crisis with a set of austerity measures similar to those prescribed to the Latin American governments in the 1980s—even though the reasons behind the Asian crisis were far different from those in Latin America.

From the IMF's perspective, fiscal as well as political austerity measures are almost always needed, even in the case of the current economic crisis. As Simon Johnson, a former IMF chief economist describes it,

> to IMF officials, all of these crises looked depressingly similar. Each country, of course, needed a loan, but more than that, each needed to make big changes so that the loan could really work. Almost always, countries in crisis need to learn to live within their means after a period of excess—exports must be increased, and imports cut—and the goal is to do this without the most horrible of recessions ... the economic solution is seldom very hard to work out. No, the real concern of the fund's senior staff, and the biggest obstacle to recovery, is almost invariably the politics of countries in crisis. Typically, these countries are in a desperate economic situation for one simple reason—the powerful elites within them overreached in good times and took too many risks ... oligarchs get carried away; they waste money and build massive business empires on a mountain of debt ... Overborrowing always ends badly, whether for an individual, a company, or a country. Sooner or later, credit conditions become tighter and no one will lend you money on anything close to affordable terms. The downward spiral that follows is remarkably steep.[55]

According to this view, "crony capitalism," where economic elites have the backing of governments even if sometimes "with a whiff of corruption," is at the root of the problem. Even in the U.S., strong economic medicine has to go hand in hand with strong political actions to break up the oligarchs and make politics and economics more transparent, accountable, and efficient.[56]

Critics argue that reality is rarely so simple, "one size fits all" solutions are not effective, and behind these poor prescriptions lay a group of inadequate economists who "are more likely to have firsthand knowledge of [a country's] five-star hotels" than of its social, political, and cultural makeup.[57] While the IMF's response to the global economic meltdown suggests it has learned key lessons from the Asian financial crisis, distrust of the organization remains.

Finally, more liberal critics claim that the IMF's policies "are a not-so-thinly disguised wedge for capital interests."[58] The fund has been criticized for being divided between the strong, Western economies and the poorer, developing member countries. Because the major economic powers are rarely forced to borrow from the IMF, they fail to foresee problems with continual expansion of the IMF's power and role. The 2009 crisis—in which more countries, including some more developed economies such as Iceland and Hungary, lined up at the doors for assistance—could potentially alter these countries' views of IMF policy. Whether this will occur remains to be seen.

To address the organization's many criticisms, critics have offered three broadly defined sets of reform proposals: abolishing the fund, significantly restructuring it, and scaling back its role to the original Bretton Woods mandate. Of course, selecting any one of these reforms would placate some groups and anger others. As Devesh Kapur joked, "If the IMF had a dollar for every criticism of its purpose and role by the Right, the Left, and the Center, it would perhaps never again have to approach its shareholders for more money to sustain its operations."[59]

The World Trade Organization

The primary purpose of the WTO is to facilitate free trade through trade agreements and negotiations, trade dispute settlements, technical assistance to developing countries on trade matters, and cooperation with other IGOs on international trade matters. The nearly 153 members, accounting for more than 97 percent of world trade, represent the WTO membership.[60]

The WTO is the youngest of the major IGOs. It also is an example of an informal institution or regime that developed into a formal IGO. WTO agreements are based on those of its predecessor, the General Agreement on Tariffs and Trade (GATT) (1947–1994), a one-time "temporary" agreement that became increasingly institutionalized over the years. Whereas the GATT focused solely on the trading of goods, the WTO agreements also include agreements on the trading of certain services (General Agreement on Trade in Services, or GATS) and the protection of intellectual property rights (Trade Related Intellectual Property Rights, or TRIPS). When creating the WTO, these future members also established the Dispute Settlement Understanding (DSU), a specific process that encourages countries to settle trade disputes through consultation or, if that fails, to bring the disputes before a specially appointed panel of experts for a ruling. Through the DSU, the WTO "has profoundly changed the nature of trade disputes" by ending a country's ability to retaliate unilaterally against another country with sanctions and various protectionist policies.[61] Under the disputed settlement rules, a country that is found to have violated its WTO commitments must either change its domestic law, regulation, or practice, or accept retaliatory trade sanctions to compensate for the aggrieved parties' losses.

A look at the WTO's membership and the list of applicant countries clearly shows the importance that governments attach to WTO membership.

China's accession to the WTO is a case in point. A sign of the WTO's success is that China's communist leaders participated in fifteen years of multilateral and bilateral negotiations with WTO members, and adopted significant market-oriented laws and trade practices to meet WTO requirements.

Yet the WTO is also one of the most controversial IGOs. Forty thousand activists and union members protested the organization and its free trade agenda at the December 1999 WTO ministerial meeting in Seattle, Washington. The result was the infamous "Battle in Seattle" during which protesters succeeded in shutting down the meeting and much of the city.

Perhaps one reason why the WTO is so controversial is that people from every part of the political spectrum can find fault with it. Problems of perception challenge the WTO's governance in global trade matters today. In the United States, some conservatives are wary of the organization because they believe it takes away U.S. sovereignty through the voting procedures and the DSU. Unlike with the IMF and its weighted vote system, the United States is a coequal in the organization: Its vote counts the same as that of Jamaica. Moreover, under the DSU, the United States can no longer respond unilaterally to trade problems and instead must bring its grievances to the Dispute Settlement Body (DSB). Of course, the United States has been the target of other countries' grievances in the WTO process and has "lost" some of these cases.

On the other hand, protesters on the left of the political spectrum deride the IGO because the WTO focuses exclusively on trade issues and not on environmental and labor concerns. Arguably, this results in a "race to the bottom"—the idea that countries and companies in the name of compliance with WTO rules will push for lower and lower environmental and labor regulations. They often cite the classic tuna–dolphin ruling that occurred under the old GATT dispute settlement process. In that case, Mexico brought a grievance against the United States for banning the importation of tuna caught with purse seine nets that were deemed unsafe for dolphins.[62] When Mexico won the case, environmentalists in the United States and elsewhere viewed this ruling as a dangerous case of free trade trumping environmental concerns.

Still another category of protesters comes from the developing countries. They argue that the WTO is biased toward wealthy countries and their MNCs. They point out that the United States and Europe pushed the developing world to accept new trade rules on services and intellectual property rights—areas where the Global North has the comparative advantage. Yet the United States and the EU were unwilling to quickly lift restrictions on textile imports or, in the case of the EU, end agricultural subsidy programs—two sectors where the Global South is more competitive. At the same time, the developing countries question the intentions of U.S. labor and environmental activists. Requiring all WTO members to adhere to stricter labor and environmental standards would raise the costs of production in the Global South—and thus keep more jobs in the United States. The developing countries' other complaint concerns the rules and informal procedures that preclude developing countries from actively and effectively participating in negotiations. For example, unlike the United States and EU, the developing countries do not have the staff or resources to participate in complex multiple negotiations simultaneously. Thus, they are either railroaded through the process or forced to delay the process through vetoes or other tactics.[63]

The most telling criticism of the WTO, however, is its perceived lack of democratic accountability and transparency. *The Economist* magazine explained the perception in the following way:

> According to skeptics, the WTO takes powers away from elected governments and grants them to faceless bureaucrats … The WTO is a kind of embryonic world government, but with none of the checks and balances that true democratic government requires. In short, it is an embryonic world tyranny. That is why, in the view of many skeptics, it is the most dangerous of all the institutions of globalisation.[64]

Not everyone blames the WTO secretariat with its 600-plus staff in Geneva for this perception. It is the member states themselves who conduct the trade negotiations, insist that they take place behind closed doors, and maintain that the DSB deliberations remain secret.[65]

In the aftermath of the 1999 Seattle ministerial meeting, the WTO began to address more seriously the criticisms and perceptions surrounding it. The need to take account of developing countries' concerns took on even greater urgency following the 2001 terrorist attacks in the United States. At the Doha, Qatar, ministerial meeting in Fall 2001, members agreed to launch another round of trade liberalization designed to address a broader range of issues of concern to developing countries. The so-called Doha Development Round (DDR) was launched to reform trade rules and, in particular, to reduce or eliminate agricultural food and cotton subsidies in the Global North, notably in the United States and the EU. The elimination of these subsidies would improve developing countries' competitiveness, allow them greater market access to wealthier countries, and promote their economic development. Whether WTO members will meet the DDR commitments, however, is debatable given farm lobby efforts and national politicians' reluctance to reform agricultural programs in the United States and the EU.

The Doha Round raised expectations for the WTO to be "reformed to serve as a vehicle for a more benign kind of globalization."[66] The question for some observers is not whether the Doha effort will be successful, but whether or not the IGO can afford not to reform itself.

The European Union

The EU is a classic example of a regional (as opposed to global) IGO.[67] Since its creation as the European Coal and Steel Community in the early 1950s, the EU has emerged as an important actor on the regional and global stage. Today, the EU represents twenty-seven countries and nearly half a billion people. Its gross domestic product (GDP) now exceeds that of the United States.[68]

The EU distinguishes itself from other IGOs in an important way. Member states "pool" their sovereignty within the EU. In effect, they share or grant part of their sovereignty to the EU itself in particular policy areas. For example, in January 2002, the twelve participating members of "Euroland" replaced their national currencies with a European currency, the euro. Instead of twelve central banks making decisions, a single European Central Bank now oversees monetary policy in much of Europe.[69]

Membership in the EU also requires significant conformity to the *acquis communautaire*—the policies, rules, and regulations that form the legal and political basis for the EU. EU law must be transposed into national law. The twelve new member states, for example, were required to rewrite—and continue to rewrite—their environmental, consumer protection, competition policy, and other laws and policies to conform to the *acquis*.

The EU is also different from other IGOs in terms of the powers granted to its supranational bodies: the European Commission, the European Parliament (EP), and the European Court of Justice (ECJ). Located in Brussels, the European Commission is the policy-making body that initiates legislation primarily in economic matters and oversees the implementation of various EU-wide policies and programs, among other duties. It is the European Commission, for example, that represents the EU in trade negotiations with the United States and in the WTO.

The European Parliament has evolved from a relatively weak assembly to a body whose voting power is equal to that of the member states in several policy areas. Scholars who study the EP argue that it is more powerful than most national parliaments in Europe.[70] The European Court of Justice, however, is arguably the most powerful supranational body in the EU.

Today, ECJ rulings have precedence over national law in matters pertaining to EU treaties and secondary legislation. Moreover, national courts in EU member states may refer questions on particular cases to the ECJ to determine how the European law should be applied at the national level.

In many regards, the EU is at a crossroads in its development. While EU member states have not relinquished sovereign authority in all policy areas—taxation is a prime example—the global fight against terrorism has prompted member states to increasingly work through the EU on matters such as border control, visas, immigration, and money laundering. And while retaining their right of policy initiation and individual veto, member states often seek European positions in Common Foreign and Security Policy (CFSP) and have appointed a "High Representative" or "Mr. CFSP" to officially present EU policy on foreign and security policy matters to the outside world.

The 2004 and 2007 enlargements in which the EU admitted twelve new members from Central and Eastern Europe remains the biggest challenge to the EU. The unprecedented enlargement poses considerable collective action problems for the EU. Governing the EU's twenty-seven members—especially when it includes countries who only recently transitioned to Western democratic ideals and capitalist markets—is considerably more challenging than governing an EU of fifteen. Some naysayers suggest that the EU will no longer be able to embrace a wide-ranging agenda and will need to focus its efforts on the maintenance of the Single Market program and the euro. For these observers, the question focuses on the extent to which the EU will dilute its powers and become more like a mini-United Nations "with much less political and legal authority, or none at all."[71] Others, however, are more confident that EU institutions and member states will embrace the challenge of enlargement and will make the reforms necessary to ensure that the EU can continue to evolve and govern effectively.

Nonetheless, there remains considerable debate over the autonomy of the EU institutions vis-à-vis that of its member states.[72] The EU's distinctive traits have led some scholars to refer to it as a *multilevel system of governance* in which certain activities or forms of governance are carried out at the supranational level, others at the national level, and still others at the subnational or regional levels. Indeed, several scholars have argued that the EU should no longer be treated as an IGO but as a "polity."[73] Thus, instead of using International Relations theory to explain member state cooperation, these scholars maintain that comparative politics theory can better explain how the EU functions. As noted earlier, for example, the European

Parliament's powers can be judged by comparing the EP to other national assemblies. Similarly, the European Central Bank's role and functions can be ascertained by comparing it to other central banking systems.

Like other IGOs, however, the EU faces many interrelated challenges. Perhaps the most fundamental is the perceived "democratic deficit" or what some term the *legitimacy deficit* of the EU. Over a fifty-plus-year period, the EU developed from a small coal and steel community to today's complex organization. During this time, political elites generally encouraged EU expansion and allowed the EU institutions to define their scope, methods, and functions—all while the mass public remained largely unaware of these developments.[74] The 1992 Danish referendum on the Maastricht Treaty, in which the Danish people voted against the expansion of EU powers, signaled the end to this permissive consensus. Public opinion polls revealed that Danes and other Europeans were increasingly wary of decisions made by unknown "Eurocrats" in Brussels (the EU capital) on such matters ranging from the size of apples to the elimination of national currencies. Government leaders who in the past found it easy to blame Brussels for forcing change on national policies now struggled to explain the functioning and relevance of the EU to their citizens. In recent years, member states and EU institutions alike have sought to better clarify their policy decisions. For example, a major sustained publicity campaign accompanied the introduction of the euro as a currency in 1999 and as legal tender in 2002.

The transparency of the EU institutions is a related problem. Critics have long complained, for example, that the Brussels machinery is too complex and obtuse to allow observers and lobbyists alike to track EU legislation. To successfully influence legislation in the early draft stages, for example, one had to develop an extensive intelligence network to monitor European Commission activities.[75] The body has endeavored to make its machinery more transparent by providing organization charts, listing contact numbers of key personnel, and issuing status reports on various pieces of legislation on its official Web site. More recently, the European Commission issued a governance paper that suggested reforms in policy making and decision making that would render the EU legislative process more efficient, open, and timely.

Compared to the European Commission, efforts by the Council of Ministers—the member states—to address the perceived democratic deficit have been less impressive. The key decision-making body of the EU has been reluctant to publish the voting records of its members. Major newspapers have sued the Council of Ministers to make its meeting and voting records more public. These actions, along with the prodding by Sweden and

Finland, have prompted the Council to begin opening up their decision-making processes. Whether or not the member states will take larger steps to address the democratic deficit remains to be seen.

Reform of EU institutions is linked to legitimacy and transparency concerns. In 1999, the European Commission resigned en masse in response to perceived mismanagement problems. Individual commissioners were alleged to have improperly hired friends and relatives and misappropriated funds. For years, the European Commission doled out management positions according to an unofficial quota to ensure the representation of all member states. As a result of the 1999 debacle, the European Commission has undergone and continues to pursue significant institutional reforms, including the establishment of a promotion process based on meritocracy instead of national quotas. The European Parliament, however, whose scrutiny of the European Commission led to the 1999 resignation, has yet to embrace such reform. EP members, for example, enjoy a questionable system of salaries and expenses that has not helped their reputation in the polls.[76] The fact that the 785-member European Parliament continues to meet in three different places—Brussels, Strasbourg, and Luxembourg—only reinforces the perception of an institution out of touch with its public.

EU leaders sought to address the challenges of legitimacy, transparency, and reform by creating a European constitution. A special Convention on the Future of Europe, led by former French Prime Minister Valerie Giscard d'Estaing, met to identify the EU's core principles and to condense the provisions of numerous EU treaties into a single document. The result was a long, detailed constitution—many would argue that it is too long and detailed—adopted by the governments on June 17 and 18, 2004. While government leaders sought to engage the European public in a dialogue over the constitution, European citizens, who historically had been excluded from EU treaty matters, remained largely disengaged from the process. As EU leaders soon discovered, the lengthy constitutional text failed to capture the European public's attention. Their decision, however, to expand the EU's boundaries to include the ten new Eastern and Central European countries did weigh heavily on people's minds as they considered the enlargement's potential impact on employment, immigration, and competitiveness policies. Thus, when French and Dutch citizens went to the polls to cast their votes on the constitution, their negative vote was as much, if not more, a protest against EU enlargement—and the failure of politicians to adequately address citizen concerns regarding the expansion—as it was against the constitution itself. In an ironic twist, EU member states' failure to engage with the public in a transparent manner over EU enlargement prompted the veto of a constitution designed to further the principles of transparency and legitimacy.

While EU observers generally consider the formal EU constitution to be a moribund issue (all twenty-seven member states must ratify the constitution before it can enter into force), they do not see its ratification as necessary for the EU to function. Legal scholars have long argued that the EU is already constitutionally grounded in the various EU treaties.[77] Others point out that many provisions in the treaty simply codified existing EU policies and practices and that many of the "new" provisions such as greater foreign policy coordination will likely take place with or without a ratified constitution. The real challenge will be for EU political leaders to allow for greater transparency and to consult with the European public on major changes facing the EU, including future enlargement. As politicians learned, constitutions alone cannot address the EU democratic deficit.

PRESCRIPTIONS

Globalization has infused new life and purpose into IGOs. Far from being the ugly ducklings of the past, IGOs now occupy center stage in addressing the most important transsovereign issues of the day. Yet globalization has also prompted increasing criticism of IGOs. Individuals and NGOs increasingly question not only IGO policies but also the raison d'être of the IGOs themselves, as evidenced by the WTO Battle in Seattle, the debates over the United Nations on the U.S. House floor, and the IMF and World Bank protests around the world. To remain relevant, IGOs and their members must address three core issues: reform, transparency, and legitimacy.

Reforming IGOs is not a question but a necessity. Indeed, there is a separate NGO—World Campaign for In-depth Reform of the system of international institutions.[78] As companies and countries adjust to globalization pressures, so too must IGOs. Many IGOs are not organized effectively to deal with today's transsovereign issues. Parts of the United Nations are prime candidates for reform because of bloated bureaucracies and poor management. However, reformers must take care to embrace efficiency without compromising the overarching values of the organization. For some countries, assessing the United Nations' performance solely in terms of an Anglo-Saxon measure of effectiveness is not appropriate. Different countries have different expectations regarding the United Nations. For some, the organization's primary role has been and still should be as a venue where dialogue can take place and where countries are treated as independent and equal—at least in the General

Assembly meetings. To reform the United Nations or any other IGO, reformers need to find a balance.[79]

Transparency is the second core issue. The WTO, for example, touts the benefits of free and open markets. The IMF demands that states develop free and open financial systems. The EU requires open borders and the free movement of goods, services, people, and capital. Yet all three organizations fail to practice what they preach, conducting their primary decision-making sessions in secrecy, behind closed doors. Who is making the decisions, why, and under what circumstances? Protesters argue that they have a right to know. Transparency allows for greater scrutiny of IGOs and "provides the basis for a highly democratic, albeit nonelectoral, system of transnational governance based on the growing strength of global civil society."[80]

Legitimacy is arguably the most important concern facing IGOs—in a sense, the umbrella issue under which all other concerns can be found. For example, whether an IGO is reforming or transparent will affect the public's determination of its legitimacy. Relations with NGOs, fairness, and adequate resources are three key factors that play an important role in enhancing the public and political support for IGOs. Today, IGOs seek to enhance their legitimacy by building coalitions and networks with NGOs and MNCs. Positive examples of such cooperation abound—from the WHO's compact with MNCs to eradicate disease, to the United Nations' alliance with the International Campaign to Ban Landmines. Relations between IGOs, NGOs, and MNCs, however, must be developed carefully to ensure that IGOs are not beholden to or co-opted by particular groups or interests.[81] Failure to do so would result in the demise of the very legitimacy IGOs sought to achieve in the first place.

IGOs—including their members—must also seek to enhance fairness as a means to promote their policies. Who does the IGO represent? Western protesters in Seattle maintained that the WTO favored MNCs at the expense of the environment and laborers. At the same time, poor countries argued that the IMF, WTO, and other economic organizations were biased toward the richer North. Of course, schisms between rich and poor countries, environmentalists, and economists are not new. However, IGO policies that fail to consider these tensions are ripe for failure.

Providing adequate resources—funding, staff, and political support—is also critical to ensuring the future health and legitimacy of IGOs. Today, IGOs serve as primary, if not the primary, entities responsible for addressing the economic, political, and cultural fallout of failed states. They are the guardians of refugees, the lenders of last resort, bulwarks against the excesses of globalization—and providers of solutions to transnational issues.

Yet they are often not given the resources to carry out these important policies in the most effective manner. Although critics and member states may complain about ill-advised programs, they often need not look beyond their own pocketbooks to explain why an IGO's performance is less than optimal.

Of course, critics of IGOS are not going away anytime soon—nor should they. Member states recognize that they are ill equipped to address today's transsovereign problems and thus, IGOs are likely to persist. Addressing the core issues of reform, transparency, and legitimacy would ensure that they are here to stay and better poised to carry out the demands of global governance.

ENDNOTES

1. Edmund Conway, "Gordon Brown Warns of Void Left by Collapse of Global Financial System," Telegraph.uk.com, March 9, 2009, <http://www.telegraph.co.uk/finance/financetopics/davos/4398124/Gordon-Brown-warns-of-void-left-by-collapse-of-global-financial-system.html>, accessed March 10, 2009.
2. A. LeRoy Bennett and James K. Oliver, *International Organizations: Principles and Issues*, 7th ed. (Upper Saddle River, NJ: Prentice Hall, 2002), 3.
3. Michael N. Barnett and Martha Finnemore, "The Politics, Power, and Pathologies of International Organizations," *International Organization*, 53(4): 699–732; Bob Reinalda and Bertjan Verbeek, *Autonomous Policy Making by International Organizations* (New York: Routledge, 1998).
4. Jeffrey Laurenti, *The World Today*, 61 (August/September 8/9, 2005): 4.
5. Clive Archer, *International Organizations* (London: Allen & Unwin, 1983).
6. Bennett and Oliver, *International Organizations* (London: Allen & Unwin, 1983), 2.
7. The actual number of international organizations varies widely, depending on various scholars' definitions of organizations and institutions. Keohane, for example, suggests there are currently more than 1,000 international institutions [Robert O. Keohane, "International Institutions: Can Interdependence Work?" *Foreign Policy* (Spring 1998): 82–94]. The term *regime* is yet another word used to describe these informal institutions. See Stephen D. Krasner, "Structural Causes and Regime Consequences: Regimes as Intervening Variables," *International Organization* 36(2): 185.
8. Keohane, "International Institutions," 86.
9. John J. Mearsheimer, "The False Promise of International Institutions," *International Security* 19(3): 5–49.
10. Barnett and Finnemore, "Politics, Power, and Pathologies," 703. See also Reinalda and Verbeek, *Autonomous Policy Making*.
11. Reinalda and Verbeek, Autonomous Policy Making, 5.
12. Bertjan Verbeek, "International Organizations: The Ugly Duckling of International Relations Theory?" in Reinalda and Verbeek (Eds.), Autonomous Policy Making, 25.
13. Ibid., 17.
14. According to Daniel Moynihan, a former U.S. representative, the United Nations itself had become "a dangerous place." See Keohane, "International Institutions," 84.
15. Ibid.

16. Oran R. Young, "Governance without Government," in *Governance in World Affairs* (Ithaca, NY: Cornell University Press, 1999), 1.

17. Thomas Friedman, *The Lexus and the Olive Tree* (New York: Farrar, Straus & Giroux, 2000).

18. Jessica T. Mathews, "Power Shift," *Foreign Affairs* (January–February 1997): 58.

19. Reinalda and Verbeek, Autonomous Policy Making, 6–7.

20. Leigh Phillips. "Leaders Seek Global Regulator," *Business Week*, January 9, 2009. <http://www.businessweek.com/globalbiz/content/jan2009/gb2009019_816873.htm>, accessed March 20, 2009.

21. Edmund Conway, "Gordon Brown Warns of Void Left by Collapse of Global Financial System," Telegraph.uk.com, March 9, 2009, <http://www.telegraph.co.uk/finance/financetopics/davos/4398124/Gordon-Brown-warns-of-void-left-by-collapse-of-global-financial-system.html>, accessed March 10, 2009.

22. Wolfgang Reinicke, "The Other World Wide Web: Global Public Policy," *Foreign Policy* (Winter 1999–2000): 44–57.

23. Oran R. Young, "Governance without Government," in *Governance in World Affairs* (Ithaca, NY: Cornell University Press, 1999), 2.

24. Donald C. F. Daniel and Bradd C. Hayes (Eds.), *Beyond Traditional Peacekeeping* (New York: St. Martin's, 1995); Lori Fisler Damrosch (Ed.), *Enforcing Restraint: Collective Intervention in Internal Conflicts* (New York: Council on Foreign Relations, 1993).

25. Bruce Russett, "Ten Balances for Weighing UN Reform Proposals," *Political Science Quarterly* 111(2): 262.

26. Steve Kobrin, "The MAI and the Clash of Globalizations," *Foreign Policy* (Fall 1998): 97–109. As Kobrin notes, NGOs were largely responsible for stopping the MAI negotiations in the OECD.

27. Martina Metzger and Birgit Reichenstein (Eds.), *Challenges for International Organizations in the 21st Century: Essays in Honor of Klaus Hufner* (New York: St. Martin's Press, 2000), viii.

28. Mathews, "Power Shift," 50–66.

29. P. J. Simmons, "Learning to Live with NGOs," *Foreign Policy* (Fall 1998): 5–6; available at <www.ceip.org/files/Publications/simmfp.asp?from=pubtopic>.

30. Corp Watch, "UN and Corporations Fact Sheet, March 2001"; available at <www.corpwatch.org/press/PPF.jsp?articleid=928>.

31. "The UN in Brief"; available at <www.un.org/overview/brief.html>.

32. Ibid.

33. David Held, Anthony McGrew, David Goldblatt, and Jonathan Perraton, *Global Transformations: Politics, Economics, and Culture* (Stanford: Stanford University Press, 1999).

34. Russett, "Ten Balances," 260.

35. UN Secretaries General Dag Hammarskjöld and Kofi Annan were also given the Nobel Prize for Peace in 1961 and 2001, respectively. Annan's prize was shared with the United Nations. The UNHCR and UNICEF have also been recipients of the Nobel Prize for Peace.

36. "Reforming the United Nations: Pope Kofi's Unruly Flock," *The Economist* (August 8, 1998): 19. See also http://www.unhcr.org.

37. See, for example, Ronald I. Meltzer, "Restructuring the United Nations System: Institutional Reform Efforts in the Context of North–South Relations," *International Organization* 32(4): 993–1018.

38. Yochi J. Dreazen, "U.N. Fires Midlevel Staffer for Oil-for-Food Role," *The Wall Street Journal* (June 2, 2005): A11.

39. "U.S. Responses to Alleged Abuse of Oil-for-Food Program," *The American Journal of International Law* 99 (January 2005): 254–255.

40. "Reforming the United Nations," 20.
41. Ibid.
42. Ibid., 22.
43. Ibid., 20.
44. "Reforming the United Nations," 19.
45. Howard LaFranchi, "Enough Reform to Satisfy Congress?" *Christian Science Monitor* (September 30, 2005), available at <www.csmonitor.com/2005/0930/p02501-usfp.htm>.
46. Charles Hill, "How to Save the U.N. (If We Really Have To)," *The Wall Street Journal* (December 7, 2004): A14.
47. David L. Bosco, *Five To Rule Them All: The UN Security Council and the Making of the Modern World* (Oxford University Press, 2009).
48. Annan, A14.
49. David D. Hale, "The IMF, Now More than Ever," *Foreign Affairs* 77(6): 107–113.
50. IMF, "IMF Pledges Stronger Partnership to Help Africa through Crisis," May 28, 2009, http://www.imf.org/external/pubs/ft/survey/so/2009/CAR052809B.htm, accessed May 29, 2009.
51. One of the most common policy criticisms of the IMF is the "moral hazard" argument in which critics fear that countries will take excessive risks knowing that the IMF will later come to their rescue. See Hale, "The IMF, Now More than Ever," 10.
52. Paul Bluestein, "At the IMF, a Struggle Shrouded in Secrecy," *Washington Post* (March 30, 1998): A1.
53. Carol Welch, "In Focus: The IMF and Good Governance," *Foreign Policy in Focus* 5(13); available at < http://www.fpif.org/fpiftxt/2832 >.
54. Joseph Stiglitz, "The Insider," *New Republic* (April 17 and 24, 2000): 56.
55. Simon Johnson, "The Quiet Coup," *The Atlantic* (May 27, 2009).
56. Ibid.
57. Ibid., 57.
58. Devesh Kapur, "The IMF: A Cure or a Curse?" *Foreign Policy* (Summer 1998): 115.
59. Ibid.
60. Another 30 countries are negotiating membership. See "The WTO in Brief" on the WTO Web site at <www.wto.org/english/thewto_e/whatis_e/inbrief_e/inbr02_e.htm>.
61. Marcus Noland, "Learning to Love the WTO," *Foreign Affairs* (September–October 1999): 81.
62. See "Beyond the Agreements: The Tuna–Dolphin Dispute" on the WTO Web site at <www.wto.org/english/thewto_e/whatis_e/tif_e/bey5_e.htm>.
63. John Audley and Ann M. Florini, *Overhauling the WTO: Opportunity at Doha and Beyond,* Policy Brief: Carnegie Endowment for International Peace (October 2001), 4.
64. "Who Elected the WTO? The Case for Globalisation Survey," *The Economist* (September 29–October 5, 2001): 26.
65. As *The Economist* argued, "The WTO is no would-be tyrant. It is democratic to a fault, and has few powers of its own." Ibid.
66. Focus on the Global South, "The End of an Illusion: WTO Reform, Global Civil Society and the Road to Hong Kong," March 31, 2005, <www.focusweb.org/Article602.html>.
67. There are still technical distinctions when referring to the *European Union* and the *European Community,* the previous name for this organization. For simplicity's sake, only the term *European Union* is used in this text.
68. Data for 2006. See "Facts and Figures" at <www.eurunion.org/profile/facts.htm>.

69. Denmark, Sweden, and the United Kingdom opted not to adopt the euro. The 10 member states that joined the EU in 2004 will have the opportunity to join the euro area once they meet the economic convergence criteria.

70. Roger Scully, "Democracy, Legitimacy, and the European Parliament," in Maria Green Cowles and Michael Smith (Eds.), *The State of the European Union: Risks, Reform, Resistance, and Revival*, vol. 5 (Oxford, UK: Oxford University Press), 228–245.

71. "A Survey of the EU's Eastern Borders," *The Economist* (June 25, 2005): 3.

72. See, for example, Mark Pollack, "Delegation, Agency, and Agenda-Setting in the European Community," *International Organization* 51(1): 99–134.

73. Simon Hix, "The Study of the European Community: The Challenge to Comparative Politics," *West European Politics* 1(1): 1–30.

74. Helen Wallace, "Politics and Policy in the EU: The Challenge of Governance," in Helen Wallace and William Wallace (Eds.), *Policy-Making in the European Union*, 3rd ed. (Oxford, UK: Oxford University Press, 1996), 3–36. See also Thomas Banchoff and Mitchell Smith (Eds.), *Legitimacy and the European Union: The Contested Polity* (New York: Routledge, 1999).

75. Maria Green Cowles, "The EU Committee of AmCham: The Powerful Voice of American Firms in Brussels," *Journal of European Public Policy* 3(3): 339–358.

76. Ian Black, "Euro Group Calls on MEPs to Reform," *Guardian* (March 15, 2001); available at <www.guardian.co.uk/europarl/Story/0,2763,452061,00.html>.

77. For example, see J. H. H. Weiler, *The Constitution of Europe: "Do the New Clothes Have an Emperor" and Other Essays on European Integration* (Cambridge: Cambridge University Press, 1999).

78. World Campaign for In-Depth Reform of the System of International Organizations, <http://www.reformcampaign.net/index.php?lg=eng&pg=que&showmenu=0>.

79. Russett, "Ten Balances," 259–269.

80. Ann M. Florini, "The End of Secrecy," *Foreign Policy* (Summer 1998); available at <www.ceip.org/files/Publications/annfp.asp?from=pubtopic>.

81. "The Non-Governmental Order," *The Economist* (December 9, 1999): 3; available at <www.economist.com/PrinterFriendly.cfm?Story_ID=266250>. See also P. J. Simmons, "Learning to Live with NGOs," *Foreign Policy* (Fall 1998): 82–96; available at <www.ceip.org/files/Publications/simmfp.asp?from=pubtopic>.

CHAPTER THREE

Nongovernmental Organizations

Politics Beyond Sovereignty

Maryann Cusimano Love

"It is extraordinary to me that you can find $700 billion to save Wall Street and the entire G8 can't find $25 billion to save 25,000 children who die every day of preventable treatable disease and hunger. Bankruptcy is a serious business and we all know people who have lost their jobs. But this is moral bankruptcy ... Providing AIDS medication to just under four million people, putting in place modest measures to improve maternal health, eradicating killer pests like malaria and rotoviruses—all these provide a leg up on the climb to self-sufficiency, all these can help us make friends in a world quick to enmity. It's not alms, it's investment. It's not charity, it's justice."

—Bono, lead singer of U2

Why is Bono at concerts, on television, on the Internet, in the halls of parliaments and Congress, at the United Nations, with his NGO The One Campaign, reminding us of our moral responsibilities to help the poor? Why is Academy Award–winning actor George Clooney a UN Messenger of Peace for Darfur, Sudan, and a founder of "Not on Our Watch," an NGO devoted to raising awareness and resources to the conflict in Darfur? Why do celebrities raise awareness with NGOs? Because it works. Consider that never before in history has half the planet tuned in to the same program on the same issue at the same time. But 3 billion people, nearly half the world's population, watched the Live 8 concerts to Make Poverty History on July 2, 2005. More than 1 million music fans packed ten concerts on four continents, another 2 billion watched on television, and the remainder tuned in online. The concerts were designed to raise awareness, mobilize citizens, and pressure governments to address global poverty. Free concerts were held in Berlin, Johannesburg, London, Moscow, Paris, Philadelphia, Rome, Tokyo, and Toronto; celebrities from Nelson Mandela, Brad Pitt, and Tom Hanks to Paul McCartney, U2, Bob Geldof, Green Day, Elton John, Coldplay, REM, The Who, Destiny's Child, Stevie Wonder, P. Diddy,

Jay-Z, Robbie Williams, and Madonna contributed their time and talent to the concerts and media campaigns.[1] The efforts largely succeeded. The G-8 leaders committed to double aid to Africa, cancel the debt of some of the world's poorest countries, provide greater access to HIV/AIDS treatment drugs, and work to reform trade practices that hurt the world's poor. The movement continues to pressure world leaders to keep and expand upon these promises in the face of the global recession.[2]

The One Campaign is a successor to the Jubilee movement, and both are curious coalitions. The pope, Bono (lead singer of the Irish rock band U2), Harvard economist Jeffrey Sachs, and a coalition of religious organizations and nongovernmental organizations (NGOs) united in an effort to get the debts of heavily indebted poor countries (HIPCs) forgiven in the millennium year and the years since. In a perverse form of foreign aid, HIPCs pay private banks and international financial institutions more in debt repayments each year than they invest in education and health care or receive in aid or foreign direct investment (FDI). Each year billions are drained away from Africa alone, more than what is needed to treat HIV and AIDS, tuberculosis, and malaria combined in Africa in one year.[3] Many of the original loans went to corrupt governments and dictators who were useful to the West during its Cold War fight against communism. For example, at least 30 percent of World Bank funds to Indonesia were pocketed by the Suharto family or its associates, according to some estimates.[4]

The idea behind these campaigns is that poor people have paid enough. Most have paid the original lending amounts three or four times over—and they will never be able to pay the escalating interest owed on loans that have profited the banks of some developed countries as well as corrupt rulers, but have deprived citizens in indebted countries of resources and basic services. Initially, the Jubilee effort was declared politically dead by officials in the U.S. Department of the Treasury, which is a strong proponent of debt repayment (U.S. banks hold some of these debts). But through dogged persistence and savvy lobbying, the Jubilee effort prevailed on several fronts in a short time. The debate moved from whether debt should be forgiven, to the questions of whose debt should be forgiven, how quickly, and using what instruments. Through a pincer movement of pressure commonly used by NGOs, these movements press democratic governments internally and externally. Through rock concerts and media campaigns, the movements appeal directly to the public, making the abstract problem of Third World poverty and debt concrete to mobilize public opinion. Leveraging celebrity activism, Bono and others worked the halls of Congress, parliaments, the

United Nations, and European Union (EU), winning over conservatives by quoting scripture and discussing religious obligations to help the poor.

In a similar story of NGOs affecting foreign policy, Canadian house-wife Jody Williams had had enough. NGOs had warned governments about the dangers of landmines for years, but governments were not tak-ing sufficient action. Long after wars were over, antipersonnel landmines remained in more than ninety countries, killing and maiming an estimated 26,000 people each year—or creating one new landmine victim every 20 minutes.[5] Landmines violate the rules of war because they cannot dis-tinguish between combatants and civilians. Many victims of landmines are children, who, out of curiosity, pick up these shiny but dangerous objects. Many governments found landmines to be cheap weapons of war. They did not want to stop using them, and they did not want to pay for difficult and often deadly mine-removal programs.

So Jody Williams used the personal computer in her kitchen to or-ganize the many NGOs that had a stake in this fight. Using e-mail and faxes, she inexpensively, quickly, and efficiently brought diverse groups on board and founded the International Campaign to Ban Landmines (ICBL). With the help of the Canadian government, the ICBL brought pressure to bear on governments to quickly ban, remove, and stop producing and stockpiling antipersonnel landmines, and to increase landmine education and reduce the pain and suffering of landmine victims. The ICBL enlisted celebrity spokespeople such as Princess Diana in a direct media campaign that bypassed obstructionist governments and made emotional appeals di-rectly to the public. Internally, governments were pressured by their own populations. Externally, they were pressed by the coalition of NGOs and states such as Canada, which led the movement to ban landmines. In record time, the ICBL succeeded in getting states to adopt an international treaty banning antipersonnel landmines in December 1997. One hundred fifty-six states have already ratified the treaty, despite opposition from the United States. In each year since the treaty's signing, landmine use, production, and stockpiling have decreased while landmine decommissioning, education, and services to landmine victims have increased. The ICBL continues to be active, using a network of over 1,000 NGOs in over 70 countries to monitor compliance with the treaty, pressuring states that have not joined the treaty, and working in coalition with others to ban cluster munitions (whose unexploded ordinance work like antipersonnel landmines). Jody Williams won the Nobel Peace Prize for her efforts.

These examples illustrate four main themes that will be explored in this chapter. First, not only are the power and number of NGOs increasing, but also they are more frequently joining forces in transnational advocacy networks, or mobilizations of principled actors who are committed to social change.[6] Second, NGOs are active in more sectors, taking on increased functions that were once the sole preserve of states (such as international finance) and serving as the legal monitors of arms control treaty compliance. Third, NGOs use tactics that are aimed directly at the public, multinational corporations (MNCs), or intergovernmental organizations (IGOs). They are not focused only on governments—and this is one of their greatest strengths. NGOs come with weaknesses, however, including democracy deficits, North–South divisions, and coordination complexity. Fourth and finally, these changing ideas and practices of transnational politics affect sovereignty.

NGOs: PEOPLE POWER

Although NGOs predate the current period of modern globalization, their numbers, sizes, budgets, ranges of activities, power, transnational networks, and levels of international recognition have drastically increased in recent years—to the point where commentators have suggested "we are in the midst of a global 'associational revolution.' "[7] NGOs are an odd category, defined negatively by what they are not rather than by positive definitions of what they are. NGOs are not governments, but they may receive resources from or offer resources to governments, or they may only involve themselves in certain areas or issues with the permission of governments. NGOs are a broad and eclectic group, however, and some never accept government aid. Other NGOs, such as Catholic Relief Services, derive significant portions of their budgets and resources from governments as states contract out developmental assistance to NGOs.

NGOs range from small, grassroots groups run on shoestring budgets to huge international organizations with deep pockets, from single-issue outfits to umbrella organizations. NGOs are private-sector organizations but are often assumed to be public interest groups, which leads to contention. Who elects NGOs and who do they speak for? Many in the United States refer to NGOs as *PVOs*, or *private volunteer organizations*. But the term *volunteer* can be misleading, because most international NGOs have permanent, full-time, paid professional staffs. NGOs are nonprofit groups. Although community development banks or Habitat for Humanity often turn a profit, the resources generated are reinvested in the community. Profit is not the organization's primary goal but a means to achieving the NGO's goals such as stabilizing communities by developing homes and businesses in poor areas where banks will not lend money.

Table 1

Worldwide NGO Growth

	1909	1951	1960	1968	
Traditional NGOs	176	832	1,268	2,577	
Special NGOs	–	–	–	741	
Total	176	832	1,268	3,318	
	1976	1978	1983	1985	
Traditional NGOs	5,155	8,347	11,523	13,768	
Special NGOs	1,067	1,174	5,507	6,866	
Total	6,222	9,521	17,030	20,634	
	1987	1989	1991	1993	
Traditional NGOs	14,943	14,333	16,113	12,759	
Special NGOs	8,305	5,730	7,522	16,142	
Total	23,248	20,063	23,635	28,901	
	1995	1997	2001/2002	2005	2008
Traditional NGOs	14,274	15,965	18,323	20,928	21,224
Special NGOs	21,780	24,341	28,775	30,581	33,153
Total	36,054	40,306	47,098	51,509	54,377

Source: Data from Union of International Associations (Ed.), Yearbook of International Organizations, vol. 1b (Brussels: K. G. Saur Verlag, 2008), Appendix 3.

Counts of NGOs vary, although scholars agree that their numbers are increasing. They are often referred to as *part of civil society* or as the *third sector* (government and for-profit businesses being the other two sectors).

The Union of International Associations tracks NGOs and IGOs (see Table 1) and listed 21,224 traditional international NGOs in 2008, such as universal membership organizations and internationally oriented national organizations. Another 33,153 special NGOs (such as religious orders) bring a total of 54,377 international NGOs.[8]

Despite their rising numbers, NGOs raise some puzzles. NGOs have no armies. They command no states. They collect no taxes and can compel no one to follow them or to contribute to their treasuries. So what is the source of their power? NGOs trade in the currency of ideas, especially ideas of good and evil, right and wrong. The ideas compel, even when the organizations cannot. NGOs attract support more than they can enforce compliance.

Many NGOs are transnational moral entrepreneurs, agents who act as reformers or crusaders to change rules out of an ethical concern to curtail a great evil.[9] Their very names are often cast as moral imperatives, proclaiming both what they value and what they do—as in Human Rights Watch and Save the Children.

Governments have legal authority, but advocacy NGOs rely on moral authority. Generally, where states have military power and MNCs have economic power, the strength of NGOs lies in their idea power. They seek to occupy the only high ground available to them, the moral high ground. If an NGO can succeed in redefining a problem as a moral issue, then it will have a greater chance of prevailing, because states and MNCs may not be able to speak credibly as bastions or brokers of morality. Religious organizations in particular often have well-developed ethics and rich institutions, resources that are useful to transnational advocacy networks and greatly needed today given the ethical and institutional gaps of globalization (discussed in Chapter 13). For example, consider the importance of church networks and leaders in abolishing slavery, as well as the importance of Archbishop Desmond Tutu in the South African anti-apartheid movement. Morally, religious organizations have legitimacy speaking on moral issues and a treasure chest of well-developed ideas available for use by transnational advocacy networks. Tactically, religious organizations can pool their power with other religious and civil society groups and use their direct pulpit access to citizens (who may be business or government decision makers) as well as their ability to attract media. Although secular NGOs may not command institutional networks (such as schools and hospitals) that are as extensive as those of religious organizations, they also develop and trade in moral ideas, such as when environmental transnational advocacy networks construct and promote environmental ethics.[10]

NGOs have information power. Especially when networked transnationally, NGOs may have access to grassroots information about how particular policies affect particular people, information that governments or IGOs overlook or do not have. People with greater and cheaper access to information technologies can force greater transparency. Transparency and sunshine politics are important tools for NGOs. By expanding the information base of a public's or elite's discussion of previously closed matters, NGOs often impose a "Dracula" test: Will a particular policy or practice be able to survive in the daylight? Transparency alone can do much to shrink both government and corporate abuses. And discussions about opening the decision-making process to greater transparency help to reframe issues as moral issues, again moving the issue to where NGOs have some home court advantage.

Some NGOs can use the power of their reputations as a "force multiplier" to enhance their values, ideas, and information power. Reputational power may derive from important, well-known, or respected figures who are members of the group, or it may come from the NGO's own track record of strong advocacy. Or, like an MNC, an NGO may build a "brand name" around the quality and reliability of the organization's information products. Some NGOs emphasize building such reputational power through quality information products—for example, Transparency International's work on corruption worldwide.

NGOs use media and communications power as a force multiplier for their values, ideas, and information power. Although NGOs vary in their skills and access to global media, they do have certain media advantages. Global media simplify issues to attract wider audiences and compete against ever-shorter sound bites to sell their products. If NGOs often emphasize how policies or practices affect particular individuals or groups, or how global issues present clear moral choices, then they may be able to attract media attention. NGOs can use media as a megaphone for their message if they understand the care and feeding of the media and can deliver compelling stories and good pictures with clear good guys and bad guys in arenas where government, IGO, or corporate responses may be slow or lack credibility. Because MNCs may have huge marketing investments in their brand names and do not want these brands sullied or their reputations trashed, even the threat of negative media coverage can bring greater attention to an NGO's ideas. It is more difficult to wield this media power against naked, anonymous commodities and unknown, unbranded companies, however. Media and communications power are important to groups that trade in ideas. NGOs, like others who can persuade but cannot compel, must be good salespeople as well as good preachers to effectively mobilize their ideas.[11]

NGOs also have female power. Women are underrepresented in the governments of states and in leadership positions in MNCs and IGOs. But women are better represented as both leaders and members of NGOs. Women make up the majority of people on the planet, but many governments, MNCs, and IGOs throw away or underutilize the talents of more than half of their populations. This can be a moral and strategic advantage for NGOs. They can provide a means for women to participate in and affect international structures that may otherwise exclude them. If women perceive NGOs as more likely to represent their interests, then this may add to popular support and reputational advantages for NGOs. Like human society in general, NGOs are certainly not free from gender conflicts; relative to other institutions, however, NGOs are more likely to be run by and for women, taking up issues—such as women's rights, human smuggling, and female genital mutilation—that other institutions ignore.[12]

NGOs also have the power of individuals. They do not accept the traditional view that states are the fundamental unit in international politics and that individuals can have little effect. Believing individuals can make a difference, they create ways for them to do so. Without getting bogged down in the question of which came first, the idea or the activist, activists are central to NGOs.[13] Individuals may start NGOs, splinter NGOs, and use NGOs as vehicles for both personal and community expression and activism. Even when NGOs network internationally in large campaigns, testimonials of how global problems affect real people are an enormous strength for NGOs, helping to put a face on global politics.

Although NGOs are generally legal groups that do not advocate violence, they share similarities with other nonstate actors that form transnational networks in pursuit of particular ideas: terrorists. For both groups, "victims" are strategically useful if a wider society empathizes with them either as innocent civilians, or because people can envision themselves in their shoes. A "poster child factor" also helps NGOs gain sympathy and concrete identification with their cause from either elites or masses. For terrorists, sympathy with the victims helps generate fear that is out of proportion to the acts they commit. The similarities end there, however, because terrorists target their victims with the intention of harming them, whereas NGOs target their groups with the intention of aiding them. The success of their very divergent strategies, however, depends on the esteem with which society regards them, their cause, and their targeted groups.

Another source of power for NGOs can be consumer power. If an NGO can credibly argue a connection between a corporate policy and some objectionable wider practice, then it can marshal the market power of customers, consumers, or shareholders through boycotts or pressure on advertisers and shareholders, among other forms of market pressures. This can put an economic price on objectionable practices that may make corporations or states notice and respond to NGO concerns. This is how "dolphin-safe tuna" came to a grocery store near you.

NGOs have network power. They are typically organized as flatter, more flexible organizations than governments, IGOs, or MNCs. This may give NGOs greater speed to respond to pressing global issues or to get their views to the media faster than some government bureaucracies. More important, networks allow NGOs to forum shop—that is, to press their issues in more favorable state or international arenas. For example, with the help of human rights NGOs, the families of four U.S. churchwomen who had been abducted, raped, and murdered while serving the poor in El Salvador in 1980 sued the generals responsible in court in the United States. Feeling that justice was blocked in the political system of El Salvador, NGOs helped to move the issue to the United States, where there are stronger legal protections on human rights and greater access to the international media, and where many of the perpetrators now reside. Those responsible for the torture and deaths of the churchwomen, and the assassin of Roman Catholic Archbishop Oscar Romero (who was murdered with a single bullet through the heart while saying mass at a hospital chapel), have been found guilty and liable.[14] What can possibly be accomplished by this? The women and the Archbishop are dead and the civil war has ended. But NGOs trade in ideas. Those involved with these cases want "to deter other would-be torturers and assassins from committing such acts," and to send "a message to military commanders around the world that they can be held responsible for their failure to act, as well as for their direct actions, and that the U.S. is not a safe haven for such people."[15] The trials help shed light on the poor human rights practices of governments, as well as open a new forum for hearing other cases blocked by local governments. Margaret Keck and Kathryn Sikkink refer to this as the "boomerang pattern":

> Governments are the primary "guarantors" of rights, but also their primary violators. When a government violates or refuses to recognize rights, individuals and domestic groups often have no recourse within domestic political or judicial arenas. They may seek international connections finally to express their concerns and even to protect their lives. When channels between the state and its domestic actors are blocked, the boomerang pattern of influence characteristic of transnational networks may occur: domestic NGOs bypass their state and directly search out international allies to try to bring pressure on their states from outside.[16]

Keck and Sikkink are correct that transnational networks often emerge as a back way around blocked local politics, but NGOs go global for other reasons as well. Even when an NGO enjoys a good relationship with the local government, as Jody Williams and the ICBL enjoyed with the Canadian government, the goal may require activating a global advocacy network. Or NGOs may perceive a better target internationally, even when local politics are not blocked.

Outlining these potential sources of power for NGOs does not mean that all organizations have all of these resources at all times. Some NGOs have denser networks that allow them to pool or access greater resources than others with fewer or sparser networks. Some issues are easier to put a face on than others. Environmentalists who are concerned with global climate change have emphasized on the effects on animals, rather than focusing on a "poster child" and the adverse impacts on people, which makes it difficult for them to translate the abstractions of climate change into more concrete concern over those who are affected. If ideas are a crucial source of power for NGOs, then clearly some ideas are better than others, and some play better to particular audiences than do others. Some NGOs can craft an easily recognizable and universally sympathetic message better than others. NGOs that promulgate values and ideas with greater resonance will have advantages over NGOs with narrower and less appealing idea bases. For example, it may be easier to mobilize against child labor than to save the dwarf wedge mussel. As in all things political, context matters in assessing NGO power. It is easier to sell the idea that child labor is wrong in rich countries than in poor countries.

Different NGOs have different resources, expertise, networks, issues, and contexts. However, NGOs use their variegated supplies of people power in several common ways. NGOs raise consciousness regarding issues with elites, masses, or both. NGOS often practice resurrection politics, taking issues previously thought dead on arrival (such as landmines and debt relief), and raising them up onto the public and political agenda. NGOs also practice ideas, information, and symbolic politics, expanding the idea base surrounding issues by introducing new or discrediting accepted information, or introducing alternative norms by which to evaluate information. NGOs frame or reframe issues. NGOs change language, beliefs, and symbols surrounding issues (which may later translate into behavioral changes). NGOs move issues to a forum more amenable to a favorable response. NGOs practice leverage politics by enlisting celebrities to bring attention and leverage to their cause.[17]

NGOs change government, IGO, or MNC policy, or individual behavior. They adapt or create institutional structures or advocacy networks to further particular issues. NGOs practice Dracula politics, transparency politics, and sunshine politics, shining a light on problems and shaming and naming perpetrators. Like Dracula, many abusive international practices can persist only in the dark, and die off when exposed to the light of day. NGOs monitor compliance with norms or regimes once created, making actors live up to the promises they make.

Yet NGOs come with their downsides as well. Coordinating action among a wide variety of eclectic organizations with different agendas, cultures, and operating procedures is difficult. The abilities of NGOs to work well with states, IGOs, and MNCs in combating transsovereign problems are often inhibited by poor communication and coordination among the various groups, who may not like, trust, or understand each other. IGOs, MNCs, and government foreign policy organizations too often deal with

NGOs in an ad hoc, nonsystematic manner. Increased numbers of NGOs in complex combinations make coordination, communication, transparency, and accountability difficult, as is determining which groups should be included in government and IGO decision processes. NGOs may compete against one another for the supremacy of their ideas, funding, and recognition. As private-sector organizations, whom do NGOs speak for or answer to beyond their own governing boards or contributors? NGOs have asymmetrical resources and influence, and even within NGO advocacy networks, conflicts arise between Northern and Southern NGOs. Who guides the network? Southern NGOs are critical of donor-driven development. However, media power and reputational power can also be tools to check and balance rising NGO power. For example, public pressure against the Red Cross decision to use funds donated to the victims of September 11 for other purposes indicates these tools can yield results. Many NGOs adopt voluntary codes of conduct and publish their budgets to encourage transparency and accountability. The same questions that plague corporate codes of conduct, however, may be raised regarding NGOs: How seriously are these codes implemented, and what are the sanctions if voluntary codes are not implemented? Because NGO power frequently derives from moral and reputational capital, NGOs may have greater incentives to address democracy deficits than other organizations.

NGOs AND GLOBALIZATION: OPEN SOCIETIES

Open societies, open technologies, and open economies make it easier to establish, organize, and run NGOs. We are witnessing an explosion of NGOs worldwide precisely when liberalizing trends are spreading. The spread of democracy lowers the barriers to forming NGOs. Some of the hallmarks of democracy are freedom of expression and freedom of association.

Certainly, the democratization process encourages the creation and spread of NGOs as part of the effort to build civil society. One Hungarian activist, Andras Biro, describes his efforts: "For the first time in forty years we are reclaiming responsibility for our lives."[18] Nondemocratic governments may make NGOs illegal, fearing they may form a base of opposition to the government. Organizing people in states with closed political systems—North Korea, for example—can be a dangerous proposition to the activist, who risks imprisonment, torture, and death.

The fears of authoritarian governments are justified because NGOs have worked to bring about the fall of nondemocratic regimes. Lester Salamon notes that "under Pope John Paul II Catholic churches in Warsaw, Gdansk, Krakow, and elsewhere in Eastern Europe provided a crucial neutral meeting ground and source of moral support for those agitating for change in the latter 1980s. The Lutheran Church played a comparable role in East Germany."[19]

NGOs also have been instrumental in pressing for open societies and advocating for human rights and democratization. During and after World War II, NGOs kept the issue of human rights on the international agenda when state representatives meeting to construct the postwar international organization (which became the United Nations) tried to exclude or water down such concerns. States were skeptical about including human rights in the UN Charter. They feared a loss of sovereignty over internal treatment of their citizens if the topic were broached in the UN Charter. But NGOs such as the American Jewish Committee, the American Bar Association, the National Association for the Advancement of Colored People, and the League of Women Voters reminded states that the failure to protect individual and minority rights after World War I had contributed to the conflict and genocide of World War II. Sustained lobbying by NGOs ensured that respect for human rights became one of the four purposes of the United Nations set forth in its Charter, and that the Charter called for the creation of a UN Commission on Human Rights. NGOs provided expert advice and research and helped to draft language and lobby for the adoption of the 1948 Universal Declaration of Human Rights and other subsequent human rights treaties.[20]

NGOs often are created as the locus of resistance to nondemocratic regimes. One dramatic example was the emergence of NGOs in opposition to the military dictatorships in Argentina and Chile in the 1970s and 1980s. Citizens who criticized or were seen as threats to these regimes, as well as many who happened to be in the wrong place at the wrong time, became the *desaparecidos*, or the "disappeared." They were kidnapped, imprisoned, tortured, and killed. In a final insult, the children of many of the disappeared were sold to childless military couples. "One torturer estimated that about sixty babies passed through [his clandestine detention center], and that all but two—whose heads were smashed against the wall in efforts to get their mothers to talk—were sold."[21]

> Children were tortured in front of their parents, and parents in front of their children. Some prisoners were kept in rooms no longer or wider than a single bed. And the torture continued for days, weeks, months, even years, until the victim was released or, more often, killed. The sadistic brutality did not always even end with the death of the victim. "One woman was sent the hands of her daughter in a shoe box." The body of another woman "was dumped in her parents' yard,

naked but showing no outward signs of torture. Later the director of the funeral home called to inform her parents that the girl's vagina had been sewn up. Inside he had found a rat."[22]

In a heroic response to such brutality, a small group of middle-aged mothers of disappeared children organized in 1977. Calling themselves the "Mothers of the Plaza de Mayo," at first they numbered only fourteen. Frustrated in their attempts to locate their children, they began a silent vigil every Thursday afternoon in the main square of Buenos Aires in front of the president's residence and seat of government. Although the women were subject to harassment and attack (some of them even disappeared themselves), they continued their efforts to draw attention to the atrocities of the military government. They were followed by the "Grandmothers of the Plaza de Mayo," who attempted to trace and recover the trafficked children and babies. Quickly, the numbers of these groups swelled across Latin America, and they soon became the NGO known as Federación Latinoamericana de Asociaciones de Familiares de Detenidos-Desaparecidos (FEDEFAM, Federation of Families of Political Prisoners and Disappeared Persons). Working with a wide transnational network of NGOs, they fought the military dictatorships and their brutality, always at great personal risk to themselves. When the dictatorships eventually fell, these groups helped to build democracies, strengthen the legal protections for human rights, and reunite political prisoners with their families.[23]

NGOs promote open societies in many ways. They expose the abuses of regimes by tracking facts and disseminating information, as well as by mobilizing public opinion to try to end the abuses and improve conditions. They communicate with decision makers locally and globally, dispensing information and advocating for legal changes. They are direct service providers, offering education, advocacy, and legal aid services. They teach citizens what their rights are and "how to act upon them."[24]

NGOs AND GLOBAL TECHNOLOGIES

Open technologies also greatly assist the formation and maintenance of NGOs, as seen in the landmines case. Any group with a personal computer can maintain a database and mailing list, post a Web site, circulate a newsletter, or e-mail information to its members. Cheap and easily available information technologies allow citizens to more easily gather and disseminate information and ideas, identify members, solicit funds, network with others, and coordinate activities. Decentralization of phone and communication companies has made it more difficult for governments to control access to or censor use of the Internet. Many governments still try to censor the Internet, although as former President Clinton put it, the attempt may be as futile as "nailing Jello to a wall."[25] NGOs also rely on independent news media to directly communicate with the public, publicize their causes, and pressure governments. For example, Greenpeace relies on satellite communications technology to launch direct media campaigns on environmental causes. When Shell Oil wanted to dump retired oil rigs at sea, Greenpeace seized one of the rigs, the Brent Spar in the North Sea, and broadcast directly from there. Media wishing to cover the controversy had to rely on Greenpeace's satellite uplinks, putting Shell and the British government at a disadvantage in getting out their side of the story. Eventually Greenpeace was successful in mobilizing public opinion to pressure the oil companies (via boycotts) and governments to stop decommissioning oil rigs at sea, in large part because of Greenpeace's effective media strategies and use of communications technologies.[26] Media attention also raises public attention and funding to NGOs.[27] Compelling media coverage of the 280,000 killed in the tsunami in Southeast Asia brought record contributions. The International Red Cross discontinued fund raising on January 26, 2005, because so much money (over 1.2 billion dollars in contributions) had been pledged in the first 30 days.[28]

NGOs also actively work to expand the reach of open technologies. Typically, international NGOs work with local counterparts, thereby spreading technology. For example, when the NGO known as Women Waging Peace began, one of the first projects it funded was equipping women's peace organizations with laptop computers and providing training in the use of the Internet and media strategies. In similar ways, environmental NGOs press for the adoption of cleaner, greener technologies, such as water- and air-filtration systems that make it possible for factories to emit fewer toxic pollutants into the environment. Public health NGOs disseminate health technologies such as filtration systems for drinking water and X-ray and diagnostic equipment as parts of their disease eradication programs. Development NGOs disseminate technologies for agriculture, irrigation, water systems, and electrification.

NGOs AND OPEN ECONOMIES

The rise in NGOs is also facilitated by open economies. The information economy brings advantages for NGOs that trade in ideas and information. Economic liberalization also allows money to flow freely across borders, allowing NGOs to solicit and contribute money across sovereign jurisdictions. In addition, capitalism encourages the growth of the private sector, of which NGOs are a part. Free-market economies tend to emphasize grassroots, private-sector responses to societal problems rather than top-down, state-sponsored solutions. NGOs thus fit with the entrepreneurial and pluralistic norms of capitalist societies. Privatization of the economy is even encouraging the growth of NGOs in China:

> The Chinese government and party have announced a new slogan. They refer to it as "small government, big society." They want to shrink government, and they want to grow society, that is, they want to shift functions from the government sphere to the private sphere. . . . The vehicle for doing this, in part, is to create a private nonprofit sector that can shoulder some of the social tasks that have traditionally, in recent Chinese history, been state functions.[29]

Although there are limits to the independence of Chinese NGOs, the small government, big society approach shows the spread of ideas concerning the value of the private sector.

NGOs vary in their receptiveness to open markets, however. While some trade and professional associations lobby to expand free-market arrangements such as the WTO and the North American Free Trade Agreement, social advocacy NGOs in the labor, development, environment, and human rights arenas are often skeptical of economic globalization—as seen in the regular protests against the IMF, World Bank, and WTO.

NGOs AND STATES

NGOs may work with donor states to aid people in weak or failing states, as relief and development organizations such as Catholic Relief Services are doing with the Afghan and Pakistani governments in ministering to the needs of Afghan refugees. Donor governments increasingly prefer to funnel aid through NGOs rather than give it directly to recipient foreign governments that may be neither efficient nor accountable in their use of the funds. In states undergoing transitions, new institutions may be weak and lack proven track records.

Governments believe that aid funneled through NGOs is more politically acceptable than direct government-to-government assistance. They believe that NGOs can better reach the grassroots level and are more efficient because they involve less bureaucratic red tape and overhead. They also believe that working with NGOs helps to develop the private sector.

Many see contracting out to NGOs as a win–win situation. The government "has found an efficient, less costly means of carrying out its legislative mandate, while the [NGO]s have discovered a relatively dependable source of money, available in large sums."[30]

There are downsides, however. NGOs risk losing the perception of their autonomy and independence from governments if they rely too heavily on state sources for funding, which can compromise an NGO's reputational power. One NGO executive director described the question of accepting funding from the United States Agency for International Development (USAID) as the dilemma of not wanting "to look like the tool or the fool of the United States government."[31]

NGOs are also concerned about the potential for conflict of interest between their goals and the goals of government donors. NGOs are concerned about becoming dependent on states for resources and potentially neglecting their traditional bases of support. They do not want to change their focus to fit more closely with government priorities in order to attract state funding. The "strings" that may come attached to accepting government funds (such as the "Buy American" requirement that goes along with U.S. aid dollars) may detract from their program principles (such as, whenever possible, to buy locally to help the local economy). And NGOs fear that the reporting and accounting procedures required of government contractors may make them more bureaucratic, entangle them in red tape, and drive up costs (which donors wanted to avoid by funneling aid through NGOs in the first place).

When recipient governments are cut out of the aid loop because of corruption or weakness, animosity may develop between state institutions and NGOs. For example, in Haiti, short-term concerns for quick and accountable projects may come at the cost of developing long-term state capacity in crucial sectors such as education and public health.[32]

As citizens turn to NGOs as service providers, the state is further undermined, which can perpetuate a feedback loop. NGOs may become involved to attend to problems that states are not addressing. In so doing, NGOs may further undermine the capacity and legitimacy of states, which can exacerbate transsovereign problems rather than fight them.

As an increasing number of states collapse, this is becoming a larger issue. Many NGOs do not wait for a state invitation before entering a country to provide services. This is especially true in countries such as Somalia, where there were no working state governments. If NGOs fulfill the functions of states where there are no functioning sovereignties, then how are sovereign states rebuilt? Some NGOs are not concerned with the question.

Individuals in need, not states, are their priorities. They regard sovereignty not only as a right to nonintervention (negative or de jure sovereignty), but also as a responsibility to provide some benefit to citizens (positive or de facto sovereignty). If states are unable or unwilling to fulfill their responsibilities toward individuals in need, then NGOs must step in.

The NGO known as Doctors Without Borders (Médicins Sans Frontières) developed specifically out of the creed that physicians would provide medical assistance where needed, regardless of whether government actors existed or welcomed them.[33] Save the Children developed out of the efforts of a British woman, Eglantyne Jebb, to provide aid to the children victimized by World War I, regardless of whether they were the citizens of a winning or losing state in the conflict.[34] Similarly, Amnesty International began in 1961 with the efforts of a London lawyer, Peter Benenson, to win the release of some Portuguese political prisoners. His campaign soon developed into a worldwide watchdog and advocacy organization for human rights. Amnesty International is fundamentally concerned with protecting the human rights of individuals and groups. It is less concerned with the effect its activities may have on state capacities. Faith-based NGOs likewise are concerned with higher principles. The major world religions existed before the advent of the modern sovereign state, and they likely will be around long after its demise. Although not necessarily antagonistic to states, faith-based NGOs feel they answer to a higher authority than the state.

Understandably, then, NGO–state relations are often adversarial because NGOs are often created to curb the abuses of states or to attend to issues that states ignore. In Central America in the 1970s and 1980s, NGOs were targeted by the state, particularly four types of NGOs—human rights, training, humanitarian, and organizations that represented those citizens uprooted by the violence and civil wars:

> Physical attacks on NGOs started in the 1970s. . . . Governments have tried to destroy human rights NGOs since their creation. They have endured because of personal courage, the mix of financial, technical, and political support received from international NGOs, and survival strategies crafted to suit local conditions. For example, the Catholic Justice and Peace Commission and El Salvador's Tutela Legal operated under the umbrella of church protection. . . . Most survived because of strong international links and small, low budget, decentralized administrative operations; some . . . perished. NGOs documenting and researching issues related to uprooted populations were also intimidated because of their infringement into policy areas considered the armed forces' preserve.[35]

One sign of the adversarial relationship between states and NGOs is the establishment of "front" NGOs by governments "to infiltrate and gather information on the NGO community. These 'government NGOs' are of particular concern in the field of human rights."[36]

NGOs AND STATE FUNCTIONS

Not only do some NGOs commandeer more resources than do many states, but also the activities of these organizations increasingly impinge on functions that previously were jealously guarded by states. NGOs carry out health, education, welfare, and development functions, especially in weak states. In abdicating educational functions to NGOs, states lose opportunities to proselytize and socialize their youth in the viewpoints of the state, as many poor Muslim states are realizing. They had welcomed Saudi charities that set up madrasas, or schools that educate students in the Wahabi form of Islam, an extreme fundamentalist version of that religion. Even in strong states, NGOs are increasingly active in issues such as economic and environmental policy making, land use, and even arms control.

Although only states make laws and sign treaties, NGOs increasingly help to write laws and treaties, lobby for their acceptance, and monitor compliance with them:

> Nongovernmental organizations play an increasingly prominent role in international environmental institutions, participating in many activities—negotiation, monitoring, and implementation—traditionally reserved to states. . . . For better or worse NGOs are now a regular part of the cooperative process. Within limits, they address delegations as a state would. They participate actively in the corridor diplomacy which is so central to negotiations, receive documents, present proposals, and are consulted by and lobby delegations. These changes are all relatively new. . . .[37]

Because environmental problems are indifferent to state borders, and the information and technical expertise needed to make environmental policy often exceeds the capacity of states, NGOs provide valuable services on environmental issues. They can track environmental problems and effects on resources across borders, presenting the wider perspective needed to write treaties and create and monitor regimes. For example, in negotiations on climate change, "NGOs set the original goal of negotiating an agreement to control greenhouse gases long before governments were ready to do so, proposed most of its structure and content, and lobbied and mobilized public pressure to force through a pact that virtually no one else thought possible when the talks began."[38] NGOs also provide policy research and development, serve on government delegations, participate in small working-group meetings at international negotiations, monitor state commitments, report on negotiations, lobby participants, and facilitate negotiations. NGOs even have legal standing in most of the major environmental treaties negotiated in the last decade.[39]

NGOs also develop and implement "soft law," or the voluntary codes that often serve as stepping stones to the eventual passage of "hard law." Finally, NGOs may change attitudes and behavior directly, changing the ideas held by individuals and institutions. In this way, NGOs may work to manage pressing global problems with or without the cooperation or capacity of states.

NGOs WORKING BEYOND SOVEREIGNTY

NGOs go beyond sovereignty not only in their organization, membership, and activities across borders, but also in their ideas and the targets of their activities. If the public sector is shrinking or not growing as fast as the private sector, then the nonprofit part of the private sector may be needed as a counterweight to the for-profit private sector. Citizens who believe globalization is out of balance or tilted in favor of corporations look to NGOs to serve as a check or counterbalance. Networks of international environmental NGOs, for example, directly pressure MNCs and the public to change environmental behavior. They do not restrict themselves to lobbying governments and IGOs for strengthened legislation or treaties. By taking their arguments directly to corporations, consumers, and public opinion worldwide, NGOs operate beyond sovereignty. McDonald's stopped using polystyrene plastic foam burger packaging largely in response to NGO-fueled direct-public and consumer-pressure campaigns.[40] NGOs often prefer direct action campaigns to legislative campaigns because state actions to pass and enforce laws on particular environmental problems can be slow and are only effective within a country's territory with enforcement measures. Direct corporate and consumer campaigns, on the other hand, can achieve results across borders without government legislation or enforcement. Convincing individuals not to purchase products made from rain-forest wood can be more effective in preserving rain forests than pursuing government legislation.

Religious organizations also work beyond sovereignty, often targeting their activities directly toward individuals and communities. Religious organizations reach globally with rich, interconnected institutions in health care, education, relief and development, and refugee and resettlement services. These institutional infrastructures are so extensive, well developed, and multifaceted that some consider it misleading to consider a religious organization "just another NGO" because NGOs may be more singular in focus and rarely run global networks of schools and hospitals, for example. Too often, when religious organizations are considered at all in international relations, they are presented as parties to ethnic and nationalist conflict and opposed to globalization, change, and modernity (or what some have termed "Jihad versus McWorld"). Samuel Huntington, among others, predicts an inevitable clash of civilizations with religious groups at war— that is, of the West versus the rest. There are alternative views, however.[41] Corporations and states are neither the only engines of globalization nor its only beneficiaries. Religious organizations have long been globalizing forces, spreading ideas, institutions, flows of people, and capital across international borders. Today, religious organizations (like other civil society groups) continue to play active roles in globalization as both global actors and mediating institutions, responding to the challenges of globalization and offering alternative ethical visions of it (beyond market or consumer dynamics).[42]

NGO ideas go beyond sovereignty. Corporations see the world as a market. In this material world, people are all customers, shareholders, or investors. States see globalization as a world to be governed. People are either governed or ungovernable, citizens or those beyond government and posing problems (for example, illegal immigrants, refugees, terrorists, and criminals). Social advocacy NGOs, however, present alternative ethical visions, seeing a world in which we are all people with fundamental human dignity. Rather than mere opposition to globalization as the clash of civilizations, "Jihad versus McWorld" formulations suggest, NGOs present more varied and constructive reactions, to create a globalization that puts people first. Their formation of transnational networks that work to acknowledge and bridge North–South conflicts may represent one of the best ways for globalization to proceed "with a human face,"[43] thereby unleashing greater human potential than can mere materialism—and for more of the planet than currently participates in the benefits of globalization.

As NGOs (sometimes in partnership with IGOs or MNCs) fill functions instead of states and challenge the ideas of states, what effect does this have on sovereignty? Keck and Sikkink note, "If sovereignty is a shared set of understandings and expectations about state authority that is reinforced by practices, then changes in these practices and understandings should in turn transform sovereignty."[44]

The state is not going away. Rather, it is increasingly contracting out. As states downsize and decentralize in response to the pressures of globalization, and as states innovate in response to global problems, nonstate actors such as NGOs perform functions previously assumed by states and promote ideas that have unintended consequences for sovereignty.

ENDNOTES

1. Reuters, "Crisis No Excuse to Ignore Poverty, Clinton, Bono," September 24, 2008; Bono interview with George Clooney, CNN Special, May 1, 2009; Michael Warner, "2 Billion Unite to Help the Starving," *The Herald Sun* (July 4, 2005).

2. The One Campaign, "ONE Hosts Press Conference at IMF Headquarters," April 23, 2009, <http://www.one.org/blog/?p=5100>.

3. Jubilee USA, "Expanded Debt Cancellation: A Key Tool to Fight Global Poverty," January 2008, <http://www.jubileeusa.org/fileadmin/user_upload/Resources/Policy_Archive/0108briefnoteedcancel.pdf>; Neil Watkins, "Foreign Policy in Focus: G20 and Global Poverty," April 8, 2009, http://www.fpif.org/fpiftxt/.

4. Rick Rowden, "A World of Debt," *American Prospect* 12(12). <www.prospect.org/print/V12/12/rowden-r.html>.

5. International Campaign to Ban Landmines, <www.icbl.org>; Richard Price, "Reversing the Gun Sights: Transnational Civil Society Targets Land Mines," *International Organization* 52(3): 613–644; Anne Peters, "The International Campaign to Ban Landmines," Case Study for the Global Public Policy Network, <www.f2.efresh.de/public/peters%20gpp%202000.pdf>.

6. Margaret E. Keck and Kathryn Sikkink, *Activists beyond Borders* (Ithaca, NY: Cornell University Press, 1998), 1.

7. Lester M. Salamon, "Interview on Global Civil Society," *Johns Hopkins Gazette*, January 3, 2000, <www.jhu.edu/~gazette/2000/jan0300/03lestxt.html>; Lester M. Salamon, *Global Civil Society: Dimensions of the Nonprofit Sector* (Baltimore: Johns Hopkins University, Institute for Policy Studies, Center for Civil Society Studies, 1999).

8. Union of International Associations (Ed.), *Yearbook of International Organizations 2008* (Brussels: K.G. Saur Verlag, 2008).

9. Howard S. Becker, *Outsiders: Studies in the Sociology of Deviance* (New York: Free Press, 1963), 148; Ethan A. Nadelmann, "Global Prohibition Regimes: The Evolution of Norms in International Society," *International Organization* 44(4): 482.

10. Paul Wapner, "Politics beyond the State: Environmental Activism and World Civic Politics," in John S. Dryzek and David Schlosberg (Eds.), *Debating the Earth: The Environmental Politics Reader* (New York: Oxford University Press, 1999), 518–519; Paul Wapner, *Environmental Activism and World Civil Politics* (Albany: SUNY Press, 1996).

11. Richard E. Neustadt, *Presidential Power and the Modern Presidents: The Politics of Leadership from Roosevelt to Reagan* (New York: Free Press, 1990).

12. Valerie Sperling, Myra Marx Ferree, and Barbara Risman, "Constructing Global Feminism: Transactional Advocacy Networks and Russian Women's Activities," *Signs: Journal of Women in Culture and Society* 26(41): 1156.

13. Martha Finnemore notes that actors and interests are constituted in interaction. Martha Finnemore, *National Interests in International Society* (Ithaca, NY: Cornell University Press, 1996).

14. Specifically, the families filed a civil lawsuit under the Torture Victim Protection Act passed by the U.S. Congress in 1991. "This federal statute permits civil lawsuits against those

accused of committing torture or murder under actual or apparent authority, or color of law, of any foreign nation. As the language intended, victims or their representatives may confront not only the perpetrators of such crimes but also their superiors who bear responsibility." Information available at <Center for Justice and Accountability, http://www.cja.org; http://www.humanrightsfirst.org/international_justice/Romerostatement_FINAL_9_04%20_2_.pdf; www.pbs.org/wnet/justice/elsalvador.html>.

15. The Center for Justice and Accountability, "What Is Hoped to Be Achieved with These Cases?" <http://www.cja.org/cases/Romagoza_News/RomagozaFAQs.htm#eight>.

16. Margaret E. Keck and Kathryn Sikkink, *Activists beyond Borders* (Ithaca, NY: Cornell University Press, 1998), 12.

17. Margaret Keck and Kathryn Sikkink, *Activists beyond Borders* (Ithaca, NY: Cornell University Press, 1998).

18. Andras Biro as quoted in Lester M. Salamon, "The Rise of the Nonprofit Sector," *Foreign Affairs* (July–Aug. 1994): 112.

19. Salamon, "The Rise of the Nonprofit Sector," 113.

20. Felice D. Gaer, "Human Rights, Nongovernmental Organizations, and the UN," in Thomas G. Weiss and Leon Gordenker (EDs.), *NGOs, the UN, and Global Governance* (Boulder, CO: Lynne Rienner Publishers, 1996) 52–53.

21. Jack Donnelly, *International Human Rights*, 2nd ed. (Boulder, CO: Westview Press, 1998), 43; John Simpson and Jana Bennett, *The Disappeared: Voices from a Secret War* (London: Robson Books, 1985), 110.

22. Donnelly, *International Human Rights*, 39; Simpson and Bennett, *The Disappeared*, 225.

23. Donnelly, *International Human Rights*, 44–45.

24. Gaer, "Human Rights," 52–53.

25. "Nailing Jello in China," *Washington Post* (August 26, 2000): A16.

26. Samuel Passow, *Sunk Costs: The Plan to Dump the Brent Spar, and Epilogue* (Cambridge, MA: Harvard University, 1997) (John F. Kennedy School of Government Case 1369), <www.ksgcase.harvard.edu/case.htm?PID=1369>.

27. Richard Morin, "Aid from the Gray Lady?", *The Washington Post* (March 13, 2005): B05.

28. "International Red Cross Needs for Tsunami Relief Met," January 26, 2005, <http://www.redcross.org/pressrelease/0,1077,0_314_4043,00.html>. Technically speaking, the International Committee of the Red Cross (ICRC) is not an NGO. It is an international organization with a mandate assigned to it by international law in the 1864 Geneva Convention and in subsequent protocols. However, unlike most other IGOs, it is not composed of states as members, and it is not part of the UN system. Instead, it is made up of national Red Cross and Red Crescent societies, which are NGOs. Thus, the ICRC resembles a hybrid NGO–IGO.

29. Salamon, "Interview on Global Civil Society."

30. Charles Downs, "Negotiating Development Assistance: USAID and the Choice between Public and Private Implementation in Haiti," in *Pew Case Studies in International Affairs* (Washington, DC: Georgetown University, Institute for the Study of Diplomacy, 1994), 7.

31. Ibid., 8.

32. Ibid., 4–5.

33. Médicins Sans Frontières, *Life, Death, and Aid: The Médicins Sans Frontières Report on World Crisis Intervention* (New York: Routledge, 1993).

34. Angela Penrose and John Seaman, "The Save the Children Fund and Nutrition for Refugees," in Peter Willetts (Ed.), *The Conscience of the World: The Influence of Nongovernmental Organisations in the UN System* (Washington, DC: Brookings Institution, 1996), 241–248.

35. Peter Sollis, "The State, Nongovernmental Organizations, and the UN," in Willetts (Ed.), *The Conscience of the World*, 194–195.

36. Willetts, *The Conscience of the World*, 6.

37. Kal Raustiala, "States, NGOs, and International Environmental Institutions," *International Studies Quarterly* 41 (December 1997): 719–724.

38. Jessica Tuchman Mathews, "Power Shift: The Age of Nonstate Actors," *Foreign Affairs* 76 (January–February 1997): 55.

39. Raustiala, "States, NGOs, and International Environmental Institutions," 726–731.

40. Wapner, "Politics beyond the State," 518–519.

41. Max L. Stackhouse (Ed.), *God and Globalization*, vols. 1 and 2 (Harrisburg, PA: Trinity Press International, 2001); Benjamin R. Barber, *Jihad vs. McWorld: How Globalism and Tribalism Are Reshaping the World* (New York: Ballantine Books, 1995); Samuel Huntington, *The Clash of Civilizations*.

42. Maryann Cusimano Love, "Globalization, Faith Based NGOs, and Peacebuilding" Presentation to the Leadership Institute Conference on Religion and U.S. Foreign Policy, Washington, DC, October 12, 2005; "Bridging the Gap: Globalization and Religion," *Journal of Social Thought,* 2003; R. Scott Appleby, "Catholic Peacebuilding," *America Magazine* 189(6) (September 8, 2003), <www.americamagazine.org/gettext.cfm?articleTypeID=1&textID=3145&issueID=449>.

43. United Nations Development Program Report, *Globalization with a Human Face* (New York: United Nations, 1999).

44. Margaret E. Keck and Kathryn Sikkink, *Activists beyond Borders* (Ithaca, NY: Cornell University Press, 1998), 37.

CHAPTER FOUR

Multinational Corporations

Power and Responsibility

Richard A. Love and Maryann Cusimano Love

Globalization makes a business such as Nike possible. The founders of Nike began by selling Tiger athletic shoes, a Japanese brand, in the U.S. market in 1964.[1] Phil Knight (later Nike's cofounder and chief executive officer [CEO]) soon realized that rather than peddle another company's brand, he could use the global supply chain to produce shoes inexpensively in Asia and sell them in developed economies for a handsome profit. Over time, Nike has shifted production from Japan and South Korea to Indonesia, Taiwan, the Philippines, Vietnam, and China in search of lower costs. While the exact labor costs are difficult to calculate and are protected as competitive business information by Nike, the trend lines are clear. One estimate noted that the labor costs for one pair of Nike shoes is $1.44 per pair. Nike buys a pair of shoes from its suppliers for approximately $20, adds transportation and marketing costs plus a profit, and sells the pair to a retailer for $40. The retailer then adds its costs and profits and sells the product to consumers for $80 and up.[2]

But why buy Nike shoes rather than another brand? The sportswear market is competitive and crowded. More than sportswear, Nike sells ideas. In Greek mythology, Nike is the winged goddess of victory, which gave rise to the company's signature winged "swoosh" symbol and the practice of making its products into wearable advertisements. Through aggressive global marketing and promotions, Nike sells an image, a lifestyle, and a creed more than a product. Close your eyes and you would be hard-pressed to tell the difference between Nike shoes and other brands. Nike is selling the dream of being a world-class athlete, the desire to belong to the club of premier athletes, and the inspiration to become the best you can be. You may never be able to play golf like Tiger Woods or basketball like LeBron James or the most famous of Nike's sports personalities, Michael Jordan, but you can wear the same brand of shoes. As one Nike official puts it, "We don't know the first thing about manufacturing. We are marketers and designers."[3] Nike pioneered the process of creating a market through product design, promotion, and innovative global advertising, and of associating the Nike brand swoosh with world-class athletes, male and female, of every race, from the inner cities to the more privileged classes. Nike went from $2 million in sales in 1972[4] to more than $18.6 billion in revenues in 2008[5]—or more than the gross domestic product (GDP) of oil-rich Bahrain and 94 other states.[6] And Nike is willing to pay for the marquee endorsement, spending over $3.4 billion for endorsements and sponsorship commitments in 2008 and famously offering a multiyear $90 million endorsement contract to LeBron James in 2003 when he was an 18-year-old awaiting the NBA draft.[7]

The same global media that made Nike a household name and a billion dollar company, however, also made it vulnerable to charges of labor and environmental abuses. NGOs and activists concerned with labor, environment, and human rights brought public attention to the sweatshop practices of Nike factories abroad and the disconnect with Nike advertising themes of empowerment, diversity, and women's equality. Reports of sexual harassment of women workers in Nike production facilities in Asia and of seven-year-old children stitching soccer balls in Pakistan gained media and consumer attention. A young woman in China making Nike shoes would have had to work nine hours a day, six days a week, for fifteen centuries to earn the yearly salary of Nike CEO Phil Knight.[8]

At first, Nike's response to the critics was denial. The factories are subcontractors to Nike, the company argued; therefore the employees who made Nike products were not company employees, and Nike was powerless to change subcontractors' behavior. When abuses at Nike's Indonesian factories came to light in the early 1990s, the Nike general manager in Indonesia responded, "It's not within our scope to investigate. I don't know that I need to know."[9] The workers were lucky to have jobs at all, Nike representatives maintained, and it was not the company's fault if governments in developing countries had poor labor or environmental laws or enforcement. By some estimates, more than 80 percent of the workers are young women. The company says these workers are good at sewing. Critics say they are more docile and easily intimidated than older workers or men. "I don't think the girls in our factories are treated badly. It's better than no job at all, than harvesting coconut meat in the tropical sun," said a company official.[10] But as the controversy grew, so did negative media coverage (undermining Nike's $280 million annual advertising budget at the time).[11] Reports continued of women being beaten by supervisors and forced to work 65 hours a week for $10 in pay without bathroom or meal breaks. Nike began to admit there were "isolated problems" that it was determined to correct, yet an internal audit done by the company and leaked to *The New York Times* revealed that workers in one factory were exposed to 177 times the legal limit of carcinogens, with 77 percent of the workers suffering from respiratory problems. Rather than being unaware, the company knew of the problem.[12]

In 1998, consumer boycotts and shareholder unrest grew while company profits fell. CEO Phil Knight announced a new course for the company. Nike would (1) increase the minimum age of its workers to 16 in apparel factories and 18 in shoe factories; (2) follow U.S. Occupational Safety and Health Administration standards for air quality at factories abroad, especially seeking substitutes for the adhesives that were causing respiratory problems in workers; and (3) allow local NGOs and independent auditors to monitor and release information about the company's subcontracting factories. Nike joined corporate responsibility groups such as the Apparel Industry Partnership, the Fair Labor Association, the Global Alliance for Workers and Communities, and the United Nations' Global Compact, and increased community development loans for small business and education projects in the areas of its overseas production facilities.[13]

Nike believes it is now a leader in corporate responsibility, and some observers credit Nike with raising standards and awareness of the issues across the apparel industry. Critics charge the pronouncements are more public relations efforts than real accomplishments and that Nike's corporate codes of conduct are voluntary and unenforceable. Nike still does not pay workers adequate wages or allow international NGOs that might be more critical to participate in monitoring. College students have organized into groups such as the Workers Rights Consortium, the Clean Clothes Campaign, and United Students Against Sweatshops to pressure suppliers of college sportswear not to use sweatshop labor. Nike has withdrawn advertising sponsorships of athletic programs at many colleges and universities such as Brown University, the University of Michigan, and even for a time Phil Knight's alma mater, the University of Oregon, due to student protests of Nike and activism in these groups. While collegiate licensing is only a small part of Nike's overall business, image is everything for a company like Nike, especially image among young athletes, the company's key market. As CEO Phil Knight acknowledged, "The brand is sacred. I messed that up."[14]

The Nike example illustrates pressing debates that will be discussed in this chapter about the rising power and global reach of multinational corporations (MNCs). Do MNCs raise labor and environmental standards internationally or are they leading a global race to the bottom? Are states effectively able to regulate MNCs, or do MNCs have increasing power over states? Are MNCs exercising their power responsibly, and how do they interact with other actors (nongovernmental organizations [NGOs], inter-governmental organizations [IGOs], and states) in setting standards for responsible corporate behavior? Are corporate codes of conduct a way to go beyond sovereignty to manage pressing global problems and to make private actors better stewards of the public good? Are they nontariff trade barriers or protectionist measures that hurt development in the Global South? Or are they merely a way for corporations to deflect state regulation and public criticism? What are the effects on sovereignty?

THE GLOBAL REACH OF MNCs

MNCs are enterprises that control and manage commercial ventures and operations outside their countries of origin.[15] Fueled by open economies and distributed technology, enhanced financial mechanisms and the ease of transborder trade, their power and influence are growing dramatically. By 2005, of the world's 150 largest economic entities, 95 (63 percent) were MNCs, not countries.[16]

MNCs are not new. Foreign investment, banking, resource extraction, trade, and production were part of imperial expansion and colonial trade by the Romans, Venetians, Genoese, English (British East India Company), and Dutch (Hudson Bay Company). What is new is the global reach and influence of modern multinational firms. In 1969, there were 7,000 MNCs.[17] By 2008, there were 79,000 multinational parent corporations with 790,000 foreign affiliates worldwide.[18] Today, the top 100 MNCs are estimated to have assets amounting to $9.239 trillion with over 15 million employees.[19] The sheer scope of these entities represents a rise in private, nonstate power across the globe.[20]

MNCs are a diverse and eclectic group. MNCs are organized internationally to achieve several corporate objectives: open new markets and gain access to new consumers, acquire natural resources at lower costs, and produce efficiencies through the reduction of production and labor costs or by taking advantage of lower environmental regulations and taxes. Some allow "host" subsidiaries greater autonomy; others insist on a high degree of "parent" company control. They range from corporations such as Royal Dutch Shell Oil and British Petroleum, which extract raw materials and natural resources; to manufacturers such as Siemens, Coca Cola, Samsung, Walt Disney Corporation, and Nokia, which produce consumer goods; to companies such as Lloyd's of London, Barclays, and Credit Suisse, which offer banking, investment, insurance, and consulting services. Many MNCs are hybrids of these functions—such as IBM, which sells computer and business products and provides consulting services.

MNCs are not simply companies that engage in foreign trade or market their products abroad. MNCs engage in foreign direct investment (FDI) and carry out production in foreign countries. They engage in FDI because local firms have a "home court advantage." They are more knowledgeable about local business practices and consumer tastes, and it is generally less costly for local firms to do business in their home markets. Foreign firms that seek entry into a locality have an incentive to "hook up" with local firms. FDI may take many forms: buyouts of a foreign subsidiary, joint ventures, licensing agreements, or strategic alliances. The top recipients of FDI are the United States, the United Kingdom, and China, while all of Africa combined receives only 3 percent of global FDI.[21]

MNCs AND THE GLOBALIZATION DEBATES

The global reach of MNCs can be a positive force for profits as well as development. MNCs can assist in transferring capital and know-how to the developing world and often bring in capital goods and technology. They may create jobs and assist in developing training and education programs. MNCs also provide avenues for access to other international markets and exposure to the region that may result in additional investment. MNCs often have the incentive to develop a host state's infrastructure to maximize commerce. For example, Nakornthon Bank works with poor villages in rural Thailand, offering training and small, low-interest loans for microdevelopment. As a result, "[i]ncome levels skyrocketed. . . . People returned to work in the village. The payoff rate for loans was 100%, and our bank now has a loyal base of customers. The project has been so successful that development agencies and the government have kept asking how it was done."[22]

But there is also a downside. MNCs can overwhelm a locality and drive traditional firms out of business. MNCs normally insist on maintaining control over technology, management, and intellectual property, which means that technology and expertise are never transferred to the host state. CEOs, boards of directors, and shareholders may all be located in developed countries so that MNC decision making and profits flow disproportionately back to developed economies. MNCs often become advocates at the local level for changing local systems in favor of gaining preferential treatment. These take the form of tax breaks, favorable laws, dispute resolution mechanisms, and ownership and property rights. In seeking lower-cost alternatives globally, MNCs exploit resources, labor, and the environment, leading critics to charge that MNCs lead a race to the bottom in worker, regulatory, safety, and environmental standards.

For example, one IGO, the UN International Labor Organization, assesses that there are 218 million child laborers worldwide, with seven in ten working in agriculture.[23] Indeed, child labor, or workers aged between five and fourteen years of age, may make up as much as 63% of Mali's labor force and could number nearly 200 million in India.[24] Some of these children work for MNCs or their subcontractors, such as in high-profile cases (e.g., Nike) and as in forced child slave labor in Africa picking the cocoa beans for major chocolate companies like Nestlé. Yet MNCs counter these arguments by noting that working conditions are generally no worse and are often better than those of the local employers, and prominent MNCs are likely to comply with standards that are higher than those maintained locally.[25] They also argue that age and wage standards cannot be universal but must be considered in the context of local economies.

MNCs AND OPEN ECONOMIES

It is no surprise that many MNCs are in the forefront of lobbying to increase free market economic systems and reduce barriers to FDI and trade.[26] Whether through regional trading blocs such as North American Free Trade Agreement (NAFTA), Central America Free Trade Agreement (CAFTA) or the European Union (EU), or multilateral free trade agreements such as General Agreement on Tariffs and Trade (GATT) and the World Trade Organization (WTO), MNCs generally seek to decrease tariff and nontariff barriers to trade and investment, as well as decrease state control of state subsidies to key industries.[27] MNCs lobby states and multinational organizations to open up economies to market forces. In the democratizing states of the former communist bloc, Latin America, and South Africa, MNCs are pressing for protections of private property and the free movement of goods and capital in their liberalizing economies. Once established, MNCs or their local affiliates often try to get the local host states to protect their advantages by enacting exclusionary laws and giving the established MNCs monopoly advantages. Host countries can be subject to intense pressure to acquiesce to MNC investment already in place and to appease international pressure to open their economies and markets. Each year, developed states spend $273 billion in agricultural subsidies to prevent goods from developing countries from reaching their markets.[28] The purpose is to distort the global market and protect or insulate a firm or sector that would lose its competitive advantage and fail when the protections or subsidies are not in place. This is why developing countries question how "free" the free market and free trade really are—free for whom?

Many MNCs have pushed hard for harmonizing international law, although some prefer to exploit differences in legal codes in local venues that profit foreign companies. For example, on the night of December 2–3, 1984, Union Carbide Chemical Corporation was responsible for the worst industrial accident in history. Its plant in Bhopal, India released 41 tons of poisonous gas, killing 14,000 people and inflicting permanent disabilities on 150,000 more:[29]

> As people ran with their families, they saw their children falling beside them, and often had to choose which ones they would carry on their shoulders and save. This image comes up again and again in the dreams of the survivors: in the stampede, the sight of a hundred people walking over the body of their child. Iftekhar Begum went out on the morning after the gas to help bury the Muslim dead. There were so many that she could not see the ground—she had to stand on the corpses to wash them.[30]

After the accident, Union Carbide worked to see that a more lenient judge in India would hear the case so that the company could avoid having to face a stricter U.S. judicial system that might have imposed hefty fines. After years of legal battles, the MNC agreed to pay survivors generally $2,857 for each death (a few received as much as $4,286). Ninety-five percent of the victims who were compensated received only $500. These are the gross figures; subtract the legal fees, administration costs, and sometimes bribes survivors had to pay to stake their claim, and most survivors actually netted much less. These settlements are low even by Indian standards. The standard compensation offered by Indian Railways is $5,714 for accidental death and $3,429 for disability, which is disbursed quickly and with minimal additional fees.[31]

While some companies prefer to take their chances with local legal codes, most MNCs have a powerful interest in harmonizing global laws to decrease transaction costs. It is costly for them to do business internationally when each country has separate standards and rules for, among other things, trade, investment, intellectual property rights, legal accountability, and contract rights. MNCs push for greater harmonization to decrease their costs and risks and create a better business climate, and they stress that developing states benefit as well from such measures. They argue that international trade, global supply chains, and FDI help developing economies, and that developing states are better served by a system of established rules with transparent and regular procedures for making rules than by trying to negotiate ad hoc agreements with more powerful actors on a deal-by-deal basis. In general, developing countries have agreed and voluntarily signed up for these international agreements out of a desperate desire to attract MNCs and FDI that may bring jobs and alleviate poverty in their countries. Often, developing states fear that not to acquiesce will mean that FDI and jobs will go elsewhere and that they will be left behind. Not surprisingly, there is unequal bargaining power among the parties. Developing states riddled with poverty cannot compete with the deep pockets of MNCs that lobby state governments and the international bodies that create the rules of the road for international trade. Developing countries often lack the resources to send delegations to the international meetings that decide the rules, thus denying them a seat at the table as the rules are debated and made.

The spread of capitalist economic systems and MNCs has also brought global pressures for deregulation, on the assumptions that markets are self-correcting and that government-imposed regulations often introduce market distortions, inefficiencies, and competitive disadvantages for regulated firms. As discussed in Chapter 1, however, the global economic recession has given new momentum to government and IGO regulation efforts, particularly regarding the previously unregulated financial derivatives "dark markets." Prior to the cascading global financial crises, efforts to regulate derivatives markets met with heavy resistance. For example, regulator Brooksley Born, chairman of the U.S. Commodity Futures Trading Commission during the 1990s, argued repeatedly that the unregulated derivatives market was ripe for fraud and abuse, and could cause a global financial meltdown. Her calls for regulation were resisted by financial MNCs, Congress, and Federal Reserve Chairman Alan Greenspan, who "explained there was no need for a law against fraud, because if a floor broker was committing fraud, the customer would figure it out and stop doing business with him." Greenspan's views prevailed before the global economic implosion, but today Greenspan has admitted he was wrong.[32]

MNCs AND OPEN TECHNOLOGIES

Cheap, easily available global information and transportation technologies make the growth of MNCs possible. New technology also creates new industries and presents the hope of "leapfrog" development for some developing countries. For example, Bangalore, India, is now a thriving center of the computer services industry. India is aided by an educated workforce that speaks English and a time zone differential that allows Indian computer programmers to service the information systems of companies in many developed countries while the companies' main workforces sleep. Although this model is not replicable everywhere, many developing countries aspire to the Bangalore model as they seek to profit from the global economy and technologies. It is not only large corporations that benefit from global technologies, but also medium, small, and even microbusinesses that can go global, thanks to the Internet and shipping companies such as FedEx and United Parcel Service. Australian sheepskin slippers, and even handicrafts produced by African refugees (and sold on-line at http://www.jrs.net/jrs/mikono) can be marketed and sold to consumers globally without large overhead investments. Access to global resources and shipping facilitate just-in-time manufacturing.

MNCs may disperse technologies in the countries where they operate as a part of their business presence, but some MNCs restrict technology transfers out of concern for retaining proprietary and competitive advantages. MNC and state interests regarding technology transfers are not always correlated either. The U.S. government wanted limits on the sale of powerful computer encryption technologies so that law enforcement officers would have the keys to crack the codes of illicit actors using encrypted communications. Businesses did not want a lucrative new market in encryption programs regulated—and business won. States often want to restrict the sale of sensitive technologies that can have military applications, whereas MNCs may favor trade in dual-use technologies. The German, British, and U.S. governments fought the Persian Gulf War in 1990 and 1991 against an Iraqi army which had weapons and the ingredients to make chemical weapons supplied by German, British, and U.S. firms.

In 1987, while the United States, Japan, and Norway were officially allied to fight the Cold War against the Soviet Union, both a Japanese and a
Norwegian MNC—Toshiba and Kongsberg—violated export restrictions
and sold technologies to the Soviet Union to help it build quieter and less-
detectable nuclear submarines.

MNCs AND OPEN SOCIETIES

The relationship between MNCs and open societies is hotly contested. In
states such as China, Indonesia, and Nigeria, MNCs have pursued a capitalist economic agenda without pushing hard for democratic political reforms. In corporatist societies (such as Chile and Argentina in the 1970s),
authoritarian regimes ally with and co-opt business elites, protecting business interests while repressing democratic rights and principles. Order is
central for the stable, efficient, and profitable conduct of commerce.
Political upheavals, even those associated with democratization, create costs
and uncertainties for the investment, production, and trade of MNCs. Do
MNCs favor repressive regimes as a way of ensuring a stable, orderly, and
favorable business environment? In Nigeria, Shell Oil was accused of helping to arm and finance a repressive military government, as long as the
government helped to keep Shell's oil flowing. According to Mr. Austin
Onuoha of the Nigerian Center for Social and Corporate Responsibility,
the oil companies claim to invest millions in "community development,"
but the money they spend to hire security forces is counted as part of their
Corporate Social Responsibility (CSR) projects. Royalty and licensing
agreements between the government and oil companies on how oil money
will be split are not made public, and Nigerians see little benefit from the
oil industry. Nigerian oil has generated estimates of over $600 billion since
1960, but corrupt business-government practices mean that the money has
not benefited the Nigerian people, 70 percent of whom live on less than
$1 a day.[33] Exxon–Mobil, Chevron-Texaco, and Petronas, with the aid of
World Bank loans, have been building and operating an oil pipeline since
July 2003 in Chad and Cameroon, extremely poor countries with two of
the most corrupt governments in the world according to ratings of government corruption by Transparency International.[34] These governments are
not democratic, and human rights and environmental abuses have been reported in the project. The government of Chad has illegally diverted World
Bank loans for military purchases. According to Fr. Antoine Berilengar, SJ,
a representative on the Petroleum Revenue Oversight and Control Committee in Chad, the oil companies do not hire local workers to build the

pipeline, but instead bring in Mexican, Egyptian, and Filipino workers, who do not pay local taxes and are less concerned about environmental and human rights abuses in Chad.[35]

Others disagree. One study analyzed MNC cash flows to developing states from 1975 to 1986 to determine whether MNCs are more or less likely to invest in repressive states with abusive human rights records. The study concluded that "MNCs in general [avoid] locating larger amounts of [foreign investment] in those [developing states] that consistently implement fewer human rights reforms. . . . [It] does not appear that MNCs view a lack of human rights reforms and the high use of repression in [developing states] as acceptable."[36] MNCs may not favor repressive regimes for several reasons. Arbitrary exercise of police powers and military brutality affect MNC executives, workers, and citizens alike. Repressive regimes may rule by force rather than law, but respect for law (and particularly for property rights) is crucial for successful business transactions. Without the rule of law, business transactions become uncertain and potentially more costly.

The effects of MNCs on human rights can cut both ways. Sometimes just the presence of an MNC can place the international media spotlight on local worker conditions, creating a "race to the top."[37] Concerned with protecting their image, companies will pressure local governments to improve workers' conditions or take the initiative to do so themselves. A multinational's instinct to protect its reputation, and thereby its bottom line, can have the beneficial side effect of exporting a concern for human rights. This may be MNC specific, however, as image-conscious branded products have a greater concern for reputation than do unbranded or extractive industries. Thus, even though MNCs generally promote open economies and open technologies, their record of promoting open societies (including respect for human rights) is contested and mixed.

RISE OF PRIVATE POWER: DO CORPORATIONS RULE THE WORLD?

We are witnessing the rise of private power. Even in developed states, private standard-setting bodies, contract law, and private arbitration mechanisms now fulfill regulatory functions once performed by states.[38] In emerging information technology sectors, this trend of private governance is particularly pronounced. For example, Internet commerce is often untaxed and self-regulated by companies, not by governments. A private body assigns Internet domain names and adjudicates disputes.

The critique that corporations rule the world[39] runs even stronger given the unequal bargaining power of developing states against MNCs. In developing states, grinding poverty leads states to court corporate investments because the private sector has more money than the public sector, and state-to-state aid and investment are drying up. Developing states often do not have the capacity to check corporate power, as law and order and institutions may be fragile at best in countries without resources to adequately pay, staff, equip, and train government officials. As corporations enter developing states, they often do so free of taxes (in export processing or free trade zones). The largest companies are also able to avoid taxes even in developed states. For example, the majority of U.S. corporations do not pay their full income tax rates and many of these firms are now benefiting from U.S. government bailout plans in order to stimulate the economy. The Emergency Economic Stabilization Act of 2008, passed to secure the U.S. financial system, authorized the U.S. Treasury to spend up to $700 billion in order to acquire risky mortgage-backed securities and make capital available to banks in order to stimulate lending, on the assumption that some MNCs were "too big to fail." Export processing and free trade zones are often free of other government regulations (environmental and worker safety law enforcement).

MNCs encourage the multilateral organizations to pressure developing states to privatize their remaining state-controlled industries, such as telephone systems. Although it is done in the name of rationalizing economies and making them more efficient, privatization may also bankrupt governments because poor countries do not have the tax bases to finance basic government services—education, public health systems, clean water, roads, public safety, customs, courts, and law and order. When telephone revenues, for example, are the primary government income and the business is privatized, after the initial windfall in money from the sale of state-owned industries, states may lack financing for basic government activities.

Many states have no tradition of payment of personal income taxes, and governments are too weak to be able to get citizens to pay taxes (this is a problem in Russia, Italy, and many Caribbean states). Because so many goods and incomes go untaxed, states charge exorbitant tax rates on those few goods or people that they are most able to tax—for example, automobile imports, or imports of washers and dryers. This creates greater incentives to smuggle, commit fraud, and evade taxes because taxes on the few pay for the services provided to the many. Inability to finance basic good governance makes all government ripe for corruption because government workers are not paid a living wage and need to supplement their income with "overtime" (the euphemism for bribery in the Caribbean). Thus, governments in developing states often do not have the capacity to challenge or contain the power of corporations, and the actions of corporations (to lower their tax rates, privatize industries, and pay government bribes) may actually contribute to the weakness of state structures and governance.

Developing states sign agreements that allow corporations to operate in their territories; such arrangements are examples of bargaining among unequal parties. A developing state is signing a contract with a gun to its head—the gun being grinding poverty, unemployment, and death—and it is trying to lure corporations with its low wages and lack of unionization. A state has less ability to wrest many guarantees of good behavior, local management power, and so on from a corporation when poverty is a state's comparative advantage. The corporation has many poor states from which to choose, and it is often not building plants and capital investments from scratch but is contracting out to local subsidiary agents. The corporation can easily find another poor country that will accept its business. Literally, beggars can't be choosers.

Even strong states cannot contain corporate power alone because MNCs operate across international borders, and jurisdiction often stops at the border. Attempts to harmonize legal codes to help law enforcement work multilaterally across borders or to rein in corporate power are weak, new, and without teeth. They often are exports of Western contract law and procedures that are advantageous to corporations. They show how corporations can get laws that work for them rather than how states can effectively counterbalance the weight of corporations.

The rise of private contract law epitomizes the rise of private power in the global age. A relatively few MNCs exercise power to create law in their own interest and for their own benefit. Developed states not only condone this practice, but also support the trend because they hope to rationalize commercial disputes and benefit from increased tax revenue from their MNCs. The result is that local governments, especially in the developing world, experience a loss of control and influence over trade practices within their borders.

MNCs worldwide are seeking ways to fashion enforceable rights. One way they do this is by expanding private contract rights in order to avoid foreign laws. This is generally not a difficult challenge. The three most common ways of doing so are through choice of law, stabilization, and arbitration clauses. These clauses ensure the protection of property rights, right of entry into new markets, and the availability of natural resources. The effect of these clauses is not only to avoid the law of a host state, but also to develop a legal system outside traditional sovereign courts. It sets up external and private law to resolve disputes, based on the concept of the sanctity of the contract and party autonomy. Courts allow these contractual decisions, often with little or no respect for the public policy concerns of host states. Courts will often refuse to hear a controversy where clauses using alternative dispute resolution (ADR) or arbitration exist in a contract. For example, when Mexico denied Metalclad, a New Jersey metal company with toxic waste by-products, permission to build a facility because of concerns about the site's environmental impact, the NAFTA court initially ordered Mexico to pay $16.7 million to Metalclad in breach of contract compensation for earnings Metalclad could have received if it had been allowed to proceed, though this amount was later reduced on appeal. The case remains an example of the tension between private contract rights and sovereign concerns such as environmental safety.

Choice of law clauses are perhaps the most common among the three and allow a party to avoid local law and remove issues from local courts by predetermining where controversies will be resolved and under whose law the controversy will proceed. Arbitration clauses determine who has the authority to decide controversies and usually include a reference to the specific rules that will guide arbitration. Arbitration courts have established procedures and remedies that can be adopted or amended by the terms of a contract, and the arbiters have powers similar to those of sovereign courts.[40] A stabilization clause freezes the law at the time the contract is entered into and prevents law made after a contract enters into force from having any effect on a controversy's ultimate disposition.

These clauses allow a contract to avoid the laws of sovereign states and propel controversies to a "supranational" legal arbitration body or to a court outside a local jurisdiction. Thus, they insulate foreign corporations from uncertain and unfamiliar locales. This facilitates predictability and reduces market uncertainty, yet this worldwide body of private law runs counter to the sovereign concept of regulating affairs within one's state borders. These contract provisions are increasingly offensive to local legal and political institutions and affront the concept of equal dignity of sovereigns. The contract terms effectively let the parties opt out of local jurisdictions. Private contract also gives MNCs a procedural advantage since many parties in the developing world lack the expertise needed to enter into agreements with a full appreciation of the costs and consequences. Firms located outside such traditional centers of commerce as New York, London, and Geneva may also lack the resources to fully protect their rights under contract. The travel costs alone may make pursuing a dispute prohibitively expensive.

While MNCs work to enlarge the private sector and earn profits, they also can facilitate the illicit economy. Money laundering, for example, is facilitated by the international banking and financial services industries. Between $640 billion and $1.6 trillion are laundered through banks every year.[41] Money laundering involves complex financial and product transactions that mask and perpetuate the underlying criminal activity that generates the illegal gains. Money laundering finances the most egregious crimes in the global age from terrorism and drug trafficking to human trafficking, illegal arms transactions, and nuclear smuggling. It propagates corruption and corrupt regimes by providing an avenue for using illegal proceeds. Money laundering also provides a way to avoid taxes.

The underlying purpose of money laundering is to conceal the true source of the funds for free use in the open market. The mechanisms for laundering money are complex and diverse and often involve multiple transactions among several (and sometimes unsuspecting) parties, fraudulent alterations of prices for goods, and outright bribes and kickbacks. Money laundering is illegal, but some MNCs prefer the benefit of the infusion of capital. The most common form of money laundering is transfer pricing, where prices are falsified on import and export transactions in order to generate artificial values. The difference between the fair market value and the artificial value is pocketed. Real estate transactions and securities trades, often between related parties and improperly priced and paid for in order to shift money across borders, offer creative avenues for generating illegal capital flight. Money laundering activities must first hide the source of the illegally received proceeds and then provide a legitimate explanation for the proceeds. Through complex, layered transactions, money laundering blends criminal proceeds into the licit economy.

Most laundered money winds up in the United States and Europe through Western banks. As the beneficiaries of such an enormous inflow of capital, the banking and financial establishment traditionally favors informal money laundering controls and reporting requirements. Government efforts to curtail money laundering have failed in the past because of the lack of "buy-in" from the private banking and business sector. The attacks of September 11 changed how many political and commercial leaders view money laundering, and they increased state and IGO pressure to regulate these industries. However, state anti–money laundering policies rely on industry self-reporting of suspicious financial activities. Even in strong, developed states, governments do not have the capacity to curtail money laundering without cooperation from the private sector, which demonstrates the extent of private power.

PRIVATE POWER AND PUBLIC RESPONSIBILITY

Does the rise in private power mean MNCs can act with impunity and with no responsibilities to the common good? No. States still regulate corporations, although, as the previous section demonstrated, MNCs may have the ability to forum shop—to have a dispute heard in a forum more amenable to their interests—and may have deeper pockets and better lawyers to evade states' regulatory capacities. However, other bodies are stepping in to fill these governance gaps. IGOs increasingly regulate global commerce, and MNCs are increasingly self-regulating, in part because of greater attention to corporate social responsibility (CSR).

There has been an explosion of CSR mechanisms for MNC voluntary self-regulation, especially in the past decade. They fall into several categories. First are internal codes of conduct and statements of company core values. Most MNCs have or are writing such in-house codes of conduct. They are frequently broad, general guidelines, such as those of Levi Strauss, which state in part that the company will embrace "Empathy, Originality, Integrity and Courage." [42] Optimists say these codes of conduct are important barometers of changing corporate culture. They are attempts to educate and socialize large workforces into common values, such as the belief that good corporate citizenship is as important as bottom-line profit margins. Even broad guidelines can be helpful as a first step to more specific standards and concrete benchmarks. They are also useful because they provide a public commitment by companies to particular values. If company behavior falls short later, then the codes of conduct and value statements give reformers a basis to discuss criticisms. Skeptics argue that the codes are little more than window dressing designed to diffuse criticism and deter regulation, that they are frequently so vague and general that they cannot be implemented or measured, and that they are unenforceable because they are voluntary.

The second genre of CSR measures are sector-wide agreements among companies within an industry to adopt certain standards or shared best practices. Sector-wide agreements can vary from narrow technical codes on specific industrial processes to broader statements of larger CSR commitments such as the Sustainable Apparel and Footwear Initiative or the Apparel Industry Partnership to improve working conditions in the garment industry. Some sectors may develop regimes or private professional bodies to monitor and report on implementation and compliance with the standards. Many rely on the companies themselves to choose methods of monitoring and transparency to show implementation and compliance with adopted codes.

The third approach is to develop general CSR codes that are not specific to particular organizations or industries. For example, the UN Global Compact challenges businesses to comply with nine principles drawn from UN treaties concerning human rights, labor, and the environment. The Global Compact is quite broad, as are other codes such as the Coalition for Environmentally Responsible Economies (CERES) principles on environmental responsibility, and the Caux Round Table Principles for Business. These set overarching corporate goals and rely on companies to decide their own monitoring and transparency measures. The International Standards Organization (ISO) has its own set of standards, such as the ISO 9000 and ISO 14000 families. The Council on Economic Priorities has Social Accountability (SA) 8000. These standards come with more specific operational guidelines and measurable benchmarks to monitor progress and implementation. As industries "buy into" ISO labeling and accreditation, they agree to undergo regular inspections and audits by accredited auditors.

There are vigorous debates over which codes, standards, and reporting techniques are more effective in raising corporate behavior and improving labor, human rights, and environmental practices. Some critics argue that internal audits are more rigorous because only people familiar with the processes and layouts of particular factories will know where to look for problems or abuses. Others argue that internal audits lack credibility because companies have few incentives to blow the whistle on themselves. This leads to arguments in favor of external auditing procedures, but again this raises questions of competence and independence. Although using professional auditors trained in particular standards sounds like an attractive way to ensure more reliability and comparability of results over time and across companies, critics argue that auditors hired and paid by industry have few incentives to issue negative reports and "bite the hand that feeds them." NGOs argue they can offer independent assessments and should be a part of the process, but this again raises the questions of which NGOs should be involved and how qualified they are to make assessments. Some corporations do not see NGOs as unbiased and believe NGOs will never acknowledge improvements in corporate practices or issue favorable assessments. Some corporations such as Nike choose to involve local NGOs as a form of outreach to the local community where facilities are located. International NGOs question whether local NGOs are more easily manipulated to issue favorable reports because they may fear losing local jobs or may not have the resources or access to complete information to make fully informed and more critical judgments. Finally, reporting varies widely. Some reports are little more than press releases, while others are substantive and concrete assessments. The Global Reporting Initiative is a UN-sponsored effort to increase the comparability, credibility, and consistency of CSR reporting and to highlight best practices.

The United Nations is taking action to increase CSR. The Secretary-General established a special representative on human rights and transnational corporations, in response to the 2005 UN High Commissioner on Human Rights' report, which noted that "there are gaps in understanding the human rights responsibilities of business."[43] Over the past decade, the United Nations has been reaching out to businesses, forming more partnerships with civil society, both MNCs and NGOs. Partnerships vary widely on topic and breadth. Development projects help provide market access for indigenous micro businesses, such as the SEED Initiative helping to create environmentally responsible businesses which help the poor, or the Shea Butter Production Initiative in Burkina Faso or the United Nations Industrial Development Organization (UNIDO) Automotive Industry Partnerships.[44]

This explosion of CSR codes and implementation techniques shows a rising acknowledgment of the power of private governance and the power of corporations to implement social and economic change. It testifies to increased attention among corporations to the "triple bottom line," a rising awareness that the environmental and social as well as economic concerns can affect business.

But why is there such growth in CSR standards and attention? Margaret Keck and Kathryn Sikkink argue that blocked politics cause activists to take their grievances to other forums,[45] including pressuring MNCs to focus on issues ignored by states. Because groups cannot lobby for environmental or human rights change in China or Burma, NGOs and moral entrepreneurs search for a forum where democratic politics, independent media, voters, and consumers can exert some pressure for change rather than be excluded. MNCs based in developed democracies are open to civil society pressures, whereas authoritarian states may be less susceptible to these pressures. Blocked politics explains some of the increased attention to CSR, but not all of it.

Corporations often argue that they are not the correct targets for labor, environment, and human rights demands and that governments should be pressured to change. Yet even in democratic countries such as the Philippines, MNCs are targeted for CSR campaigns rather than governments, even though politics are not blocked and procedures exist for citizen advocacy. Moving away from state activism and toward CSR campaigns focused on MNCs is a way for NGOs to focus their resources and to get more bang for the buck. NGO resources are constrained, so dividing them among 191 countries may mean there will be too few resources for any one NGO to be effective, reach critical mass, and overcome threshold effects of inertia and the status quo. Just as opponents of the U.S. civil rights movement in the 1960s tried to splinter the movement by arguing that local state governments should decide the civil rights of African Americans, NGOs find that if they successfully lobby MNCs to raise standards, the effects will be felt broadly across borders, rather than in one country only.

There are other reasons for the increased number and attention to CSR codes as well. Virginia Haufler studied private standard setting across a variety of sectors and industries and concluded that risk assessments, concern for reputation, and corporate learning were critical factors in adoption and implementation of CSR standards.[46] Previous crises certainly can alert decision makers to the risks of ignoring CSR. In this way, the CERES principles were created in response to the Exxon Valdez oil spill.[47]

Only publicly traded companies are vulnerable to shareholder activism, and unbranded products are less vulnerable to consumer boycotts and negative publicity. But ideas matter in pressuring corporations to address global issues. Even unbranded food products are vulnerable to claims about health and safety. And not all brands are equally vulnerable to CSR pressures. It matters what values and ideas the brand proclaims. Nike was vulnerable not just because it was an identifiable brand, but also because it advertised values of diversity, emancipating young people, and women's equality. This made it more vulnerable to brand devaluation by charges that women were being abused and children were forced to work in diverse countries. Similarly, Mattel Toys has been a leader in the Business Anti-Smuggling Coalition because, as its chief security officer puts it, "The last thing we can afford is Barbie on drugs." A shipment of Barbie toys compromised by drug traffickers would be extremely harmful to the toy's wholesome role model identity in a way that would be less damaging to a shipment of Lysol toilet bowl cleaner. It is not just the brand, but the ideas behind the brand that give traction to CSR efforts.

Several factors are important in determining whether an MNC will adopt CSR standards. The internal leadership of the company is important. Anita Roddick, founder of The Body Shop, was a force for CSR within her global franchise and throughout the wider business community.[48]

Company culture, the competitive environment, and consumer demand are important. Chiquita Brands International, the banana importer and exporter, changed its company practices and adopted some of the industry's most enlightened age and wage policies. But if grocery stores and consumers do not factor CSR into buying decisions, then CSR policies may not be sustainable,[49] either because leadership will backside if companies believe CSR policies are a drag to their costs that competitors avoid and consumers do not reward, or because the company goes under.

Shareholder activism also can spur attention to CSR as investments are withdrawn from companies with poor practices or ratings. For example, the Interfaith Center on Corporate Responsibility, a coalition of 275 religious investors from the Catholic, Jewish, and Protestant communities with a combined investment total of over $110 billion, promotes socially responsible investing. TIAA-CREF (Teachers Insurance and Annuity Association-College Retirement Equities Fund), the largest private pension fund in the United States, negotiates directly with companies regarding their CSR records. The U.S. Jesuit Conference negotiated with Occidental Petroleum, accused of questionable human rights practices in Colombia. As a result of this shareholder activism, Occidental agreed to write and implement a corporate code of conduct.[50] Shareholder activism does not produce quick results, but it can produce great effects over time. Media attention to corporate shortcomings spurs MNC attention. Companies engage not only in immediate damage control within a targeted company but also in long-range policy change across companies as MNC leaders learn lessons from the crises of others. NGOs threaten to use the sticks of negative media publicity, protests, consumer boycotts, and shareholder activism, but they can also offer the carrots of positive attention to favorable examples of CSR. Too often, however, NGOs rely more on the sticks than the carrots. Finally, IGOs and states can offer incentives for positive CSR behavior and threaten regulation or adversarial treatment to companies with negative CSR records. A combination of these factors leads companies to decide whether and which CSR policies may enhance their reputation, change their market share, or reduce their risks of adverse consumer, media, IGO, government, or shareholder reactions.

Through the CSR movement, MNCs are finding that open societies, open technologies, and open economies cut both ways. These infrastructures facilitate the operations and profits of MNCs. Yet global technologies that broadcast MNC advertising also serve as an instant and global megaphone for news of corporate abuses. Open societies allow critics to organize and apply political pressure to MNCs, and open economies allow consumer and shareholder market pressures to be brought to bear on MNCs.

MNCs, STATE FUNCTIONS, AND SOVEREIGNTY

Beyond social, environmental, and economic regulatory and arbitration functions, MNCs are also performing security functions that traditionally have been reserved for states, such as arms control negotiations, homeland security, disarmament, demining operations, and military activities. Functions traditionally reserved for the state are increasingly contracted out. For example, in 1978, when the negotiation process for the chemical weapons convention (CWC) began, few government officials had more than superficial knowledge of the chemical industry. U.S. arms control negotiators requested assistance in the negotiation process from the chemical industry. Recognizing the importance and effect of the chemical weapons ban for their industry, the chemical manufacturers assisted the U.S. government. An industry group, the Chemical Manufacturers Association (CMA), helped develop procedures for on-site inspections and participated in special sessions of the Conference on Disarmament. What resulted was an unprecedented industry–government partnership in forging an effective treaty. For industry, opposition to the treaty not only would have resulted in negative publicity but also would have risked the creation of a treaty that was technically unsound and detrimental to industry interests.

The private sector has a critical role to play in protecting critical infrastructure from illicit activities, from terrorism to cybercrime. Between 85 and 90 percent of critical infrastructure in the United States is privately owned. Critical infrastructures are systems whose incapacity or destruction would have a debilitating effect on a state's defense or economic security. They include telecommunications, electrical power systems, gas and oil industries, banking and finance, transportation, water supply systems, government services, and emergency services. The events of September 11, 2001, highlighted security concerns over physical and electronic threats to critical infrastructures. Such threats are global, blur public–private distinctions, and render states, commercial interests, and individuals mutually vulnerable and interdependent.

There are limits to what governments can effectively do to provide adequate security in the absence of private cooperation. Private infrastructure owners are in the best position to understand the technology and vulnerabilities and must recognize their stake in infrastructure protection. Many challenges to effective public–private cooperation exist. Trust needs to be established between stakeholders. Public–private lines of communication and response activities need to be clarified. Technical training and expertise needs to be furthered in both sectors. Government and industry leaders must recognize the need for cooperation. Process buy-in is essential to success.

Governments of the strongest states are ceding security functions to private companies, despite concerns about the transparency, accountability, and human rights abuses of these companies.[51] For example, the British and U.S. governments extensively contract to private security companies to work alongside and often instead of British and U.S. troops. With the U.S. government's blessing, mercenaries trained the Bosnian and Iraqi armies. The U.S. government uses private security companies to disassemble former Soviet nuclear weapons through the Cooperative Threat Reduction program, as well as to conduct demining operations in support of U.S. troop deployments. Over 310 private security companies with over 30,000 employees have provided military services in Iraq, from securing the U.S. embassy to interrogating prisoners.

Private organizations are increasingly seen not just as contributors to global problems but as crucial players in designing and implementing effective global solutions. We are witnessing a creative period as new private organizations arise and increased partnerships are formed with business to manage pressing global problems. As MNCs become the target of citizen demands for social, environmental, and economic goods, ideas of authority change. As governments cede or contract functions to the private sector (even security functions), state power, capacity, legitimacy, and authority change relative to other actors—and thus sovereignty is changing.

ENDNOTES

1. Phil Knight and Bill Bowerman, the head coach of the University of Oregon's track and field teams, each contributed $500 to start Blue Ribbon Sports Company, Nike's predecessor. As conflicts grew with Tiger concerning control over the company and exclusive rights to U.S. distribution, Knight ordered 6,000 pairs of shoes with the now-familiar "swoosh" logo in 1971. The company subsequently broke with Tiger and became Nike.
2. Peter Schwartz and Blair Gibb, *When Good Companies Do Bad Things: Responsibility and Risk in an Age of Globalization* (New York: Wiley & Sons, 1999), 52.
3. Miguel Korzeniewicz, "Commodity Chains and Marketing Strategies: Nike and the Global Athletic Footwear Industry," in Frank J. Lechner and John Boli (Eds.), *The Globalization Reader* (Malden, MA: Blackwell, 2000), 158–159.
4. Ibid., 157.
5. Nike, Inc. Annual Report, <http://invest.nike.com/phoenix.zhtml?c=100529&p=irol-finReporting>.
6. World Bank, 2007 World Development Indicators Database, May 27, 2009, <http://siteresources.worldbank.org/DATASTATISTICS/Resources/GDP.pdf>.
7. Daniel Kaplan, "Nike's Tab for Endorsements Spikes to $3.4B", *Sports Business Journal* (April 14, 2008): 01; available at <http://www.sportsbusinessjournal.com/article/58660>.
8. Schwartz and Gibb, *When Good Companies Do Bad Things*, 51, 53.
9. Michael Clancy, "Sweating the Swoosh: Nike, the Globalization of Sneakers, and the Question of Sweatshop Labor," in *Pew Case Studies in International Affairs* (Washington, DC: Georgetown University, Institute for the Study of Diplomacy, 2000), 5.
10. Ibid.

11. Schwartz and Gibb, *When Good Companies Do Bad Things*, 51, 53.
12. Clancy, "Sweating the Swoosh," 9.
13. Nike Web site, Corporate Responsibility Page, <www.nikebiz.com/labor/index. shtml>.
14. Clancy, "Sweating the Swoosh," 13.
15. "Firms are considered to be more multinational if (1) they have foreign affiliates or subsidiaries in foreign countries; (2) they operate in a wide variety of countries around the globe; (3) the proportion of assets, revenues, or profits accounted for by overseas operations relative to total assets, revenues, or profits is high; (4) their employees, stockholders, owners, and managers are from many different countries; (5) their overseas operations are much more ambitious than just sales offices, including a full range of manufacturing and research and development activities. MNCs are firms that have sent abroad a package of capital, technology, managerial talent, and marketing skills to carry out production in foreign countries." Joan E. Spiro and Jeffrey A. Hart, *The Politics of International Economic Relations* (New York: St. Martin's Press, 1997), 96, 98.
16. "Corporations among Largest Global Economic Entities, Rank Above Many Countries; Corporations Make Up 63% of 150 Largest Global Economic Enterprises," Report summary of *Fortune Magazine*, July 18, 2005; available at <http://news.mongabay. com/2005/0718-worlds_largest.html>.
17. *The Economist* (July 30, 1994): 57, reprinted in James Lee Ray, *Global Problems* (New York: Houghton Mifflin, 1998), 465.
18. United Nations Conference on Trade and Development (UNCTAD), World Investment Report 2008, <http://www.unctad.org/en/docs/wir2008overview_en.pdf>, 10.
19. Ibid., 27.
20. Ibid, 10.
21. UNCTAD, World Investment Report 2005, Overview, <http://www.unctad.org/en/ docs/wir2005overview_en.pdf>.
22. Schwartz and Gibb, *When Good Companies Do Bad Things*, 85.
23. Megha Bahree, "Child Labor", *Forbes*, March 10, 2008, <http://www.forbes.com/ global/2008/0310/062.html>. Of these, 61 percent are in Asia, 32 percent in Africa, and 7 percent in Latin America. Human Rights Watch, Child Labor, <http://www.hrw. org/children/labor.htm>.
24. Megha Bahree, "Child Labor", *Forbes*, March 10, 2008, <http://www.forbes.com/ global/2008/0310/062.html>.
25. For example, MNCs are under growing pressure to conform to higher environmental standards from home country regulations and consumers. See UNCTAD, *World Investment Report: Foreign Direct Investment and the Challenge of Development, Overview* (New York: United Nations, 1999), 46; UNCTAD, *World Investment Report, 1999* (New York: United Nations, 1999).
26. A. Claire Cutler, Virginia Haufler, and Tony Porter, *Private Authority and International Affairs* (Albany: SUNY Press, 1999), 16.
27. In practice, this varies by MNC and country. Companies that receive subsidies favor continuing them, and industries that are hurt by foreign competition pressure governments for protection.
28. World Bank, World Development Report 2008, <http://siteresources.worldbank.org/ INTWDR2008/Resources/2795087-1192112387976/WDR08_08_ch04.pdf>, 97.
29. Ward Morehouse and M. Arun Subramaniam, *The Bhopal Tragedy: A Report for the Citizens Commission on Bhopal* (New York: Council on International and Public Affairs, 1986); William Board, *The Bhopal Tragedy: Language, Logic, and Politics in the Production of a Hazard* (Boulder, CO: Westview, 1989); Paul Shrivastava, *Bhopal: Anatomy of a Crisis*

(Cambridge, MA: Ballinger, 1987); Rama Lakshmi, "India Seeks to Reduce Charge Facing Ex-Union Carbide Boss," *Washington Post* (July 8, 2002): A12.

30. Suketu Mehta, "Bhopal Lives," *Village Voice* (December 3, 1996): 51.

31. Ibid., 55; Lakshmi, "India Seeks to Reduce Charge Facing Ex-Union Carbide Boss." Warren Anderson, CEO of Union Carbide at the time of the accident, was charged with culpable homicide in India and faced a civil suit in the United States over the accident. In June 2003, the Indian government requested Anderson's extradition to stand trial. A year later, on July 13, 2004, the U.S. government rejected Anderson's extradition request on technical grounds. He currently resides in Long Island, New York.

32. Manuel Roig-Franzia, "Unheeded Regulator Warned of Derivatives Debacle," *The Washington Post*, (May 26, 2009): C2; Darrin W. Snyder Belousek, "Greenspan's Folly," *America*, (March 30, 2009).

33. Amnesty International, "Nigeria: Petroleum, Poverty, and Pollution in the Niger Delta," June 20, 2009, p. 9, <http://amnesty.org/en/library/asset/AFR44/017/2009/en/e2415061-da5c-44f8-a73c-a7a4766ee21d/afr440172009en.pdf>; Mr. Austin Onuoha, "African Oil and Poverty," Speech at Catholic University of America, Washington, DC, October 17, 2005.

34. The Global Corruption Report 2005, *Transparency International*, <http://www.global-corruptionreport.org/gcr2005/download/english/country_reports_a_j.pdf>.

35. Fr. Antoine Berilengar, SJ, "African Oil and Poverty," Speech at Catholic University of America, Washington, DC, October 17, 2005.

36. Bret L. Billet, "Safeguarding or International Morality? The Behavior of Multinational Corporations in Less Developed Countries, 1975–86," *International Interactions* 17 (1991): 171, 184; quoted in Ray, *Global Problems*, 476.

37. Deborah L. Spar, "The Spotlight and the Bottom Line: How Multinationals Export Human Rights," *Foreign Affairs* 77 (March–April 1998): 7–12.

38. Cutler, Haufler, and Porter, *Private Authority and International Affairs*.

39. David C. Korten, *When Corporations Rule the World* (West Hartford, CT: Kumarian Press, 1995).

40. These include the power to compel discovery, dispose of property and property rights, order monetary damages, and, depending on the nature of the contract and the rules of arbitration chosen, even order specific performance.

41. Raymond W. Baker, *Capitalism's Achilles Heel* (Hoboken, NJ: Wiley & Sons, 2005), 163.

42. Schwartz and Gibb, *When Good Companies Do Bad Things*, 92.

43. United Nations, "Report of the United Nations High Commissioner on Human Rights on the Responsibilities of Transnational Corporations and Related Business Enterprises with Regard to Human Rights," February 2005, <http://www2.ohchr.org/english/bodies/hrcouncil/docs/11session/A.HRC.11.13.pdf>.

44. Jan Martin Witte and Wolfgang Reinicke, "Business UNusual," 2005, UN Global Compact Office <http://globalpublicpolicy.net/businessUNusual/>; Witte and Reinicke, "Partnerships: Opportunities and Challenges of Partnering with the UN," Global Compact, July 10, 2005, <www.globalpublicpolicy.net>; Sarah Murray, "UN Partnerships: Mistrust of Corporate World Wearing Off," *Financial Times* (September 13, 2005).

45. Margaret E. Keck and Kathryn Sikkink, *Activists Beyond Borders* (Ithaca, NY: Cornell University Press, 1998).

46. Virginia Haufler, *A Public Role for the Private Sector: Industry Self-Regulation in a Global Economy* (Washington, DC: Carnegie Endowment for International Peace, 2001), 106.

47. "The Coalition for Environmentally Responsible Economies (CERES) was formed in 1989 as a groundbreaking partnership between leading environmental groups and institutional investors. Ceres emerged just as the Exxon Valdez oil spill in Alaska motivated

the environmental and investor communities to push for higher standards of corporate environmental performance and disclosure. That work resulted in the creation of the Ceres Principles, a pioneering ten-point code of corporate environmental conduct that has led to the widespread adoption of environmental principles by companies worldwide." <http://www.ceres.org>

48. Jack Quarter, *Beyond the Bottom Line* (Westport, CT: Quorum Books, 2000), 119–133.

49. Presentation to the Humanizing the Global Economy Conference of the Latin American, Canadian, and US Catholic Bishops, Washington, DC, Catholic University, January 29, 2002.

50. Schwartz and Gibb, *When Good Companies Do Bad Things*, 77; John Kleiderer, US Jesuit Conference, "African Oil and Poverty," Speech at Catholic University of America, Washington, DC, October 17, 2005.

51. Joby Warrick and R. Jeffrey Smith , "CIA Hired Firm for Assassin Program," The Washington Post, August 20, 2009; United Nations Office of the High Commissioner for Human Rights, "UN human rights chief welcomes US appointment of prosecutor to investigate alleged abuse of terror suspects," August 25, 2009, < http://www.ohchr. org/EN/NewsEvents/Pages/media.aspx>; Haroon Siddique, "Private security firms face tough times in Iraq," August 10, 2009, <http://www.guardian.co.uk/world/2009/ aug/10/iraq-murder-security-firms >; British Government Foreign and Commonwealth Office, "Public Consultation on Private Military Companies," April 2009, http://www.fco.gov.uk/en/newsroom/latest-news/?view=PressS&id=16784533

CHAPTER FIVE

Networked Terror

Martha Crenshaw and Maryann Cusimano Love

Terrorism is not new. What is new is the way terrorists today can take advantage of globalization. Terrorists use cheap and instant global infrastructure to recruit members; raise money; train individuals and cells; gather intelligence; move people, money, and material; conduct operations; and spread their messages. Terrorists do not respect sovereign borders. But governments do respect sovereign borders in their efforts to stop, arrest, and eliminate terrorists.

Consider these examples. Al Qaeda uses mobile phone to Web applications in conducting terrorist attacks. Training is now available cheaply and globally on the Internet 24/7, despite the efforts of U.S. and coalition forces who raided and shut down al Qaeda training camps in Afghanistan in 2001 and 2002. According to Osama bin Laden biographer Hamid Mir, as al Qaeda scattered from Afghanistan into exile, Mir watched "every second al Qaeda member carrying a laptop computer along with a Kalashnikov." Internet training videos and manuals include "how to's" for building and wearing a suicide bomber belt; creating biological weapons and spreading the plague; poisoning techniques; extracting and recycling explosives from missiles and land mines; bomb recipes, instructions, and country-by-country explosives shopping lists and availability information; hostage taking; assassination; shooting a rocket-propelled grenade; firing an SA-7 surface-to-air missile; blowing up cars; and using the Internet to organize a cell and plan an operation. In 1998 there were 12 terrorist-related Web sites; today there are over 5,000, and about 50,000 when including social networking sites, forums, blogs, video sites, and virtual world sites. As government authorities shut down a terrorist Web site, hundreds of successors crop up with mirror postings. Concerned that fixed Web sites are too vulnerable, al Qaeda uses more mobile and difficult to track postings on bulletin boards, in Internet storage sites, and chat rooms.[1]

Seized laptop computers offer a window into al Qaeda. After a failed assassination attempt on the Pakistani president, Pakistani officials cracked down on al Qaeda operatives in Pakistan and made a series of high-profile arrests in July 2004. Among those arrested was Muhammad Naeem Noor Khan, a British computer engineer of Pakistani descent. He was caught with laptops containing scouting reports, detailed surveillance information, and hundreds of photographs of financial institutions in the United States, including the World Bank headquarters in Washington, DC. Khan cooperated with law enforcement officials and sent e-mails in a "sting" operation to gather evidence on other al Qaeda operatives. Khan's Pakistan arrest led British authorities to arrest his cousin Babar Ahmad, another British citizen of Pakistani descent.[2]

In another example of global networks, consider the case of the millennium bomber. On the evening of December 14, 1999, U.S. Customs agent Deana Dean decided to search the last rental car leaving the ferry from Vancouver, British Columbia, into Washington state. The driver had a Canadian driver's license that identified him as Benni Antoine Noris of Montreal, but his answers to her routine questions seemed hesitant and nervous. Customs agents removed the cover over the spare tire in his trunk and found garbage bags of white powder, as well as aspirin containers and olive jars filled with liquid resembling honey. The suspect bolted, ran across lanes of traffic, bounced off a moving vehicle, and tried to commandeer a car. Customs agents apprehended and handcuffed him and continued to search his vehicle. Thinking they had found drugs, the border guards lifted, examined, and shook the containers, while the suspect ducked behind a car. Later they learned they had by chance apprehended a 32-year-old Algerian man named Ahmed Ressam, who was wanted in France and Canada for suspected terrorist activities. Rather than narcotics, Ressam was carrying 100 pounds of volatile, high-powered explosives that could have detonated if accidentally dropped by the customs agents. His intended target had been the Los Angeles International airport. The press quickly dubbed him the "Millennium Bomber."[3]

Ressam worked with his father in a coffee shop in Algeria until intrastate hostilities intensified in Algeria in 1992. An Islamic fundamentalist party was on the verge of winning national elections, but the government prevented it from taking power and a civil war broke out. Ressam became associated with Islamic militants and then moved to France for the next two years. During that time, Algerian terrorists calling themselves the Group Islamique Armé (GIA), or Armed Islamic Group, conducted a series of bombings of the Paris Metro subway system, killing 22 people and injuring more than 200 others. In an eerie preview of the September 11 attacks, in 1994 they hijacked an Air France plane, which they intended to crash, fully loaded with fuel and passengers, into a Paris landmark, preferably the Eiffel Tower. French commandos successfully stormed the plane, freed the passengers, and shot the hijackers, thus spoiling the plan.[4]

Ressam left France, using a fake French passport, and applied for political asylum in Canada. He moved in with a group of Islamic extremists in Quebec, where he supported himself on Canadian welfare assistance and petty theft and fraud, usually by robbing tourists and using or selling their traveler's checks, cash and credit cards, passports, driver's licenses, and other identification papers. When French police upset a GIA plot to bomb a G-7 economic meeting in France, they seized an electronic organizer filled with phone numbers and addresses of others in the terrorist network. Ahmed Ressam in Montreal was included in the electronic records. Bureaucratic obstacles and delays between the French and Canadian governments and within the Canadian government kept law enforcement from apprehending Ressam. In the meantime, he forged a false Canadian birth record and obtained a Canadian driver's license and passport as Benni Noris. Posing as Noris, he traveled to Pakistan, where he met with al Qaeda members and was taken to Osama bin Laden's terrorist training camps in Afghanistan. He received training in explosives manufacturing, destruction of a country's infrastructure, use of chemical weapons, and other terrorist activities. He left with new skills, $12,000 in "seed money" from the al Qaeda network to pursue terrorist activities, and a request from one of bin Laden's chief lieutenants to steal and send them original Canadian passports so they could help establish operatives in the United States. As investigating French Judge Jean-Louis Brugiere noted, "You can't move around if you don't have false papers and passports. For these groups, passports are as important as weapons."[5] Ressam returned to Canada via South Korea, with a layover in Los Angeles International Airport. While there, he surveyed the site, calculating how long he could leave explosives-laden luggage before it would be discovered and moved, and the length of time he would have to escape the premises (apparently, he did not plan a suicide bombing).[6]

Ressam was arrested days before the millennium, and his cooperation with law enforcement helped secure the arrests of some of his associates in Canada and Brooklyn, NY. International law enforcement efforts foiled other millennium plots in Jordan, Yemen, the Philippines, and elsewhere.[7] After the September 11 attacks, Ressam was again interrogated in a high-security prison in Seattle. He said he did not know any of the September 11 hijackers, but he gave authorities additional information about terrorist sleeper cells and about al Qaeda's interest in chemical and biological weapons. In return, he sought reduced prison time.[8]

These examples illustrate many trends in modern terrorism: global operations, use of cheap and easily available modern technologies, networked organizational structures, and a desire to increase casualties. The Ressam case also demonstrates how difficult it is for states to cooperate effectively to combat terrorism in a timely fashion. The purpose of this chapter is to put the transsovereign problem of modern terrorism in context:[9] in the context of the debates over defining terrorism compared to other forms of political violence, in the context of globalization,[10] in the context of what the private sector and states can do to prevent and respond to terrorism, and in the context of how terrorism ends.

DEFINING TERRORISM

Terrorism has been around for centuries. The word *terrorism* was first used in describing the Reign of Terror phase of the French Revolution in 1793–1794 as a newly installed regime systematically attempted to consolidate power. In nineteenth-century Russia, the People's Will proudly admitted using terrorism in its fight against the autocracy, seeing its members as "noble, terrible … the martyr and the hero." A successor group later proclaimed, "The terrorists are the incarnation of the honor and the conscience of the Russian revolution."[11]

Using the term *terrorism* has always been controversial. The British army in Palestine in 1947 banned use of the word *terrorist* to describe members of Menachem Begin's Irgun group, the principal Jewish rebel force, because it implied that British forces had reason to be terrified by the resistance fighters.[12]

Defining terrorism today is no less controversial, in part because the concept is "overlaid with questions of value, usually centered on the legitimacy of the use of violence. Attitudes toward terrorism are frequently based on deep moral commitments ... the morality of political systems and governments; one has to ask what values are to be defended."[13] Because of the word's pejorative connotation, many people seek to label any use of violence they perceive as illegitimate or with which they disagree as terrorism. Israel tends to refer to any Palestinian violence as *terrorism*, whereas Palestinians call Israel a *terrorist state*. Pakistan regards Muslims fighting for the autonomy of Kashmir as freedom fighters, yet India regards them as terrorists. Al Qaeda contends that the United States engaged in terrorism because of civilians killed in Iraq, and because the United States used weapons of mass destruction against civilian populations—as when it dropped atomic bombs on Hiroshima and Nagasaki in 1945.

Distinct from the word's use as an insult, however, is some core of agreement about the definition of terrorism. Why is terrorism considered to be an illegitimate use of force? One reason is that terrorism typically refers to *force directed against noncombatants*, which violates centuries of natural law and international law regarding the rules of war.[14]

Unlike other "isms"—communism, fascism, socialism—terrorism is a strategy or tactic, not an ideology. It is used by widely divergent groups, from Maoists in the mountains of Peru to conservative Islamic extremists in the Arabian desert. Combating terrorism is similar to other efforts to delegitimize particular tactics internationally, such as the efforts to ban the use of antipersonnel landmines and cluster munitions. Similar to these campaigns to ban landmines and cluster munitions as illegitimate tools of force against noncombatants, international coalitions, treaties, and conventions against terrorism also seek to globally undermine the use of terrorism as a tool against noncombatants. Combating terrorism is not a fight against a particular state, territory, group, person, or ideology. It is a battle to curtail the use of a specific method of violence.[15]

Terrorism can be defined as organized and purposive political violence that is perceived as unacceptable by society because of its cruelty and unexpectedness:

> Terrorism usually occurs in situations of peace rather than war, and comes as a surprise to its victims ... who are noncombatants, not prepared to defend themselves against attack and only in the most tenuous way responsible for the actions of the governments that terrorists oppose. ... Terrorists intend, if not to terrorize (that is, to create the emotion of terror, a form of panic), at least to produce outrage and shock. Terrorism is a strategy of surprise. It is meant to ... produce

psychological and political effects far out of proportion to the magnitude of physical destruction. . . . [T]he physical victims of terrorism are not the targets. That they are terrorized is important only in so far as their terror is communicated to a watching audience, whose emotions the terrorists seek to manipulate.[16]

Terrorism depends on surprise to gain attention and generate fear, so terrorists must constantly be innovative in their means of attack or they lose the power to shock. If terrorist violence becomes routine, then their actions will not pressure change and their goals will no longer receive attention. Surprise is one way of compensating for what they lack in numbers. "Terrorists rarely attack well defended targets. The two factors of weakness and the desire to excite passions encourage terrorists to attack ordinary civilians."[17]

Terrorism is an inherently political act designed to achieve particular goals, generally to bring public pressure to bear on government decisions. For example, al Qaeda's terrorist campaign against the United States is an attempt to pressure the United States to withdraw its support from the Saudi and Egyptian regimes, which al Qaeda regards as illegitimate. The calculus assumes that raising the costs to the United States will undermine support and encourage change of U.S. policies in the Middle East. Thus, even though some people regard such terrorists as "mad" due to their morally reprehensible means, terrorist groups are engaged in conscious, goal-directed, and premeditated rather than random behavior.

As opposed to mass uprisings or spontaneous violence, "Terrorism is clandestine violence organized by small groups. ... [T]errorism is highly intentional or purposeful violence. It is not spontaneous or unplanned."[18] For example, the four simultaneous hijackings of September 11, and the 10 coordinated attacks in Mumbai, India in November 2008, revealed a vast, complex, and highly organized conspiracy.[19]

Because terrorism aims to arouse or intimidate civilian audiences more than reduce an opponent's military effectiveness, "Victims are representative and symbolic. Their usefulness to the terrorist lies in the regard society has for them," as evidenced by attacks on "everyday" train commuters in Mumbai, London, and Spain. [20]

There are other official definitions of terrorism. The International Convention for the Suppression of the Financing of Terrorism sponsored by the United Nations defines terrorism as "an act intended to cause death or serious bodily injury to any person not actively involved in armed conflict in order to intimidate a population, or to compel a government or an international organization to do or abstain from doing any act."[21] Other UN documents stress that terrorists are nonstate actors motivated by political goals.[22]

The U.S. Department of State defines terrorism as

> premeditated, politically motivated violence perpetrated against noncombatant targets by subnational groups or clandestine agents, usually intended to influence an audience. The term "international terrorism" means terrorism involving citizens or the territory of more than one country. The term "terrorist group" means any group practicing, or that has significant subgroups that practice, international terrorism.[23]

The definitions generally share the idea that terrorism is the use of violence against noncombatants, generally by nonstate actors to generate fear in furtherance of other political goals. The "nonstate" component of the definition is important, though controversial. If terrorism is conducted only by nonstate actors, then by definition U.S. and Israeli actions against noncombatants are not terrorism, whereas similar actions by Palestinians may be so termed. If states deliberately and intentionally target and terrorize noncombatants, it is a violation of the laws of armed conflict, not terrorism. International conventions, because they are signed by states, are likely to support definitions of terrorism that are more favorable to states.

It is important to note that all uses of violence by groups labeled as terrorist may not be terrorism, and not all violence by nonstate actors is terrorism. Terrorism is distinct from other low-level forms of political violence by nonstate actors such as guerrilla warfare, ethnic or nationalist separatist violence, and violent efforts to overthrow governments, among others. Depending on the context, nonstate groups may use a medley of tactics that includes both terrorism and other forms of political violence.[24] Sometimes terrorist groups may engage in traditional insurgent activities of using force against military and government targets in order to gain territory or strategic advantage, not to strike at noncombatants in order to cause fear. Terrorism means not only conducting illegal actions (such as killing noncombatants), but also having certain intentions behind those actions (causing fear and psychological reactions to achieve political or other goals rather than destroy something of material value). Traditional guerrilla or insurgent actions to diminish a government's abilities to project power into a disputed region may not be terrorism. These distinctions between terrorism and other forms of low-level violence can confuse policy makers and the public, because generally once a group is labeled as terrorist, all its actions are labeled as terrorism, even though groups may employ a variety of tactics, only some of which are terrorism. If Osama bin Laden orders a cup of coffee, is it an act of terrorism? If a vendor was forced to give bin Laden a cup of coffee at gunpoint, is the vendor illegally giving material support to terrorism? These are not trivial questions—the USA PATRIOT Act, as currently and over-broadly interpreted, categorizes such a person as a criminal who gives material support to terrorists.[25]

Developing common definitions of terrorism is important as antiterrorism laws are increasingly enacted domestically and internationally. In the case of the millennium bomber, what difference does it make whether we call his actions terrorism? He committed fraud, theft, illegal immigration, and perjury, and he created and carried illegal explosives across state lines in a conspiracy to commit multiple homicides. Unlike many acts of cybercrime, which are not illegal in some states, terrorism is not primarily a problem of a lack of law. Most everything terrorist organizations do is already illegal: fraud, theft, murder, hijackings, bombings, and conspiracy. What value is added by enacting additional domestic and international legislation that labels these activities as terrorism? The purpose of additional antiterrorism legislation is primarily political: to help free additional resources to combat terrorism, to build international political consensus and harmonize international law regarding these acts, and to further undermine the tactic's legitimacy.

GOING GLOBAL

Additional international legal conventions are also sought against terrorism because, although terrorist networks are increasingly global, intelligence, military, and law enforcement efforts are still stymied by state borders and jurisdictions. For example, the U.S. government complains that European governments are more lax in prosecution of suspected terrorists. Many of those apprehended in Germany in connection with the September 11 plot were either released or served minimal jail sentences. In contrast, the Saudi government beheaded suspects apprehended in connection with the USS *Cole* bombing. This was also a blow to officials in the U.S. government, who were not afforded an opportunity to question the suspects. Because the suspects were Saudi citizens in Saudi territory, the Saudi government was well within its sovereign rights. Terrorists may go global, but state actions to pursue terrorists are constrained by sovereignty.

Although terrorism has existed for centuries, the modern period of globalization changes it. If terrorism is a form of "advertising discontent,"[26] then globalization offers terrorists the opportunity to easily and cheaply take their complaints to a global stage.[27] For example, al Qaeda's attacks on U.S. targets can be seen as a strategic reaction to American power in the context of a globalized civil war. The United States is susceptible to international terrorism because of its global engagement and its choice of allies, most of whom face significant opposition at home.

> For many of the militants now engaged in al Qaeda, opposition to authority at home, whether peaceful or violent, was ineffective. Local regimes countered dissent with severe repression. As a result, radical frustrations apparently were transferred to the United States as a symbol of both oppression and arrogance. As a free and affluent society, America is a target-rich environment, and one where sensational attacks elicit gratifying media attention. Portraying the United States as an immoral enemy justifies terrorism to the audiences of the dispossessed, especially young men without life prospects whose only education is religious. These various strands have been knitted together in the transnational conspiracy that is al Qaeda. One cannot understand al Qaeda without understanding the domestic politics of Egypt and Saudi Arabia, or now much of the Muslim world.[28]

Globalization takes local fault lines farther afield. Terrorists can go global by using global media as shrewdly as other political actors. Journalist Peter Bergen recalls being contacted by Osama bin Laden's media advisors, who were considering appropriate venues for bin Laden's first television interview. The advisors had a large stack of media requests, but they had narrowed it down to the BBC, CBS News's 60 Minutes program, or CNN. Bergen, employed by CNN, recalled, "I pointed out that CNN's programs were shown in over a hundred countries, while CBS was broadcast only in the United States."[29] A month later, CNN was called on to do the interview. Bergen and his crew were blindfolded and escorted to an undisclosed location in Afghanistan and allowed to use only al Qaeda's video equipment in case their cameras were bugged or rigged with explosives.[30] After the interview, the media advisor reviewed the tape and cut out any unflattering footage of bin Laden.[31]

Besides global media, terrorists use other cheap and easily available off-the-shelf technologies. A laptop computer left behind by one of the terrorists responsible for the 1993 bombing of the World Trade Center revealed an evidence trail to other coconspirators, as well as an al Qaeda "how-to" terrorist manual. The September 11 hijackers used the Internet to download specific airport maps, directions, flying instructions, and information about the targeted buildings. They even purchased many of their tickets online. To hide their trail, they often used general access computers in public libraries. Terrorist groups routinely set up Web sites and broadcast their political aims and encourage recruits. They create and copy home-made videotapes for use in international recruitment. From fax machines to Blackberries and cell phones, terrorist networks use the same technologies that global business networks use.

Globalization increases terrorists' casualties, due to greater access to lethal technologies and reduced taboos on killing. Experts have noted rising casualties and increased lethality in terrorist violence in recent years. Although the Japanese group Aum Shinrikyo's release of poisonous sarin gas into the crowded Tokyo subway system in 1995 killed "only" twelve people, more than 5,500 were injured. Many more would have died if the group had been more expert in its use of chemical agents. Local terrorist groups in the past faced diminishing returns on increased bloodshed. If their activities caused too many casualties, it could decrease critical social support, recruitments, financial support, and legitimacy. The Irish Republican Army (IRA) often faced this dilemma. But today, terrorism experts fear greater casualties in coming years as terrorist groups train in and explore the use of chemical, biological, and nuclear devices. Because terrorist groups are increasingly networked globally, with training, recruitment, financing, and operations carried out in several countries, increased deaths of one country's citizens may not reduce sympathy, support, and recruitment for the group in other countries. Increased casualties may actually build support as the group gains media exposure and international recognition that it is a force to be reckoned with. Terrorists may also capitalize politically on governments' increased use of violence to combat terrorism. For example, increased violence by British troops and Protestant paramilitary units in Northern Ireland—including the British Army's firing into a crowd of unarmed Irish Catholic demonstrators in Londonderry on "Bloody Sunday" (January 30, 1972)[32]—led to the establishment of the Provisional IRA and increased sympathy for the IRA's cause for a time, as many people asked, "Who are the real terrorists here?"[33] Similarly the Iraq War proved to be a huge rallying point and recruitment tool for jihadist terrorists.

Globalization also facilitates the financing of terrorist groups, because dirty money moves in the same cross-border financial flows as clean money. Terrorists can finance their operations through private charitable foundations. These NGOs may conduct social service works (such as education, health care, and care of widows, orphans, war victims, and refugees), but some of the funds raised may be diverted to illicit activities. Terrorists also engage in strategic cooperative ventures with transnational criminal groups.

Terrorist groups in Latin America, for example, often derive significant financial benefit from the drug trade, just as al Qaeda profited from the Afghan heroin trade.

Terrorist organizations may also conduct legal businesses. The Aum Shinrikyo sect used its software development companies as a major source of revenue. The Japanese defense ministry even used Aum-developed communications programs at twenty ground bases across Japan to gain more rapid access to the Internet. Aum programs were also used for airline-route management and mainframe computer operations. The software companies earned the business through indirect subcontracting relationships and by underbidding competitors by 30 to 40 percent because their employees, all Aum members, worked for virtually no pay. In an incredible irony, the Japanese government purchased software from the very group that perpetrated the sarin gas attacks in the hope of causing chaos that would lead to the overthrow of the Japanese government.[34]

Terrorist organizations may also network with other terrorist organizations. For example, the Provisional IRA historically has prized "its links with foreign terrorist movements such as the Popular Front for the Liberation of Palestine, the Red Brigades, the Red Army Faction, and the ETA [Euskadi Ta Askatasuna, a Basque separatist group that inhabits the Spanish–French border region]. Italian terrorists shared a huge consignment of Palestinian weapons between the ETA and the IRA."[35] IRA members have been arrested in Colombia, helping to train the Revolutionary Armed Forces of Colombia (Fuerzas Armadas Revolucionarias de Colombia, or FARC).

THE MISSING LINK: THE PRIVATE SECTOR AND CURTAILING TERRORISM

Global infrastructures were built for speed and profit, not security. People and packages now move faster, farther, more easily, and for a lower price than ever before—but at the cost of preventive, multilateral security measures.[36] Although attention has been placed on increasing government activities against terrorism after September 11, the private sector remains key in safeguarding infrastructure from terrorist attack. Eighty-five percent of U.S. critical infrastructure are privately owned and operated—everything from roads and bridges to power plants, nuclear facilities, and chemical and pharmaceutical manufacturers. Much of U.S. critical infrastructure is old, and was not built with security concerns in mind. Investments in critical infrastructure yield dividends every day whether or not a terrorist attack ever occurs, from better roads and bridges to better responses in hurricane or flu season.

While greater cooperation with the private sector is necessary, it is difficult. Businesses say they have few incentives to change the system and engage in greater public–private cooperation with government on security issues. They are rarely required to do so by law. Their clients, customers, and shareholders are concerned more with the bottom line than with security measures. They do not trust government competence or motives. Would information volunteered to government land in the hands of their competitors or result in higher tax bills? Without action by businesses, however, terrorists can easily exploit the vulnerabilities of the global trade and transportation infrastructure, as they did on September 11. Because terrorists seek easy targets, private sector responses are crucial. The private sector is increasingly partnering with states. For example, the financial sector is working to curtail money laundering, and pharmaceutical companies are rapidly producing smallpox vaccine to prepare for potential bioterrorist attacks. Yet more private sector cooperation is needed in the war on terrorism.

Border control has improved in the last decade, but greater real-time transparency within transportation and shipping infrastructure systems is still needed. Increasing the number of border control agents and the amount of equipment and increasing searches and seizures at borders are efforts that are still bound to fail because even the most up-to-date and efficient government agents cannot keep up with the volume of global trade flows. Speed and volume are crucial to maintaining the economic health of global trade and transportation systems. Just-in-time shipping and narrow profit margins that are dependent on speed and volume mean that closing down borders for old-fashioned search and seizures is an unsustainable approach and equivalent to imposing an economic embargo on ourselves.[37] Luckily we have other choices.

Rather than focusing efforts on border control, security checks should be done at the point of origin in trade and transportation flows. As Stephen Flynn, a senior fellow at the Council on Foreign Relations and a retired Coast Guard commander, notes trying to manage security at borders is like "trying to catch minnows at the base of Niagara Falls."[38] Border checks should be the last defense, not the first or main check for security. Thorough security background checks should be required of all private-sector employees in the shipping and transportation sectors. Governments and private-sector actors need to employ smarter technologies, such as bar coding, GPS transceivers, sensors, smart cards, and advance electronic manifests; these would allow real-time transparency and accountability about the contents of the shipping or transportation stream at any given time. This is how United Parcel Service and FedEx track packages in transit to customers. Businesses that comply with standards and do thorough and strict self-policing can be accorded fast-track processing at borders that would be the equivalent of an "EZ pass" electronic toll collection lane. Border checks would continue but be based on intelligence and risk management baselines rather than purely on hunches.

STATE RESPONSES: HOW TERRORISM ENDS

So far the discussion has focused on how to manage or curtail terrorism. More international cooperation, greater information sharing and cooperation across and within government bureaucracies, and more sustained and systematic cooperation between governments and the private sector are all needed.[39] But how does terrorism end? No democratic regime has ever been conquered by terror. Over time, terrorist groups often go out of business. Context matters. As we try to formulate governmental policies aimed at ending terrorism, we must ask how such policies are likely to affect the evolution of terrorism.

The first set of questions involves the terrorist groups themselves. First, internal factors must be assessed. How does the organization make decisions? How does the organization perceive its environment? What are its internal psychological dynamics? Is the organization divided internally? The answers to all of these questions are important to know but often difficult to ascertain.

Next, external factors must be considered. How does the relative strength of the terrorist organization compare with that of the government it opposes? Are the terrorists ideologically or ethnically motivated? What kinds of ties do they have to outside groups that may support them? Is the conflict best characterized as a secessionist struggle or does it involve a battle over civil society and representation?

The options that a government uses to respond to terrorism, many of which can be pursued simultaneously, must be adapted to the type of group and situation. There is no one-size-fits-all policy.

First, governments can try deterrence. They can use their coercive capacity to make terrorism too costly for those who seek to use it. They can do this by military strikes against terrorist bases, assassinations of key leaders, and collective punishment. There are several drawbacks to this approach, however. It can lead to unacceptable human rights violations, and groups may not come to government attention until their movements are so well developed that containing them through deterrent methods is insufficient.

An alternative is to use the criminal justice system to end terrorist activities and groups. Governments can treat terrorism primarily as a crime and therefore pursue the extradition, prosecution, and incarceration of suspects. One drawback to this approach is that the prosecution of terrorists in a court of law can compromise government efforts to gather intelligence on terrorist organizations. For example, al Qaeda members drastically reduced their usage of cell phones after court testimony revealed that governments could easily intercept cell phone conversations. In addition, criminal justice efforts (like deterrent efforts) are deployed mostly after terrorists have struck, meaning that significant damage and loss of life may have already occurred.

Governments can enhance prevention and defense. They can make targets harder to attack, and they can use intelligence capabilities to gain advance knowledge of when attacks may take place. As targets are hardened, however, some terrorist groups may shift their sights to softer targets. An example is the targeting of the U.S. embassies in Kenya and Tanzania in August 1998 by truck bombs. Although the attacks were coordinated by al Qaeda, targets in Africa were chosen because of their relatively lax security compared with targets in the Middle East.

States also may try negotiations. Governments can elect to negotiate with terrorist groups and make concessions in exchange for the groups' renunciation of violence. The Good Friday Peace Accords and the associated peace process in Northern Ireland, and the Colombian government's outreach to insurgency and terrorist groups are attempts to reach negotiated settlements and end violence. Governments are often reluctant to do so when terror campaigns begin, but negotiations may be the only way to resolve long-standing disputes, especially ethnonationalist claims that have significant popular support.

The end of terrorism may result from one or more of the following situations. Success may end it. The terrorists may accomplish their objectives, such as the overthrow of a government, the end of an occupation, or a policy change. Terrorism per se cannot achieve long-term goals such as revolution or independence, but it can sometimes do so in conjunction with less violent political action. The terrorists may also achieve partial or preliminary success. A corollary to achieving objectives is having at least achieved public recognition for an organization and the cause it espouses.

It can put the issue on the public agenda. In this case, continued terrorist actions may alienate supporters, sponsors, or key third-country actors for whom continued violence is unacceptable.

Terrorists may experience organizational breakdown, as has been the case for the Tupac Amaru group in Peru. After some of its members died when a four-month siege of the Japanese embassy in Peru was put down by Peruvian forces in 1997, the group has not mounted a significant terrorist action and appears to be in organizational disarray, with dwindling numbers focused mainly on freeing their imprisoned compatriots.[40] Terrorist organizations, like any organizations, must constantly work to maintain themselves. If recruiting dries up, or if funding becomes unavailable, then the organization may be unable to sustain itself. On the other hand, the necessity of self-preservation may force organizations to continue terrorist activities even if the leadership otherwise wishes to give them up. It may be that the only way for the organization to continue to attract new recruits and financial support is to continue to gain publicity for its terrorist actions.

Terrorist groups also may face dwindling support. Organizations may lose the support of their various constituencies—the populations they seek to represent or the governments or other organizations that support them. They can do so for reasons of ideological or strategic differences, personality clashes, or simple fatigue. Terrorist actions can also provoke moral outrage and undermine support.

New alternatives to achieve political or other goals may emerge. At times, other options for political change emerge. They can include more traditional forms of warfare or revolution, mass protests, or political negotiations.

As suggested earlier, many of the factors and consequences already outlined may occur simultaneously. Both governments and terrorist organizations can pursue many tracks at once, and organizations may confront a wide series of challenges simultaneously.

Governmental decisions about how to confront terrorism are made more difficult by the frequently high degree of uncertainty governments have about the nature of terrorist organizations, their motivations, and the effects of government actions on those organizations. The need for understanding terrorist organizations is highlighted by the fact that such groups' calculations are based on their perceptions of costs and rewards, not those of the authorities who confront them or of objective observers.

So called get-tough measures against terrorist groups can have unintended consequences. Trying to decapitate a movement may radicalize the whole movement or some splinter faction. Assassinations and military force can provoke a desire for revenge, and raids and arrests can reinforce martial images, create mythologies of martyrdom, and feed paranoia and secretiveness (which makes the movements even harder to penetrate for reasons of either understanding motivations or foiling actions). Success in combating terrorism in one place may merely push it to another region. After the assassination of Egyptian President Anwar Sadat, Egyptian authorities cracked down on the Egyptian Islamic Jihad group. Many of its members fled Egypt and joined forces with Osama bin Laden's al Qaeda organization, becoming bin Laden's chief lieutenants. Success in routing al Qaeda fighters from Afghanistan pushed the organization into Pakistan, Yemen, Sudan, and Somalia.

In the event that organizations are primarily motivated by a desire for recognition, how should policy makers respond? Should the government recognize the organizations and eliminate their motivation for terrorism? Because terrorist actions most often are considered newsworthy events by media organizations, governments cannot control whether the actions garner attention. Governments can play an effective role, however, in influencing how terrorist events are portrayed to the public and thus influence (but not control) how the public interprets those events.

Public opinion is important because it can determine the amount of financial and operational support the terrorists enjoy. In some cases, support comes from abroad and is difficult for governments to control. In other cases, governments have control over populations that are sympathetic to the terrorists. In this event, they must walk a difficult line. On the one hand, repressive measures can encourage antigovernment hostility and support for the terrorists. On the other hand, fear of punishment for the terrorists' excesses can undermine a population's willingness to support terrorist activities. In this balance, the terrorists have two weapons on their side. The first is their ability to mete out punishment against those who do not support their actions, and the second is their ability to build on group solidarity to overcome reservations about their methods.

One effective tactic against many terrorist organizations may be to promote their disintegration from the inside. Governments can demonstrate to such groups that their support among the populations they supposedly represent is waning. Even where such allegations are true, however, groups may resolutely believe they enjoy support even after it has dissipated.

Governments can also try to split off members from a group either by offering large rewards for information that undermines group solidarity or by making promises of leniency for imprisoned group members. Finally, governments can unilaterally enact reforms that reduce public support for the terrorists without rewarding the terrorists directly, or they may choose to negotiate with terrorist leaders.

Another tactic may be to put pressure on states that are sympathetic to a terrorist group's goals, even if the states are not outright sponsors of the group. Expulsion from a haven often causes financial pressures or logistical difficulties and can sometimes end a group's viability. In many cases, however, affected countries lack the necessary ties to effect such pressure, or laws that govern free expression make it difficult to crack down on an organization's activities.

If the efforts to eliminate a terrorist group through compulsion fail, however, governments are left trying to reach a peaceful settlement with that group. In civil conflicts, such a settlement usually entails negotiations for amnesty of both individuals and the group. In trying negotiations, governments must confront opposition on two fronts: from the group's rank-and-file members, who may be more disposed toward violence than the leadership; and from the inside—that is, from their own populations, who may oppose the government sitting down with killers and "rewarding violence." Groups that are opposed to a peaceful reconciliation will act to undermine the peace, often by undertaking terrorist actions of their own, as has been the case in the peace process in Northern Ireland. In this event, governments that have only a precarious grip on power will find it difficult to move decisively toward peace.

In addition, governments must time their peace overtures carefully: first, by making such gestures when their ability to reward good behavior and punish bad is strong; and second, by making them when the terrorist organization is going through some period of internal questioning. In such situations, effective intelligence can be crucial in identifying auspicious times for a peaceful gesture and in defining the context of that gesture. Yet lack of timely intelligence is often cited as the crux of the problem.

CONCLUSIONS: CONSIDER THE CONTEXT

Deciding when to employ what strategy is one of the hardest problems facing government officials who deal with terrorism.[41] There is no single solution. Governments must carefully consider the nature of their terrorism problem in context. Negotiations with those who are perpetrating violence are not the solution to every problem. By the same token, many terrorist campaigns cannot be stopped by military or law enforcement actions alone. Many people suggest that a decisive factor that determines the effectiveness of law enforcement activities is the support that the terrorist groups enjoy among their base. Narrowly based terrorist groups can be rooted out, but groups that rely on a broad base of support (some of them from beyond a nation's borders) have a durability that may defy such efforts. For that reason, ethnically based groups may be harder than class-based groups to eliminate through force because ethnicity has proven a stronger tie than class in most cases.

If negotiations are pursued, then two conditions should be present. First, the government should enjoy a strong popular mandate. Political opponents often portray negotiating with terrorists as "giving in" to terrorism. Such an attack can topple a weak government or, short of that, block whatever agreement has been reached through negotiations. Second, the terrorist organization should be undergoing a period of self-evaluation. In such a circumstance, the government may be able to successfully split off pragmatists from hardline terrorists, bring the population along with the pragmatists, and dry up popular support for those who continue to pursue violence.

Intelligence is important throughout. In confronting terrorism, the nature of the grievance does matter, as does the nature of the organization that puts forth the grievance. Intelligence is important not only to prevent terrorist attacks but also to understand how the organization works and how its decision-making processes can be affected. Because terrorism is global, intelligence becomes an almost intractable problem. How can intelligence collection, analysis, and dissemination be conducted or shared globally? This is resisted by sovereign states.

Terrorism is an international problem and therefore requires policies that go beyond unilateral state actions. Money and weapons flow across borders, and supporters of terrorism (if not the terrorists themselves) often have established bases in other countries. Increasingly, law enforcement efforts aimed at stemming terrorism have an international component, and such a strategy will only require more international cooperation in the future. The nature of the terrorists' grievances matters. Although political violence by itself can rarely achieve its aims, it can sometimes do so in conjunction with less violent political action. By the same token, deterring terrorism and prosecuting terrorists may be insufficient to end terrorism, especially when a large population supports the terrorists' cause. In this regard, the war on terrorism may be as unsuccessful as the war on drugs if efforts to curtail terrorism focus exclusively on military, defensive, and law enforcement approaches. Without addressing underlying factors of what terrorists are fighting for, where they draw their strength from, and how to address their grievances or separate organizations from their base, it will be difficult to manage or end terrorism. The means and targets of terrorism may be global, but grievances are often still local, ensuring that governments will need to use a range of responses to manage networked terror.

Which measures are chosen will depend on the nature of the terrorist threat as well as the domestic political context. The diffusion of power in democratic governments poses a challenge for formulating and coordinating policy.[42] In addition, democracies generally promote the idea of protection of the rights of the individual, bringing pressure on governments to respond to terrorist attacks on innocent civilians. "Democracies can survive the assassinations of leaders . . . but they cannot tolerate public insecurity."[43] However, choosing a response must be tempered by the fact that no democratic regime has ever been conquered by terrorism. Terrorists often miscalculate. Their attacks may rally support for their opponent and strengthen rather than undermine the power of the state. The magnitude of terrorist destruction must also be considered in context. Terrorist destruction "is small compared not only to other forms of political violence such as civil wars or communal rioting but also to other sources of casualties in modern societies."[44] This is particularly true after September 11. The public perception of risk from terrorism generally far exceeds the reality. Citizens in developed countries are more likely to die from firearms or car accidents than from terrorism. In 2007, 41,059 Americans died in traffic accidents.[45] Citizens in developing countries are more likely to die from tuberculosis, malaria, or AIDS than from terrorism. The spread of democracy and global media make open societies more vulnerable to terrorist attacks and place great pressure on governments to respond. Yet in choosing a response, democracies must be careful not to overreact. In fighting the war on terrorism, we must not become more like our opponents than we would like and less able to address the underlying vulnerabilities and grievances of globalization that can fuel terrorism.[46]

ENDNOTES

1. Chen Hsinchun and Cathy Larson, "The Dark Web Terrorism Research Project," University of Arizona Artificial Intelligence Lab, <http://ai.arizona.edu/research/terror/index.htm>; Weimann, Gabriel, "Using the Internet for Terrorist Recruitment and Mobilization," in Boaz Ganor, Katharina Von Knop, and Carlos Duarte (Eds.), *Hypermedia Seduction for Terrorist Recruiting* NATO Science for Peace and Security Series Vol. 25, (Fairfax, VA: IOS Press, 2007), 47–58; U.S. Army Intelligence, "Al Qaeda's Use of Web to Mobile Technologies," October 16, 2008, <http://www.fas.org/irp/eprint/mobile.pdf>; Steve Coll and Susan B. Glasser, "Terrorists Turn to the Web as Base of Operations," *The Washington Post* (August 7, 2005): A01.

2. Craig Whitlock, "Briton Used the Internet as His Bully Pulpit," *The Washington Post* (August 8, 2005): A01.

3. Terrence McKenna, "Trail of a Terrorist," Transcript of Frontline documentary, Public Broadcasting Service [PBS], October 25, 2001, <www.pbs.org/wgbh/pages/frontline/shows/trail/etc/script.html>; Ahmed Ressam testimony in July 2001 as a witness for the prosecution at the New York trial of coconspirator Mokhtar Haouari, federal district court of the Southern District of New York, <www.pbs.org/wgbh/pages/frontline/shows/trail/inside/testimony.html>.

4. McKenna, "Trail of a Terrorist"; Ahmed Ressam testimony, July 2001.

5. McKenna, "Trail of a Terrorist." 4. Ibid.; Ahmed Ressam testimony, July 2001.

6. Ibid.

7. Vernon Loeb, "Terrorists Plotted Jan. 2000," *The Washington Post* (December 24, 2000): A01; *Frontline*, "Other Millennium Plots," PBS, October 25, 2001, <www.pbs.org/wgbh/pages/frontline/shows/trail/inside/attacks.html>.

8. McKenna, "Trail of a Terrorist." Ressam later recanted his statements implicating other terror suspects. Associated Press, "Judge Affirms 'Millennium Bomber' Sentence," Dec. 3, 2008, <http://www.msnbc.msn.com/id/28028799/>

9. Martha Crenshaw, "Terrorism in Context," in Martha Crenshaw (Ed.), *Terrorism in Context* (University Park: Pennsylvania State University Press, 1995).

10. Maryann Cusimano Love, "Globalization, Ethics, and the War on Terrorism," *Notre Dame Journal of Law, Ethics, & Public Policy* (Violence in America issue, 2002): 65–80; Maryann Cusimano Love, "Morality Matters: Ethics, Power, Politics, and the War on Terrorism," *Georgetown Journal of International Affairs* (Summer–Fall 2002): 7–16.

11. Martha Crenshaw, "Organized Disorder: Terrorism, Politics, and Society," in Ray C. Rist (Ed.), *The Democratic Imagination* (New Brunswick, NJ: Transaction Publishers, 1994), 140.

12. Ibid., 141.

13. Ibid., 143.

14. Saint Augustine, *City of God*. Translated by Thomas Merton. (New York: Modern Library Paperback Classics, 2000).

15. Cusimano Love, "Globalization, Ethics, and the War on Terrorism," 65–80; Cusimano Love, "Morality Matters."

16. Martha Crenshaw, *Terrorism and International Cooperation* (New York: Institute for East-West Security Studies; Boulder, CO: Westview, 1989), 6–7.

17. Crenshaw, "Organized Disorder," 150.

18. Ibid., 143–144.

19. Martha Crenshaw, "Why America? The Globalization of Civil War," *Current History* (December 2001): 425.

20. RAND, "Mumbai Terror Attacks Show Rise of Strategic Terrorist Culture," January 16, 2009, <http://www.rand.org/news/press/2009/01/16/>; Crenshaw, "Organized Disorder," 143.

21. United Nations, "International Convention for the Suppression of the Financing of Terrorism," December 9, 1999, <http://untreaty.un.org/English/tersumen.htm#4>.

22. Jonathan R. White, *Terrorism and Homeland Security* (Belmont, CA: Wadsworth, 2005), 12.

23. U.S. Department of State, *Country Reports on Terrorism 2008* (Washington, DC: U.S. Government Printing Office, April 27, 2009); available at < http://www.state.gov/s/ct/rls/crt/2008/122450>.

24. Crenshaw, *Terrorism and International Cooperation*, 8.

25. Maryann Cusimano Love, "Broken Promises," *America* (May 14, 2007); Senator Patrick Leahy, "The Material Support Bar: Denying Refuge to the Persecuted?" Senate Judiciary Committee, Subcommittee on Human Rights and the Law, September 19, 2007.

26. Irving Louis Horowitz, "Political Terrorism and State Power," *Journal of Political and Military Sociology* (Spring 1973): 145–157.

27. Cusimano Love, "Globalization, Ethics, and the War on Terrorism," 65–80.

28. Crenshaw, "Why America?" 425.

29. Peter L. Bergen, *Holy War, Inc.: Inside the Secret World of Bin Laden* (New York: Free Press, 2001), 6.

30. It is ironic that Afghan rebel leader Ahmad Shah Massoud, an ardent opponent of the Taliban government and the al Qaeda camps in his country, was later assassinated by opponents disguised as a camera crew.

31. Bergen, *Holy War, Inc.*, 23.

32. Prime Minister Tony Blair, "Prime Minister's Statement, Bloody Sunday Inquiry," House of Commons Official Report (January 29, 1998), Parliamentary Debates (Hansard) (London); available at <www.bloody-Sunday-inquiry.org.uk/index2.asp?p=7>.

33. Paul Wilkinson, "The Orange and the Green," in Martha Crenshaw (Ed.), *Terrorism, Legitimacy and Power* (Middletown, CT: Wesleyan University Press, 1983), 117.

34. Maryann Cusimano Love, Public Private Partnerships and Global Problems: Y2K and Cybercrime. Paper delivered at International Studies Association, Hong Kong meeting, July 2001; Calvin Sims, "Japan Software Suppliers Linked to Sect," *The New York Times* (March 2, 2000): A6.

35. Wilkinson, "The Orange and the Green," 120.

36. This section is derived from Cusimano Love, "Globalization, Ethics, and the War on Terrorism," 65–80.

37. Stephen Flynn, "Homeland Insecurity," *The American Interest* (May/June 2009); *The Edge of Disaster: Building a Resilient Nation.* (New York: Random House, 2007); Stephen E. Flynn, *America the Vulnerable: How Our Government Is Failing to Protect Us from Terrorism* (New York: Harper Collins/Perennial, 2005); Stephen E. Flynn, *The Age of Disaster: Terror, Catastrophe, and the Unmaking of a Great Nation* (New York: Random House, 2006).

38. Ibid.

39. This section is drawn from Martha Crenshaw, *How Terrorism Ends* (Washington, DC: U.S. Institute of Peace, May 25, 1999); available at <www.usip.org/oc/sr/sr990525/sr990525.html>.

40. U.S. Department of State, Patterns of Global Terrorism 2000.

41. This section is drawn from Crenshaw, *How Terrorism Ends.*

42. Martha Crenshaw, "Counterterrorism Policy and the Political Process," *Studies in Conflict & Terrorism* (October 2001): 329–337.

43. Crenshaw, "Organized Disorder," 149; Irving Louis Horowitz, "The Routinization of Terrorism and Its Unanticipated Consequences," in Martha Crenshaw (Ed.), *Terrorism, Legitimacy, and Power* (Middletown, CT: Wesleyan University Press, 1983).

44. Crenshaw, "Organized Disorder," 145.

45. U.S. Department of Transportation, National Highway Traffic Safety Administration, "2007 Traffic Safety Annual Assessment."

46. Cusimano Love, "Globalization, Ethics, and the War on Terrorism," 65–80; Cusimano Love, "Morality Matters," 7–16.

CHAPTER SIX

Global Crime Inc.

Louise Shelley, John Picarelli, and Chris Corpora

Afghanistan's poppies are deadly. Afghanistan supplies over 93% of the lucrative global market in opiates. Heroin is one of the world's most valuable commodities; the U.S. Drug Enforcement Administration estimates a ton of heroin costs between $360 million and $900 million in New York, more valuable than oil or gold by many orders of magnitude. At this writing, crude oil is selling for under $300 a ton, and gold for $30 million a ton. These narco-profits fund sophisticated weapons, training, and soldiers for al Qaeda terrorists, the Taliban, and local and regional warlords, and make governing Afghanistan difficult to impossible.[1] Drugs are smuggled out of Afghanistan through Iran, Pakistan, Tajisktan, and other neighbor countries, creating problems of violence and addiction all along the opium trail en route to markets in Europe and the United States; Iran is the world's worst abuser of opium; opiates are also the most abused drugs in populous India, China, and Malaysia.

"The fight against drugs is actually the fight for Afghanistan," said Afghan President Hamid Karzai when he took office in 2002. The Afghanistan National Development Strategy for the 2008–2013 period aims to cut the illegal economy while growing the legal economy through crop replacement and other economic development strategies; this is difficult to do in practice. Opium poppies grown in just 7 provinces of Afghanistan account for 97% of all Afghanistan's poppy crop. But fighting the opium trade is dangerous; deaths of poppy eradication workers in Afghanistan increased sixfold in 2008.[2]

Steve MacQueen, the Chief of the World Bank's Microfinance Investment and Support Facility for Afghanistan, found this out when he stepped out of a bar called the Elbow Room and into his Ministry of Rural Rehabilitation's 4-wheel-drive vehicle one chilly Monday evening in March 2005. This was meant to be his last week in Kabul, but it turned out to be his last few moments of life.[3] MacQueen oversaw the World Bank project aimed at converting poppy farms into other, legal activities. The Ministry of Rural Rehabilitation was universally understood to be the financial arm of the opium eradication efforts in Afghanistan, and MacQueen embodied an activity many resisted. It is nearly impossible to know who drove the two black Toyota Landcruisers that approached MacQueen in expert fashion and boldly killed the 41-year-old directly in front of the Dutch Embassy. The complexity of determining the actual killers, or those who had arranged for the murder, stems from the transnational nature of the opium trade in Afghanistan.[4] The poppy trade has long been a crucial commodity for raising much-needed funds for forming necessary strategic alliances across the divided country. These activities clearly crossed the borders of the shattered country in the early 1990s, when Afghanistan jumped past Myanmar as the world's largest opium exporter.[5] This tainted success could come only with the corrupt support of government officials, within and surrounding Afghanistan, and with a growing international smuggling interest that was finding new access in the post-Soviet North. The threat MacQueen and his activities posed to the multibillion-dollar transnational trade in heroin went deeper than the fledgling Afghan Anti-Narcotics Teams, which were already limited by corruption, or the solemn rhetoric of many international leaders.[6] MacQueen represented a true and direct threat that could cause international traffickers' business costs to rise, which would in turn shrink the funds available for bribes and equipment. The message sent through MacQueen's assassination could have come from any number of entities threatened by the program he oversaw: narcotics-funded Taliban, Pakistani-trained terrorists, Central Asian smugglers, or corrupt government officials whose wealth and power would be compromised by the program's success. Each of these potential instigators exemplifies the complex nature and challenge of transnational organized crime and corruption to legitimate, transparent governance and security; the rule of law and a vibrant civil society; and regional development. It also explains why this purposefully public and violent crime remains unsolved.[7] The UK Select Committee on Foreign Affairs, in its Sixth Annual Report of 2005 on Afghanistan, suggested that the lack of resolution in the MacQueen affair, and other kidnappings and murders linked to the Afghan drug trade, demonstrated the pervasive nature, power, and close cooperation of the criminal organizations and corrupt public institutions and officials involved.[8]

TRANSNATIONAL ORGANIZED CRIME: DIFFERENT VIEWS

The *global Mafia*, the *next war*, the *pax mafiosi*, the *dark side of globalization*, the *illicit global economy*, the *retreat of the state*—all are recent terms and expressions in the literature of world politics that describe the appearance of transnational organized crime. However, such crime has a lineage that scholars have traced back to the times of pirates on the high seas and the African slave trade. So is this a new phenomenon or something that scholars of world politics have just begun to notice and explore? Furthermore, what makes the phenomenon "transnational"? Finally, what is the significance of using a term such as *transnational* or, in the context of this volume, *transsovereign*?

These are valid and often asked questions about the study of transnational organized crime. In the span of some 2 decades, practitioners and scholars alike have begun to explore and analyze the different activities and processes that compose the phenomenon, developing and revising definitions as they go along. Furthermore, especially in the scholarly realm, we have attempted to explain transnational criminal groups, focusing both within the traditional analytical unit of world politics—the state—as well as the state system. Finally, we have sought to identify objects and methods for responding to these criminal enterprises. This chapter will address these important issues while engaging the debates throughout the literature. It concludes by fashioning a framework for composing strategy that will respond to transnational organized crime.

TRANSNATIONAL ORGANIZED CRIME

Over the past 2 decades, scholarship that addresses the phenomenon of transnational organized crime has blossomed. This has accompanied analyses of globalization and the fact that transnational criminals are major beneficiaries of globalization. In the 1990s, the scholarly literature began a more serious focus on transnational organized crime as a phenomenon unto itself, whereas earlier literature had focused on domestic organized crime or organized criminal activities that span borders, such as the trafficking of narcotics. The scholars and practitioners who have contributed to this growing corpus of knowledge have sought to answer fundamental questions: What is transnational organized crime? Why the label *transnational* versus others such as *international*? What kinds of activities compose this area of inquiry? In what ways does transnational organized crime interact with the state? What kinds of approaches are most appropriate for examining transnational organized crime? Each question leads us to important answers that affect the ways we view and approach world politics.

Definitional Issues

One of the first major issues that researchers and practitioners tackled was defining transnational organized crime. The United Nations established the term *transnational crime* more than 25 years ago, but it was a catchall term that incorporated some 18 categories of activity, including terrorism and hijacking, alongside organized crime activities.[9] The distinction between domestic forms of organized crime and transnational organized crime developed from the increased study of narcotics trafficking and the growth in organized crime operating across international borders during the 1980s. The generation of a definition had to overcome traditional and novel hurdles ranging from the minimum number of individuals in a group to the basis for considering a group a transnational criminal entity—decisions that greatly affect the inclusiveness of the definition.

The definition of organized crime has evolved, reflecting the increasing complexity and international nature of the phenomenon. One of the first definitions of organized crime came from U.S. law enforcement, primarily the Federal Bureau of Investigation (FBI), which states that organized crime is "continuing and self-perpetuating criminal conspiracy, having an organized structure, fed by fear and corruption, and motivated by greed."[10] With time, the FBI began to use this definition to describe what it referred to as *international organized crime*—that is, organized crime groups operating in more than one country. Note, however, that this definition retains the notion of organized crime operating internationally, and it does not seek to identify the criminal activity as a transnational phenomenon.

Thinking of crime as transnational better illustrates the ways in which these criminal organizations seek to operate outside of the state system— in essence, transcending the sovereignty that organizes the modern state system and leveraging it for their own gain. One of the first to make this distinction was Phil Williams, who in 1996 demonstrated that organized crime was recasting itself by leveraging the changes in global political economy and society being rendered by globalization and the technology revolution.[11] What resulted were criminal organizations that came to "resemble transnational corporations" that operated across the globe from a home base using networked structures to perpetuate their activities, all the while seeing borders as hindering law enforcement more than their own activities.[12]

More recently, the United Nations Convention on Transnational Organized Crime sought to provide a unified definition that is likely to serve as the benchmark for identifying transnational criminal organizations:

> "Organized criminal group" shall mean a structured group of three or more persons, existing for a period of time and acting in concert with the aim of committing one or more serious crimes or offences established in accordance with this Convention, in order to obtain, directly or indirectly, a financial or other material benefit. "Serious crime" shall mean conduct constituting an offence punishable by a maximum deprivation of liberty of at least four years or a more serious penalty. "Structured group" shall mean a group that is not randomly formed for the immediate commission of an offence and that does not need to have formally defined roles for its members, continuity of its membership or a developed structure. ... [A]n offence is transnational in nature if: (a) It is committed in more than one state; (b) It is committed in one state but a substantial part of its preparation, planning, direction or control takes place in another state; (c) It is committed in one state but involves an organized criminal group that engages in criminal activities in more than one state; or (d) It is committed in one state but has substantial effects in another state.[13]

The United Nations' definition is one of the most comprehensive, addressing the issue of size, duration, and the transnational nature of criminal groups. Furthermore, it provides the flexibility to examine transnational organized crime outside of such traditional ethnic groups as the Russian Mafiya, Chinese Triads, Japanese Yakuza, and Italian Mafia families.

Transnational Criminal Activities

Transnational criminal activity involves a broad range of activities in both the legitimate and illegitimate sectors of the economy. The associated activities of money laundering and corruption are vital to the conduct of transnational organized crime because criminals need to dispose of their profits and to neutralize law enforcement and facilitate their illicit transactions.

Some criminal groups function primarily in the illegitimate sector, such as drug trafficking groups, and arms and human smugglers, whereas others span both sectors of the economy searching for high profits. The massive privatizations of the 1990s have given many transnational organized crime groups a large and important foothold in the economies of their home countries and in many others. This occurred in Colombia, Mexico, the former Soviet Union, and many Eastern European countries. In the financial crisis that began in 2008, organized crime groups stand to benefit significantly because they were excluded from banks and financial markets after 9/11 when strict regulations were placed on financial institutions regarding receipt of criminal profits. Holding large amounts of cash, they are in the position to hire many unemployed, to buy businesses at bargain prices, and to influence the political leadership of key states.

TYPES OF CRIMINAL ACTIVITIES

Experts and practitioners have identified more than a dozen criminal activities engaged in by transnational criminal organizations. The major component of most of these activities is smuggling of diverse commodities and the provision of illicit goods and services. Narcotics trafficking is the most common and profitable activity. Many organizations and countries cite narcotics trafficking as the most significant transnational organized crime in terms of annual profits.

Furthermore, scholars such as Pino Arlacchi have demonstrated that narcotics trafficking has often served as the gateway for domestic organized crime groups to enter the transnational realm.[14] Hence, it comes as no surprise that the drug trade is often cited as the most commonly known transnational organized criminal activity. Important regional criminal actors such as Colombia and Mexico now operate on a global scale with numerous international connections.[15]

The next most significant transnational organized crimes are trafficking in persons and in arms. An important distinction characterizes these forms of organized crime. Arms deliveries involve the transfer of inanimate goods that are used to commit other crimes or to arm regional conflicts. In contrast, trafficking in persons involves the movement of live human beings who are exploited continuously after their delivery. Likewise, human trafficking provides ongoing revenues for transnational organized crime, whereas the arms trade, if it is to be sustained, requires the perpetuation of conflict.

Trafficking in persons and migrant smuggling, a similar activity that does not incorporate the pernicious aspects of slavery, both involve the recruitment, movement, and delivery of migrants from a host to a destination state. The profits from such activities are significant and believed to be rising—a recent FBI estimate placed the annual profits of trafficking in persons at $9.5 billion.[16] Crafting even inexact estimates of the number of people trafficked annually is difficult at best, and thus few solid estimates exist. Yet most every expert on trafficking in persons—practitioner and scholar alike—agrees that the problem is significant and increasing as both demand and supply are rising. The rise in demand for cheap services and labor in developed countries and the growth of population in developing countries without adequate employment will result in a rise in this phenomenon in coming decades.

Trafficking and smuggling in persons is pernicious because of both the large profits and the physical and emotional toll it takes on the victims. Numerous trafficking studies note the physical violence and mental strain that victims suffer at the hands of their captors. For example, it is not uncommon for these victims to become addicted to alcohol or narcotics, contract HIV and AIDS or other diseases, or die from strain or violence. Those that do survive often face difficult and time-consuming recoveries.

The fact that transnational criminal organizations are increasingly gravitating toward the trafficking in persons as a source of profits is even more pernicious as it is these groups that have a profound interest in perpetuating the trade in persons. A range of transnational criminal organizations are trafficking in persons, particularly Chinese and Taiwanese, Thai, Indian, Pakistani, Japanese, Russian-speaking, and Balkan organized crime groups.[17] Indeed, Shelley has identified at least 5 business models for trafficking syndicates globally, and another study highlights the integration of trafficking and smuggling enterprises in organized crime's portfolio.[18]

None of this activity can function without the complicity of some law enforcement and the corruption of officials in source, transit, and destination countries. This telling quote from Kevin Bales also applies outside the Thai context: "To be sure, a brothel owner may have some ties to organized crime, but in Thailand organized crime includes the police and much of the government. Indeed, the work of the modern slaveholder is best seen not as aberrant criminality but as a perfect example of disinterested capitalism."[19]

Arms trafficking is another significant form of transnational organized crime. The rise of regional conflicts in the postwar era has provided transnational organized crime groups with a huge market for small arms. In some cases, transnational organized crime groups help foment regional conflict to increase demand for weapons.[20] This has been particularly true in Africa but also applies in the Balkans, Latin America, and Asia. Many of the weapons come from former Soviet states and Eastern Europe. The trafficking in arms has also led to an insidious partnership between military forces and Mafia groups, especially in the post-Soviet transition states of Eastern Europe and the former Soviet Union. Graham Turbiville, Jr., for example, outlines the ways in which organized crime and the Russian military coalesced after the end of the Soviet Union, going so far as to refer to the Russian armed forces as mafia in uniform.[21]

Transnational criminal organizations have found a niche supplying arms to areas suffering from continued conflict with small arms and even major arms systems. Organized crime has also positioned itself as the arms supplier of last resort, oftentimes delivering arms to regions under arms embargo. For example, in April 2001, Italian authorities arrested members of a Russian and Ukrainian criminal network that, for more than 7 years, had supplied more than 13,500 tons of arms, including thousands of assault rifles and hundreds of missiles and antitank shells, to groups fighting in the Balkans, including the Croatian army.[22] Italian authorities then dismantled a similar Russian organized crime controlled network soon afterward that was supplying arms to Charles Taylor's forces in Sierra Leone.[23] The problem is very apparent in the Caucasus where the smuggling of arms and other commodities has prolonged the conflict in Abkhazia and Ossetia regions. In both areas, border controls are weak and individuals guarding the borders are profiting significantly from the trafficking of contraband. This contraband, comprised of both arms and different commodities, makes it difficult to solve these conflicts.[24] In 2008, Thai authorities arrested Viktor Bout, a notorious arms trafficker identified as an arms supplier to conflicts in Africa and Colombia.[25]

The largest profits for organized crime have been in the small weapons area, but the threat of organized crime trafficking in nuclear materials and biological and chemical weapons remains a major concern. This became ever more apparent after the arrest of Oleg Khintsagov in Georgia trying to sell weapons-grade nuclear material.[26] Richard Love has identified organized crime as a potential facilitator for the theft and smuggling of strategic weapons and materials.[27] In the end, transnational organized crime involvement in arms smuggling is a major concern for states and international organizations concerned with maintaining international security and peace.

Smuggling and trade-related transnational criminal activities are a major profit source for transnational organized crime. For example, trade in cigarettes, once a national trade, has been internationalized by transnational criminal groups, who have worked with legitimate cigarette manufacturers to obtain their commodities. These links between crime groups and legitimate corporations have been the subject of major criminal investigations within the European community.[28] Since these investigations, there has been an effort by some cigarette manufacturers to vigorously fight this illicit trade. Such illicit trade also thrives across the U.S.–Canadian border where the territories of Native Americans are used to evade traditional border controls.[29] All too often this trade is tied to the financing of terrorism.[30]

Furthermore, organized crime groups are important actors internationally in the illicit trade in environmental products, ranging from banned chlorofluorocarbon-based refrigerants to toxic waste, and even endangered fauna and flora.[31] Likewise, scholars have identified transnational organized crime as a player in the theft and smuggling of art and antiquities and have linked the latter to international money laundering.[32] The thefts from the Iraqi Museum, many of which were unregistered antiquities, provided money for the skilled thieves who were able to smuggle the antiquities out of the country.[33] These antiquities could then be translated into cash once they had been sold to collectors outside the country. Finally, there is the smuggling of stolen automobiles, an activity that is especially prevalent in Central Europe and the southwestern United States.[34] Roughly $1 billion worth of stolen vehicles are removed from the United States annually and sent to other countries.[35] The theft of vehicles exists in Asia as well. Stolen Japanese vehicles are transported to Russia for sale in the Far East and parts of Siberia.[36]

The return of a trade-related organized criminal activity that many had thought was relegated to the past—the piracy of ships in international waters—also involves the activities of transnational criminal organizations. The coast of Somalia has become a major focal point of piracy with the seizure of ships with oil and arms and their ransoming for enormous profits for the criminals.[37]

Pirating now benefits from cheaply available global technologies. "One pirate ship captured recently in Indonesia was outfitted with bogus immigration stamps, tools to forge ship documents, and sophisticated radar, communications, and satellite-tracking equipment."[38] According to the Piracy Reporting Center (PRC) of the International Chamber of Commerce International Maritime Bureau, piracy in 2008 surpassed all figures for hijacked vessels and hostages taken recorded by the PRC since it began its worldwide reporting function in 1992.[39] Organized crime is closely linked to these incidents, either conducting the piracy itself or supporting piracy. The benefits for the organized crime groups are significant as they can move cargo and illegal immigrants and engage in insurance fraud.

The problem is most pronounced in Asia but also is common in Latin America and Africa. The crime groups are increasingly focusing on the theft of high-technology cargo.[40] Hijacking of cargo is not confined to the sea. Analysts have identified transnational organized crime involvement in the theft of land-based cargo, such as hijackings of truck and rail cargo.[41]

Increasingly, analysts have documented links between transnational organized crime and terrorism. Although it is clear that international terrorist organizations have routinely used organized crime tactics to raise money and move equipment and personnel, it was historically rare to find an alliance between groups separately motivated by economics and politics.[42] However, some recent studies on Abu Sayyaf, Islamic Jihad, and Hizb-I Islami Gulbuddin (HIG) suggest that these activities overlap increasingly beyond convenient opportunities. The conflict in Afghanistan has revealed the importance of the drug trade for the funding of the re-emergent Taliban.[43]

Many significant transnational criminal activities are now linked to the licit economy. Fraud scams originating in western Africa, primarily Nigeria, use official-looking fax and e-mail correspondence to obtain banking information from victims that is then used to steal funds from their accounts.[44] Transnational criminal organizations have also engaged in massive credit card and identity theft rings using stolen account numbers and identities to amass millions in fraudulent charges. Arrests in Spain of members of a terrorist cell revealed that they supported themselves by producing fraudulent documents and airplane tickets.[45] Al Qaeda profited from heroin trafficking. The MacQueen assassination was only one act of violence aimed at challenging the slow-starting international anti-narcotics effort in Afghanistan. Slowly, international institutions are beginning to understand the depth and breadth of the Afghan poppy problem—ranging far beyond an Afghan-centric drug cultivation issue into international terrorism and regional politics. Therefore, organized crime for profit not only is the domain of criminals who seek profits but also is being used by politically motivated groups.

Crime groups cash counterfeit checks, trade in bearer bonds, and manipulate the stock market in the United States, Canada, and Italy. Asian organized crime groups operating in Las Vegas were earning close to $500,000 monthly from the cashing of counterfeit checks in casinos.[46] Finally, some organized crime groups in the United States have recently infiltrated the U.S. stock markets, purchasing or creating their own brokerage houses to engage in "pump and dump" and other types of stock manipulations for illicit gains. For example, a scandal occurred in Canadian markets with the manipulation of stocks by Russian organized crime in the metals trade. Italian organized crime, according to Italian investigators, is now also active in market manipulation.[47]

Violence and corruption, the traditional methods of organized crime once applied on the local level, are now being applied internationally. Protection rackets, the backbone of domestic organized crime groups, have been retained as an important activity for transnational criminal organizations, who also frequently engage in contract killings for profit or power projection. For example, the use of violence for protection rackets and other purposes is referred to as the *defining characteristic* of Asian organized crime groups operating in the United States.[48] Furthermore, Russian-speaking organized crime groups have used threats of violence to extort Russian hockey players in the National Hockey League.[49] Contract killers have been sent from Russia to carry out their hits and returned home after carrying out their missions. The violence from Mexico spills across the border reaching many locales in the United States.[50]

A significant area of growth for transnational criminal activity is within the realm of information and high technology. Just as pirates are now focusing on high-technology cargo, criminals are realizing high profits from pursuing the hardware of technology, and their Internet schemes reveal their capacity to engage in cybercrime.[51] For example, John Picarelli and Phil Williams have identified several ways criminals can use information technology as a criminal milieu, as a tool, and even as a weapon to further their activities.[52] Likewise, a conference that examined the ways in which organized crime, terrorist, and other groups use information technology noted that such technology can assist in the conduct of traditional criminal activities as well as serve as the gateway to new criminal endeavors. For example, panelists noted that Nigerian criminal gangs were abandoning fax machines and using e-mail in their elaborate fraud schemes, and that criminal groups were becoming increasingly involved in the piracy of intellectual property such as compact discs and computer software.[53] Finally, Richard Love notes in Chapter 9 how criminal organizations are operating online rather than in the bricks and mortar world.

ACTIVITIES THAT SUPPORT TRANSNATIONAL CRIME

Transnational criminal activity cannot survive solely in the illicit realm. Its profits must be moved into the legitimate economy to be invested. Furthermore, it requires corruption to function—to fend off arrests, obtain lucrative contracts, and obtain legitimacy in the community.

Money Laundering

Money laundering is a universal and crucial activity for transnational criminal organizations. The previous section described the numerous methods by which transnational organized crime generates profits. These profits remain useless, however, unless the criminal groups can somehow place them into the licit global financial infrastructure without the knowledge of law enforcement or regulators. Hence, almost all transnational criminal organizations engage in some form of money laundering to dispose of their profits.

Money laundering has increased in both scope and sophistication. Although the estimates of global money laundering have continued to prove difficult to quantify, estimates of $500 billion to $1 trillion annually is a commonly held figure.[54] More anecdotal estimates provide a basis to demonstrate the significant size of money laundering. For example, in 1995 Australian officials estimated that close to $3 billion of laundered funds passed through their country.[55] Canada estimated that laundered funds from the narcotics industry alone accounted for roughly $5–$14 billion annually from Canada.[56]

The methods that money launderers use range from placement in the licit financial sector through phony corporations, bank accounts, and the use of offshore banking centers to less traditional means such as using Internet-based banking and informal banking systems, including the hawala.[57] This informal remittance system is used to move funds into and from South Asia and the Middle East, and it has gained attention because of its uses by terrorist organizations such as al Qaeda.[58] One study showed that because increases in crime have been coupled with a decrease in the demand for currency, money launderers apparently are "moving away from the banking system and cash and toward parallel financial markets, sophisticated nonmonetary instruments (such as derivatives), and possibly barter (such as an exchange of boats and guns for drugs)."[59]

In the end, money laundering is the bridge that connects the illicit and licit global economies. Money laundering uses licit financial markets as a method of transfer and placement for illicit funds. Such activities, more importantly, skew economic indicators and policy in significant ways. Tanzi, for example, demonstrates that large capital inflows and outflows from money laundering affect interest rates, that the demand for dollars from money launderers supports an implicit seigniorage for U.S. currency markets, and that money laundering generates distrust in markets, which then amplifies reactions to rumors or false statements.[60]

International investigations have gone after the proceeds of organized crime. In the United States, drug-related assets seized by the federal government have tripled since 2004, going from $567 million to $1.6 billion annually by 2007. Individual states seize more, with $125 million seized in Texas alone in 2007.[61] In Georgia, a case was discovered involving $1 billion of laundered money in which the money moved through the bank was entirely illicit. The laundered money was the proceeds of organized crime activity from crime groups from the former Soviet Union who were active in crime all over the world.[62]

Extensive money laundering was detected at Riggs Bank, which received the largest fine ever imposed in the United States on a banking institution for money laundering. The bank was disclosed to have laundered money for the dictator of Equatorial Guinea and for former President Pinochet of Chile, and some of the accounts of the Saudi embassy may have facilitated the financing of terrorism. The ease with which Riggs Bank continued to engage in this activity even after the PATRIOT Act was initiated is indicative of the relative ease with which it is still possible to launder money in the United States.[63] But increasingly the money is laundered outside of the banking system, where there is less risk of detection.

Most of the proceeds of the drug trade have gone into the national treasuries of the countries where they have been seized. In Italy, unique legislation authorizes the use of seized assets for community development and drug treatment.[64]

Corruption

Corruption is an important tool for organized crime, and transnational organized crime groups have exploited such relationships with politicians and government officials. Put broadly, corruption is "the misuse of office for personal gain" and "means charging an illicit price for a service or using the power of office to further illicit aims."[65] Corruption differs from clientelism in that the latter retains a vertical separation between the patron and client, and is based on an exchange for unspecified services. Corruption blurs the line between the state and transnational criminal organizations. Some states are so thoroughly corrupt that scholars refer to them as *criminal states*.

Two significant and related phenomena are important for our purposes—political and economic corruption. Political corruption has received strong consideration in the literature. Now the links between political corruption and organized crime also have been analyzed—for example, the differing views on the connections between corruption[66] and political parties.[67]

Economic corruption hinges on the desire for industries to collude and establish cartels within markets, as when firms use organized crime to organize and maintain cartels among them.[68] Recent studies tackle the thorny issue of corruption within the sector of international development aid.[69]

For what ends does organized crime engage in corruption? To answer this question, we refer to the triangular relationship between organized crime, the state (i.e., government), and firms.[70] Organized crime provides electoral support and intimidation powers to politicians in return for protection and legitimization of its activities. Likewise, organized crime provides protection and assistance with cartels in return for money. Finally, an important part of this equation is public contracts, which politicians can use to seek rents from both firms and criminal organizations. In turn, these contracts are a major source of Mafia profits. Hence, corruption is a key factor to consider when we analyze the behavior of transnational criminal organizations.

Along with the necessity to understand the relationship between organized crime and corruption is the need to fully address the broader complex that brings these together in association with terrorism and insurgency. Studies addressing post-conflict environments and organized crime suggest that the merging of these efforts is often found in areas poorly governed or still under the informal control of a faction.[71] The post-Yugoslav conflicts still suffer from the rule of informal political control that finds its support in its ability to generate much-needed funds, employment, and political influence through illicit activities. Often this is a continuation of business as conducted during conflict, as the primary way to obtain materials and personnel and move these in a clandestine manner.[72] Post-conflict Iraq and Afghanistan demonstrate a high correlation with these findings and have given rise to a broader research program—ranging from a postmortem of past conflicts to those only recently coming to an end or protracted pause. Despite the fact that these conflicts are often contained within discrete regions, their impact with regard to transnational organized crime transcends the bounds of the physical conflict.

EXPLAINING TRANSNATIONAL ORGANIZED CRIME

Transnational crime, once neglected in the study of International Relations, is now studied in different parts of the discipline because of its far-reaching effects on political systems, national sovereignty, and international political economy. The relationship between transnational crime and the state is central to this entire analysis. The following section surveys some of the approaches to studying transnational crime. Such crime can be considered from 2 levels of analysis: the community level and the international level with globalization.

A significant difference exists between the strategic studies literature that identifies transnational organized crime as a threat to the industrialized world and world order and the literature that focuses on the societal level at which transnational organized crime operates, shaped by the local community. Whereas organized crime has proliferated with globalization, many of the groups are still deeply entrenched in their home societies where their effects are particularly strong. It is important to consider both aspects when calculating effective responses.

Internal Analysis: Trust and Civil Society

Organized crime usually develops and operates in areas where civil society is weak or nonexistent. For example, in a landmark study, Robert Putnam describes how civil society arose in northern Italy but failed to take hold in southern regions where 4 organized crime groups are based.[73] In another example, Russian-speaking organized crime has emerged with potency in the states of the former Soviet Union where the communists wiped out all elements of civil society.[74]

Other related factors are trust in intrapersonal societal relations and the effects of trust on governance.[75] Weak states have poorly formed civil societies, which leads to a lack of trust in the state and a dependence on surrogate actors to address civic needs. For example, organized crime in Sicily arose when state control was absent; organized crime substituted itself for the state and provided the protection that substituted for trust in society.[76]

Trust and civil society factors help explain how transnational criminal organizations embed themselves within societal structures. A successful response must consider the societal context within which crime groups operate, particularly within the state, and at the local level where they are based. For example, Sicilian society has mobilized against the Mafia for the past century.[77] In recent decades, the movement has mobilized all levels of society simultaneously and has attempted to reeducate citizens at the local level on the need for alternatives to the Mafia. The primary objective of nearly all the anti-Mafia associations is to educate children to know and respect the law and to prevent them from acquiring a "Mafia mentality" of distrust and antagonism toward public institutions—which may lead to a life of crime.[78] Such programs were introduced in the early 1980s by the first anti-Mafia groups but obtained additional impetus in the early 1990s in response to the Anti-Mafia Commission and the pressures of the mass anti-Mafia organizations of civil society. Libera, the umbrella of 800 nationwide anti-Mafia organizations, works with urban communities, schools, and the churches to implement anti-Mafia curricula.[79]

External Analysis: Globalization

Globalization is a key factor in the rise of transnational organized crime. There are several competing notions regarding how to theorize transnationality, marking a different way to configure social spaces.[80] Transnational organized crime cuts across the globalization discourse, ranging from notions of informal markets and new authoritarianism to ideas about global criminal networks.[81] The majority of the globalization literature captures transnational phenomena as dynamic, cross-sectoral, and embedded in global markets, making the concept more than a new level of analysis.

Globalization provides a theoretical boost to historical notions of national or international organized crime, emphasizing the ascendance of nonstate actors as legitimate objects of political inquiry. However, the concept of globalization is far from a settled theory and stirs great debate, ranging from downplay, through social transformation, to near chaos or turbulence.[82]

The categories of state, economics, and institutional structures are useful for capturing the majority of analysis on transnational organized crime in the globalization context. Globalization benefits the capabilities, resources, and strategies that are available to transnational organized crime.

The neoliberal understanding of globalization stresses the role played by global free market capitalism and representative democracy in making the world richer, more connected, and peaceful, as represented in the writings of Francis Fukuyama and traditional political economic interpretations.[83] In this light, transnational organized crime and other similar issues often are seen as the last vestiges of resistance to this "new world order" that eventually will be brought under control.[84]

THE ROLE OF THE STATE

What effects do globalization processes have on the modern state? These academic discussions directly affect our consideration of transnational organized crime. For example, Saskia Sassen posits that globalization is transforming the logic of sovereignty without eliminating the role of the state,[85] a view shared by James Mittelman and James Rosenau. Combined with weak state scenarios, such as Robert Jackson's concept of "negative sovereignty" and Susan Strange's "retreat of the state," these provide the theoretical backbone for analyzing transnational organized crime and corruption in the globalization context.[86] Several scholars have suggested some governments and other formal powers politicize or securitize the term *transnational organized crime* as a way to create political capital to justify further coercive actions.[87] Peter Andreas and Ethan Nadelman provide several cases in which political crimes, like terrorism and sabotage, have been "securitized, desecuritized and resecuritized over time."[88]

Most often, scholars have posited that the weakening of state structures, either caused or enhanced through globalization processes, has created spaces that have allowed transnational organized crime to flourish.[89] Louise Shelley has examined the interplay of weakened states, civil society, and transnational organized crime, viewing criminal groups as taking advantage of new technologies and global opportunities to amplify the weakening of states.[90] Nikos Passas finds that the demise of states is a necessary part of the globalization of organized crime because it erodes the bonds of trust between state and citizenry and provides transnational organized crime with the opportunity to play surrogate for the state.[91] Peter Andreas points out how globalization processes, embodied in the North American Free Trade Agreement (NAFTA), directly affected the increase of transnational organized crime in Mexico by liberalizing markets without sufficient regulation and oversight.[92] The growth of organized crime in Mexico in the period since the adoption of NAFTA has been phenomenal as the illicit has moved along with the licit.

THE ROLE OF THE ECONOMY

The political economic approach addresses how the "illicit global economy" affects the state and the licit economy.[93] For example, the illicit Colombian economy distorts the legal economy.[94] Economic markets shape transnational organized crime, taking organizational form based on the economic context.[95] Transnational business strategies of the illicit actors increasingly mirror those in the licit economy. Specialists such as lawyers, accountants, and transportation experts now work for organized crime as they do for the legitimate economy.[96]

As the share of the international economy controlled by organized crime increases, there will necessarily be more attention to the political economy of the drug trade and other diverse forms of illicit activity. Especially since September 11, the interaction of the illicit and licit economies is receiving greater attention.

HYBRID ANALYSIS: SECURITY STUDIES

The security studies literature views organized crime as a threat. Its involvement in the weapons trade, its deleterious effects on state sovereignty, and its corruption of state structures are seen as serious threats to individual states, regional stability, and the international order. Security scholars have used several methods to explore the threat transnational organized crime poses to people, the nation–state, and global stability. Researchers of the "Copenhagen School" focus on how threats are formed and the effects they have across the social experience,[97] providing a flexible approach for looking at a broader spectrum of threats.[98] The military and state continue to be an important sector, but they are evaluated in conjunction with the economic, societal, and environmental sectors. Transnational organized crime and other negative consequences of globalization are seen as a cross-sectoral threat. Buzan and Waever take this analytic a step further in their recent monograph, breaking out regions and conflicts and applying the analytic to demonstrate its power in helping to understand and explain security complexes.[99] A growing number of security scholars, who focus on asymmetric and nontraditional threats, have advanced concepts and methods suggesting a clearer place for study of organized crime in the security context. K. M. Fierke suggests that organized crime and terrorism are the kinds of issues that force scholars and practitioners to recognize the need to address the individual and the state as potentially threatened and/or the threat in a wide array of complex cases.[100]

However, security experts are increasingly concerned about the linkages between organized crime and other threats like terrorism and proliferation—a view that has obtained more currency since September 11, 2001. A study has concluded that the range of potential cooperation between crime and terror groups is much broader than security planners had once considered.[101] Recent analysis of crime and terror groups demonstrates the spectrum of potential interactions between crime and terror groups as well.[102] Other analyses of these alliances focus on the capacity to acquire and deploy weapons of mass destruction.[103] Others have addressed the growing links between organized crime and terrorist groups.

MULTIPLE APPROACHES ARE NEEDED

Transnational crime operates on the global level but is embedded in many societies at the local level. International policies that address transnational crime at only a single level are doomed to failure. As the previous analysis has indicated, a multidisciplinary perspective is needed to understand trans-national crime—one that incorporates economic, social, political, and strategic studies analyses. Yet these perspectives must also include an understanding of the historical and cultural context that led to the rise of organized crime groups in particular locales. Transnational crime has local and global, and societal and state components. Effective responses to manage transnational crime must deal with each of these elements. Furthermore, new theories, methods, and policies should be developed to address the increasing empirical data suggesting the overlap of issues, such as crime, terror, and proliferation. Traditionally these were studied as separate issues, and the corresponding "counter" activities, were funded through different governmental programs.[104]

Globalization helps to turn once locally and regionally contained phenomena into transnational crime problems. The profits and effects of these groups are so significant in some regions that they pose threats to nation-states and undermine the national sovereignty of many countries. The global illicit trade has assumed massive proportions, and its effects are particularly great in smaller economies where the profits of this illegal trade can undermine and distort the economy. Likely the epitome of this asymmetry is found in Afghanistan, where the narcotics trade represents some 60 percent of the economy and, as the opening anecdote attests, continues to undermine the process of democratization and state-building. An additional 20 percent of the economy is believed to be attributed to the illicit trade in timber and antiquities.[105] For example, tax rates escalate as the size of the illegal economy grows. Because less economic activity is conducted in the sphere where states can levy taxes, states raise rates on the remaining licit economy to recoup lost tax income and sustain government budgets. In a vicious circle, government's attempts to sustain its revenue base can push more businesses into the illicit economy (through fraud, tax evasion, and transfer pricing) to avoid the high tax rates in the licit economy. Weakened state treasuries reduce the resources that are available to states to fight organized crime.

Organized crime is necessarily, in part, a covert phenomenon. Therefore, analysis and information on the phenomenon is partial and often misinterpreted by individuals who do not understand the context in which it functions. Policy makers from one arena—law enforcement, economics, or security studies—often believe that their perspective holds the "answer" without understanding that a multidisciplinary approach is needed.

Effective strategies to control and contain transnational crime cannot address only one aspect. For example, as peacekeepers have discovered in the Balkans, Colombia, and elsewhere, transnational crime groups are now the defining actors in the political environment. Traditional military strategies cannot be used to contain their activities. As anti-Mafia activists have discovered in Sicily, the legal system can prosecute and isolate the Mafia bosses, but civil society must change community attitudes toward organized crime and must prove to the citizens of their island that there are tangible benefits for them in fighting organized crime.[106]

CONCLUSION: A WAY AHEAD?

We propose the following framework for addressing the transnational organized crime problem through a dynamic and multidisciplinary perspective. First, any serious researcher or policy maker must ask the following questions before developing a policy. What is the process of social transformation at play? What unique and general aspects of a particular manifestation of transnational organized crime are present in the local context, and how are they embedded within it? How does the transnational crime group connect with regional, international, and multilateral actors of the legitimate and illegitimate economy? To what extent does the community understand the problems of transnational crime and have the willingness and the capacity to help address the problem? What are the costs on the local, regional, and national level of the group's continued criminality?

Because globalization reshapes both international dynamics and the local community, attempts to manage transnational organized crime must acknowledge both levels. Part of this process of social transformation is that time, space, and boundaries are collapsed or compacted. Relationships on an international scale occur more rapidly and commercial relations are more frequent. The illicit can be facilitated and more easily commingled with the licit. On the local level, culture, ideas, and society are affected. Local control can be challenged in weak states (places where significant social upheaval exists), which leads to deeper divisions. Therefore, transnational groups face fewer obstacles on the local level and more ability to operate in the global economic environment.

Individual states cannot solve their problems alone. Whether one considers the rise of the European Union (EU), the collapse of border controls of the once territorially immense Soviet state, or the rise of regional conflicts that blur national distinctions, states alone are less important. All of these changes have provided opportunities for transnational crime to work and to expand its operations. With globalization, the central state in many countries has become a less effective institution of control. It cannot sufficiently absorb the shocks, limit the dislocations, or regulate the transformation. Deepening local insecurity further strains the bonds of trust between state and citizen.

Under these circumstances, resistance to social transformation, like that found within globalization, can create the space for the proliferation of organized crime and corruption in a given locale. Local control is assumed, and services are rendered through an informal transaction between people playing the roles of criminal and citizen in exchange for certain rents and permissions. Crime groups based in the local community are not impervious to the logic of global social transformation, which changes the organization and its methods of operation. The transformation of organized criminality into a transnational phenomenon is often a logical response to the effects of globalization on the local level.

Understanding transnational crime at the different levels at which it operates requires the engagement of many different sectors of the policy and legal communities, civil society, and the media. Transnational crime groups often provide services at the local level and fulfill demands for illicit commodities and cheap services at the international level. Therefore, any strategy to address transnational crime must convince individuals that it is not in their interest to support or be complicit in its operations. To achieve this objective, media must be mobilized, independent, and supported in their efforts to report on this phenomenon. Civil society must be mobilized to address transnational crime, a mobilization that often comes only with enormous personal loss and even tragedy. Finally, legal measures must be harmonized. This includes both the criminal codes and the procedures needed to combat transnational crime. For example, much has been achieved in this area in money laundering, but the passage of needed legislation is not sufficient. Unless implementation strategies are achieved, laws remain on the books and have no practical effects.

A resource and intelligence gap divides the capacity of developed and developing and transitional countries from addressing the range of problems caused by organized crime. Affluent societies have the legal tools, personnel, and intelligence resources to pursue transnational criminals. Less affluent societies that are faced with critical health, social welfare, and other concerns often cannot allocate the financial and human resources to address transnational organized crime. Unless strategies address the enormous capacity gaps that exist between developed countries and the rest of the world, there can be little success in achieving a global effort to address this issue.

Transnational crime groups are major actors in areas with significant regional conflicts. The demand for arms and quick profits and the lack of territorial control are fertile grounds for the rise of organized crime. Unless military and peacekeepers begin to integrate the problem of transnational crime into their strategies for conflict management, the problem will undermine conflict resolution and postconflict stability.

Organized crime and corruption issues have not traditionally been part of the discourse of international relations, strategic studies, or economic development. Until these elements are integrated into these disciplines and policy planning, organized crime will continue to proliferate. Incorporating these problems into the needed framework is not a guarantee of success, but the failure to address them ensures their continued growth.

Since September 11, 2001, terrorism has received enormous attention in the United States and transnational crime has received much less attention from governmental authorities. In Europe, transnational crime continues to receive more attention, and terrorism less. For Europeans, the pressing problems of illegal migration, human trafficking, and the consequences of opening their borders have made them much more sensitive to the problems of transnational crime and the implications for the EU and their individual countries. In the international context, transnational crime and terrorism are major problems of international concern, especially in countries where citizens are most affected by their prevalence. Recent analysis has shown that transnational crime and terrorism are more closely linked than many acknowledged. The relationship is more complex than the ability of terrorists to support themselves through transnational criminal activity. Therefore, transnational crime has repercussions that far exceed the individual crimes of document fraud, criminal abuse of the Internet, or trafficking in small arms. These issues merit far more attention in all spheres of education, research, and policy in the international community.

ENDNOTES

1. Joel Hafvenstein, *Opium Season: A Year on the Afghan Frontier* (Guilford: The Lions Press, 2007).
2. The International Narcotics Control Board Report 2008, <http://www.incb.org/pdf/annual-report/2008/en/AR2008_Chapter_III_Asia.pdf>.
3. Torcuil Crichton, "To Die For," *The Sunday Herald* 13 (March 13, 2005): 15.
4. UNODC, "The World Drug Report 2008," <http://www.unodc.org/unodc/en/data-and-analysis/WDR-2008.html>; United Nations Drug Control Program (UNDCP), *Global Impact of the Ban on Opium Production in Afghanistan (Second Update)*, Vienna, 2001; UNODC, *The Opium Economy in Afghanistan*, (New York and Vienna: UNODC, 2003).
5. Alain Labrousse, "The FARC and the Taliban's connections to drugs," *Journal of Drug Issues* 35 (Winter 2005): 169–184.

6. Andrew North, "Afghan Murder Inquiry Draws Blank," BBC News (online service), January 30, 2006, <http://www.ask.com/bar?q=%22Steve+MacQueen%22+and+corruption&page=1&qsrc=0&ab=0&u=http%3A%2F%2Fnews.bbc.co.uk%2Fgo%2Frss%2F-%2F2%2Fhi%2Fsouth_asia%2F4662850.stm>.

7. As of the date of this writing the MacQueen case remains open with few solid leads reported. However, Kabul-based international officials and the press regularly express their certainty that this issue is not only linked to the drug trade, but also demonstrates the depth of narco-corruption in Afghanistan.

8. House of Commons, Select Committee on Foreign Affairs, 6th Annual Report on Afghanistan, 2005. Further testimony to the same Committee on 25 March 2009 suggests that security sector reform is stagnant due to the high levels of corruption throughout the Afghan government; available at <http://www.publications.parliament.uk/pa/cm200809/cmselect/cmfaff/uc302-ii/uc30202.htm>.

9. Gerhard O. W. Mueller, "Transnational Crime: Definitions and Concepts," *Transnational Organized Crime* 4(3–4): 13–21.

10. National Security Council, International Crime Threat Assessment Web site, <www.terrorism.com/documents/pub45270/pub45270chap1.html>, accessed 2003.

11. Phil Williams, "Transnational Criminal Organizations and International Security," *Survival* 36(1): 96–113.

12. Ibid., 97.

13. UN General Assembly, "Convention against Transnational Organized Crime," (New York: United Nations Publications, November 2, 2001), 25–26.

14. Pino Arlacchi, *Mafia Business: The Mafia Ethic and the Spirit of Capitalism* (London: Verso, 1986), 187–210.

15. Juan Carlos Garzón, *Mafia & Co. La Red Criminal en México, Brasil y Colombia* (Bogotá: Editorial Planeta, 2008).

16. U.S. Department of State, Trafficking in Persons Report, June 2005, 13–14; available at <www.state.gov/g/tip/rls/tiprpt/2005/>, accessed April 4, 2009. The source or methodology used to produce this estimate is unstated.

17. Amy O'Neill, *International Trafficking in Women to the United States: A Contemporary Manifestation of Slavery* (Washington, DC: Center for the Study of Intelligence, 1999), 55–62; Donna Hughes, "The 'Natasha' Trade: The Transnational Shadow Market of Trafficking in Women" (available at <www.uri.edu/artsci/wms/hughes/natasha.htm>, accessed April 4, 2009); James O. Finckenauer, "Russian Transnational Organized Crime and Human Trafficking," in Kyle and Koslowski (Eds.), *Global Human Smuggling* (Baltimore, MD: The Johns Hopkins University Press, 2001), 166–186; Pasuk Phongpaichit, "Trafficking in People in Thailand," *Transnational Organized Crime* 3(4): 74–104; U.S. Department of State, Trafficking in Persons Report, 2005.

18. Louise Shelley, "Trafficking in Women: The Business Model Approach," *The Brown Journal of World Affairs* 10(1) (Summer/Fall 2003): 119–133; Andreas Schloenhardt, "Organized Crime and the Business of Migrant Trafficking," *Crime, Law and Social Change* 32(3) (October 1999): 203–233.

19. Kevin Bales, *Disposable People* (Berkeley: University of California Press, 1999), 50.

20. See World Bank, "Understanding Civil War, Crime and Violence through Economic Research," <www.worldbank.org/research/conflict> for research papers that discuss this relationship.

21. Graham Turbiville, Jr., "Organized Crime and the Russian Armed Forces," *Transnational Organized Crime* 1(4): 57–104 (quote on 62–63).

22. CNN, "Italy Cracks Arms Smuggling Network," broadcast April 19, 2001.

23. Jon Swain and John Follain, "Sierra Leone Arms Ring Broken," *Sunday Times* (UK) (July 8, 2001): N24.

24. Alexandre Kukhianidze, Alexandre Kupatadze, and Roman Gotsiridze, "Smuggling through Abkhazia and Tskinvali Region of Georgia," <policy-traccc.gmu.edu/publications/publications_georgia.shtml>, accessed April 4, 2009.

25. Bruce Falconer, "Viktor Bout's Last Deal," <http://www.motherjones.com/politics/2008/03/viktor-bouts-last-deal>, accessed April 4, 2009; Douglas Farah and Stephen Braun, *Merchant of Death: Money, Guns, Planes, and the Man Who Makes War Possible* (Hoboken, NJ: John Wiley and Sons, 2007).

26. Michael Bronner, "100 Grams (and counting)" <200806_belfercenter_100gramsandcounting.pdf>, accessed April 4, 2009.

27. Rensselaer Lee, III, *Smuggling Armageddon* (New York: St. Martin's Griffin, 1998), 47–72. See also, Phil Williams and Paul Woessner, "Nuclear Material Trafficking: An Interim Assessment," *Transnational Organized Crime* 1(2): 206–238.

28. See Guardian, "BAT Exposé" (special report) (available at <http://www.guardian.co.uk/bat/>, accessed April 5, 2009); the International Consortium for Investigative Journalists, "Tobacco Companies Linked to Criminal Organizations in Lucrative Cigarette Smuggling" (available at <http://projects.publicintegrity.org/Content.aspx?context=article&id=351>, accessed April 5, 2009).

29. Criminal Intelligence Service Canada, "Contraband Smuggling" (2001 annual report) (available at <www.cisc.gc.ca/annual_reports/documents/2001_annual_report.pdf>, accessed April 4, 2009); "Tobacco Underground New: Big Tobacco's American Indian Connections" (available at <http://www.publicintegrity.org/projects/entry/887/>, accessed April 8, 2009).

30. Louise Shelley and Sharon A. Melzer, "The Nexus of Organized Crime and Terrorism: Two Case Studies in Cigarette Smuggling." *International Journal of Comparative and Applied Criminal Justice* 32(1) (Spring 2008), 43–63.

31. Svend Søyland, "Criminal Organizations and Crimes against the Environment." Report for the UN Interregional Crime & Justice Research Institute, June 2000; available at <www.unicri.it/pdf/cocae.pdf>, accessed 2003.

32. Lauren L. Bernick, "Art and Antiquities Theft," *Transnational Organized Crime* 4(2): 91–116.

33. Elizabeth Olson, "Sending the F.B.I. to Art School," *New York Times* (March 30, 2005): E2.

34. Royal Canadian Mounted Police, "Organized Crime and Automobile Theft," September 1, 1998 (available at <www.rcmp-grc.gc.ca/crim_int/sparkplugeng.html>, accessed 2003); Rosalva Resendiz and David M. Neal, "International Auto Theft: The Illegal Export of American Vehicles to Mexico," in Delbert Rounds (Ed.), *International Criminal Justice: Issues in a Global Perspective* (Boston: Allyn & Bacon, 1998), 7–18; Interpol, "Vehicle Crime Profits Can Be Used to Support Terrorist Organizations, Interpol's Chief Says," November 19, 2001 (available at <www.interpol.int/Public/ICPO/PressReleases/PR2001/PR200136.asp>, accessed April 4, 2009).

35. Anthony Lake, *Six Nightmares: Real Threats in a Dangerous World and How America Can Meet Them* (New York: Little, Brown, 2000), 46.

36. V. A. Nomokonov and Y. A. Aminyeva, "Two Aspects of the Interrelation of Migration and Crime in the Russian Far East and the Primorya"; available at <http://www.crime.vl.ru/docs/stats/stat_121.htm>, accessed October 5, 2005 (it was posted on the Web on October 27, 2004).

37. "Q and A: Somalia Piracy," January 9, 2009, <http://news.bbc.co.uk/2/hi/africa/7734985.stm>, accessed April 8, 2009.

38. Kevin Sullivan and Mary Jordan, "High Tech Pirates Ravage Asian Seas," *The Washington Post* (July 5, 1999): A18.

39. International Chamber of Commerce International Maritime Bureau Piracy Reporting Center, "IMB Reports Unprecedented Rise in Maritime Hijackings,"

January 16, 2009; available at <http://www.icc-ccs.org/index.php?option=com_content&view=article&id=332:imb-reports-unprecedented-rise-in-maritime-hijackings&catid=60:news&Itemid=51>, accessed April 14, 2009.

40. "Overview of Maritime Crime," *Trends in Organized Crime* 3(4): 68–71.

41. Julie Salzano and Stephen Hartman, "Cargo Crime," *Transnational Organized Crime* 3(1): 39–49.

42. John T. Picarelli and Louise Shelley, "Methods, Not Motives: Implications of the Convergence of International Organized Crime and Terrorism," *Police Practice and Research* 3(4) (2002): 305–318.

43. Matthew Levitt and Michael Jacobson (Eds.), *Countering Transnational Threats Terrorism, Narco-Trafficking and WMD Proliferation*, Policy Focus #92, Washington Institute for Near East Policy, February 2009, <http://www.washingtoninstitute.org/pubPDFs/PolicyFocus92.pdf>, accessed April 8, 2009.

44. U.S. Department of State, Bureau of International Narcotics and Law Enforcement, "Before You Go" (information on Nigerian advanced fee fraud), April 1997; available at <www.state.gov/documents/organization/2189.pdf>, accessed April 4, 2009.

45. "Spain Arrests Members of Terrorist Cell," *The New York Times* (September 26, 2001): B4.

46. Karen Zekan, "Chinese Crime Ring Ripping off Strip," *Las Vegas Sun* (January 21, 1999); available at <www.lasvegassun.com/news/1999/jan/21/chinese-crime-ring-ripping-off-strip/>, accessed April 4, 2009.

47. Nichole Christian, "Officials Say Stock Scheme Raised Money for the Mob," *The New York Times* (March 9, 2001): B3; Thomas V. Fuentes, "Organized Crime: Statement on the Record before House Subcommittee on Finance and Hazardous Materials," September 13, 2000, <http://www.encyclopedia.com/doc/1P1-32174321.html>, accessed April 4, 2009.

48. James O. Finckenauer, "Chinese Transnational Organized Crime: The Fuk Ching." (Report to the UN National Institute of Justice, International Center); available at <www.ncjrs.gov/pdffiles1/nij/218463.pdf>, accessed April 4, 2009.

49. Robert I. Friedman, *Red Mafiya* (Boston: Little, Brown, 2000), 173–201.

50. Brandi Grissom, "Homeland Security Official Affirms Mexican Drug Cartel Violence has spilled over into Texas," February 24, 2009, <http://www.elpasotimes.com/newupdated/ci_11770847>, accessed April 8, 2009.

51. P. N. Grabosky and Russell Smith, *Crime in the Digital Age: Controlling Telecommunications and Cyberspace Illegalities* (Brunswick, NJ: Transaction, 1998).

52. John Picarelli and Phil Williams, "Information Technologies and Transnational Organized Crime," in David Alberts and Dan Papp (Eds.), *Information Age Anthology: National Security Implications of the Information Age*, vol. II (Washington, DC: NDU Press, 2000), 365–402.

53. Transnational Crime and Corruption Center, Transnational Crime, Corruption, and Information Technology (2000 Annual Conference Report), 4–5; available at <http://policy-traccc.gmu.edu/resources/publications/variou01.pdf>, accessed April 4, 2009.

54. Raymond Baker, "The Biggest Loophole in the Free Market System," *Washington Quarterly* 22(4): 30.

55. Financial Action Task Force on Money Laundering, "1996–1997 Report on Money Laundering Typologies," February 1997; available at <www.fatf-gafi.org/dataoecd/31/29/34043795.pdf>, 3, accessed April 4, 2009.

56. Canadian Security Intelligence Service, Report No. 2000/07, Transnational Criminal Activity: A Global Context, August 17, 2000, <http://www.csis-scrs.gc.ca/pblctns/prspctvs/200007-eng.asp>, accessed April 4, 2009.

57. Nikos Passas, *Informal Value Transfer Systems and Criminal Organizations* (The Hague, Netherlands: Netherlands Ministry of Justice Research and Documentation Center, 1999), 13–16.

58. Kathleen Day, "U.S. Islamic Cash Outlets Investigated: 'Hawalas' Suspected in Terror Funding," *The Washington Post* (November 7, 2001): A1; Vincent Schodolski, "Terror Networks Rely on 'Hawala,'" *Chicago Tribune* (September 26, 2001): 10.

59. Peter Quirk, "Money Laundering: Muddying the Macroeconomy," *Finance and Development*, 34(1); available at <www.worldbank.org/fandd/english/0397/articles/0110397.htm>.

60. Vito Tanzi, "Macroeconomic Implications to Money Laundering," in Ernesto Savona (Ed.), *Responding to Money Laundering: International Perspectives* (Netherlands: Harwood Academic, 1997), 91–106.

61. John Burnett, "Seized Drug Assets Pad Police Budgets," June 26, 2008, <www.npr.org/templates/story/story.php?storyid=91490480>, accessed April 15, 2009.

62. International Narcotics Control Strategy Report 2005, Volume II: Money Laundering and Financial Crimes Country Reports—Georgia; available at <http://www.state.gov/p/inl/rls/nrcrpt/2005/vol2/html/42394.htm>, accessed April 4, 2009.

63. For a fuller discussion of this topic, see Peter Reuter and Edwin Truman, *Chasing Dirty Money: The Fight against Money Laundering* (Washington, DC: International Institute for Economics, 2004), 135.

64. Alison Jamieson, *The Antimafia: Italy's Fight against Organized Crime* (London: Macmillan, 2000), 128–129, 144.

65. Robert Klitgaard, R. Maclean-Abaroa, and H. L. Parris, *Corrupt Cities: A Practical Guide to Cure and Prevention* (Oakland, CA: Institute for Contemporary Studies, 2000), 2.

66. Samuel Huntington, *Political Order in Changing Societies* (New Haven, CT: Yale University Press, 1969), 59–71.

67. Donatella Della Porta and Yves Meny, "Conclusion," in Donatella Della Porta and Yves Meny (Eds.), *Democracy and Corruption in Europe* (London: Pinter, 1997), 166–180.

68. Diego Gambetta and Peter Reuter, "Conspiracy among the Many: The Mafia in Legitimate Business," in Gianluca Fiorentini and Sam Peltzman (Eds.), *The Economics of Organized Crime* (Cambridge, UK: Cambridge University Press, 1995), 116–135.

69. Dr. Georg Cremar, *Corruption and Development Aid: Confronting the Challenges* (Boulder, CO: Lynne Reinner, 2008); Raymond Fisman and Edward Miguel, *Economic Gangsters, Corruption, Violence—The Poverty of Nations* (Princeton: Princeton University Press, 2008).

70. The concept is taken from Donatella Della Porta and Alberto Vannucci, *Corrupt Exchanges: Actors, Resources, and Mechanisms of Political Corruption* (New York: Aldine de Gruyter, 1999), 236–240.

71. Mats Berdal and Monica Serrano, *Transnational Organized Crime and International Security: Business as Usual?* (Boulder: Lynne Rienner, 2002); Peter Andreas, "The Clandestine Political Economy of War in Bosnia," *International Studies Quarterly* 48(1): 29–52.

72. Three distinct trends in this literature have emerged. First, the results-oriented track, exemplified by the writings of Michael Dzeidzic and Phil Williams, takes a direct rule of law and legal institutional approach to addressing this problem. Second, the clandestine political economy approach, best demonstrated through the recent writings of Peter Andreas and captured in the Mats Berdal and Monica Serrano edited volume, focuses on discovering and understanding the range and scope of the association. Finally, the European peace approach, highlighted by the work of Michael Pugh,

suggests that early detection of these illicit alliances could curb the chances for regional conflict. In each case, the 3 approaches provide a useful web for understanding and dissecting the relationship between conflict, post-conflict, and organized crime, marking one of the newer and intellectually vibrant tracks in the study of the issue.

73. Robert Putnam, Robert Leonardi, and Raffaella Y. Nanetti, *Making Democracy Work* (Princeton, NJ: Princeton University Press, 1993).

74. Louise Shelley, "Post-Soviet Organized Crime," *Demokratizatsiya* 2(3): 354–355.

75. Valerie Braithwaite and Margaret Levi (Eds.), *Trust and Governance* (New York: Russell Sage Foundation, 1998); Francis Fukuyama, *Trust: The Social Virtues and the Creation of Prosperity* (New York: The Free Press, 1995).

76. Louise Shelley, "Mafia and the Italian State: The Historical Roots of the Current Crisis," *Sociological Forum* 9(4): 661–672. For more, see Raimondo Catanzaro, *Men of Respect: A Social History of the Sicilian Mafia* (New York: The Free Press, 1992), and Diego Gambetta, *The Sicilian Mafia: The Business of Private Protection* (Cambridge: Harvard University Press, 1993).

77. Umberto Santino, *Storia del Movimento Antimafia* (Rome: Editori Riuniti, 2000).

78. Jamieson, *The Antimafia*, 148.

79. Rita Borsellino, "In Spite of Everything: The Popular Anti-Mafia Commitment in Sicily," *Trends in Organized Crime* 5(3): 58–63.

80. For a representation of the treatment of complexity, see Saskia Sassen, *Globalization and Its Discontents* (New York: New Press, 1998); Gwyn Prins, "Notes Toward the Definition of Global Security," *American Behavioral Scientist* (May 1995): 820–821; Robert D. Kaplan, "The Coming Anarchy: How Scarcity, Crime, Overpopulation, Tribalism, and Disease Are Destroying the Social Fabric of Our Planet," *Atlantic Monthly* (February 1994): 44–76.

81. Sassen, *Globalization*, 153–158; Louise I. Shelley, "Transnational Organized Crime: The New Authoritarianism," in H. Richard Friman and Peter Andreas (Eds.), *The Illicit Global Economy and State Power* (Lanham, MD: Rowman & Littlefield, 1999), 26–33; Phil Williams, "The Nature of Drug Trafficking Networks," *Current History* 97(618): 155.

82. The globalization debate is wide, contentious, and marked by a variety of skeptics and believers. For further treatment, see Paul Hirst and Grahame Thompson, *Globalization in Question* (Oxford, UK: Blackwell, 1996); James Mittelman, *The Globalization Syndrome: Transformation and Resistance* (Princeton, NJ: Princeton University Press, 2000); James Rosenau, *Along the Domestic-Foreign Frontier: Exploring Governance in a Turbulent World* (Cambridge, UK: Cambridge University Press, 1997); David Harvey, *The Condition of Postmodernity* (Oxford, UK: Blackwell, 1989); Richard Falk, *Predatory Globalization: A Critique* (Cambridge, UK: Polity Press, 1999); Thomas Friedman, *The Lexus and the Olive Tree* (New York: Farrar, Straus & Giroux, 1999).

83. Francis Fukuyama, *The End of History and the Last Man* (New York: Avon Books, 1992), 39–51.

84. In this regard, power is understood as an act of will that manifests itself through material and ideational expressions: coercion and knowledge. For an articulation of complex power along these lines, see Robert Cox, "Social Forces, States, and World Orders: Beyond International Relations Theory" in Robert Keohane (Ed.), *Neorealism and Its Critics* (New York: Columbia University Press, 1986), 204–254.

85. Sassen, *Globalization*, 81–82, 87–90, 92–97.

86. Robert Jackson, *Quasi-States: Sovereignty, International Relations and the Third World* (Cambridge, UK: Cambridge University Press, 1989); Susan Strange, *The Retreat of the State* (Cambridge, UK: Cambridge University Press, 1986).

87. See Willem van Schendel and Itty Abraham (Eds.), *Illicit Flows and Criminal Things: States, Borders and the Other Side of Globalization* (Bloomington: Indiana University Press, 2005) and Margaret E. Beare (Ed.), *Critical Reflections on Transnational Crime, Money Laundering, and Corruption* (Toronto: University of Toronto Press, 2003).

88. Petre Andreas and Ethan Nadelmann, *Policing the Globe: Criminalization and Crime Control in International Relations* (Oxford: Oxford University Press, 2006), 238.

89. Rosenau, *Along the Domestic-Foreign Frontier*, 114–117, 349–358.

90. Shelley, "Mafia and the Italian State," 664–669. It is important to note that Shelley's work approaches this triad from the perspective of each place, allowing for a multi-spectral analysis that can be tested in a variety of empirical contexts. Most recently, Shelley used this framework to investigate and comment on human trafficking, especially in conjunction with the global sex trade. In this same vein, Sassen (*Globalization*) examines the women and immigrants as "undervalorized" in the globalization dynamic.

91. Nikos Passas, "Global Anomie, Dysanomie, and Economic Crime: Hidden Consequences of Neoliberalism and Globalization in Russia and Around the World," *Social Justice* 27(2): 19–24. Passas's construction is similar to Pino Arlacchi's and Raimondo Catanzarro's, each of whom find the Sicilian Mafia a direct result of weak central authority and poor land reform; and in essence, the landowners looked for protection, creating a historical link between legitimate business and organized crime, and thus creating the Mafia.

92. Peter Andreas, "The Political Economy of Narco-Corruption in Mexico," *Current History* 97(618): 162–164.

93. Most of this scholarship owes and pays homage to the work of Susan Strange, namely, *Casino Capitalism* (Oxford, UK: Blackwell, 1986) and *The Retreat of the State*, and a handful of scholarly essays that challenged the mainstream notion of international relations that the state is the only or best legitimate object of inquiry.

94. Francisco E. Thoumi, *Political Economy and Illegal Drugs in Colombia* (Boulder, CO: Lynne Rienner, 1995).

95. Gambetta and Reuter, "Conspiracy among the Many," 118, 121–123.

96. Friman and Andreas (Eds.), *The Illicit Global Economy and State Power*, 7.

97. Bill McSweeney, "Identity and Security: Buzan and the Copenhagen School," *Review of International Studies* 22(1): 81–93.

98. Barry Buzan, Ole Waever, and Jaap de Wilde, *Security: A New Framework for Analysis* (Boulder, CO: Lynne Rienner, 1998); Barry Buzan, *People, States, and Fear* (Boulder, CO: Lynne Rienner, 1990).

99. Buzan and Waever, *Regions and Powers: The Structure of International Security* (Cambridge: Cambridge University Press, 2003).

100. K. M. Fierke, *Critical Approaches to International Security* (Cambridge: Polity Press, 2007), 99, 144.

101. Louise Shelley and John Picarelli, "Methods, Not Motives: Implications of the Convergence of International Organized Crime and Terrorism," *Police Practice and Research* 3 (2002): 305–318.

102. Shelley and Picarelli; Phil Williams, "Terrorism and Organized Crime: Convergence, Nexus or Transformation?" in Jervas (Ed.), *FOA Report on Terrorism* (Stockholm: Defence Research Establishment), 69–92; Makarenko, Tamara, " 'The Ties that Bind': Uncovering the Relationship Between Organized Crime and Terrorism," in Dina Siegel et al. (Eds.), *Global Organized Crime: Trends and Developments* (Dordrecht: Kluwer Academic Publishers, 2003), 159–170; Chris Dishman, "Terrorism, Crime and Transformation," *Studies in Conflict and Terrorism* 24(1) (2001): 43–58.

103. Lake, *Six Nightmares*, 1–32.
104. Christopher A. Corpora, "The Tangled Relationship between Organized crime, Terrorism and Proliferation," in Michael Tanji (Ed.), *Threats in the Age of Obama* (Ann Arbor: Nimble Books, 2009), 6.
105. Conversation with former Minister of Finance of Afghanistan, World Economic Forum, Dubai, November 2008.
106. Peter T. Schneider and Jane C. Schneider, *Reversible Destiny: Mafia, Antimafia and the Struggle for Palermo* (Berkeley and Los Angeles: University of California Press, 2003).

CHAPTER SEVEN

God and Global Governance

Resurgent Religion in World Politics

Maryann Cusimano Love

"We have a responsibility to join together on behalf of the world we seek ... a world where governments serve their citizens, and the rights of all God's children are respected ... We have the power to make the world we seek. ... The people of the world can live together in peace. We know that is God's vision. Now, that must be our work here on Earth."

—President Barack Obama[1]

"Everyone has the right to freedom of thought, conscience, and religion, and this right includes freedom to change his religion or belief and freedom to manifest his religion or belief in teaching, practice, worship and observance."

—Article 18, Universal Declaration of Human Rights

"If religion is unimportant, it can be tolerated. If it is important, governments will insist on controlling it, regulating it, suppressing or prohibiting it, or manipulating it to their own advantage."

—Samuel Huntington[2]

"From the 18th century onwards a succession of European sages predicted that modernization would produce the end of religion. ... Today it is secularization theory that is dead rather than religion. Religion continues to flourish ... The answer to *Time* magazine's question back in 1966——Is God Dead?——is thus an emphatic 'no.' God has not only survived the acids of modernity. He has learned how to use the tools of modernity to spread His message."

—John Micklethwait and Adrian Wooldridge[3]

"The religious impulse, the quest of meaning that transcends the restricted space of empirical existence in this world, has been a perennial feature of humanity. It would require something close to a mutation of the species to extinguish this impulse for good ... The critique of secularity common to all the resurgent movements is that human existence bereft of transcendence is an impoverished and finally untenable condition."

—Peter L. Berger[4]

When Bono and the Pope joined a host of other religious and civil society actors in demanding debt forgiveness and essential medicines for poor, the leaders of most countries did not believe the issue would go anywhere. The U.S. Treasury secretary advised the religious and nongovernmental organization (NGO) groups to spend their scarce resources elsewhere, as these issues were dead on arrival. The Clinton administration and conventional wisdom were wrong. In the decade since, the world has seen more debt forgiveness and access to essential medicines for the poor than ever before. There is still more to do, but the view that religiously motivated groups were impotent was wrong.

Similarly, when religious and NGO actors joined forces across borders to work to ban landmines, many academics and world leaders were dismissive. With the government of the world's most powerful state (the United States) against the International Campaign to Ban Landmines (ICBL), why bother? Conventional wisdom said the effort was bound to fail; but that view was wrong. The international Mine Ban Treaty was signed in record time, banning the production, sale, and use of antipersonnel landmines, mandating mine removal and assistance to landmine victims, and international transparency and reporting regarding landmines. The treaty is monitored by the same transnational advocacy network that was instrumental in developing this international treaty.

When U.S. President George W. Bush assumed power in 2000, he and his administration were briefed on the immediate threat that al Qaeda posed to the United States and allies. But those who attempted to warn the administration were brushed off as "alarmist" and off-base. Domestically, the administration believed that conservative religious voters were a key component to the Republicans maintaining a permanent majority in domestic politics. Internationally, the administration viewed religiously motivated nonstate actors as unimportant; instead, the militaries of powerful states were what counted in international politics. On September 11, 2001, a handful of suicide bombers who believed their reward would come in heaven, killed nearly 3,000 citizens in 4 simultaneous, coordinated attacks in the political and financial capitals of the United States. Even after the "impossible" occurred, the Bush administration could not believe that nonstate, religiously motivated actors were responsible. On the very day of the attacks, Vice President Cheney and Defense Secretary Rumsfeld pressed for the invasion of the secular state of Iraq in retaliation for 9/11, despite the utter lack of evidence linking Saddam Hussein's government to the attacks. When the Bush administration ordered the invasion of Iraq in 2003, they believed victory would be easy. They failed to anticipate prior, or respond afterwards, to the sectarian conflicts in Iraq that would tear the country apart.

In all of these important cases, leaders of powerful states and many mainstream academics were totally wrong. They failed to understand the importance that religiously motivated actors can play in world politics, in saving lives or in destroying them.

Why? Why do so many people who should know better consistently and spectacularly get religion wrong in international affairs?

GETTING RELIGION WRONG IN WORLD POLITICS

The reasons go back over 2 millennia. In his *History of the Peloponnesian Wars*, the Athenian general and historian, Thucydides, warned against the corrosive impact of religion in world affairs. Thucydides was impatient with the traditional Greek practice of attributing success in battle to having the favor of the gods. He argued that religious ideas and ethical norms had no place in world affairs, where material military power reigned supreme. Long before the creation of the modern sovereign state system, he articulated many components of what would later be incorporated into the "Realist" world view.

This view of world affairs gained traction after the Crusades, the Inquisition, pogroms, and the religious wars of the Middle Ages. The Roman Empire spread Christianity globally, and the collapse of the Roman Empire led to centuries of overlapping and contested political organization and authority. In the medieval world, rule was spiritual not spatial, religion was communal not individual, and religious and secular authority were intertwined and overlapping. But such ultimate power led to corruption, undermining the legitimacy of both church and government, and fueling opposition. The Reformation created new ideas about religion and authority, including individual autonomy and freedom from outside interference. A century of wars in Europe were fought over these new religious ideas and authorities, and these wars such as the Thirty Years War in turn undermined the old system. Changes in technology also undermined the old system. The invention of the printing press meant that individuals could own, read, and interpret scriptures on their own. They could also disseminate scientific information, free of the communal interpretations of Church authorities and their monk and religious scribes. During the Enlightenment, religion was often at odds with science, as Catholic and Protestant churches opposed scientific and academic inquiry that seemed to challenge literal readings of the Bible, such as Copernicus's, Kepler's, and Galileo's views that the earth revolved around the sun. Changes in the economy added fuel to the fire; the Roman Catholic Church was against loaning money and swearing oaths, even though contracts and currency were required by the new economic system of long-distance trade. The modern sovereign state was born in the 1648 Treaty of Westphalia, in which the boundaries of rule were no longer determined by religion but by geography. The principle of noninterference in the domestic affairs of sovereign states originally referred to *respecting the religious preferences of other states.*

Many believed Westphalia signaled the final separation of the sacred from the sovereign in world affairs. It did not. The bloody history of colonization around the globe showed that Westphalian noninterference applied primarily to Western countries organized as sovereignties. Non-Western peoples and other forms of political and religious systems were ripe for forced religious conversion and military and political conquer. Westphalia did not guarantee religious freedom, as is sometimes mistakenly inferred. States were, and are, still free to try to control and mandate religious practices within their borders, and also still try to promote these ideas and systems abroad.

The French and American Revolutions struck blows for religious freedom, furthering the separation of church and state. For example, the First Amendment of the U.S. Constitution states that "Congress shall make no law respecting an establishment of religion, or prohibiting the free exercise thereof; or abridging the freedom of speech, or of the press; or the right of the people peaceably to assemble, and to petition the Government for a redress of grievances." Thomas Jefferson felt so strongly about this that his authorship of Virginia's Statute of Religious Freedom (which preceded the U.S. Constitution and First Amendment) was 1 of only 3 accomplishments he dictated be listed on his tombstone (the others were his authorship of the Declaration of Independence and his founding of the University of Virginia, *not* his service as the third president of the United States). It was not until 1948, however, that respect for religious liberty was recognized internationally, in Article 18 of the Universal Declaration of Human Rights. Religious freedom is still abused and restricted, serving as a powerful component of religious conflict today. Marxism and Communism believed religion to be an unscrupulous scam on the poor and working classes, and worked hard to stamp out religion from the people and large territories they controlled in the 20th century. By their economic materialist view, religion was the destructive "opiate of the masses" that would quell demands of the poor and working classes for justice and revolution and con them out of better conditions, by convincing them that it didn't matter if the rich oppressed them, since material possessions didn't matter anyway, and their rewards would come in heaven.

Ironically, throughout the 20th century (through wars against German imperialism, Nazism and fascism, and Marxism and Communism), both the so-called Idealist and Realist approaches to international politics believed that religion ought to be kept out of politics. Idealists believed in the importance of ideas such as democracy, but believed states should promote only secular ideas; religion belonged in the private, personal sphere, not in the arena of public or world affairs. While many Cold War Realists denounced the rise of "Godless" Communism, they were also "Godless" in their approaches to world politics. They believed that religious ideas and actors were unimportant in world politics. Only the material military and economic power of states mattered, therefore religious ideas and identities ought to be a private matter, not the concern of secular states. The Realist view formidably dominated both the theory and practice of world politics in the past century. One study of International Relations (IR) scholarship showed that 92 percent of hypotheses and 94 percent of variables used by scholars were Realist.[5] Competing theoretical approaches, such as idealism, complex interdependence theory, Marxism/dependency theory, postmodernism, etc., all likewise discount the role and study of religion in international politics. Methodology plays its part, as quantitative approaches dominate the IR academy, while studies of religion often use more historical and qualitative methods.

Not only IR scholars were wrong about religion. Sociologists also practiced and promoted the "secular theory," that modernization meant the demise of religion.[6] Since religion was based on primitive, primal, and superstitious views, as societies modernized and science and technology advanced, religion would recede.

> Voltaire predicted that Christianity would wither as man became more enlightened. Marx argued that religion was a tool of ruling class exploitation that would disappear with the birth of a classless society. Nietzsche proclaimed that "God is dead. God will remain dead. And we have killed him." By the 1960s it looked as if the prophets of secularization were being proved right. Christianity was withering in the former heartland of Christendom—Europe. Developing countries from India to Iran were in the hands of avowedly secular governments. And two of the world's biggest countries——Russia and China—— were run by Communist Parties that were dedicated to proving that Marx was right ... But the great secular "isms"—socialism, capitalism and Pan-Arabism——all lost their luster. In fact secularization theory always underestimated the power of religion.[7]

These views were not restricted to universities, but were widely held by statesmen, soldiers, and government bureaucrats as well. *The Economist* magazine published an obituary for God. No wonder that one survey of major world politics journals from the last 20 years of the 20th century found a mere 6 articles on religion.[8] Why study religion if it is dying and unimportant in world politics?

All these views minimizing the importance of religion in world affairs, from Thucydides to Communists, Idealists, and Realists, are based on several misconceptions. First, they confuse prescription with empirical description, an "ought" (religion ought to be kept out of world politics) with an "is" (religion is unimportant in world politics). Second, the belief that religion ought to be kept out of world politics was based on a false assumption that religion could play only a destructive role in world affairs. By definition (because little careful empirical or analytical work was done to investigate these claims), religions caused wars, poverty, and oppression. The ways in which religion aided peace, democracy, human rights, and development were not given much attention. Third, they confuse the demise in the power of the Roman Catholic and Protestant churches over affairs of state since Westphalia, and the demise in attendance at mainstream religious houses of worship primarily in Europe, with the demise of religion writ large. They also confused belonging with believing. People who don't attend church, synagogue, mosque, or other religious communities and services, still believe in God and religious principles. The growth in religion in populations outside of Europe (including the United States), and the growth in new religions and non-Western religions were erroneously deemed as anomalies, temporary exceptions that would eventually succumb to the European trends. Fourth, they believed that advances in technology and economics undermined religion, creating a more material and individual-focused consumer world, more opposed to the divine. They failed to understand the ways in which religions could flourish using the new economies and technologies. Finally, the prevalence of materialist views (power politics or economics matter, not ideas) and Realist views (states are the primary actors in world politics) meant that religious actors and dynamics had 2 strikes against them. Since religious actors are nonstate actors who thrive on and promote ideas, they were consistently ignored, underestimated, and misunderstood by most of the leading scholars and practitioners of world politics over the past several centuries. Soviet leader Josef Stalin dismissively asked "How many divisions does the Pope have?"[9] His point was that leaders without armies are powerless. Ironically, many leaders and scholars who vehemently opposed Stalin nevertheless agreed with his assessment of the unimportance of religious actors. In further irony, just a few decades after Stalin's dismissive comment, the Soviet Union hired assassins to try to murder Pope John Paul II, because the first Polish Pope inspired and supported the anti-Communist Solidarity movement in Poland. The Pope was wounded but lived, helping to bring about the demise of Communist rule in Poland followed by the death of the Soviet Union itself. The Pope never commanded any divisions in Poland against the Soviet military superpower, but religious ideas and organizations, in combination with other factors, helped to end the Soviet empire and the Cold War. This history is very much on the minds of Chinese leaders as they repress religious groups in China today.[10]

The world has been ill-served by this dismissal of the role of religion in world politics. The secular government of the Shah of Iran was replaced by a fundamentalist Shi'a Islamist theocracy in 1979. Thirty years later, the world is still perplexed in navigating relations with the Iranian regime. From Iran's Middle Eastern neighbors to its former European colonial conquerors to its former ally the United States, few have clear insights into the religious dynamics and institutions that underlie the Iranian regime. Progress would be improved on critical issues from nuclear power and weapons to terrorism and drug trafficking with better understanding and engagement of religious factors and actors.

The end of the Cold War, the Balkan Wars of the 1990s, and the rise of violent strains of Islamic fundamentalism and terrorist groups like al Qaeda give new appreciation to the role of religion in world politics.[11] But as one fallacy loses ground (that religious actors and dynamics are unimportant), another fallacy remains, that religious actors and dynamics can play no constructive role[12] in world politics. The one-sided theory extols only the destructive qualities of religion, even though in practice, people, governments, and intergovernmental organizations (IGOs) rely extensively on religious actors in response to the problems of failed and failing states. Religious actors provide a host of critical functions, from providing humanitarian relief during wars and natural disasters, economic development, education, health care (from maternal and child health to immunization, HIV/AIDS care and prevention, to malaria prevention), providing on-the-ground information about human rights abuses, protecting refugees, and displaced persons, to building peace and reconciliation in conflict-prone areas, and safeguarding the environment. Religious actors in coalition with civil society groups form effective transnational networks. Religious groups operate in and across state borders, and they are less inhibited by the Westphalian nonintervention principle that can often cripple the responses of states and IGOs to pressing human needs.

Unfortunately our ideas about how the world works have not yet caught up with these practices. In a 2-year analysis of the U.S. government's understanding of religious factors and engagement with religious actors in U.S. foreign policy, the Center for Strategic and International Studies concluded that "miscalculating religion's role has led to failure to anticipate conflict or has actually been counterproductive to policy goals. It has kept officials from properly engaging influential leaders, interfered with the provision of effective development assistance, and at times harmed American national security." From diplomacy to development to defense, "policymakers and practitioners have largely been wary of directly addressing religion." Concerns over separation of church and state; prevalence of the Realist worldview; lack of education and training in religion; failure to recruit individuals for government service with education and expertise in religion; and failure to create career tracks for soldiers, intelligence analysts, or statesmen specializing in religion and international affairs (as there are career tracks for economic expertise for example) are some of the many reasons for the failure to effectively engage with religious factors and actors. Others include:

- ❏ U.S. government officials are often reluctant to address the issue of religion, whether in response to a secular U.S. legal and political tradition, in the context of America's Judeo-Christian image overseas, or simply because religion is perceived as too complicated or sensitive.

- ❏ Current U.S. government frameworks for approaching religion are narrow, often approaching religions as problematic or monolithic forces, overemphasizing a terrorism-focused analysis of Islam and sometimes marginalizing religion as a peripheral humanitarian or cultural issue.

- ❏ Institutional capacity to understand and approach religion is limited due to legal limitations, lack of religious expertise or training, minimal influence for religion related initiatives, and a government primarily structured to engage with other official state actors.[13]

These critiques of the U.S. government apply equally well to many governments and IGOs around the world, who struggle in determining how secular states and organizations can account for and interact with religious actors and factors.

RELIGION, WAR, AND PEACE

Does religion incite violence or bring peace? It depends. This context-driven ambiguity is the "Ambivalence of the sacred," as Scott Appleby notes.[14] Wars are sometimes fought directly over religious dogmas and the extent of religious control, as in the Crusades. But religions can also be a source of peace, nonviolence, and reconciliation, as in the Velvet Revolutions ending Communism and Soviet control, and the experiences of religious peacemakers worldwide. Contrary to the widespread view of religions as a source of war, the secular wars and violence of the 20th century, the most violent century in human history, caused much greater loss of human life than religious wars by many orders of magnitude.[15] Atheistic Communist regimes alone caused over 100 million deaths. This does not excuse religiously based violence, but merely puts the issue in context as a corrective to popular misperceptions.

Differing definitions of "war" and "religion" also make answering the question difficult. Many of the major studies and databases define war as an event resulting in over 1,000 battle deaths in a year.[16] This definition is criticized for underestimating the casualties of war for several reasons. Most deaths do not occur directly to military personnel on the field of battle, but are civilians killed in war by other means—forced starvation by parties to the conflict, deaths from the disruption of public health infrastructure that the warring parties deliberately bombed and disrupted, etc. Most wars are civil wars, not international wars, and civil conflicts often use methods of extermination—ethnic cleansing, forced moves, and denial of food or services, that do not count as battlefield deaths. Official death figures offered by parties to the conflict may be incorrect due to deliberate distortion (to make it appear that losses were not high and one's forces were not "losing"). Or the parties may be unable or unwilling to keep an accurate count (as U.S. General Tommy Franks noted regarding Iraqi civilian deaths during the U.S.–Iraq war, "We don't do body counts"). One widely cited study notes that "The biggest death tolls do not come from the actual fighting, however, but from war-exacerbated disease and malnutrition. These 'indirect' deaths can account for as much as 90% of the total war-related death toll."[17] Counts that only include 10 percent of deaths and exclude 90 percent are understandably seen as problematic. Many conflicts simmer for many years just short of the 1,000 battle deaths threshold, so are never counted, even though thousands die over time.

As conflict researcher Dr. Milton Leitenberger notes,

> Restrictive criteria that serve to exclude large numbers of people that
> die during wars and conflicts simply produce grossly misleading

conclusions regarding the consequences of the event. Conflicts that produced comparatively small numbers of battlefield or combat deaths but hundreds of thousands and even a million or more civilian casualties appear to be trivial events if only combat mortality is tabulated ... It is particularly pertinent to include deaths caused by starvation and disease during war and conflict when such deaths are a direct concomitant of the conflict. This is especially important because food denial has become an explicit and very significant strategic policy in several wars and conflicts in recent decades (Biafra, Angola, Ethiopia, Somalia, Cambodia, Sudan). It accounts for some of the highest mortalities, and that mortality is, of course, overwhelmingly civilian.[18]

Combatants who deliberately target civilians violate international and national laws of armed conflict, and so understandably try to hide and deny their actions to avoid any countermeasures against them and prosecutions for war crimes and crimes against humanity. Unfortunately when scholars count only military combat deaths, they may unintentionally aid those committing atrocities with a shroud of silence about these acts.

It is also difficult to determine whether a given war or conflict is religious. According to a recent United Nations University study, all the world's major religions place premiums on peace and limitations on war and violence. Yet political leaders often manipulate and pervert religious identities and language for their own gain, to justify war and try to motivate followers to risk their lives for causes that are not particularly religious in nature. What is often referred to as *religious war* is instead a false, deliberate, and cynical perversion of religion to gain a veneer of legitimacy to mask the self-interest or national interest reasons for pursuing conflict.[19]

There is some truth to this claim. Many of what are often referred to as religious wars either are not, or have only partial or tangential relation to religious disagreements. For example, most journalists and pundits described the cause of conflict in the Balkans as a combination of "ancient ethnic and religious hatreds."[20] But the leaders who plunged the region into conflict, such as war criminal Slobodan Milosevic, were Communist political leaders with no religious ties or credentials before the breakup of the Soviet Union. After the end of the Communist system, these leaders sought to reinvent themselves as nationalists who also invoked religious identities, to justify themselves to anti-Communist voters and save their political careers. Poor economics and leaders who stoked conflict were pivotal in bringing violence to Yugoslavia. As the economic situation deteriorated in Yugoslavia, politicians sought to protect their own groups. Leaders exploited identity differences to blame scapegoats, explain away economic woes, and distance themselves from their Communist pasts, often magnifying their messages of hate via the media. Thus while groups from different religions (among other differences) fought in the Balkans, the conflict drivers were more secular than sacred.[21]

While one can question the religious motivations and qualifications of nationalist leaders such as Milosevic, the problem with this analysis is that it diminishes the deep power of religion once unleashed into conflict, even if unleashed for cynical and self-interested purposes. In the Balkans, "between them the Croat and Serb nationalists demolished an estimated 1,400 mosques. They destroyed birth records, work records, gravesites, and other traces of the Bosnian Muslim people ... Mass expulsions (of Catholics and Muslims by Serbs) and a campaign of terror including murder, forced labor, beatings, and other abuses nearly erased the Croat, Muslim, and Roma (gypsy) populations from the region." Yes, the religious elements of violence were manipulated by nationalist leaders, and they were not "inevitable." Nevertheless, "the sad truth is that the war in the former Yugoslavia featured a prominent religious element."[22]

It is true that all the major world religions arrive at similar conclusions regarding the primacy of peace and limitations on war and killing, particularly the protection of civilian noncombatants. These religious norms held by all the Abrahamic religions—Christianity, Islam, and Judaism—as well as non-Abrahamic traditions—Buddhism, Hinduism, and so on—informed the development of international and national laws limiting conflict and defining war crimes. The Geneva Conventions, the Laws of Armed Conflict, and the United States and other countries' military codes of justice, portions of the UN Charter, as well as the charters of many regional security organizations such as North Atlantic Treaty Organization (NATO), all owe a debt to religious traditions concerning the primacy of peace and limitations on conflict.[23] It is important to both note and encourage the vast common ground that exists among world religions on issues of peace, war, and human development. These shared values are underappreciated and underutilized in the quest for peace and development.

It is also true that the violence of many religiously motivated extremists is decried and not sanctioned by the world's mainstream religions. Christian leaders condemn the violence of the Lord's Resistance Army in Uganda. And Muslim leaders condemn al Qaeda's violence.[24] The perpetrators of religious violence are generally minority groups acting without the blessing of the majority of their coreligionists, because these groups pervert religious teachings by overturning the religious injunctions against violence.

However, there are problems with this logic. The very religious pluralism that is upheld and applauded by modern and Western governments has a downside: who speaks for Christianity, Hinduism, Buddhism, Judaism, and Islam? The ever-growing diversity and the "splinter sect" phenomenon facilitated by modern technologies and communications mean every person has the ability to interpret religious texts and traditions in their own ways, and the ability to more easily gain like-minded followers using the tools of globalization. Decrying "This is not *true* Christianity," or "this is not *true* Islam" does not get us very far. It may be helpful to deny mainstream legitimacy to violent cults, and to try to clarify and contain the spread of violence from the wider audience of adherents to a religious tradition. But it does not stop the activities of violent religious groups.

Further it glosses over the problematic passages that offend other faith groups and are often used as religious justifications for violence. Rabbi David Meyer, Imam Sohaib Bencheikh, and Jesuit priest Rev. Yves Simoens, SJ enumerate a number of these "painful verses" within each of their own faith traditions. Too often interfaith dialogue stresses the commonalities among religious groups but avoids the tough issues that are sources of division. In Christianity, some translations of the gospel of John emphasize that "the Jews killed Jesus," justification that has been used in anti-Jewish pogroms (even though Jesus and his apostles were also Jews). One of Islam's "painful verses," is the Prophet Mohammed's saying "Kill he who changes his religion," used by some to threaten ex-Muslims with death. The Jewish Torah tells the Israelites to wipe out the rival Amalekite tribe in Palestine, which some use to justify killing their modern descendants. For believers who do not hold literal interpretations of sacred texts, but who engage in contextual and historic interpretation, these passages do not justify violence.[25] Fundamentalists from all religious traditions hold to more literal interpretations, but the vast majority of fundamentalists also do not espouse violence, and instead interpret these passages with greater priority to the much more frequent passages urging love of neighbor, peace, and unity.[26] But religiously motivated groups who espouse violence often use these problematic passages to overcome religion's traditional prescriptions against violence, and to fuel the fires of conflict. Ignoring these passages or downplaying them as "not representative of *real* religion" does not do much to douse the fire.

Part of the problem in determining whether a war is a religious war is that violence is usually overdetermined. Wars and other forms of violence have many causes—routinely economic and political, at times abetted and intensified by religious factors. One problem in deciphering the issue of religious violence is in separating the rhetoric from the reality. The conflict between Israel and the Palestinians is commonly referred to as a *Holy War*. However, the conflict centers over sovereignty, land, borders, water rights, freedom of movement, property rights, citizenship rights, demographics, and government control. The vast majority of Israeli Jews are secular, not practicing Jews. Not all Palestinians are Muslims; Christian Palestinians are also quite adversely affected by Israeli policy. Certainly, control over religious sites and movement of religious leaders are contentious, polarizing issues. But by no means is the conflict exclusively or even primarily religious.

Conflicts in northern Nigeria between Christians and Muslims have troubled this populous African oil state. At first glance the violence would seem to be clearly religious. Conflicts over the introduction of Muslim Shariah law left 1,000 dead in Kaduna in 2000, and 2,000 dead in Jos in 2001, and over 600 in 2009. More died in the late 2008 clashes over local elections of a Christian party than died in the Mumbai terrorist attacks which occurred at the same time, although international attention focused on the violence in Mumbai. However, the Sultan of Sokoto, His Eminence Alhaji Muhammad Sa'adu Abubakar III, and Nigerian Archbishop John Onaiyekan of Abuja, serve as cochairs of the Nigeria Inter-Religious Council. Together, these 2 religious leaders represent about 95 percent of Nigerians, and they do not believe the conflict is over religion, but over land, water, frustration with corrupt and incompetent government, and frustration with persistent poverty despite the riches of an oil economy. In the Yoruba lands of southwest Nigeria, Christians and Muslims intermarry, share extended families, and live harmoniously. "When people start fighting, it is rarely for religious reasons," says Archbishop Onaiyekan. Yet they believe religion can be used to intensify conflicts, if religious leaders are not vigilant to stop this. The Sultan of Sokoto notes that many "religious intensification" factors in Nigeria come from abroad, such as Pentecostals who create huge gatherings of hundreds of thousands of Nigerians while predicting that apocryphal end times call for extreme actions, and extremist Wahhabi Muslims from the Middle East and Taliban elements from Chad and Niger who also polarize. Nonreligious factors may form the roots of conflict, but religious factors can serve as tinder to spread and intensify conflict.[27]

The problem isn't religion per say, which is neither always peaceful nor always violent. The problem is determining the specifics: Under what conditions will what sorts of religions in what sorts of contexts aid peace or war? The answer seems to turn significantly on religious freedom and the autonomy between church and state, or the lack thereof. Conventional wisdom views religious freedom at the margins of foreign policy, a subset of human rights concerns to be trumped by more pressing strategic or security concerns. However, research shows that religious freedom is actually a security concern. Where states seek to repress religion, violence often ensues—violence by the state against religious minorities, violence by majority groups who take their cues from state policy, and violence by religious minorities trying to protect their communities and beliefs.[28] Political scientist Daniel Philpott shows 2 important variables in whether religions will aid war or peace: differentiation and political theology, meaning institutions and ideas. Differentiation is the degree to which state and religious institutions are autonomous, separate, and draw on their own sources of authority. When such differentiation is consensual (both state and religious organizations desire and seek differentiation), peace is likely. Neither party uses violence to subjugate the other, and minority religious groups are likewise secure from repression so they also do not seek violent redress. When state and religious organizations are integrated and not differentiated (when state and religious authority overlap or are merged), trouble begins. If integration is not consensual (if the status was forced by either party), conflict remains either openly or repressed as parties would prefer greater autonomy. Even if the integration of state and religious institutions is consensual, if the political theology of the religion is exclusionary, conflict also ensues, as other religious groups seek protection from repression. Religion aids peace and democracy when institutions are differentiated and ideas embrace human rights and tolerance.

In practice, there are usually 3 types of religiously motivated violence: religion as a component of nationalist identity politics; violent fundamentalist groups (some of whom use the technique of terrorism, sometimes due to apocalyptic views); and "just war."[29]

The most common form of religious violence is when religion is one component of the Molotov cocktail of violent nationalism. Recall that a nation is not a state. A nation is a group bound together by ethnic, racial, linguistic, cultural, historic, or religious identity. There are over 8,000 national groups around the world, and only 192 internationally recognized sovereign states. Most war is civil war, that is, violence inside states rather than between states, and most civil wars involve conflicts over whether particular national groups should secede from or take over leadership of the state. National groups may be excluded from economic and political opportunities; their language or cultural traditions or human rights may be repressed by majority or ruling groups; or they may have previously ruled and be seeking a return to power. Religion is often invoked as one of the components of national identity, as in the Balkans. Religious differences may pale next to economic or political conflict triggers, and religious differences may not matter when economic times are good and politics are stable. But because religious differences are easier to name and target than perhaps other more entrenched but less transparent economic and political factors, religious identity can be used to spread, intensify, legitimize, and sacralize nationalist identity violence. It can be invoked (and often manipulated) by leaders of nationalist violence, although it is rarely the stand-alone or tent pole factor driving all nationalist violence. Nationalist identity violence spiked with the end of the Soviet empire. While recently this type of violence is receding, it is too early to tell whether the downward trend will continue.

The second form of religious violence perhaps most dominant in media headlines and in the minds of political elites today is violence by fundamentalist religious groups. Fundamentalists are themselves minorities within their larger religious traditions, and those who promote violence are minorities within the minorities. Nevertheless, very small groups can have large impacts, particularly when they use the techniques of made-for-media terrorism and suicide bombings as force multipliers, to gain publicity and generate fear far in excess of the actual damages done by the attacks, as explained in Chapter 5. The term *fundamentalism* is hotly contested. Many within the religious traditions from which fundamentalist groups hail decry the term, saying these groups do not represent the basic "fundamentals" of the faith at all but instead distort the faith. But the term can be useful across a wide variety of faith traditions to denote a "pattern of religious militance by which self-styled true believers attempt to arrest the erosion of religious identity, fortify the borders of the religious community, and create viable alternatives to secular structures and processes."[30] They feel endangered by secular and religious outsiders (who can be foreigners, those of another or no religion, as well as insufficiently zealous members of their own religion), in danger of losing members and their traditions dying off. They believe that the world is divided unambiguously into good and evil, pure and impure, orthodox and infidel, often seen through "an apocalyptic framework: the world is in spiritual crisis, perhaps near its end, when God will bring terrible judgment on the children of darkness." They "tend to be exceptionalists," believing "themselves to living in a special dispensation—an unusual, extraordinary time of crisis, danger, or apocalyptic doom: the advent of the Messiah, the Second Coming of Christ, or the return of the Hidden Imam; and so on."[31] The urgency of this "special time requires true believers to make exceptions, to depart from the general rule of the tradition." Fundamentalists are minorities within their own religious traditions; a multiyear, multivolume study on fundamentalism by scholars such as Scott Appleby, Gabriel Almond, and Martin Marty, found only 10 fundamentalist movements.[32] The vast majority of adherents to fundamentalist religious views are not violent. They feel their group and values are under siege, and they want to safeguard and advance their group and values, but they do not espouse violence. However, for the minority of fundamentalists who do preach violence, this is how they do it: They select passages and elements from their religious traditions that seem to justify violence against evil-doers (for example, by cherry-picking elements from various religious traditions' versions of just war tradition); they ignore the religious traditions' injunctions against violence, arguing that "extreme times call for extreme measures"; they chastise as "heretics" religious leaders and authorities who call for peace; and they convince particularly young, marginal, vulnerable, aggrieved people who have little or incomplete education or formation in their faith traditions, that violence is a sacred duty and that the glories of martyrdom await. In Philpott's terms, these groups hold exclusionary political theologies that espouse violence, and they seek to integrate their religion with the institutions of the state so as to repress other religions and nonbelievers.

In the 10 years since the September 11 attacks in the United States, this type of religiously motivated violence is high on the minds of policy makers because of the greater lethality of terrorist attacks (discussed in Chapter 5). While terrorist attacks are rare overall, their number and lethality per incident have been rising, resulting in greater attention to these types of violence. Much of the surge in terrorist attacks comes from insurgent violence in Iraq, so again it is unclear whether future trend lines will resemble the past. Greater political and religious reconciliation in Iraq would lessen all violence there, including religiously motivated violence and terrorist attacks.

The final, most rare, form of religiously motivated violence is when violence is sanctioned as a self-defensive "just war" necessary to oppose grave evil.[33] Just war tradition (JWT) is a centuries-old guide to thinking about when it is morally justifiable to go to war (*jus ad bellum*) and how to fight war in an ethical manner (*jus in bello*). The morality of war is "always judged twice," considering both just reasons for going to war and means to fight war.[34] Before entering combat, there must be a just cause such as self-defense, discerned by a right authority intent on peace and protecting the common good, using force only as a last resort, when success is possible and the harms of war will not be disproportionate to the reasons for going to war. Upon conducting hostilities, the means used must protect noncombatants and be proportionate and discriminate, not total. These JWT criteria offer a means for soldiers, statesmen, and citizens alike to consider whether and how to ethically use force. JWT stakes out the middle ground between committed nonviolence (pacifism) on the one side, and political realism (realpolitik) on the other. In contrast to both, JWT holds that even under the extreme conditions of warfare, we are all moral beings capable of moral behavior and required to live up to our capacity for ethical treatment of other human beings. While JWT was honed by Western Christians (often Europeans), many of the key elements of just war are thought to pre-date Christianity and are shared by a wide variety of cultures. JWT owes a debt to Africa,[35] to pre-Christian Greek and Roman law and customs, and to Judaic traditions which parallel JWT. The Islamic tradition of jihad (or justifiable holy war) also contains many parallels with JWT,[36] including just cause (self-defense and protection of the global Muslim community from threatened extinction), right authority, and protections on noncombatants and limitations on the conduct of war.[37] Parallels to JWT are found across cultures and religious traditions, from ancient Indian, Chinese, Hindu, Persian, Japanese Samurai, and Aztec traditions, to the Shaolin kung fu monks and the Plains Indians.[38]

Religiously sanctioned just wars are extremely rare. In the most violent 20th century, only World War II met the criteria of a just war of self-defense, made necessary because of the failure of a decade's worth of nonviolent means to combat and contain Nazi evil. Most wars are not just wars, but are civil wars in which moral breaches occur on all sides, both prior to and during the conflict.[39] However, elements of JWT are routinely hijacked by the previously described violent fundamentalist groups. Different groups in different places distort JWT in common patterns: They claim an "emergency" context, in which the supposed threatened extinction of their group and their values justifies the resort to violence in a common obligation to resist great evil. They ignore the components of the tradition that require that war be a last resort, invoked by right authority. And they not only disregard the prohibitions on deliberately targeting and killing noncombatants and other restrictions (proportionality, etc.), they do so intentionally, to attract greater attention to their causes precisely because they are flagrantly violating entrenched norms and laws shared universally.

There are also 3 typical religious approaches to peace: nonviolence (sometimes called pacifism); just war attempts to stop and limit violence; and peacebuilding attempts to prevent violence, end violence, and rebuild societies after violence in just and sustainable ways so that violence will not return.

While the previously described JWT is often thought of as an approach to war, it is also a religious approach to peace, because it reminds us that peace is always the ultimate objective, and that war is almost never justified. JWT also works to lessen and contain conflicts already begun. Regardless of whether the prior *jus ad bellum* conditions were met (and usually they are not), JWT still works to try to contain the conflict by limiting the means of warfare.

The second religious approach to peace is frequently called pacifism. But many practitioners of this approach believe the term *nonviolent resistance* to be more accurate, as there is nothing "passive" about choosing nonviolence, and action is required to oppose great evil. This approach was practiced most memorably by Hindus led by Mahatma Gandhi to overturn British colonial rule in India in the 1940s, and by Christians led by Rev. Martin Luther King to oppose discriminatory rule in the United States during the Civil Rights movement of the 1950s and 1960s. Nonviolent resistance was also effective during the collapse of the Soviet empire, and of the South African apartheid state. People may espouse nonviolent resistance for secular reasons, and often nonviolent groups partner with others, for example with peacebuilders engaged in preventing or ending violent conflicts.

The final religious approach to peace is religious peacebuilding.[40] *Peacebuilding* refers to a wide variety of practices during the entire conflict cycle, from conflict prevention to mediation and conflict resolution to postconflict reconstruction. States have severe capacity gaps in peacebuilding— states know how to fight wars, but they have little institutional capacity to prevent violence and to carry out postconflict reconstruction. Recognizing these failures, states and IGOs are creating a host of new peacebuilding institutions, from the UN Peacebuilding Commission, to new peacebuilding units and missions in existing state foreign and defense ministries. The bad news is that these institutions have severe capacity gaps[41] and normative gaps. None of the new institutions have adequate resources to effectively pursue their missions. The peace they seek is constrained by state sovereignty, national interest, and short time horizons, and emphasizes construction of material and state infrastructure, rather than reconciliation among conflicting groups, post-trauma healing, and rebuilding of human relationships and communities. Religious organizations bring considerable capacity and legitimacy to these tasks, particularly reconciliation, healing, and relationship building. Because most conflicts are internal, state institutions are often inadequate to the tasks of peacebuilding; they may be seen as illegitimate (as one of the parties to the conflict) and incapable (weak, failed, and failing states are often the sites of violent conflicts). Resurgent religions can be extremely helpful to states challenged by peacebuilding. Failures to engage with religious groups in conflict prevention, conflict mediation, and postconflict reconstruction cost lives and lengthen wars. In conflicts with religious components, as in Nigeria today, religious groups can be invaluable guides to the contours of the conflict (which states often do not understand), and partners in helping to defuse the religious components. But even in conflicts which are not religiously based, such as the Congo, religious peacebuilding can be invaluable as states lack the capacity and moral authority to build peace while religious organizations may have both. In many parts of the globe, like the Congo, religious institutions are the only ones left in the vacuum created by failed and failing states.

RESURGENT RELIGION AND CHALLENGED STATES

Religion is resurgent around the world at precisely the time when states are challenged. Strong global religious networks meet weakened and stressed state institutions, with a variety of results.

States are under siege externally from a host of global problems that easily cross borders, facilitated by globalization's open economies, societies, and technologies. Global problems such as disease, terrorism, drugs and crime, environmental degradation, refugee flows, cyber threats, and the proliferation of weapons of mass destruction (WMD), plague strong and weak states alike. The problems do not stop at state borders, but state capacities and authority to address these problems usually do stop at the borders. States are charged with responding to these problems, but they lack effective capacities and institutions to do so. No one state can solve or manage any of these problems alone, yet states lack effective means of coordinating or compelling action across borders. Failures to adequately address global problems undermine the authority and legitimacy of states (and associated IGOs), as citizens become dissatisfied with the institutions' continued inability to adequately meet pressing challenges. Even the strongest states in the system find their sovereign institutions are inadequate to meet global challenges.

The weaker states in the system have an even more tenuous grasp on these problems. In addition to external challenges, these states also face grave internal challenges, as reinforcing crises of poverty and security further undermine capacity, authority, and legitimacy of state institutions, creating failed and failing states with ungoverned and ungovernable territories. One-third of the world's population live in failed or failing states, without basic governance capacities to meet citizen demands. People still face problems, but state institutions are less able to meet and manage these problems alone.

At precisely the moment when state institutions struggle to meet pressing global problems, religious institutions and networks are resurgent worldwide. Global religious networks have both physical resources (personnel, money, technical competence, institutional structures from hospitals to schools) and moral resources (ethical and legal codes, popular support, moral legitimacy) to address many global problems. In regions of continued, prolonged conflict (such as Colombia) and areas of postconflict reconstruction (Burundi, Rwanda, Afghanistan, Iraq), when old regimes have been discredited but new institutions have not yet been built, religious institutions and leaders often step into the vacuum to help bridge these institutional gaps.

Strong and weak states alike "contract out" a host of social service functions to religious organizations. From emergency relief and development programs that serve the poor, to a host of health and education functions, states partner with religious organizations in providing needed social services for a variety of reasons. Religious organizations, with their long-standing grassroots networks, including low-paid clerics and volunteers, may simply be able to deliver social services more cheaply and effectively than state institutions. These efficiency gains are often the motivating force when strong states (including developed democracies) partner with religious organizations to provide services. In weak, failed, or failing states, religious organizations may have capacities, reach, and legitimacy that states lack. Strong religious networks and institutions (hospitals, schools, universities, relief and development organizations) may be active in places where state institutions are weak or nonexistent. For example, faith-based organizations have been key in global efforts to reduce HIV/AIDS, malaria, and TB, particularly in Africa; religious health networks have effectively delivered health services in areas without state public health institutions. Whether partnerships develop by choice or by necessity, usually such public–private partnerships are consensual, and serve the interests of both state and religious organizations. Religious organizations may have mandates to serve the poor and feed the hungry, and government service contracts or partnerships may allow them to serve more needy people. Governments may have authorities and responsibilities to aid people, but may lack the institutional capacities, so turning to religious and other private sector actors is a way to quickly "rent" and use networks and capabilities that would take states much longer to try to build.

For example, in Pakistan, Muslim clerics are working with NGOs and the government to reduce maternal and infant mortality rates by increasing health education and the use of health services. Ahsan Akbar Dhani, district coordinator of the National Programme for Family Planning and Primary Health Care, notes that "Without involving the clerics, it's not easy to get our message across. People already have these misconceptions that the vaccination drops, Tetanus Toxoid (TT) shots, or even ORS [oral rehydration salts] will affect their reproductive system or make them impotent. Even the Imams have children and wives, and the health issues faced by them are also faced by people in their locality. In the communities here, the word of a cleric carries more power than anyone else. Why not use their influence and clout for a healthy cause." Health brochures distributed in madrasas and mosques emphasized that protecting public health is a religious concern. "Cleanliness is important in Islam. By acting according to the Islamic injunctions, we can create a healthier environment. May Allah always give us the strength to stay clean and protect ourselves and others from diseases as well as disseminate information with regards to health and hygiene, Amen." Local hospitals reported that more people used free public health services as a result of the messages from the Imams.[42]

Similarly, mosques and churches serve as important distribution points for mosquito nets and information in the fight against malaria in Nigeria. One quarter of all African malaria cases come from Nigeria. Malaria routinely stunts worker productivity in adults, but it is deadly to children. Working with international NGOs and IGOs, Archbishop Onaiyekan and the Sultan of Sokoto have formed the Nigeria Interfaith Action Association in order to distribute 60 million insecticide-treated bed nets to 30 million families via their respective religious networks. Religious leaders are a trusted source of information regarding how mosquito nets must be consistently used to be effective. Mosques and churches are critical distribution points, reaching areas where no public health clinics exist.

States often turn to religious organizations for services in the economic and social realms, where liberal, capitalist states have the least reach. Yet religious organizations are increasingly active even in the law and order, security, and peacebuilding realms. For example, Chapter 6 discusses cases in which religious actors were key in combating organized crime in Italy. Mexico now faces increasing violence from global drug cartels, and Mexican churches are turning to their religious colleagues in Italy and Colombia to share their expertise in combating organized crime. Italian and Colombian clerics with experience fighting international crime cartels are training and sharing lessons learned with their Mexican church colleagues. It is dangerous work, and many Mexican priests have been slain for standing up to the crime cartels. But in the absence of effective state institutions, religious institutions often step in to fill the gap. Religious organizations may be able to bring their moral authority and legitimacy to bear on problems in ways states cannot, especially where state institutions are seen as corrupt and part of the problem, as in Mexico and Colombia.

There are challenges when states contract out to religious organizations, as discussed in Chapter 3. Does reliance on religious networks serve the short-term goal of providing needed services, while ignoring or delaying the long-term goal of developing adequate state institutional capacity to provide essential services? Religious organizations must avoid "capture" or "neutering" of their creeds and practices at the hands of the state. Countries that do not establish a state religion must avoid establishing religious monopolies, and ensure that religious organizations do not favor their own congregants or use state monies to proselytize.

Religious organizations and states operate differently regarding sovereignty. Religious organizations have a moral mandate to help "God's children," and do not stand on the sidelines and wait until state institutions are ready and able to provide services. Westphalia created a nonintervention norm for other states that does not apply to religious actors, who answer to a higher authority than state sovereignty. Some NGOs, like "Doctors Without Borders," also act wherever people are in need, whether or not it has the prior permission of the sovereign state. But a key difference with the NGO comparison is that religious organizations are both domestic and external actors; global religious organizations have believers and branches in countries around the world, and are not only external actors. Thus religious organizations often put people before states. Many religious organizations would concur with the position stated in Vatican II, The Church in the Modern World, "The social order and its development must constantly yield to the good of the person, since the order of things must be subordinate to the order of persons and not the other way around, as the Lord suggested when he said that the Sabbath was made for man and not man for the Sabbath."[43] Religious organizations often begin with the protection of human life and dignity over deference to sovereignty.[44] The United Nations and the U.S. government have moved toward this position in adopting the Principle to Protect, "the idea that sovereign states have a responsibility to protect their own citizens from avoidable catastrophe, but that when they are unwilling or unable to do so, that responsibility must be borne by the broader community of *states*." But putting that principle into practice has been limited by state interests and concerns of state sovereignty.[45] In Philpott's terms, the political theology of some religions is more liberal in the protection of human rights than some sovereign states, which can lead to pressures from religious groups for more democratization and protection of human rights, as will be discussed later.

In a minority of cases, religious groups and actors seek to take over either all or part of the governing functions of states; they seek to integrate their religion in the governing institutions of states. Religious groups and institutions in some areas of the world, scandalized and discouraged by the corruption and incompetence of state structures, have sought to overturn and fill the functions of states themselves as theocracies, in places such as Iran and Afghanistan under the Taliban. In other areas, short of fully establishing theocracies, states "contract out" the law to religious codes such as sharia law governing Muslim communities in some states of northern Nigeria. When resurgent religions with exclusionary and integrationist political theologies meet the vacuums created by weak and failing states, peace and democratization are endangered, as well as the lives and religious freedom of nonmembers to the resurgent exclusionary faith. This occurs in a dangerous minority of cases, but this potential is why religious actors in politics are often seen as "enemies of the state."

RELIGION AND GLOBALIZATION

Religion and globalization have always gone hand-in-hand. The quest to understand and encounter the transcendent runs deep in humans; because we are social animals, the impulse to share religious ideas and practices with others also runs deep. Religions have track records of spreading globally, from the spread of Confucianism and Zoroastrianism in earlier millennia, to the work of Paul and the disciples to spread Christianity from a small swath of Galilee to large tracts of the globe in just a few years, to the rapid spread of Islam and evangelical Protestantism today. That process continues, but with a few modern wrinkles. As discussed in Chapter 1, globalization is not new; traders and missionaries left their marks in previous periods of globalization. But globalization today is quicker, thicker, deeper, and cheaper than previous periods of globalization. Ideas move at the speed of a keystroke, as fast as the mobile or Internet or satellite connection, and so cheaply as to create much greater global volume. This creates a tipping point for today's global interactions; the difference between modern globalization and its predecessors is not just one of quantity, but of kind, quality, intensity, and scope. More people in more strata of societies are affected by more aspects of global networks more quickly than in previous periods, when people, ideas, and goods spread with the speed of frigates.

This fast modern phase of globalization, spreading interdependent open society, open economy, and open technology networks, creates unintended challenges for states for which states are not well equipped to handle.

The very principles of sovereignty are being challenged in theory and in practice. One-third of the world's population live in weak, failed and failing states, where sovereign states lack the capacity to provide citizens with basic necessities: security, law and order, food and clean drinking water, access to health, education, and opportunities for jobs. An overlapping set of half the world's people live in states with repressive governments that do not protect citizens but abuse the basic human rights of their own people. The worst of these are predatory states engaged in genocides or democides, killing their own citizens they are charged with protecting. Even strong states and rich, developed, democratic states struggle in responding to a host of global problems from nuclear threats to the spread of diseases to environmental threats.

Chapter 3 described the ways in which transnational civil society networks come together to address many of these global issues, and gave examples of religious organizations effectively joining forces with secular NGOs from debt relief to the landmine campaign. Faith-based groups now have historic opportunities to practically and importantly influence international and local politics. This is due to the intersection of several related trends: the modern period of globalization, the falling costs and rising opportunities presented by communications technologies, the rising power of NGOs, including faith-based organizations, and the rising power of transnational advocacy networks. The results are important opportunities for what I refer to in Chapter 3 as *resurrection politics*, a politics of life and hope, in which faith-based groups in coalition with secular NGOs take issues previously thought to be dead on arrival, raise them up onto the political agenda, reframe issues with values and powerful images, and thereby change the political space to include those previously marginalized, by drawing on the language and symbols of faith.

While religious organizations can and do work with NGOs, they are in many ways not "just another NGO." Global religious networks *can* function as transnational advocacy networks, yet the category does not quite fit. Global religious networks have much greater institutional and ideological depth than most transnational advocacy networks. They work across wider time and issue horizons. They have longer histories of continuously working as networks across a wide range of issue areas; they are not assembled ad hoc primarily for single issue advocacy. They are not only advocacy networks, but have great functional capacity across a wide range of functional areas. For example, the Catholic Church is the largest single sect religion in the world (Islam has slightly more followers, but these are divided among Sunni and Shi'a sects). The Catholic Church operates over 200,000 schools, serving more than 52 million students. The Church also runs more than 5,000 hospitals; 16,000 clinics, 14,000 homes for the aged and disabled, 8,000 orphanages, 11,000 nurseries, and 25,000 other social service agencies.[46] Catholic relief and development organizations serve needy populations in every country. This kind of institutional breadth and depth is not quantitatively or qualitatively comparable with NGO structures.

Conventional wisdom is that globalization sets the forces of modernity against the forces of tradition, in ways that undermine religious groups.[47] I take issue with that view.[48] Religion is resurgent around the world, and many faith-based groups are facilitated and empowered by globalization.[49] Religious organizations work beyond sovereignty, often targeting their activities directly toward individuals and communities. Corporations, NGOs, and states are neither the only engines of globalization nor its only beneficiaries. Religious organizations have long been globalizing forces, spreading ideas, institutions, flows of people, and capital across international borders. Today, religious organizations, in partnership with other civil society groups, are opening up new political space, responding to the challenges of globalization and offering alternative ethical visions of it.

RELIGION AND OPEN ECONOMIES

God and money have been on mixed terms over the millennia. On the one hand, religions sometimes seem discouraging about money. All of the world's major religions emphasize that humans should not enslave themselves to money and possessions. All the Abrahamic faiths (Judaism, Christianity, Islam, and all their offshoots) share teachings that humanity should pursue God, not pursue "idols" and "false gods" such as the pursuit of economic gain at the expense of spiritual development. It is lawful to own property if economic gain is pursued and used ethically. Money should serve the purposes of God and community, and not be gained or used in ways which exploit persons or for personal aggrandizement at the expense of pressing communal needs. The same teachings hold in non-Western religions, that the pursuit of money and possessions can corrupt human beings and communities, leading people away from enlightenment, enslaved by their possessions and by performing nonmeaningful work only for the purpose of earning money. For these reasons, all the major religions prescribe charity and generosity toward the poor, and limitations on debt (which is why religious organizations joined NGOs in a transnational advocacy network pressing for debt relief). The stance toward lending money has been a particularly provocative point. Early Christianity and Islam placed prohibitions on money lending for interest, while Judaism placed restraints on the amount of interest that could be charged and to whom. The Torah also urges debt forgiveness every 7 years. Charging interest raises concerns about abuse of the poor, as well as concerns about greed and excessive wealth creation without work. Catholic restrictions on money lending were one of the economic factors that led to the creation of the sovereign state. The rise of long-distance trade and merchant classes required economic activities that previously had not been sanctioned by the Church. Over time both Christianity and Islam allowed for money lenders to earn some profits, but profits were restricted in scale to the work and risks investors added to the enterprise (leading to a separate Islamic banking system, so that Muslim communities could be certain that financial services followed Islamic values, much as many Jews turn to "kosher" products to be certain that food is prepared consistent with Jewish dietary restrictions). Money lending often contributed to anti-Semitism and violent pogroms over the centuries, as non-Jewish communities turned to Jewish money lenders as a means to circumvent the money-lending restrictions placed by their own religious faiths, but then faulted "greedy Jewish money lenders" for providing needed financial services.

On the other hand, today it may sometimes seem difficult to discern the impact of ancient religious restrictions on the use of money. Religious organizations and leaders have often amassed great wealth, in land, church buildings including universities and hospitals, artwork, as well as cash donations. The fall of Communism in the USSR and the old Soviet empire has created resurgent opportunities not just for capitalism in previously Communist countries, but also for capitalist religions, for religious organizations to fund raise and offer church members economic as well as spiritual counseling. Religious organizations and leaders apply the principles of open markets and modern capitalism to their churches, and reap great benefits. Religious books (such as the best-selling *Left Behind* novel series, and Rick Warren's *A Purpose Driven Life*), music, movies, and even health clubs and theme parks are big businesses. More than one thousand megachurches exist internationally, each drawing congregations of over 3,000 worshipers per week, using organizational methods that consciously mimic corporate culture. Megachurch leaders describe themselves as "pastorpreneurs,"[50] using the same niche marketing and economies of scale principles as other successful businesses. As megachurch pastor and televangelist T. D. Jakes describes it, "Jesus is the product. When the product is excellent, it doesn't require a big sales pitch."[51]

The advancement of open economic systems worldwide greatly aids the spread of religious ideas and organizations globally. As John Micklethwait and Adrian Wooldridge argue, "The God Business" is huge. Global market competition now applies to religions, each vying for followers by providing "total service excellence. These pastorpreneurs don't just preach on Sundays. They don't just provide services for the great rituals of birth, death, and marriage. They keep their buildings open 7 days a week, from dawn to dusk, and provide a mind-boggling array of services," from banks, pharmacies, and schools, to tax and real estate services and skateboarding parks.[52] Religious organizations offer franchises more flexible than McDonald's, with boutique branches to serve specific demographics, such as biker churches or sports-enthusiast churches. New religious franchises are making big in-roads against the traditional religions, such as mainstream Protestant and Catholic faiths, but are also attracting followers who were previously nonreligious or "unchurched." This is not just a U.S. phenomenon. South Korea is home to 5 of the world's 10 biggest megachurches.

The spread of capitalist economic forms has advanced the development, number, and capacity of all private sector organizations, including religious organizations, even in "Godless" Communist China. The opening of the Chinese economy has coincided with the rise in religion in China. Despite the state's official stance against religion, 56 percent of Chinese polled say that religion is very or somewhat important in their lives. "There are probably close to 100 million Christians in China," following a very individualistic style of Christianity or in small congregations of "house churches," which are groups that meet to worship in people's homes to avoid the persecution that might ensue from meeting publicly in official churches. "Nobody reports us as long as we don't sing," explains one congregant.[53] Because the state still officially persecutes many believers and restricts religious practice, the numbers in China may actually be much higher. Some estimate that China could be the world's biggest Muslim country, as well as the biggest Christian country, by 2050.[54]

Religion's resurgence is also aided by global capitalism in another way. As capitalism spreads its market values globally, many look to religions as a counterweight to the market's excesses, as a source of values that the market does not supply. In China, many look for a source of values which they do not see in corrupt market and government institutions. A Chinese government economist, Zhao Xiao, argues that market values are not enough; they can encourage efficiency, but not honesty or selflessness, for example. For these the market needs God. "Only through faith can the market economy have a soul."[55]

This view is shared by many in less-developed countries, who look to religion as a source of social justice. Economic and political systems favor elites, while some religious organizations speak courageously on behalf of the poor.[56] Religion thrives among the poor, with religious organizations often serving the poor in basic ways (provision of food, health services, education) which state and other institutions do not provide. Pippa Norris and Ronald Inglehart argue that religion is most important in the least-developed majority of the world, but they echo the Marxist and secularist arguments that as scarcity decreases so does religion. This ignores evidence from emerging economies such as China, India, and the former Soviet Union, where religious institutions and practices are increasing while prosperity also increases.[57] The problem in recognizing religious resurgence in developed economies may stem from measurement errors and differing religious expression. It may be that religion is practiced differently from poor countries to rich countries.[58] The poor may be more communal as they reach out to extended family and neighbors in the quest for survival; and they may likewise be more communal in religious expression, joining and attending religious organizations and services. Demography shows the poor may have little choice, as they are often highly concentrated and crowded. Religious practices in rich countries may be more individualistic and personal, less defined by congregating face-to-face in brick-and-mortar places. For many, religion may be a matter of "Believing Without Belonging," according to sociologist Grace Davie.[59] This is evident in the volume of people who watch religious programs and read religious books, but may not regularly attend religious services. The poor may not be able to afford religion by technology or through buying religious products, so the old-fashioned (and free) brick-and-mortar route may be the more available and therefore more prevalent means of religious expression. The rich have more options, and so may express their religious behavior more like their consumer behavior. This is true in the United States and many Latin American countries, where people frequently change religions just as they change consumer brands. In some places, people may practice "vicarious religion"; they may not regularly attend services, but neither do they change brands. They engage virtually, but expect their traditional religious brand to be there for them when they need it (i.e., for a family funeral), like a public utility. Lived religion is a moving target. These behaviors may be different from historic measures of religion (weekly attendance in churches/mosques/synagogues), but it may not signify a loss of religion.

Still, the triumph of the market has led to some concern that the search for money overwhelms the search for the divine, and that the importance of material possessions in a global consumer culture crowds out spiritual concerns. With the global economic meltdown of 2009, many religious organizations are reporting huge increases in attendance and requests for social services. This can be interpreted in 2 ways. As Norris and Inglehart note, people can turn to religion when they have few other options to deal with problems of resource scarcity. But also, even prosperous people still see in religion a source of social justice that may be lacking in market and government structures. Concern for social justice and for changing unjust social structures can be attractive to poor and prosperous alike. All the major world religions have always had a focus on care for the poor, leading to a focus among religious groups on both short-term charity and emergency assistance and long-term economic development. A large percentage of foreign aid funding is channeled through religious NGOs. Religious actors and organizations' concern with the poor and social justice fueled the Jubilee Debt relief and eradicate poverty campaigns, discussed in Chapter 3. Because of this historic association, religious organizations who align too closely with market forces without sufficient care for the poor may lose legitimacy, as their behavior is perceived as inauthentic.

Consistent with religious traditions of care for the poor, religious organizations and leaders often raise concerns about whether global financial institutions such as the International Monetary Fund (IMF), World Trade Organization (WTO), and World Bank, as well as specific free-trade agreements, adequately address the needs of the world's poor.[60] Religious leaders often pressure the leaders of multinational corporations (MNCs) to protect the poor and the environment in the areas in which they do business. For example, religious leaders are concerned that the poor often bear the costs of oil or natural mineral extraction, but do not share in the economic benefits that derive from exploiting these natural resources. Therefore African Jesuit priests from the Congo to Cameroon are engaged in transparency and shame and name projects, gathering information on the profit-sharing agreements between MNC oil and mining companies and governments, to follow the money trail, learn why the poor did not benefit, and pressure changes so that the poor will benefit more from such arrangements in the future.[61] Catholic Relief Services Extractive Industries programs likewise urge MNCs to "publish what they pay," and to fully respect human rights and the environment.[62] Religious organizations engage in shareholder activism to encourage MNCs to adopt more socially responsible business practices with better impacts on the poor and the environment.[63] Thus many religious organizations attempt to use the tools of the global economy, in order to create a global economy that better serves the needs of the world's poor and vulnerable people.

RELIGION AND OPEN TECHNOLOGIES

Conventional wisdom holds that religion and science and technology are opposed. This view is mistaken. Some religious organizations oppose some scientific theories and technological practices, exemplified by the debates over cloning, stem cell research, abortion, and evolution. Religious groups continue to monitor and challenge the ethical bases of technologies, from nuclear weapons to health care. But religious organizations are also significant beneficiaries of global transportation and communication technologies. Technologies from papyrus scrolls to Phoenician ships have always been the backstory of religious advancement and dissemination. Twenty-first century global technologies help religious groups organize, proselytize, mobilize, and conduct their core ministries in ways that are revolutionizing religion.

At the time of Westphalia, the dawn of new technologies created problems for organized religious hierarchies. Specifically, the Gutenberg printing press undermined the authority of clerics' views of scriptures, the Bible, and religious texts, and literally allowed laymen and laywomen for the first time to hold and read their own copies of holy books, and reach their own conclusions. This technological opening created religious and organizational openings, as new Protestant and reform religious groups were formed based on individual, not communal, ideas of faith and authority.

The Internet and other cheap, decentralized, and readily available information technologies are creating similar changes today. The "Gutenberg Bible" of the 21st century is no single text in a single medium; instead there are thousands of religious texts and videos from all the world religious traditions available through a myriad of mediums, low- and high-tech, new- and old-tech applications—Facebook, Twitter, cell phones, travel drives, iPods, radio, and TV. Today's connective information technologies from computers to televisions to wireless devices bring religious materials from the Koran and the teachings of the Dalai Lama as well as the Bible to exponentially more people than ever read a Gutenberg Bible. People now have more religious resources than ever before available to them at the touch of a keystroke or the push of a button on their TV. This not only allows them to reach their own conclusions on religious matters with less intercession from traditional religious hierarchies and clerics, but it also allows individuals to partake in religious ceremonies and practices from the comfort of their homes, without ever having to set foot in a mosque, synagogue, or church. People who have never been persecuted have house churches. This further privatization of religion creates challenges and opportunities for religious organizations. For old-brand religions that do not adapt to new technologies, attendance is diminishing at their traditional religious services. Why travel to an inconvenient brick-and-mortar location for a service whose music and sermon may not be as compelling as what is readily available online, on the television, or on DVD? Why go, on Sunday morning or Saturday night or any inconvenient time when one can participate in religious ritual at any hour, any day? For new religious organizations and religious organizations that adopt a variety of new technologies, this creates opportunities for new outreach and new services (including the vast array of one-stop-shopping services, from counseling to theme parks to food courts and child care available at many megachurch complexes). Many religious organizations have been very successful by creating new "value-added" attractions not available through remote venues. Believing without belonging has reached a new expression; believing with virtual belonging, to listening, viewing, or online communities.

Humans are social animals, and religious organizations offer supportive social communities, therefore there will always be a market for "old-time" religion, offered up face-to-face and hand-to-hand. Big ticket religious rituals—births, deaths, marriages—will always be in-person events. However, even "old-time religion" services are taking cues from corporate and entertainment culture, with more friendly Walmart-type "greeters" rather than stoic ushers helping congregants to seats, and more professional high-quality audio and video performances replacing lower-quality music and visuals.

Religious organizations are scrambling to keep up with the speed of technological revolutions, a race made difficult by the age discrepancies between many older clerics and younger congregants with different technological skills and expectations. Religious organizations that do not use the new technologies (that retain paper religious bulletins rather than creating sophisticated Web sites and online presences) often find they may have difficulties attracting younger followers, who look for information about religious services and activities online, using the same technologies for the sacred as they use in the secular areas of their lives. Religious organizations without virtual presences do not exist to many younger believers.

Religious organizations that skillfully adapt and use the new technologies find efficient force multipliers for their ministries and messages. These networks and communications are not totally free but are mediated, by service and content providers and users, who combined, define the search terms and content. But mediation is decentralized and diffuse, especially compared with more hierarchical controls of previous media and religious authorities. Buddhist monks challenging the Burmese military leaders in the Saffron Revolution, Iranians challenging election results by chanting "God is good," all use Facebook, Twitter, blogs, cell phone photos, and uploads to disseminate real-time information about their religious groups' activities to a global audience, despite government attempts to restrict their communications. Ironically, even conservative, orthodox, and fundamentalist religious groups use the new technologies to reach more people. Small sects in remote locations are no longer prisoners of their geography, but can preach views and reach followers cheaply at a distance to a potentially global audience. As discussed in Chapter 5, religiously motivated terrorist groups like al Qaeda also skillfully use new technologies to promote their views, plan operations, raise funds, train, and communicate among members.

Because religious groups often attract followers across class and generational lines, many must remain literate in both old and new technologies, using print media, radio, television, and other older media to communicate with followers, in addition to streaming video, social networking sites, and podcasts. Used well, these new technologies can be a vital way to connect more of the human family in new ways, and sensitize followers to global religious issues, for example to problems of global poverty, in ways that might otherwise be more difficult. The resurgence of religion has been facilitated by cheap, widely available, global communication technologies. This helps people find God in cyberspace, and helps religious organizations to efficiently communicate, organize, do their work, and raise funds.

The cheaper cost and wider availability of global transportation technologies also dramatically change the lived experiences of the world's religions. Many more Muslims now make pilgrimages to Mecca, Buddhists travel to Lumbini (where Buddha was born), and Catholics travel to the Vatican than ever before. According to the fifth principle of Islam, Hajj, Muslims are required once in a lifetime to go on a pilgrimage to Mecca in Saudi Arabia, if the individual has the means to do so. So many Muslims now have the means to do so (thanks to the cheaper cost and wider availability of global transportation technologies), that Saudi authorities now must use 1,500 cameras to monitor and manage the crowded pilgrims, to avoid congestion and stampedes, as millions converge on the holy sites at the same time.

Similarly, anyone can now be a missionary. Millions do so for short periods of time, given the opportunities afforded by "Twinning" relationships of religious communities in developed and developing countries and global "mission trips" and the service-learning voluntourism industry. Religious

201

tourism and mission-centered "voluntourism" are thriving industries, complete with their own trade shows and trade associations. The World Religious Travel Association and Expo estimates that religious tourism is an $18 billion-per-year industry involving over 300 million tourists. Their estimate is likely too low, capturing primarily international travel costs to major pilgrimage sites (such as Mecca), given the UN estimates of tourism as an $856 billion-industry annually with nearly 1 billion tourists. Over 1 million Americans volunteer overseas each year, many through religious organizations and programs.[64]

Global technologies also help religious organizations in another way, as people turn to religion as a counterforce to the destructive concerns raised by technologies. For example, religious organizations are increasingly active to combat global climate change. They are concerned that overconsumption and toxic technologies are polluting "God's green earth," and that we have religious responsibilities to address environmental problems, which disproportionately harm the world's poor. Abrahamic religions believe that God created the world and entered into a covenant with humanity to be careful stewards of God's creation. The Coalition on the Environment and Jewish Life notes that "For Jews, the environmental crisis is a religious challenge. As heirs to a tradition of stewardship that goes back to Genesis and that teaches us to be partners in the ongoing work of creation, we cannot accept the escalating destruction of our environment and its effect on human health and livelihood. Where we are despoiling our air, land, and water, it is our sacred duty as Jews to acknowledge our God-given responsibility and take action to alleviate environmental degradation and the pain and suffering that it causes. We must reaffirm and bequeath the tradition we have inherited which calls upon us to safeguard humanity's home."[65]

Global environmental technology concerns dovetail with religious concerns with caring for the poor. Rev. John McCullough, Executive Director of Church World Services, and Ken Hackett, Director of Catholic Relief Services, note that the "real inconvenient truth" is the effect of climate change on the world's poor. "Island nations are grappling with relocating their citizens as the sea level rises. The IPCC [Intergovernmental Panel on Climate Change] estimates that if left unchecked, climate change may cause acute water shortages for up to 3 billion people, increase hunger for 30 million people, expand exposure to malaria for up to 60 million more Africans, and increase heat-related premature deaths ... Ninety-seven percent of all natural disaster-related deaths already occur in developing countries, and estimates of climate change's contributions to worsening conditions are disturbing. The poorest 1 billion people are responsible for producing just 3 percent of green house gas emissions causing these shifts. Yet, they bear the brunt of global climate change's impact and have the fewest resources to deal with its consequences." Climate change legislation ought to "support coping and adaptation strategies in poor communities around the world."[66]

Religious groups are not only concerned about the ethical repercussions of technology, but also with the ethical distribution of technology. Religious groups work to mitigate the "digital divide," by offering access and training in technologies at religious schools and centers. For example, Jesuit Refugee Services, Catholic Relief Services, Church World Services, and other faith-based NGOs offer livelihood and development programs for the poor in rural areas via access to the technologies of religious organizations. Sudanese refugees sell their handicrafts online via Web access and training provided by religious organizations. Resurgent religions are filling functions not filled by challenged sovereign states.

RELIGION AND OPEN SOCIETIES

Led by Buddhist monks and nuns, hundreds of thousands of protesters marched through the streets of Myanmar (also known as Burma) in 2007. Myanmar has been ruled by a brutal military junta since 1962. The ruling regime, called (in Orwellian fashion) the State Peace and Development Council, is one of the worst abusers of human rights in the world, according to human rights NGOs and the U.S. Department of State. The predatory military routinely pillages villages, rapes women, forcibly conscripts child soldiers, abducts people into slave labor, and trades in drugs. They also practice ethnic cleansing, destroying the villages of minorities who either oppose the government or who stand in the way of state infrastructure development projects. Dissenters are subject to prison or death. Nevertheless, in the fall of 2007, the country's Buddhist monks and nuns led pro-democracy protests in what has been dubbed "the Saffron Revolution" (invoking the color of many Buddhist monks' robes). Burma should be a rich country, with extensive resources in natural gas, minerals, and precious stones. Yet Burma is poor, due to incompetent and corrupt leadership. Protests began over skyrocketing prices of bread and fuel, but quickly turned to democratization. Bearing banners with the words "Love and kindness must win over all," monks on megaphones chanted their concerns. "We want the people to join us, we want national reconciliation, we want dialogue with the military, we want freedom for Aung San Suu Kyi and other political prisoners." The marchers responded by raising their hands in the air and shouting, "Our God!" The monks urged people "to struggle peacefully against the evil military dictatorship till its complete downfall and to banish the common enemy evil regime from Burmese soil forever." The monks' message was broadcast to the world using the new technologies of cell phones and the Internet. Democracy has not yet come to Burma. But if it does, the country's Buddhist monks and nuns will likely play a key role. There are 400,000 soldiers in Burma, nearly the number of Buddhist monks in the country. The soldiers have a preponderance in arms, but religious organizations have greater legitimacy and moral authority among the people, so the government persecutes religious organizations and shuts down monastaries, seeing religious organizations as a threat to the state. As a senior monk whose monastery was closed after the uprising said, "The authorities have destroyed the economy, public health and the environment. Now Buddhism itself has come under attack."[67]

International Relations theory traditionally has had little to say to cases like this. Religion was viewed as either unimportant in world politics, or as undemocratic; both views are false. With modern globalization, the opening of societies has greatly aided the advancement of religion. Religion is resurgent in formerly Communist states, showing "godless communism" to have had a much more tenuous grasp on the populations than many previously imagined. But religious organizations have also helped to bring about democratization, in places such as the Philippines and Poland.

Historically, analysis of religion and democratization quickly turned to discussions of *which* religions helped democratization, and which ones did not. Conventional wisdom was that Protestant religions aided democratization, while hierarchical Catholicism and human-rights hindered Islam did not. "As an egalitarian religion profoundly opposed to hierarchy, Protestant Christianity would seem to enjoy a powerful affinity with democracy."[68] The facts did not always substantiate this thesis; from Cromwell to colonialism to Apartheid, in many cases Protestant religions did not advance democracy. Today the world's largest democracy, India, is a predominantly Hindu and Muslim country. The world's largest Muslim country, Indonesia, is also the world's third largest democracy. A more nuanced research focus is needed, which explores which elements of religions under what conditions help or hurt democratization.

The answers parallel the results on religion, war, and peace. Religious groups that hold political theologies that embrace human rights and democracy, and which work toward differentiation of political and religious institutions, advance democratization. Religious groups that hold exclusionary political theologies and that prefer integration with state institutions do not advance democracy. For example, the Catholic Church used to prefer integration with state power, and often supported nondemocratic regimes that supported the Catholic religion, in places like Spain, Portugal, Brazil, and Chile. When the Catholic Church's political theology dramatically changed after the Second Vatican Council (1962–1965) to become more clearly supportive of institutional separation with state structures, and of human rights, religious freedom, democracy, and development, the Catholic Church became a powerful aid to democratization in many places around the world. Seventy-five percent of the 30 countries that democratized after the Second Vatican Council were predominantly Catholic countries.

The question many raise today is whether Islam can make a similar transition. As Indonesia, India, and Turkey illustrate, Islam is compatible with democracy. The issue is in the details: Which specific version of Islam is espousing which ideas and political institutions, in which contexts? The record of democracy in Arab Islamic states is quite poor, untouched by the waves of democratization that have upended authoritarian regimes in all other parts of the globe. Yet nearly half of the world's Muslims live in democratic or partly free states, suggesting alternative futures should more variants of Islam emerge in Arab countries which espouse institutional separation and "Islamic concepts that favor democracy such as *shurah* (consultation), *ijma* (consensus), and *ijtihad* (independent interpretive judgment)."[69]

Put another way, how can religious and state institutions each develop what Alfred Stepan calls the "twin tolerations?" "Democracy is a system of conflict regulation that allows open competition over the values and goals that citizens want to advance,"[70] including religious values and religiously motivated goals. The challenge is not banishing religion from politics, but negotiating the boundaries within which the competition can take place, in ways which respect the institutions of both state and religious organizations. There is no exact one-size-fits-all answer, but stable democracies have to address the questions of "the minimal degree of toleration democracy needs from religion and the minimal degree of toleration that religion needs from the state for the polity to be democratic. Religious institutions should not have constitutionally privileged prerogatives which allow them authoritatively to mandate public policy to democratically elected officials. The minimal degree of toleration religion needs from democracy … is not only the complete right to worship, but the freedom of religious individuals and groups to publicly advance their values in civil society, and to sponsor organizations and movements in political society, as long as their public advancement of these beliefs does not impinge negatively on the liberties of other citizens, or violate democracy and the law, by violence."[71]

Nonviolence and religious freedom go hand in hand, and help form the basis of stable democracies.

Even where nonviolent religions are free to flourish, however, religion alone does not bring democracy. Other conditions matter. Catholicism was the majority religion in Poland with a long tradition of autonomy from the state. This gave church structures greater impact in their battles with the Communist regime. Minority religions may not have the same impact or legitimacy. As Nigerian Archbishop Onaiyekan describes the Catholic Church's role in advancing democracy and anticorruption in Nigeria,

> In my country, people at times accuse us of not doing enough to in-
> fluence the political fortunes of our nation. They point to the example
> and the record of Church action in a country like Philippines or
> Poland. I always remind them that Nigeria is neither the Philippines
> nor Poland. The Archbishop of Abuja does not have the same politi-
> cal clout as the Archbishop of Manila or of Warsaw. In the countries
> where the church is a dominant force, by mere fact of her relative
> numerical strength, the responsibility to be pro-active and indeed to
> be very much in the front line of peace building activities is clear and
> evident. In other countries, where the church is just one out of many
> religious groups, it will be up to the local church to assess and work
> out how far it can effectively move. In my country Nigeria, Catholics
> form no more than about 25 percent of the population. We know that
> we can only offer our own suggestions to the solutions of the prob-
> lems of the nation. We have no way to force our position on anyone,
> not even our Catholic members in public office. I must say however,
> that because of the coherence and objective merits of what we have to
> say, our message generally receives very good reception, well beyond
> the confines of the Catholic faith. Experience has shown that the
> church can always bear witness to justice and peace even in situations
> where it may be of very weak numerical strength.[72]

Minority religious groups can play important roles, with the help of modern technologies and global networks. They can be "eyes and ears," windows into authoritarian regimes, providing information about inter-nal conditions in countries (including human rights abuses and breaches of peace) when states cannot or will not do so, for example in Sudan or Sri Lanka. This information can be invaluable, and over time can aid de-mocratization and protection of human rights.

Again, religious freedom turns out to be a kind of "canary in the coal mine" for other human rights and freedoms necessary for democracy to function; perhaps this is why religious freedom was the first item on the U.S. Bill of Rights. "Throughout most of history the demand for religious freedom has come from religious minorities, dissenters ... this is not good enough. Let us make religious freedom the demand of majorities who understand that their own fates hang in the balance as well, if not today, then tomorrow. If we do not protect the religious freedom of even the smallest and weakest religious minorities, we are setting a precedent that will come back to haunt us. For if religious freedom—freedom of conscience—is not protected, the political freedoms of the right to vote, as well as freedom of speech, assembly, and press are certainly not safe."[73]

CONCLUSION: GETTING RELIGION RIGHT

The trends of resurgent religions in a world of challenged states mean the opportunities are increasing for religious groups, of all persuasions, to influence politics. The impact of religion in world politics is neither always good nor always evil, everywhere a cause of war or peace, democracy, or authoritarian rule. We have to make more distinctions than that. To "get religion right" in world politics, states and citizens will need to think and act in more serious and nuanced ways, and build the institutional capacities to engage with religious actors and factors.

Religion can be a source of peace and democratization when religious groups seek separation from state structures and espouse liberal political ideas including the protection of human rights. When states control or restrict religion, violence is more likely. Religious identity markers are often co-opted and manipulated in conflicts that are primarily about control over resources or political power, not souls and dogma, but once these religious elements are unleashed in nationalist and ethnic conflicts, the conflicts can be more difficult to solve. Religious peacebuilding is an important and underappreciated tool by states that lack institutional capacity in peacebuilding.

Globalization does not staunch religion, but may increase the quest for tradition and meaning in a material, uncertain, and fast-changing world. And globalization offers new tools to religious organizations that adapt and harness the technology, markets, and social networking possibilities of globalization to the traditional focus of faiths. Religious maps are changing, as demographics change; some traditional religions adapt or do not, while new groups compete. Religious practices and expressions change, as technologies and economies change, and many become those who believe but do not belong. But the part of human nature that seeks to understand the relation of humans to each other, to the cosmos, and to the Divine seems in no danger of extinction. Religions have always gone beyond sovereignty, but that process is now on steroids, aided by the technologies and ideas prominent in our age. And as religious organizations respond to the failures of states and to globalization's gaps, loyalties may be created or intensified that do not coincide with the boundaries of states, and are causing complications for states that seek to control or stamp out religious impulses and organizations. To borrow from Mark Twain, news of the death of religion has been overstated. Modernization and globalization have redrawn the map of religion in society, but they have not erased religion from society. Actually, the opposite has occurred. How to engage with resurgent religious actors and factors in a world of challenged states, how to extend the map of religious freedom, peace, and democracy to more areas of the world—these are the challenges of our time. We will continue to pay a high price if we fail to "get religion right," to engage with religious actors and factors in world politics.

ENDNOTES

1. President Barack Obama, "Speech at Cairo University," June 4, 2009.
2. Samuel P. Huntington, *The Clash of Civilizations and the Remaking of World Order* (New York: Simon & Schuster, 1996).
3. John Micklethwait and Adrian Wooldridge, *God Is Back* (New York: The Penguin Press, 2009), and book excerpt, "God Is Back," The Fox News Forum, April 9, 2009, <http://foxforum.blogs.foxnews.com/2009/04/06/god_faith_religion/>
4. Peter Berger, *The Desecularization of the World: Resurgent Religion in World Politics* (New York: Eerdmans, 1999).
5. Daniel Philpott, *Revolutions in Sovereignty* (Princeton, NJ: Princeton University Press, 2001), 5.
6. Sociologist Peter Berger's 1999 book, *The Desecularization of the World*, turned away from his previous decades of work promoting secularization theory.
7. John Micklethwait and Adrian Wooldridge, *God Is Back* (New York: The Penguin Press, 2009), and book excerpt, "God Is Back," The Fox News Forum, April 9, 2009, <http://foxforum.blogs.foxnews.com/2009/04/06/god_faith_religion/>
8. Daniel Philpott, *Revolutions in Sovereignty* (Princeton, NJ: Princeton University Press, 2001), 9.
9. Quoted in Winston Churchill, "The Gathering Storm," in *The Second World War*, vol. 1 (New York, NY: Houghton Mifflin Company, 1948), ch. 8.
10. Anna Machowska, "Soviets sent Bulgarian assassin to kill Pope John Paul II during Cold War," *The Daily Mail UK*, February 16, 2009, <http://www.dailymail.co.uk/news/worldnews/article_1146559/Soviet_spies_sent_Bulgarian_assassin_kill_Pope_John_Paul_II_Cold_War_claims_priest.html#>
11. Scott Appleby, *The Ambivalence of the Sacred* (Lanham, MD: Rowman and Littlefield, 1999); Thomas Farr, *World of Faith and Freedom: Why International Religious Liberty Is Vital to American National Security* (New York: Oxford University Press, 2008); Daniel Philpott,

"Explaining the Political Ambivalence of Religion," *The American Political Science Review* 101(3) (August 2007): 505–525; Daniel Philpott, "The Challenge of September 11th to Secularism in International Relations," *World Politics*, vol. 55 (Baltimore, MD: Johns Hopkins University Press, October 2002), 66–95; Scott M. Thomas, "Taking Religious and Cultural Pluralism Seriously: The Global Resurgence of Religion and the Transformation of International Society," *Millennium Journal of International Studies* 29(3) (Sage: 2000): 815–841; Thomas Farr, "Diplomacy in an Age of Faith: Religious Freedom and National Security," *Foreign Affairs* (New York: Council on Foreign Relations, April/May 2008); Max L. Stackhouse, *God and Globalization*, vols. 1–4 (Princeton: Center of Theological Inquiry, 2000–2009); Karen Armstrong, *The Battle for God* (Toronto: Ballantine Books, 2001); Gabriel Almond, Scott Appleby, and Emmanuel Silvan, *Strong Religion: The Rise of Fundamentalisms around the World* (The Fundamentalism Project) (Chicago: University of Chicago Press, 2003); Scott Thomas, *The Global Resurgence of Religion and the Transformation of International Relations* (New York, NY: Palgrave Macmillan, 2007); Robert Seiple and Dennis Hoover, *Religion and Security: The New Nexus in International Relations* (Lanham, MD: Rowman and Littlefield, 2004); Jonathan Fox and Schmuel Sandler, *Bringing Religion into International Relations* (Palgrave Macmillan, 2006); Eric O. Hansen, *Religion and Politics in the International System Today* (London: Cambridge University Press, 2006); Jeff Haynes, *An Introduction to International Relations and Religion* (Boston: Longman, 2007); John Micklethwait and Adrian Wooldridge, *God Is Back* (New York: The Penguin Press, 2009); and similar works.

12. Benjamin R. Barber, *Jihad vs. McWorld: How Globalism and Tribalism Are Reshaping the World* (New York: Ballantine Books, 1995); Thomas Friedman, *The Lexus and the Olive Tree* (New York: Farrar, Straus, & Giroux, 1999); Samuel Huntington, *The Clash of Civilizations* (New York, NY: Touchstone, 1996).

13. Liora Danon and the Center for Strategic and International Studies, "Mixed Blessings," August 2007, 2–3.

14. Scott Appleby, *The Ambivalence of the Sacred* (Lanham, MD: Rowman and Littlefield, 1999).

15. Milton Leitenberg, "Deaths in Wars and Conflicts Between 1945 and 2000" (Cornell University Peace Studies Program, Occasional paper #29, June 2006), <http://www.cissm.umd.edu/papers/files/deathswarsconflictsjune52006.pdf>; Walter Wink, *The Powers that Be* (New York, 1998).

16. David Singer and David Small, *The Correlates of War*; The Stockholm International Peace Research Institute (SIPRI) *Annual Yearbook of Major Armed Conflicts* (Stockholm: SIPRI, 2009); Monty Marshall and Ted Robert Gurr, *Peace and Conflict: A Global Survey of Armed conflicts, Self-Determination Movements, and Democracy* (College Park, MD: Center for International Development and Conflict Management University of Maryland, 2007).

17. Andrew Mack, *The Human Security Report, 2005: War and Peace in the 21st Century* (Oxford: Oxford University Press, 2005).

18. Milton Leitenberg, "Deaths in Wars and Conflicts Between 1945 and 2000" (Cornell University Peace Studies Program, Occasional paper #29, June 2006), <http://www.cissm.umd.edu/papers/files/deathswarsconflictsjune52006.pdf>

19. Vesselin Popovski, Gregory M. Reichbert, Nicholas Turner (Eds.), *World Religions and Norms of War* (New York: United Nations University Press, 2009).

20. Robert D. Kaplan, *The Coming Anarchy: Shattering the Dreams of the Post Cold War World* (New York: Vintage Books, 2001); Robert D. Kaplan, *Balkan Ghosts: A Journey through History* (New York: Vintage Books, 1994).

21. Susan Woodward, *Balkan Tragedy* (Washington, DC: Brookings Institution, 1995).

22. Scott Appleby, *The Ambivalence of the Sacred:* (Lanham, MD: Rowman and Littlefield, 1999), 70–71.

23. Maryann Cusimano Love, *Morality Matters: Ethics and Combating Terror* (Ithaca, New York: Cornell University Press, forthcoming).

24. Maryann Cusimano Love, *Morality Matters: Ethics and Combating Terror* (Ithaca, New York: Cornell University Press, forthcoming).

25. Associated Press, "A Rabbi, an Imam, and a Priest Discuss Their Painful Verses," May 6, 2008, <http://www.haaretz.com/hasen/spages/990622.html>.

26. Karen Armstrong, *The Battle for God* (Toronto: Ballantine Books, 2001).

27. Michael Gerson, "The Sultan and the Archbishop," *The Washington Post* (May 22, 2009); John L. Allen, Jr., "Tough Love With Islam: Church in Nigeria may be a model of dialogue," *National Catholic Reporter* (March 30, 2007).

28. Thomas Farr, *World of Faith and Freedom: Why International Religious Liberty Is Vital to American National Security* (New York: Oxford University Press, 2008); Daniel Philpott, "Explaining the Political Ambivalence of Religion," *The American Political Science Review* 101(3) (August 2007): 505–525; Philip Jenkins, "The Politics of Persecuted Religious Minorities," in *Religion and Security: The New Nexus in International Relations* (Lanham, MD: Rowman and Littlefield, 2004); Robert Seiple and Dennis Hoover (Eds.), *Religion and Security: The New Nexus in International Relations* (Lanham, MD: Rowman and Littlefield, 2004).

29. Scott Appleby, *The Ambivalence of the Sacred:* (Lanham, MD: Rowman and Littlefield, 1999).

30. Ibid., 86.

31. Ibid., 88.

32. "(1) multigenerational Protestant fundamentalism in North America; (2) Comunione e Liberazione, the Roman Catholic movement active in Italy and other parts of Europe; (3) international branches or offshoots of the original Egyptian Muslim Brotherhood, including Hamas and Hassan Turabi's National Islamic Front of Sudan; (4) the Sunni jama'at extremist cells influenced by the ideology of Maududi and Qutb and led by charismatic figures such as Omar Abdel Rahman of Egypt and Marwan Hadid of Syria (Algeria's Islamist movement, as it developed in the 1970s and 1980s, was also influenced by this ideological strain, as are the aforementioned global terrorist networks of bin Laden); (5) Shi'ite movements in Iran (led by the Ayatollah Khomeini and his successors) and Lebanon (Hizbullah); (6) Maududi's Jamaat-i-Islami organization in southern Asia, which remains strongest in Pakistan; (7) the Haredi, or ultra-Orthodox Jewish enclaves in Israel and North America; (8) Habad, the movement of Lubavitcher Hasidim, another Jewish messianist enclave but with missionary outreach toward the larger Jewish community; (9) Gush Emunim, the extremist backbone of the Israeli settler movement; and (10) the Sikh extremists agitating for a separate state (Khalistan) in the Punjab." Scott Appleby, *The Ambivalence of the Sacred* (Lanham, MD: Rowman and Littlefield, 1999), 103.

33. Adapted from Maryann Cusimano Love, *Morality Matters: Ethics and Combating Terror* (Ithaca, New York: Cornell University Press, forthcoming), ch. 2.

34. Michael Walzer, *Just and Unjust Wars: A Moral Argument with Historical Illustrations*, 3rd ed. (New York: Basic Books, 1977), 21.

35. Clement and Augustine (whom many consider the "father" of JWT), were Africans whose thought inspired later generations of European just war thinkers.

36. John Kelsay and James Turner Johnson (Eds.), *Just War and Jihad: Historical and Theoretical Perspectives on War and Peace in Western and Islamic Traditions* (New York: Greenwood Press, 1991); Karen Armstrong, *The Battle for God* (New York: Random House, 2000);

George W. Gawrych, "Jihad, War, and Terrorism," (Fort Leavenworth, KS: U.S. Army Command and General Staff College, Combat Studies Institute, n.d.), October 29, 2002, <http://www_cgsc.army.mil/csi/research/writing/JihadGawrych.asp>.

37. The greater jihad (to which all Muslims are called) is personal conversion and continued spiritual transformation. The lesser jihad (which is only necessitated under limited circumstances) is the defensive resort to arms to protect the Islamic community from attack. "The defensive jihad (*jihad al-dafaa*) is a widely accepted concept that is analogous to international norms of self-defense and Judeo-Christian just war theory. According to most Islamic scholars, when an outside force invades Muslim territory, it is incumbent upon all Muslims to wage jihad to protect the faith and the faithful. Mutual protection is seen as a religious obligation intended to ensure the survival of the global Muslim community. At the root of defensive jihad is a theological emphasis on justness, as embodied in Chapter 6, Verse 151 of the Quran: "Do not slay the soul sanctified by God except for just cause." Defending the faith-based community against external aggression is considered a just cause *par excellence*." (Quintan Wiktorowicz and John Kaltner, "Killing in the Name of Islam: Al-Qaeda's Justification for September 11," *Middle East Policy Council Journal* X(2) (Summer 2003). Defensive jihad not only parallels the *jus ad bellum* condition of just cause, but "the jihad tradition also requires right authority. Historically, the leader of the community—the caliph for the Sunnis and the imam for the Shiites—had to authorize the use of force ... to defend against an attack on Islamic society. But there were very stringent restrictions placed on this ... Furthermore, the jihad tradition includes very explicit limits on whom you may fight. There are a number of traditions associated with Prophet Mohammed which include the language 'you shall not kill the women and children.' Some of the traditions also include other groups of people: the aged, the infirm, the mentally incompetent. These are exactly the same kinds of lists we find in the just war tradition and in the contemporary international law of armed conflict." (James Turner Johnson, in Pew Forum on Religion and Public Life Panel Discussion, "Just War Tradition and the New War on Terrorism," (New York, October 2001). <http://pewforum.org/publications/reports/PFJustWar.pdf>, 8). Citing Islamic tradition concerning limitations on war, many prominent Islamic scholars and clerics condemned the September 11 terrorist attacks as inconsistent with Islam.

38. Shannon E. French, *The Code of the Warrior: The Values and Ideals of Warrior Cultures Throughout History* (Lanham, MD: Rowman & Littlefield, 2003).

39. Maryann Cusimano Love, *Morality Matters* (Ithaca, NY: Cornell University Press, forthcoming), ch. 2. Currently approximately 17 major armed conflicts are going on around the world, most taking place in Africa and Asia. That number is down from a high of 33 major armed conflicts immediately after the Cold War ended, but the number has been rather stable over the past 10 years. Most of these conflicts are civil or internal wars fought between government and rebel groups over who will control the country. In most of these wars serious *jus in bello* violations are routinely committed by both government and rebel groups (and are well documented by many NGOs and IGOs, such as the International Committee of the Red Cross (ICRC) and Red Crescent societies, Amnesty International, Human Rights Watch, Doctors Without Borders, and the UN High Commission for Human Rights and the UN High Commission for Refugees). Wars in which noncombatant immunity and discrimination are routinely and deliberately violated are not just wars (*jus in bello* criteria are not met), regardless of the rationales behind these conflicts. Further, we know that many wars are conducted for personal power or aggrandizement, by brutal, corrupt, self-interested dictators, governments, and rebel groups, at times supported by private mercenary groups; these wars do not meet *jus ad bellum* conditions (just cause, right intention, legitimate authority).

Yet we also know that sometimes innocents are slaughtered and in need of protection (e.g., September 11; Rwanda). So the empirical record of recent decades has been that while most wars are unjust, under rare conditions, war may be just. This rough, rule of thumb generalization can serve as a baseline to evaluate whether commentators (or we ourselves) are applying JWT responsibly. If all wars are deemed just, or all wars are deemed unjust, we should be suspicious. Similarly, since no country or decision maker has a lock on virtue or vice, we should be similarly skeptical should all wars by one country or leader be judged just or unjust (for example, the United States only fights just wars, or all U.S. military interventions are unjust). While the evaluation in any particular case may prove true upon further inspection, it may also be a red flag that jingoist, nationalist, ideological, or political biases are distorting judgment.

40. Maryann Cusimano Love, "What Kind of Peace Do We Seek? Emerging Peacebuilding Norms and Institutions," in Scott Appleby (Ed.), *The Ethics and Theology of Peacebuilding* (New York and London: Oxford University Press, forthcoming).

41. Capacity gaps are shortfalls in organizations or organizational strength, resources, personnel, competence, or standard operating procedures that hinder an institution's ability to effectively respond to problems.

42. IRIN, "Pakistan: Imams Involved in Health Drive," May 3, 2009, http://www.irinnews.org/PrintReport.aspx?ReportId=84206.

43. Second Vatican Council Promulgated by His Holiness Pope Paul VI, Gaudium et Spes, Pastoral Constitution on the Church in the Modern World, December 7, 1965, 26, <http://www.newadvent.org/library/docs_ec21gs.htm>.

44. As the U.S. Catholic bishops put it, "The church is not bound to any particular economic, political, or social system; it has lived with many forms of economic and social organization and will continue to do so, evaluating each according to moral and ethical principles: What is the impact of the system on people? Does it support or threaten human dignity?" U.S. Bishops, "Economic Justice for All," 1986, <http://www.osjspm.org/economic_justice_for_all.aspx>, 130. This is not an exclusionary or triumphalist position. Other nonstate actors, both religious and secular institutions, privilege attention to humans and communities over the interests of sovereign states, in both principles and practices. Because the Catholic Church is so large and has UN observer status and diplomatic missions, the higher levels of the Church (The Vatican and the various bishops' conferences) have sustained relations with states. But the dominant focus of the Church's work is not at the state, but at the community level.

45. Although recognizing the importance of human rights, the U.S. government and the United Nations begin from the default position of recognizing sovereign states regardless of the government's treatment of its own citizens. While a "responsibility to protect" norm is emerging at the United Nations and within the United States to justify humanitarian response in cases of genocide, war crimes, ethnic cleansing, and crimes against humanity, in practice this is controversial, partial, and difficult to implement, as the anemic responses to the ongoing genocide in Darfur indicate. The International Commission on Intervention and State Sovereignty in 2001 recommended to the UN secretary general " 'The Responsibility to Protect,' the idea that sovereign states have a responsibility to protect their own citizens from avoidable catastrophe, but that when they are unwilling or unable to do so, that responsibility must be borne by the broader community of *states*."; available at <http://www.iciss.ca/report-en.asp>. This principle was established in the UN Security Council 1674, adopted April 28, 2006, accepting "the responsibility to protect populations from genocide, war crimes, ethnic cleansing, and crimes against humanity."; available at <http://daccessdds.un.org/doc/UNDOC/GEN/N06/331/99/PDF/N0633199.pdf>. This moves the United Nations and the United States a step

closer to the position of the Church and other nonstate actors. But the fact that such a principle is only recently emerging and was needed shows the established default position is a deference to state sovereignty over protection of human persons.

46. Vatican, "Catholic Population Slightly Up, Annual Report Shows," Catholic News Service, October 25, 2004.

47. Benjamin R. Barber, *Jihad vs. McWorld: How Globalism and Tribalism Are Reshaping the World* (New York: Ballantine Books, 1995); Thomas Friedman, *The Lexus and the Olive Tree* (New York: Farrar, Straus, & Giroux, 1999); Samuel Huntington, *The Clash of Civilizations.*

48. Previous versions of the arguments in this article appeared in Maryann Cusimano Love, *Beyond Sovereignty: Issues for a Global Agenda* (New York: Thomson/Wadsworth, 2006); Address to Georgetown University, The International Conference Prayer for Peace, "Religion and Terrorism: Resurrection Politics," Washington, DC April 27, 2006; Keynote address to the International Conference of the World Union of Catholic Women's Organizations, "Women Peacemakers," Arlington, VA, June 1, 2006; Address at the Chicago Theological Union, to the Catholic Peacebuilding Network Conference, "Emerging Peacebuilding Institutions and Norms," Chicago, IL, April 19, 2006; Address to the Executive Leadership of the Roundtable, Georgetown June 16, 2006; and Address to Catholic University Conference on Globalization, "Globalization and Faith-Based NGOs: Opportunities for Political Action," Washington, DC, April 15, 2005.

49. Margaret E. Keck and Kathryn Sikkink, *Activists beyond Borders* (Ithaca, NY: Cornell University Press, 1998).

50. John Jackson, *Pastorpreneur* (Friendswood, Texas: Baxter Press, 2003).

51. Tyler Mathisen, "Do God and Money Mix?" *CNBC*, April 1, 2005, <http://www.msnbc.msn.com/id/7346446/>.

52. John Micklethwait and Adrian Wooldridge, *God Is Back: How the Global Revival of Faith Is Changing the World* (New York: The Penguin Press, 2009), 189.

53. John Micklethwait and Adrian Wooldridge, *God Is Back: How the Global Revival of Faith Is Changing the World* (New York: The Penguin Press, 2009), 19.

54. John Micklethwait and Adrian Wooldridge, "God Still Isn't Dead," *The Wall Street Journal* (New York: April 7, 2009), A15.

55. John Micklethwait and Adrian Wooldridge, *God Is Back: How the Global Revival of Faith Is Changing the World* (New York: The Penguin Press, 2009), 9.

56. Woodstock Theological Center, "Project on Globalization, Culture, and Ethics," Washington, DC: Georgetown University, 2006.

57. Pippa Norris and Ronald Inglehart, *Sacred and Secular: Religion and Politics Worldwide* (London: Cambridge University Press, 2004).

58. Grace Davie notes that Americans and Europeans "are *differently* religious." A similar point may hold for developed and developing countries. Grace Davie, "Pew Forum on Religion and Public Life: Believing without Belonging—Just How Secular Is Europe?" (FL: Key West, December 5, 2005), <http://pewforum.org/events/?EventID=97>.

59. Grace Davie, *Religion in Britain since 1945: Believing without Belonging* (New York: Blackwell, 1994).

60. USCCB, "Catholics Confront Global Poverty," <http://www.usccb.org/sdwp/globalpoverty/ccgp_index.shtml>; "A Place at the Table," <http://www.usccb.org/bishops/table.shtml>.

61. Fr. Ferdinand Muhigirwa, SJ, Centre d'Etudes Pour l'Action Sociale (CEPAS), Democratic Republic of Congo, "Natural Resource Extraction and Conflict in the Democratic Republic of Congo," Conference on The Future of Catholic Peacebuilding, Washington, DC: The Catholic University of America, April 7, 2008.

62. Catholic Relief Services, "Catholics Confront Global Poverty: Natural Resources and Our Catholic Response," <http://www.usccb.org/sdwp/globalpoverty/pdfs/Natural_Resources.pdf>.

63. Mike Sweitzer-Beckman, "Shareholder Activism Really Does Work," *National Catholic Reporter*, April 30, 2009; Interfaith Center on Corporate Activism, "ICCR Marks 40th Anniversary Chronicling the History of Faith-Based Shareholder Activism," June 18, 2009.

64. United Nations World Tourism Organization, "World Tourism Barometer," June 2009, <http://www.unwto.org/facts/eng/barometer.htm>; World Religious Travel Association, http://www.religioustravelassociation.com/; "Voluntourism," <http://www.voluntourism.org/index.html>; Corporation for National and Community Service, "Volunteering in America," July, 28 2008, <http://www.volunteeringinamerica.gov/press/press_releases.cfm>.

65. Coalition on the Environment and Jewish Life, "What's Jewish about Protecting the Environment? Ten Year Report," <http://www.coejl.org/~coejlor/about/TenYearReport.pdf>.

66. Ken Hackett and Rev. John McCullough, "Poorest People Need Resources to Deal with Climate Change," *Roll Call* (Washington, DC: June 3, 2009), <http://catholicclimatecovenant.org/wp_content/uploads/2009/04/crs_cws_rollcall.pdf>.

67. *Frontline*, "Burma and the Saffron Revolution: What Comes Next?" September 25, 2008.

68. Timothy Shah and Robert Woodberry, "The Pioneering Protestants," *The Journal of Democracy*, 15(2), (April 2004), 47.

69. Daniel Philpott, "Explaining the Political Ambivalence of Religion," *The American Political Science Review* 101(3) (August 2007), 515.

70. Alfred Stepan, "Religion, Democracy, and the 'Twin Tolerations,'" in Larry Diamond (Ed.), *World Religions and Democracy* (Baltimore: The Johns Hopkins University Press, 2005), 5.

71. Alfred Stepan, "The Multiple Secularisms of Modern Democracies," September 2006, SSRC Working Group paper for a forthcoming volume *Rethinking Secularism*, to be edited by Mark Juergensmeyer, October, 2007, 1.

72. Archbishop Onaihekan, "The Future of Catholic Peacebuilding Conference," The University of Notre Dame, South Bend, Indiana, April 13–15, 2008, <http://cpn.nd.edu/papers_2008CPN/Role%20of%20Bishops%20in%20Peacebuilding%20_%20Onaiyekan.pdf>

73. Elliot Abrams, "Religious Freedom: An American Perspective," International Coalition for Religious Freedom Conference on "Religious Freedom and the New Millenium," Tokyo, Japan, May 23–25, 1998.

CHAPTER EIGHT

People on the Move

Refugees, IDPs, and Migrants

Maryann Cusimano Love

Over a million people in the Swat Valley of Northwest Pakistan fled fighting between Taliban and government forces in May 2009. Unable to cross an international border, they sought emergency shelter and assistance outside their home region but within their country. As an aid worker for Catholic Relief Services (CRS) described it, "people just ran out of the house with nothing more than a blanket. Some piled onto trucks to get out of the region; others walked with young children for miles to get to the safety of camps and temporary shelters. They're traumatized. One mother told me she had to leave a handicapped child behind in order to save other family members. Another woman had to leave her father-in-law behind for the same reason."[1]

This experience is familiar to Denisa Baransata, a refugee in the Jesuit Refugee Services camp in Zimbabwe. Like many from the Great Lakes region in Central Africa of Burundi, Rwanda, and the Congo, she bundled up her family and fled the violence. As she describes her experience,

The war in Burundi is a war against civilians ... when I saw a group of soldiers coming towards our home, I knew this would not be the only visit. I left immediately, carrying my two-year-old baby on my back. I took nothing else with me, no clothes, no shoes, nothing. After walking for some time, I arrived at the outskirts of a town called Gasamanzuki, where I met so many people in distress. We stayed there without aid of any sort. We could not sleep, our children were crying because of hunger, cold, and rain. People died, especially children and pregnant women during delivery as there was no one to assist them ... After some days, the area was attacked by soldiers, and many people were killed. Some parents escaped without their children, some women who had twins took one and left the other behind. It was very painful. The survivors of the attack were marched by the armed forces into camps where they could be more effectively controlled, and subject to extensive rape and beating. People who resisted entering the camps were killed ... I decided to flee the country. On my way out, I saw bodies lying on the roadside, many of women and children. Today, I am a refugee in Harare, Zimbabwe. I have bad memories, it may be too hard for me to go back home. I do not even know if my husband is alive or dead. I prefer to have nothing, to be destitute, but to live in peace.[2]

Other people cross borders in search of economic opportunities. Looking for jobs, education, and a better life for themselves and their families, immigrants from Muslim and Arab countries came to Europe as part of post–World War II guest worker reconstruction programs. People from these countries continue to be the majority of immigrants to Europe today. Approximately 20 million Muslim immigrants now make Europe their home, accounting for about 5 percent of the total population.[3] According to the UN Arab Human Development Report, Arab countries are the youngest on the globe, with almost 38 percent of the population under the age of 14, significantly younger than the global average. Income and jobs are not growing commensurate with the population, however; more than half of Arab young people surveyed said that they wanted to emigrate outside the region.[4]

In contrast to this steady migration for economic reasons, others hastily flee environmental and natural disasters, often with only the clothes on their backs and without knowing the whereabouts of other family members and friends. Aminah and her 5 children survived the tsunami that killed 280,000 in South and Southeast Asia and washed away their Breuh Island home in Aceh, Indonesia, in December 2004. They lived on Sumatra Island, Indonesia, in a camp with 3,000 other storm survivors, until new homes could be built in partnership with the nongovernmental organizations (NGOs), CRS, and Jesuit Refugee Services.[5] Rebuilding so many homes and infrastructure after such total devastation takes time, and most must remain scattered in temporary housing or camps for years. Thousands living in southwest Pakistan suffered an earthquake on October 29, 2008. Some 225 are estimated dead, and another 15,000 have been left homeless.[6] Similarly, a million people fled the path of Hurricane Katrina along the Gulf Coast of the United States in the final days of August 2005, in the largest sudden displacement of Americans since the U.S. Civil War. Neither the San Francisco fire of 1906 nor the Dust Bowl in the 1930s forced as many people out of their homes.[7] The news media referred to this as an *exodus of U.S. refugees.*

But of the preceding examples, only Denisa from Burundi is a refugee. Those who fled the tsunami or the Taliban or earthquake in Pakistan or Hurricane Katrina are not refugees but internally displaced persons (IDPs), never crossing an international border. The millions who emigrate to find a better life are migrants, not refugees; they cross an international border but are not fleeing because of a well-founded fear of persecution.

According to international law, the 1951 UN Convention on Refugees defines a refugee as any person who "owing to well-founded fear of being persecuted for reasons of race, religion, nationality, membership of a particular social group, or political opinion, is outside the country of his nationality, and is unable to return to it." Those escaping natural or economic disasters, and those displaced within their countries, are not refugees. Consider the musical "The Sound of Music." The Von Trapp family, on the run from the Nazis, certainly was fleeing a well-founded fear of political persecution. But while they were hiding in the nunnery or climbing the Alps, they were not yet refugees but IDPs. Only when they crossed an international border did they satisfy the international legal definition of refugee, and qualify for asylum status in the country they entered.

WHY DOES IT MATTER HOW REFUGEES ARE DEFINED?

For people on the move, the legal definition of refugee seems full of arbitrary distinctions that only lawyers understand or love. People move to save their lives from a variety of threats to their survival: war, famine, violence, persecution, natural disasters, failed economies. But only some death threats count in international law as a "well-founded fear of persecution," and only some of those who are fleeing qualify for asylum and for international protections as refugees.

The refugee definition matters because 147 countries are signatories to the UN Convention and thus by international law are not supposed to turn away refugees but are expected to offer them asylum. The Convention commits the signatories not to return someone to a country where s/he would be in danger, in addition to offering protection to refugees by granting them the same rights as other foreigners living in their society. It also stipulates that states should not impose penalties on refugees when they have entered the country illegally or return a refugee to a country "where his life or freedom would be threatened on account of his race, religion, nationality, membership of a political social group or political opinion."[8] This does not mean that receiving countries are obligated to offer refugees citizenship. The law states only that host countries are not allowed to forcibly return refugees to their countries of origin, since to do so would be serving as an accomplice to murder, akin to sending Jewish refugees back to the Nazis during the Holocaust.

Based on the definition of a refugee as a person with a "well-founded fear of persecution" for reasons of race, religion, nationality, political opinion, or membership in a particular social group, the refugee definition is commonly understood to include 3 essential elements: (1) there must be a form of harm rising to the level of persecution, inflicted by a government or by individuals or a group that the government cannot or will not control; (2) the person's fear of such harm must be well-founded—the U.S. Supreme Court has ruled that a fear can be well-founded if there is a one-in-ten likelihood of its occurring; (3) the harm, or persecution, must be inflicted upon the person for reasons related to the person's race, religion, nationality, political opinion, or membership in a particular social group.[9]

The international definition of "refugee" has been interpreted primarily in the context of male asylum-seekers, to the prejudice of women refugees. Male political dissident Andrei Sakharov of the former Soviet Union, who was persecuted for denouncing totalitarianism, was the classic image of a refugee. In these Cold War cases, an adjudicator had little difficulty recognizing that the harm suffered amounted to persecution, forming the basis for refugee protection.

But women and children make up 80 percent of refugee and internally displaced populations, and the claims of women asylum-seekers often differ from those of men. "First, women often suffer harms which are either unique to their gender, such as female genital mutilation or forcible abortion, or which are more commonly inflicted upon women than men, such as rape or domestic violence. Second, women's claims differ from those of men in that they may suffer harms solely or exclusively because they are women, such as the policies of the Taliban in Afghanistan. And third, women often suffer harm at the hands of private individuals such as family members who threaten them with 'honor killings' or abusive spouses who batter them, rather than government actors."[10] For example, women in Eastern Congo are routinely raped and mutilated as a weapon of war; over 5.4 million people have died in the past 10 years in the Democratic Republic of Congo, in conflict fueled over natural resources such as the coltan used in cell phones. UN Special Rapporteur on violence against women, Ms. Yakin Erturk notes, "the scale and brutality of the atrocities amount to war crimes and crimes against humanity." Girls as young as 5 and grandmothers as old as 80 are not immune to gang rapes, rapes with tree limbs, guns, machetes. Mothers are raped while their husbands and children are tied to trees and forced to watch. In a stunning betrayal, the victims are shunned, blamed for their own attacks which humiliate the family, or because they are infected by the attacks with HIV/AIDs and other diseases, or because many are impregnated with the children of these criminals and enemies.[11]

Do women fleeing rape or female genital mutilation (FGM)[12] qualify as refugees? They are fleeing a well-founded fear of persecution due to membership in a social group (their gender), and they cross international borders and cannot return. But the UN Convention does not mention gender specifically, and various courts have ruled differently. International law cases are generally heard by domestic systems and courts, so each country (and sometimes different courts within the same country) can apply or interpret the law differently, and there is no "International Supreme Court" to appeal to for final decision or arbitration among conflicting decisions by lower courts. Some judges, concerned that allowing refugee status to women fleeing FGM would open up the floodgates to new refugee claims, have argued that FGM is an accepted "cultural practice" and does not rise to the threat status protected by the UN Convention. Others have ruled that the practice threatens the life and health of women due only to their membership in a social group (their gender), and therefore constitutes a well-founded fear of persecution as covered by the UN Convention.

What about women fleeing domestic violence? Should they be accorded refugee status? Rodi Alvarado was 16 when she married Francisco Osorio in Guatemala. Her husband brutally beat her and vowed to kill her. "Osorio raped and sodomized Rodi, broke windows and mirrors with her head, dislocated her jaw, and tried to abort her child by kicking her violently in the spine. Besides using his hands and his feet against her, he also resorted to weapons—pistol-whipping her and terrorizing her with his machete." Rodi's repeated attempts to obtain protection failed.

The police and the courts refused to intervene because it was a "domestic matter" and because her husband was a former army soldier. Rodi fled to the United States, where her case was unresolved for over a decade. Under the Clinton administration she was granted asylum, and the government "issued proposed regulations clarifying that victims of domestic violence and other gender-related persecution are eligible for asylum. However, these proposed regulations never became final."[13] Bush administration attorney general John Ashcroft considered deporting Ms. Alvarado back to Guatemala, but Justice Department attorneys prevailed and Obama administration officials recommend granting asylum.

Unfortunately, Ms. Alvarado's case is not an exception. "Honor killings" are the practice of murdering a woman in order to reclaim the family's "honor." A woman who is accused of socially unacceptable behaviors may be killed or brutally mutilated in order to wipe out the "blemish" on a family's good name. Offenses include walking without a male relative escort, being a victim of rape, kissing or engaging in sexual behavior out of wedlock, flirting, failing to serve a meal on time, seeking divorce, or seeking to choose one's own marriage partner rather than accede to an arranged marriage. In one case, "a husband murdered his wife based on a dream that she had betrayed him. In Turkey, a young woman's throat was slit in the town square because a love ballad had been dedicated to her over the radio . . . a 16-year-old mentally retarded girl who was raped in the Northwest Frontier province of Pakistan was turned over to her tribe's judicial council. Even though the crime was reported to the police and the perpetrator was arrested, the Pathan tribesmen decided that she had brought shame to her tribe and she was killed in front of a tribal gathering."[14] In some countries the practice is legal; in others, the law looks the other way as vigilante practice takes over. Estimates are that 5,000 women are killed in honor killings each year, but as the crime is generally unreported and unprosecuted, firm statistics are scarce. In India alone, for example, the United Nations cites that 5,000 women are murdered each year because their bridal dowries are deemed insufficient. Honor killings have been reported to the United Nations in Afghanistan, Bangladesh, Great Britain, Brazil, Ecuador, Egypt, India, Iraq, Iran, Israel, Italy, Jordan, Pakistan, Morocco, Sweden, Turkey, and Uganda.

Slaves and victims of human trafficking are other people on the move who are accorded little protection. There are 27 million slaves in the world today, more than ever before in human history. Slavery is nowhere legal, but the practice persists, and is on the rise due to the economic recession, according to the United Nations. Seventeenth-century slaves were considered valuable property to be defended, but 21st century slaves are primarily women and children; they cost little and are easy to replace and thus are considered disposable.[15] Eighty percent of people trafficked are women and girls, and more than 50 percent are minors. Human traffickers use a variety of methods. Children are kidnapped to work as child soldiers, as laborers in the Indian carpet industry, and as camel jockeys in the Gulf states. Women and girls in poor countries answer employment ads for legal jobs in developed countries as domestic workers, waitresses, and so on. When they report to the employer, they hand over their passports and ID so the employer can supposedly photocopy and verify the information, and use the documents to arrange border crossings. The girls soon learn they have been enslaved into the sex trade. They have no documents, are moved illegally across borders and sold in slave markets, are brutally beaten, and are told that if they work hard they can pay back their debt to the brothel owners for room and board and earn their freedom. Many do not know their whereabouts, do not speak the language to be able to ask for help, are incarcerated in the brothels, and report that the police are often customers, not would-be rescuers. Those that do risk beatings or death and are able to escape may find themselves imprisoned for prostitution and illegal immigration (even though they were forced into both). If deported back to their home countries, they are often ostracized by their families and communities for being prostitutes (and/or for being infected with HIV/AIDS, a common fate of those in the sex industry), and are then vulnerable to fall back into the hands of traffickers. Whereas the victims of trafficking are too often prosecuted rather than protected, traffickers often bribe local law enforcement and avoid prosecution. The United States works to pressure foreign governments to do more to prosecute human trafficking and protect victims through the Trafficking Victims Protection Act. But while the U.S. government spends nearly $76 million a year to aid antitrafficking efforts internationally, it has issued temporary visas to only 700 trafficking victims out of the estimated 50,000 women and children trafficked into the United States each year.[16]

While human rights groups argue that women fleeing honor killings, domestic violence, genital mutilation, or human trafficking meet the standard of "a well-founded fear of persecution," many governments have disagreed. An Afghan woman fleeing the abusive practices of the Taliban government, a Jordanian woman fleeing the practice of honor killing, and a Somali woman fleeing genital mutilation were all denied political asylum and refugee status and were ordered returned to their persecutors.[17] The legal definition of refugee matters quite intimately to people on the move.

GLOBALIZATION HELPS PEOPLE MOVE

Today there are more than 42 million refugees and displaced people[18] around the world. With an estimated 26 million IDPs in at least 50 countries, there are more than twice as many IDPs as refugees, which are estimated at 11.4 million.[19] Eighty percent of refugees are women and children. Many are victims of protracted conflicts and have not been able to return home for several years or even decades.

People are pushed into leaving home by war, violence, persecution, disease, environmental degradation, famine, economic crises, and natural disasters. People are pulled into leaving home by more attractive circumstances elsewhere (peace, jobs, and educational opportunities), compared to less-promising conditions at home. Countries court rich or educated workers from abroad. But countries resist foreign population flows of refugees and economic migrants, viewing poor and more vulnerable populations as a liability, a strain on public services and budgets, and a source of societal instability and violence. Trying to prevent population flows, many countries keep refugees warehoused in camps, separated from society, unable to farm or work or return to normal social patterns. Food to the camps may be rationed or cut back to encourage refugees to return home (whether or not conditions are safe for them at home). Families may be separated in camps, crime and rape too often occur, and the armies or militants who chased refugees from their homes may enter the camps and continue their violence.

Refugee flows mostly originate in the developing world. Sadly, the top sending countries reads like a Who's Who of conflict and instability: Afghanistan, Iraq, Colombia, Sudan, Somalia, Burundi, Democratic Republic of Congo, and Palestine. More than 27 percent of all refugees in 2008 were from Afghanistan, and Iraq and Afghanistan combined account for almost half of all refugees.[20] Those seeking refuge are usually headed for neighboring countries. The largest receiving countries in the world are Pakistan, Syria, Iran, Germany, Jordan, Tanzania, China, the United Kingdom, Chad, and the United States.

In addition to these continual refugee flows there are an estimated 192 million migrants around the world, and their numbers have been rising by about 2 percent per year, although the recession has slowed migration.[21] Migrant flows usually are headed toward developed countries and facilitated by open societies, open economies, and open technologies. As many state borders and trade barriers have been removed to encourage the free exchange of goods and services, information technologies facilitate digital communications and transactions beyond borders. Due to labor shortages in the information technology and health care sectors, many Western countries have practiced selective recruitment of skilled migrant workers; many other immigrants have made their way illegally into Europe and the United States.

Developed states have resorted to ever-new technologies and strategies intended to deter, divert, and preempt migrant flows along their porous borders. Aiming to detect illegal "human freight," British border authorities in Calais send trucks through X-ray scanners and use carbon monoxide tests to identify breathing inside freight containers.[22] In a highly controversial example of extraterritorial "punitive preemption," the Australian military intercepts boats with asylum-seeking refugees and migrants to prevent them from coming ashore; in one case in 2001, an Indonesian ship was sunk, killing 352 people.[23] In theory, the creation of a new frontier would thus add to the protection of the host country's borders, because asylum seekers would have to overcome an additional geographical barrier. Critics note that moving the processing centers to the places people are trying to escape from undermines the very concept of asylum. Additionally, these measures are no guarantee for keeping people out. Thousands risk their lives every year by crossing the Mediterranean Sea in rubber boats, walking across the Mexican desert, or jumping onto Eurochunnel trains; it is far from clear that new frontiers will deter people from coming. Located at the coast of Morocco, the Spanish enclave Ceuta has served as the "southernmost gateway" to Europe for thousands of asylum seekers who manage to overcome barbed wire fences with sensory lights and 24-hour guards.[24] Even after increased security to the Eurochunnel tunnels, refugees and migrants continue to come to the French frontier town of Calais.[25]

Sovereign borders do not keep out people flows. As it has become both more cumbersome and costly to distinguish between wanted and unwanted border flows, migrants and asylum seekers often benefit from the same information, technology, and dwindling transportation costs that made globalization possible in the first place. They can resort to services provided by illegal smuggling networks that specialize in human trafficking via air and road transportation, or global container trade.[26] And they can "get lost among thousands of other undocumented immigrants."[27]

Sovereign institutions are unwilling or slow to respond to the needs of migratory populations. Plagued by application backlogs, the often-inefficient systems have created a general "impression of governmental incompetence and incapacity."[28] Applications might take years to process—one asylum-seeker in Britain has been detained for 8 years[29]—but asylum seekers and migrants do not have a voice or a vote in the democratic politics of their host countries.[30]

Economic migrants, however, are becoming increasingly powerful in the political systems of the countries they left. Monies sent home from emigrants are "one of the most visible manifestations of today's migration,"[31] and have become a huge income source in many developing countries. Remittances to developing countries total more than $251 billion. Mexico is the world's largest recipient of remittances, receiving more than $25 billion per year.[32] After foreign direct investment (FDI), it is the second largest component of external financing in the Latin America, and the largest form of income for countries such as El Salvador and Honduras.[33]

"Remittance management" serves as an example for an emerging public–private partnership beyond sovereignty, involving the governments and the private sector in both home and host countries. As remittances have surpassed official development assistance since 1996, Western governments like to think of the monies sent to local communities as development aid that can alleviate poverty in developing countries.[34] Because these flows could be even higher if the transfer was handled more efficiently, governments are working to cut transfer costs by reducing exchange rates in receiving countries and fostering competition between banks.[35] Banks, too, are eager to increase their share in a market that has been dominated by transfer agencies like Western Union and informal operators. Currently the World Bank is supporting efforts to transmit remittances via mobile phones, making transfers faster and cheaper.[36] Banks in origin and receiving countries have started joining forces so both can profit from a greater network and visibility.[37] While both parties are interested in improving existing channeling structures, Western governments are also seeking to stop informal and anonymous money transactions beyond sovereignty. Known as black market peso exchange in Latin America and hawala in the Islamic world, these transactions are impossible to track and usually take place in venues used by money laundering and other organized crime networks.[38] On the receiving end, Latin American governments and banks have designed remittance plans that can be used to secure long-term loans and credit, and even home ownership in Peru. In Ecuador, people can use remittances to qualify for mortgages and to build education and retirement funds.[39] Guatemalan, Mexican, and Salvadoran expatriates have formed hometown associations through which remittances are pooled and eventually used for local community projects in their respective home countries, provinces, and villages.[40] Programs have been largely successful, and according to the World Bank, monies "appear to be a more stable source of external financing and to be more evenly distributed among and within countries" than other foreign investment sources.[41]

Once they are registered voters in their home countries, many migrants retain voting rights in sending countries and are a powerful and much sought after constituency. Elections now go beyond sovereignty, as Mexican Presidential candidates campaign in California, Texas, and Florida to earn the votes of Mexicans who have emigrated to the United States, but can cast absentee votes by mail.[42] From the Philippines to Iraq and South Africa, overseas citizens vote in state and federal elections.[43]

NGOs SERVING PEOPLE ON THE MOVE

NGO numbers and capabilities to serve as advocates and provide services for the displaced have increased as a result of the expanded communications and networking capacities allowed by globalization. On the pro side, NGOs provide much-needed services to vulnerable populations who are truly beyond sovereignty, often not served well by either the governments of sending countries or host countries. NGOs can be powerful advocates and watchdogs for the rights of people on the move, providing a voice for those who otherwise would have no voice in international politics, and bringing attention and pressure on abusive and corrupt governments and policies. On the con side, NGOs operate at the intersection between the global and the local, and are challenged to walk on that fault line when international practices or concerns do not match local ones. Do international NGOs impose one-size-fits-all packages of services, or do the people served have an ability to articulate and participate in meeting their own needs, both short and long term? Are the practices of NGOs transparent and accountable? When governments are corrupt or abusive, do NGOs have the ability to challenge this, or must they "go along to get along," looking the other way or participating in corrupt practices in order to be able to do their jobs and serve people on the move?

NGOs provide services for people on the move at all stages of their movements: NGOs provide instant emergency relief and everyday food, clothing, shelter, medical, legal, and educational services to refugee settlements and IDP camps, assist in post-conflict resettlement and reconstruction efforts once they can return home, as well as guide them through the complex asylum jungle in receiving countries. Suffering from budget cuts, the UNHCR (the Office of the United Nations High Commissioner for Refugees, traditionally the lead agency for refugee relief) increasingly relies on NGOs for the work on the ground. At the same time, donor governments have shown a tendency to directly contact and work through NGOs, which are frequently viewed as a more flexible and cheaper alternative to working through governments.[44] Unlike the UNHCR, NGOs also do not need the permission of sovereign governments to assist IDPs in relief efforts that go beyond sovereignty.[45]

Field NGOs, both indigenous and international, play a crucial role in the on-site assistance of refugees and IDPs. Their very presence can be essential for the safety of displaced people, as they serve as a deterrent against violent attacks inside and outside the confinements of their camps.[46] Basic on-site services generally include the distribution of food rations and provision of health care to meet everyday needs. NGOs may provide trauma and psychological counseling, human rights education, and legal assistance.

Other NGO activities are geared toward the future and designed to increase the self-reliance and dignity of displaced persons. Jesuit Refugee Services offers education, sewing, carpentry, farming, small business, and handicraft opportunities to help refugees return to work and become self-sufficient. In Tanzanian camps, NGOs offer workshops so refugees can develop baking, weaving, and carpentry skills.[47] Refugees in Guinean camps received loan services and business training. The American Refugee Committee managed to continue this service even after the refugees had returned to their homes in Sierra Leone so their credit history would not get lost.[48] In Mozambique and Rwanda, World Relief has successfully introduced microfinance programs, allowing refugees and displaced persons to take out loans, keep savings accounts for remittances, or even transfer money between camps.[49] NGO work on the ground often involves long-term development projects as well. While assisting in the resettlement of refugees in Ethiopia, environmental protection, including reforestation and soil conservation, is a core responsibility of local NGOs.[50] NGO projects involving the construction of roads, schools, and health centers improve local infrastructures and have "strategic" implications, as the facilities benefit displaced and local populations alike.[51]

While many of these initiatives can revive local economies and reduce strains between local and refugee populations, NGO supply structures can also have detrimental effects. NGO services may undermine state structures that are already too weak to perform these functions and provide for their own people. In the case of Tanzania, the local benefits of NGO services were so dramatic that the United Nations called the full repatriation of the refugees to their home countries "the worst-case scenario for the [nearby villages] in terms of access to services utilized in the camps for local populations who have no other facilities to turn to."[52] Governments are not oblivious to the possible effects of these parallel NGO structures.

For example, government agencies closely monitor NGOs in Eastern Tigray because "their population usually feels more related to (foreign) NGOs, who are, after all, their main service providers, than to their government. This erodes the government's base of support."[53] The Ethiopian government has also been suspicious of any NGO projects involving civic or human rights education, fearing that it might lead people to question the ruling elite.[54]

NGO relationships with local governments are usually complicated. NGOs walk a fine line: cooperation with local governments may be necessary to help provide refugees with security and access local economic systems. However, NGOs serve as watchdogs and advocates for refugees, and must be accountable to their donors, so NGOs are often critical of government actions, which may put their personnel and programs in danger, as when the government of Sudan expelled many foreign NGOs assisting refugees from Darfur.[55] Field NGOs might also decide to follow local rules out of fear that governments might take revenge and close them down.[56] In these situations, international NGOs have an advantage over indigenous NGOs because it is easier for them to join forces with human rights agencies, publicizing and decrying abuses and fraud without revealing sources.[57] The collaboration between Jesuit Refugee Services and Human Rights Watch is an example of this kind of symbiosis.

The sheer number of different NGOs, both local and international, creates competition between NGOs and poses challenges for the coordination of relief efforts and long-term development.[58] NGOs need to coordinate their activities among themselves and with fellow international actors. In times of emergency, local organizations may be "pushed aside" and "cannibalized" by larger and better-equipped international NGOs, which might also seek to recruit their personnel.[59] Sometimes collaboration between NGOs is further complicated by the fact that some NGOs have become hybrid organizations with diffuse agendas, and might also be accountable to their donors (DONGOs) or the local government (GONGOs).[60] As field NGOs are attuned to their community's needs and problems, their "embeddedness" can also affect their "objectivity." There is a risk that NGOs might become entangled in power politics as humanitarian operations can be used to justify foreign interventions and facilitate convenient supply lines for troops and warring factions.

Conversely, critics argue that NGOs (as the operational arm of the international donor community) too often acquiesce to local practices and fail to use the "power of the purse" to ensure basic rights of those refugees whose status has remained in limbo for sometimes whole generations. The U.S. Committee for Refugees campaigns against *refugee warehousing*, which refers to refugees who have been living in refugee camps for 5 or more years and are deprived of the right to work or move freely; 9 million refugees "are *warehoused*, confined to camps or segregated settlements or otherwise deprived of these basic rights, in situations lasting 10 years or more."[61] Host governments often isolate refugees, who remain cut off from local markets and dependent on international aid, in an attempt to reduce the attractiveness of their country as a permanent resettlement site. As conflicts in Somalia, Burundi, or Myanmar have dragged on for more than a century, these camps have served as recruitment centers for future generations of soldiers and terrorists who are interested in perpetuating the conflict that caused the displacement in the first place.[62] The camps can serve as a breeding ground for conflicts to spill over into the host country and destabilize an entire region, as the example of Rwandan refugee camps in Zaire illustrated in the 1990s. IDP camps breed similar problems.[63]

NGOs face a number of "balancing act" challenges: short- versus long-term activities; relief and development versus justice and peace-building activities; activities that address symptoms or underlying causes. For example, CRS had been active in relief, development, refugee, and IDP work in Rwanda for more than 3 decades when the Rwandan genocide broke out in April 1994, killing 800,000 and displacing over a million more. CRS had known of the underlying fault lines in Rwandan society but had not attempted to resolve them, instead working around them to deliver relief and development services. As Fr. Bill Headley of CRS describes it,

> Peace had not been part of the mission of CRS. It had not been part of what we did. We had competencies in agriculture, health, education and a number of other social service disciplines … And so, CRS did its development work and did it well. What we were not prepared to do was make peace. When the genocide occurred, CRS' projects were wiped out in days; many of the people we had served became the 'well-fed dead.' After and partly because of the genocide, CRS took a hard look at itself. This introspection called us to realize that we could no longer just address the symptoms of conflict-stimulated crisis: burned out houses, food shortages and refugee movements. We also had to attack the systems and structures that underlie oppression and poverty …
> Today, peacebuilding is an agency-wide priority for CRS. Aided by U.S. government funding, CRS brought a group of 21 Burundians, including bishops, priests, sisters and a range of lay leaders, to the Baltimore area. They were offered three weeks of joint planning and preparation for practical peacebuilding back in Burundi. It was reasoned that in a

predominantly Catholic country, where a decade-old conflict still smolders, the church with its array of institutions could play a critical role.[64]

CRS's story is not unique among NGOs. All organizations must balance concerns over mission-creep with questions of long-term effect and sustainability. Is success providing emergency food assistance reliably for years to refugees who are in limbo, restricted to camps, not allowed to move forward or move back? Or is success helping refugees to make new lives abroad and resolving conflicts so they may repatriate back home, creating sustainable livelihoods so they will not need future emergency food aid? Organizations which serve refugees must adapt with the needs of changing populations and situations.

NEVER AGAIN: WWII AND THE HISTORY OF THE UNHCR

The Office of the United Nations High Commissioner for Refugees was created with the experience of the Second World War and the Holocaust in mind, but has had to adapt since its inception. On May 13, 1939, the S.S. *St. Louis* passenger ship set sail from Hamburg, Germany. Nine hundred of its 937 passengers were German Jews fleeing Hitler's Nazi regime to join relatives or start new lives in the Americas. But when the ship arrived in Havana, the Cuban government refused entry to the passengers. The captain then sailed the ship to Florida, but the U.S. government also refused to admit the refugees; the Coast Guard even fired a warning shot to turn the ship away from the U.S. coastline. The ship's passengers, dubbed "the Voyage of the Damned," then appealed to other countries to save them from the certain death awaiting should they be returned to Nazi Germany. Belgium, Holland, France, and England eventually admitted the refugees, but the first 3 countries were overrun by the Nazis within months. The *St. Louis* passengers died in the Holocaust along with other European Jews who were unable to escape. Only the few passengers admitted into England survived.[65]

After the Nazi regime's ouster and the end of World War II, memory of the Holocaust galvanized international human rights groups. The establishment of the Universal Declaration of Human Rights, the International Convention to Prevent Genocide, and the UNHCR were all informed by the Holocaust and the motto "Never again." The 1951 UN Convention on Refugees' definition of a refugee as any person who "owing to well-founded fear of being persecuted for reasons of race, religion, nationality, membership in a particular social group, or political opinion, is outside the country of his nationality, and is unable to return to it," becomes more understandable in the context of the Holocaust. Had this treaty been in force before World War II, the thinking went, countries would not have been allowed to turn away Jews fleeing Nazi persecution. People fleeing persecution, refugees, ought to be allowed protected status and not be forcibly returned to their home countries and the peril that awaits them there.

The Cold War left its mark on the Refugee Convention. As the world became split into the Communist East and the Democratic West, the refugee definition was used to embarrass the Soviet Union and Eastern bloc countries. Defectors leaving the Soviet bloc by definition were welcomed into the West as refugees. They did not have to prove that they particularly or personally had a well-founded fear of persecution, as did those coming from Africa or other regions. Soviet defectors were welcomed as refugees simply because they hailed from a communist state, and the existence of these defectors was used in the propaganda war between East and West to show the deficiencies of the communist system (how good could the communist dream really be if people were fleeing it?). This policy was abruptly changed when the Berlin Wall fell in 1989 and the USSR dissolved in 1991. The reversal shocked many defecting from Russia shortly after the political changeover, who were surprised to find they no longer had special treatment, and had to show a well-founded threat of persecution to themselves particularly, as did any other asylum applicant.

The UNHCR began in this climate after World War II. With a 3-year mandate, it was believed to be a temporary agency that would close its doors after having resettled those people displaced by World War II. Unfortunately, wars and persecution continued. The UNHCR mandate was extended every 5 years to serve the growing number of people that were displaced in the wars of colonial independence in Asia and Africa during the 1950s, '60s and '70s.[66] As an international agency of the United Nations, the UNHCR dealt with refugees displaced across borders, tending to refugees' needs in the relatively sheltered environment of their new host countries. Toward the end of the Cold War, the increase in civil wars in which civilians were a common target of violence brought new challenges to the UN relief agency. Originally with a mandate to serve only refugees, the United Nations extended the organization's mission to also serve IDPs in 1992 in response to the war in Bosnia and Herzegovina, and appointed Francis Deng as the Representative on Internally Displaced Persons.[67] The decision heralded the beginning of a new era in which the UNHCR's mandate of assisting and protecting refugees was expanded to include IDPs, thus going beyond sovereignty.

As the former state of Yugoslavia broke apart in civil wars in the Balkans, the problems associated with only helping refugees became apparent. Slobodan Milosevic, President of the former Republic of Yugoslavia and head of its armed forces, was the first head of state to be placed on trial for crimes against humanity and violations of the Geneva Conventions and the laws of war; he died in prison before the trial's end.[68] Milosevic's charges were due to his acts of ethnic cleansing, attempting to force ethnic Bosnians, Croatians, and Albanians out of lands he wanted to claim for Serbia. In this case, if the UNHCR tended to people's needs only after they left their homes and crossed an international border, was the UNHCR in some way aiding and abetting ethnic cleansing? Some argued that the UNHCR should attend to the needs of IDPs before they crossed international borders and became refugees. It was not enough to help refugees after the fact; UNHCR should be working to prevent the dire circumstances that caused people to flee. More narrow political interests were also in play. Western European countries were interested in preventing refugee flows. If people could be encouraged to stay in their home countries, it would relieve the strain on host countries caused by refugee flows.[69] In Bosnia, the UNHCR was thus tasked with creating safe areas of "humanitarian space" for civilians so they would not have to leave. Once the fighting broke out, however, the UNHCR faced an impossible mission. As the conflict moved, previously "safe areas" became areas of war. UNHCR often had to negotiate with the warring parties in order to get aid shipments through to the civilian population, and the UNHCR could not protect civilians from hostile factions determined to implement ethnic cleansing.[70] The United Nations introduced peacekeeping troops, United Nations Protection Force (UNPROFOR), to try to stabilize the situation. But the introduction of UN peacekeeping troops undermined UNHCR's role as a neutral provider of humanitarian aid, and the peacekeepers' limited mandate made them ineffective and unable to provide the support UNHCR needed.[71] A mission to save people from refugee miseries thus "took on the characteristics of preventing flight rather than changing conditions."[72]

The case of the former Yugoslavia illustrates the ongoing difficulties the United Nations and relief agencies face in trying to deliver humanitarian assistance in the midst of conflict. It also shows that while people and relief agencies move beyond sovereign borders, state actors can undermine attempts to help IDPs and refugees. States pushing people out may not want outsiders "meddling" in their affairs, and states receiving refugees may not want them and may try, despite the Refugee Convention, to make it difficult for refugees to enter their countries and unattractive for them to stay.

MIGRATION TRENDS AFTER SEPTEMBER 11

Not one of the September 11 bombers entered the United States as a refugee claiming asylum. The London and Madrid bombers appear to have been British and Spanish citizens, respectively. Nevertheless, after September 11 and other attacks, refugee and asylum and immigration programs came under increased scrutiny and anti-immigration platforms thrived in the politics of Western countries. The U.S. government initially placed a moratorium on refugee admissions while a comprehensive review of procedures was undertaken and new security measures were developed and implemented. As Arthur Dewey, then Assistant Secretary of State for Population, Refugees, and Migration, noted, "demented individuals" might use the U.S. refugee admissions program as "a soft underbelly for such entry."[73] Refugee admissions dropped precipitously. A decade ago, the United States typically allowed about 130,000 refugees into the country each year. In 2001, the United States admitted 69,304. This fell to 27,110 in 2002 and 28,422 in 2003, even though the presidential authorization for 70,000 refugees had not changed.[74]

Even after new security screening procedures were in place, many previously approved refugees remained frozen out of the United States, in limbo. A group of 230 Lebanese approved for refugee resettlement into the United States, and a group of Iraqi refugees waiting to be processed, were shut out for several years. Statistics cannot do justice to the suffering that is behind these cases, notes Lavinia Limon, executive director of Immigration and Refugee Services of America and the U.S. Committee for Refugees, a nonprofit resettlement agency in Washington, DC. Limon expressed grave concern about many refugees who were murdered, who died of diseases, who were raped, deported, or incarcerated because they were kept in limbo in the aftermath of the September 11 attacks. In spite of years of delays and detailed background checks, not a single refugee applicant has turned out to be a security threat, said a State Department official, speaking on condition of anonymity. That does not surprise people like Limon who believes that no terrorist would waste his or her time sitting for 10 years in a refugee camp waiting to win the lottery for resettlement into the United States. Furthermore, Limon thinks that the plummeting rate of refugees has been triggered by "bureaucratic inertia ... or perhaps even more scary is the fact that people are more comfortable saying nothing than saying yes, because everyone is so afraid they are going to be the one to sign the visa for someone who might turn out to be a terrorist."[75]

Initially bureaucratic inertia seemed to be the stumbling block for resumption of the U.S. refugee resettlement program. Then the program was underfunded. Today refugee admissions are again creeping upward at 48,282, although they still fall far short of the 70,000 ceiling and previous levels.[76] But today the USA PATRIOT anti-terrorism law itself is an obstacle to legitimate refugees. A provision of the Patriot Act excludes from refugee admission anyone who has provided "material support" to any organization involved in terrorist activities. Unfortunately this clause has been broadly interpreted without exceptions for "support" forced at gunpoint or under duress, or for minimal or unknowing support. This means that Colombian families forced to pay ransom for the return of kidnapped loved ones are deemed to be terrorist supporters rather than being recognized as victims of terrorism. Most Colombians identified by the UNHCR as in need of resettlement are thus excluded, as extortion by paramilitary forces is routine. Even Iraqis who worked with U.S. forces to overthrow the government of Saddam Hussein were excluded by this law that was intended to catch terrorists.

PROSPECTS FOR THE FUTURE

People are hardwired to survive. Thus people have always moved to flee violence, persecution, disease, famine, disaster, and to find a better place in the world for themselves and their families. The modern period of globalization makes it easier than ever before for people to move across sovereign borders. The challenges presented by people on the move will not go away on their own, but will only intensify.

The push factors of war, violence, persecution, disease, environmental degradation, famine, economic crises, and "natural" disasters show no signs of abating. In fact quite the opposite has been true: as people build large and permanent nonsustainable settlements (in coastal areas, flood plains, cliffs, earthquake zones, wild fire plains, mud slide areas, deserts, and barrier islands, using inexpensive and impermanent building materials and techniques) weather cycles are ever more deadly and costly. As global climate change increases, sea levels rise and weather patterns change, forcing people to move. The UN Intergovernmental Panel on Climate Change (IPCC) estimates 150 million environmental refugees will exist by 2050, dwarfing the numbers of "political" refugees by orders of magnitude. We are already seeing these "environmental refugees"; residents of Pacific Islands have had to move as rising seawaters have submerged their lands. As one evacuating islander put it, "All those big countries like America and Russia and in Europe are making all the pollution, but we are the ones who are suffering for it." New Zealand, one of the few countries to acknowledge and plan for environmental refugees, has agreed to accept 11,000 Tuvaluan island residents who will be forced to leave their home.[77]

Additionally, the flow of 24/7 information gives pull factors a loud megaphone with global reach. There has always been inequality in the world. But people today are more likely to know that there are places in the world where people don't suffer from war, violence, persecution, disease, environmental degradation, famine, economic crises, and disaster, and to know how to get there. Demographic trends ensure that pull factors will be with us for some time. Developed countries are graying, while developing countries have majorities of young people of working age. Developed countries need to import labor to sustain their economies, lifestyles, and aging populations.

Alleviating push factors addresses the root causes that force people unwillingly out of their homes. To protect people in their home communities from forced dispersion, governments and the private sector must work together to foster peace, build sustainable economies and stable environments, and protect human rights. CRS and Mennonite peace-building activities are examples of public–private partnerships to address underlying causes that force people from their homes.

Stopping and prosecuting practices such as female genital mutilation, honor killings, human trafficking, and other violence against women, will help protect women and allow them and their children to remain in their homes. Some progress has been made,[78] as the United States and the UN have enacted anti-trafficking laws and conventions that pressure action by other states.[79] Much work remains to be done, however, as millions are still victims of these practices, in developed and developing countries alike.

These issues are linked. For example, people may be forced from their homes due to food shortages, but famines are political rather than natural disasters; no democracy with a free press has ever suffered a major famine. Even when crops fail or drought prevails, food is generally available in other parts of the country or region, but food is not distributed to vulnerable populations for political reasons. Food may be used as a weapon by conflicting sides, as in the Somali famine of 1992.[80] Starvation may be used to punish rebels, to achieve ethnic cleansing, to make a population docile or to weed out insurgents, as in Sudan, or the Irish potato famine of 1846–1850. And refugee camps may be deprived of food in order to push refugees out of host countries. Alleviating the underlying conflicts and environmental degradation that cause food shortages prevents not only starvation, malnutrition, and the related diseases that prey on compromised immune systems, but it also prevents refugee flows.

Lessening push factors also decreases pull factors, which are often a matter of relative gains. Leaving home is never easy and extracts a host of social, political, economic, emotional, familial, and spiritual costs. These costs loom larger and life abroad looks less attractive when life at home holds more promise.

But minimizing push and pull factors will not eradicate them. People will vote with their feet as long as global inequalities persist in human security; political and religious rights and freedoms; education, job, and economic opportunities; and safe environments. Personal security will always trump deference to sovereignty. As long as people continue to move, and governments respond insufficiently to the needs of people on the move, NGOs and IGOs will continue to step into the gap, serving in critical capacities and at times challenging states. Larger networks of people, money, and services exist and work in these gaps of sovereignty.

Previous forms of political organization took a more flexible approach toward migratory populations. As sovereignty tied territory to jurisdiction, people were no longer defined as "children of God" or other more mobile identities, but primarily as citizens of a particular geographic space. Civic rights and governmental responsibilities depended on where you lived. Counterintuitively, today attempts to harden and militarize borders against population flows have the unintended consequence of increasing the number of permanent illegal aliens resident in developed countries. When borders are more permeable, people prefer to move back and forth with circumstances or with the employment market, retaining their homes abroad. But as immigration becomes more restrictive, the cost and danger of border crossings make trips back and forth too difficult and risky. Families become split, and efforts to keep out illegal aliens work perversely to wall them in. Attempts to manage population flows must begin with the recognition that developed economies critically depend on imported labor and will continue to do so as their populations age. A globalization that protects and defends capital flows but not people flows is highly problematic, leads to pernicious injustices, and fuels security problems. The growth of al Qaeda in Europe is fueled by resentments of Muslims whose parents emigrated to Europe via guest worker programs. These Muslims are European citizens who feel they have not been respected, welcomed, or fairly treated by other Europeans. From Burundi and Rwanda to Europe, improperly handled population flows can lay the groundwork for conflicts to come.

The growth of international humanitarian law, such as the International Conventions on Refugees and Human Rights, and the practices of NGOs and IGOs, are expanding the notions of human rights and governmental responsibilities regardless of a person's residence or country of origin. As states increasingly contract out aid and social service functions to NGOs, they aid the growth of nonstate actors, which work to promote ideas of portable human rights regardless of geographic borders. People have fundamental human rights regardless of the countries they find themselves in. States and MNCs have an interest in expanding human rights beyond sovereign borders, if only to protect their own industries and populations from conflict and instability. We need to move from reactive responses to flows of people after the fact, to more proactive responses to the underlying causes that force people to move.

ENDNOTES

1. Liz O'Neal, "Desperate Pakistanis Flee Fighting in Swat Valley," CRS, May 2009, <http://crs.org/pakistan/swat-valley-violence/>.
2. Jesuit Refugee Services, "War Has Changed Our Life, Not Our Spirit: Experiences of Forcibly Displaced Women," Rome, Italy, 2001, <www.jrs.net/jrs/>.
3. Robert S. Leiken, "Europe's Angry Muslims," *Foreign Affairs* (July/August 2005).
4. United Nations, "Arab Human Development Report," 2003, <www.undp.org/rbas/ahdr/englishpresskit2003.html>.
5. Catholic Relief Services, "Rebuilding after the Tsunami," *The Wooden Bell*, 16(5) (Aug. 2005): 3.
6. Liz O'Neil, "Pakistan Earthquake Puts Women, Kids at Risk," CRS, October 31, 2008, <http://crs.org/pakistan/baluchistan-earthquake-2008/>.
7. David Von Drehle and Jacqueline Salmon, "The Refugees: Displacement of Historic Proportions," *The Washington Post* (September 2, 2005): A1.
8. United Nations Conference of Plenipotentiaries on the Status of Refugees, April 22, 1954, Preamble; available at <http://www.refugee.net/legal/un.html>.
9. UNESCO (United States Educational, Scientific, and Cultural Organization), 2004, [Convention of 1951, Article 1A (2)] The United Nations High Commissioner for Refugees (UNHCR) and the Executive Committee of the High Commissioners Programme, <http://portal.unesco.org/shs/en/ev.php-URL_ID=3138&URL_DO=DO_TOPIC&URL_SECTION=201.html>.
10. Karen Musalo, Director, "Gender Asylum Facts: Background on Gender and Asylum," Center for Gender & Refugee Studies (CGRS), <http://cgrs.uchastings.edu/about/facts.php>.
11. Maryann Cusimano Love, "Against All Odds," *America* (May 5, 2008).
12. Robin M. Maher, "Female Genital Mutilation: The Modern Day Struggle to Eradicate a Torturous Rite of Passage," *Human Rights* 23(4) (Fall, 1996). Maher suggests that the term *female genital mutilation* generally describes 3 different forms of genital mutilation. The most common form is female circumcision, in which the clitoris is partially or

completely cut away, often with razor blades or broken glass, and rarely with anesthesia. The most extreme form of FGM is infibulation, in which the entire genital area and outer tissues are cut away. The external sides of the vagina are then sewn together using catgut or thorns, leaving only a tiny opening for the passage of urine and for menstruation. The procedure, often performed by female family members, is carried out in nonsterile conditions and frequently results in serious and sometimes fatal infections. In some areas in West Africa, dirt, ashes, or pulverized animal feces are thrown into the wound to stop the bleeding, which contributes to the opportunity for infection, shock, and uncontrolled hemorrhaging. Following the procedure, the girl's legs are bound together for as long as 40 days, during which time (if she survives) her wound heals and scars. The long-term effects of this procedure include complications and pain with menstruation, urination, intercourse, and childbirth. The association suggests that it is no coincidence that the highest maternal and infant mortality rates in the world are recorded in regions where FGM is practiced. The scarring and complications associated with FGM frequently result in delayed and obstructed labor, tearing, and hemorrhaging. Unassisted childbirth is impossible following infibulation; many women and infants die during childbirth as a consequence of the procedure.

13. Karen Musalo, "Gender Asylum Facts: Background on Gender and Asylum," Center for Gender & Refugee Studies (CGRS), <http://cgrs.uchastings.edu/about/facts.php>; "Update on Rodi Alvarado's Case," Center for Gender & Refugee Studies (CGRS), September 2008, <http://cgrs.uchastings.edu/campaigns/alvarado.php>.

14. Hillary Mayell, "Thousands of Women Killed for Family 'Honor,'" National Geographic, February 12, 2002, <http://news.nationalgeographic.com/news/2002/02/0212_020212_honorkilling.html>.

15. UNODC, "Global Report on Trafficking in Persons," February 12, 2009, <http://www.unodc.org/unodc/en/frontpage/unodc-report-on-human-trafficking-exposes-modern-form-of-slavery-.html>; Anderson Cooper, "Modern Day Slavery on the Rise," February 19, 2009, <http://ac360.blogs.cnn.com/2009/02/19/modern-day-slavery-on-the-rise/>; UNODC, Kevin Bales, "Modern-Day Slavery," Testimony Before the Congressional Human Rights Caucus, June 17, 2003, <www.house.gov/lantos/caucus/TestimonyBales061703.htm>; Kevin Bales, "How We Can End Slavery," National Geographic, September 2003, <http://magma.nationalgeographic.com/ngm/0309/feature1/online_extra.html>; Andrew Cockburn, "Twenty-First Century Slaves," National Geographic, September 2003, <http://magma.nationalgeographic.com/ngm/0309/feature1/index.html>.

16. "Release of the Annual Trafficking in Persons Report," U.S. Department of State Briefing, Washington, DC, April 3, 2009, <http://www.state.gov/g/tip/rls/fs/2009/121359.htm>; Lise Olsen, "Sex Trafficking Victims' Lives in VISA Limbo," Houston Chronicle (November 24, 2008).

17. Karen Musalo, "Gender Asylum Facts: Background on Gender and Asylum," Center for Gender and Refugee Studies (CGRS), <http://cgrs.uchastings.edu/about/mission.php>.

18. These figures include the UNHCR numbers of 11.4 million refugees and 26 million IDPs, plus 4.6 million Palestinian refugees from United Nations Relief and Works Agency (UNRWA) numbers. The total population of concern to the UNHCR includes refugees, asylum-seekers, returnees (returned refugees), IDPs, returned IDP's, and stateless persons. UNHCR, 2007 Statistical Yearbook, December 2008, <http://www.unhcr.org/4981b19d2.html>, 23–25.

19. Internal Displacement Monitoring Center/Norwegian Refugee Council, Internal Displacement: Global Overview of Trends and Developments in 2008 (Geneva: Global IDP Project, May 2009), 9.

20. All figures taken from UNHCR, *2008 Global Refugee Trends* (Geneva: UNHCR, December 2008).

21. International Organization for Migration, *World Migration 2008* (Geneva: IMO, 2008).

22. Charles M. Sennott, "An Immigrant Rush Stirs British–French Friction Eurotunnel Lure Draws Foreigners," *The Boston Globe* (June 9, 2002): A6.

23. Leanne Weber, "Policing the Virtual Border: Punitive Preemption in Australian Off-Shore Migration Control," *Social Justice* (June 22, 2007): 12,

24. Sara B. Miller, "Migration Station," *Christian Science Monitor* (June 26, 2003): 11.

25. UK Mail Online, "Illegal Immigrants Walk Three Miles through Channel Tunnel in Attempt to Sneak into UK," (January 3, 2008).

26. Richard Bernstein, "One African's Ten-Year Odyssey Reflects a Growing European Concern," *The New York Times* (December 5, 2004): 10.

27. Miller, "Migration Station"; See also Jeff Crisp, "Refugees and the Global Politics of Asylum," Political Quarterly, January 12, 2004, Volume 74, Issue s1, p. 83.

28. Crisp, "Politics of Asylum," 83.

29. Louise Hunt, "The Mental Distress of Detained Asylum Seekers," *Community Care* (April 9, 2009); "Home at Last," *The Economist* (June 25, 2005): 42.

30. UNHCR, *2008 Global Refugee Trends*, 5.

31. The United Nations Economic Commission for Latin America and the Caribbean (ECLAC), *Productive Development in Open Economies*, June 18, 2004, <http://www.eclac.org/publicaciones/xml/2/15082/DGI-2234-Chapter11.pdf>, 53.

32. World Bank, Migration and Remittances Team, "Migration and Development Brief 5: Remittances Trends," July 10, 2008, <http://siteresources.worldbank.org/INTPROSPECTS/Resources/334934-1110315015165/MD_Brief5.pdf>.

33. ECLAC, Productive Development, 93. See also Richard Lapper, "For a Few Dollars More, a Better Life Back Home," *Financial Times* (April 13, 2005): 2.

34. UN, *World Economic Survey 2004*, 105, 111; "Dollars without Borders," *The New York Times* (May 13, 2004): 26; Peter Wise, "A Mainstay of the Economy: Portugal's Banks Have Been Singled Out as Model for How Remittances Can Be Used to Build National Wealth," *Financial Times* (October 20, 2004): 3.

35. Krissah Williams, "U.S. Banks Hope Money Transfers Attract Hispanics," *The Washington Post* (October 6, 2005): D5; Christopher Swann, "Helping More Cash Reach the Families Back Home: The US Treasury Is Encouraging Cheaper and Easier Methods for Foreign Workers to Send Remittances," *Financial Times* (June 10, 2004): 11.

36. "World Bank to Support Remittance Transfer Via Mobile Phones," *The Financial Express* (May 5, 2009).

37. John Authers, "Mexican Wave of Remittances for US Banks: Big Four Target the Tide of Money Sent Home by Migrant Workers," *Financial Times* (June 18, 2004): 29; Betsy Cummings, "Cash Flow across Border Starts to Get More Savvy," *The New York Times* (July 28, 2005): 6.

38. Motoo Noguchi, "Help Needed for the 'Unbanked,' " *The Washington Post* (March 26, 2004): A23; Elizabeth Becker, "Adding Value to Immigrants' Cash," *The New York Times* (June 6, 2004): 4; Bei Hu, "Remittance Firms Wary of Backdoor Channels; Competition Concerns Foreign Money-Movers as They Eye Larger Share of Transfers," *South China Morning Post* (August 11, 2005): 2.

39. Lucien O. Chauvin, "With Money Sent from US, Peruvians Buy Homes," *Christian Science Monitor* (July 13, 2005): 4.

40. UN, World Economic Survey, 109.

41. UN, World Economic Survey, 105.

42. Benedict Mander, "Mexicans Abroad Win the Right to Vote by Post," *Financial Times* (June 30, 2005): 6.

43. BUA, "Ex-Patriot Voters Acknowledged," *South Africa Information*, April 24, 2009, <http://www.southafrica.info/abroad/voters.htm>; Roel Landingin and Justine Lau, "Philippine Presidential Race Moves Overseas," *Financial Times* (February 16, 2004): 2; Simon Montlake, "Filipinos Abroad Get Vote," *Christian Science Monitor* (March 17, 2004): 7.

44. Mark Raper, "Changing Role of NGOs in Refugee Assistance," in Leonore Loeb Adler and Uwe P. Gielen (Eds.), *Migration: Immigration and Emigration in International Perspective* (Westport, CT: Greenwood Publishing Group, 2003), 355; Stephen C. Lubkemann, "Refugees," in *World at Risk: A Global Issues Source Book* (Washington, DC: CQ Press, 2002), 531.

45. Raper, "Changing Role," 359.

46. Ibid., 356–357.

47. Gregory Chen, "Confinement and Dependency: The Decline of Refugee Rights in Tanzania," in *U.S. Committee for Refugees and Immigrants, World Refugees Survey 2005*, <www.refugees.org/uploadedFiles/Investigate/Publications_&_Archives/WRS_Archives/2005/gregory_chen.pdf>, 3.

48. Karen Jacobsen, *The Economic Life of Refugees* (Bloomfield, CT: Kumarian Press, 2005), 80–81.

49. Jacobsen, *Economic Life*, 77–78.

50. Benjamin Gidron, Phillip Quarles van Ufford, and Abdulhamid Bedri Kello, NGOs Dealing with Refugee Resettlement in Ethiopia, NIRP Research for Policy Series 12 (Amsterdam, NE: Royal Tropical Institute, 2002), Netherlands-Israel Development Research Programme (NIRP), 24–25.

51. Chen, "Confinement and Dependency," 9–10.

52. Quoted in Chen, "Confinement and Dependency," 10.

53. Benjamin Gidron, Phillip Quarles van Ufford and Abdulhamid Bedri Kello, *NGOs Dealing with Refugee Resettlement in Ethiopia, NIRP Research for Policy Series 12* (Amsterdam, NE: Royal Tropical Institute, 2002), 40.

54. Benjamin Gidron, Phillip Quarles van Ufford and Abdulhamid Bedri Kello, *NGOs in Ethopia*, 19.

55. Reuters, "NGOs Expelled from Darfur," March 16, 2009, http://www.reuters.com/article/latestCrisis/idUSN16528406

56. Chen, "Confinement and Dependency," 7–8.

57. Raper, "Changing Role," 358.

58. Ibid., 360.

59. Ibid., 352.

60. Benjamin Gidron, Phillip Quarles van Ufford and Abdulhamid Bedri Kello, *NGOs in Ethopia*, 41.

61. U.S. Committee for Refugees and Immigrants, "Statement Calling for Solutions to End Warehousing of Refugees," August 2008, <http://www.refugees.org/uploadedFiles/Investigate/Anti_Warehousing/statement.pdf>; World Refugee Survey 2004—Warehousing Issue, May 2004, <www.refugees.org/data/refugee_reports/archives/2004/0504.pdf>; "Warehouses for Refugees," *The New York Times* (September 28, 2004): 24.

62. See, for example, Gil Loescher and James Milner, *Protracted Refugee Situations: Domestic and International Security Implications, Adelphi Paper 375* (International Institute for Strategic Studies, London: 2005).

63. U.S. Agency for International Development, *USAID Assistance to Internally Displaced Persons Policy*, USAID Policy (October 2004).

64. Fr. William Headley, *Catholic Relief Services, Caritas Internationalis and Catholic Peacebuilding Network as 'Practical Peacebuilders*, San Diego, CA, June 9, 2005; available at <http://cpn.nd.edu/beyond_merton.htm>.

65. U.S. Holocaust Memorial Exhibit, and Frank Davies, "Ill-Fated WWII Voyage Created a Mini Holocaust," *The Miami Herald* (June 1, 1999).

66. In 2003, more than 50 years after the UNHCR was founded, the UN General Assembly decided to change it into a permanent mandate until the resolution of all refugee problems was achieved. UNHCR, Basic Facts: Helping Refugees, <www.unhcr.ch/cgibin/texis/vtx/basics/opendoc.htm?tbl=BASICS&id=420cc0432>.

67. Stephen C. Lubkemann, "Refugees," 530.

68. United Nations, "Milosevic Case Information Sheet," April 5, 2005, <www.un.org/icty/glance/milosevic.htm>.

69. Jolene Kay Jesse, "Humanitarian Relief in the Midst of Conflict: The UN High Commissioner for Refugees in the Former Yugoslavia," Institute for the Study of Diplomacy, Case 471 (Georgetown University, 1996), 1–7.

70. Jesse, 6–7.

71. Ibid.

72. Ibid., 8.

73. Arthur E. Dewey, "Remarks to the American Society for International Law," April 3, 2003, <www.state.gov> (September 13, 2005), 1.

74. U.S. Department of State, Bureau of Population, Refugees, and Migration, "Refugee Admissions and Resettlement," March 6, 2009, <http://www.state.gov/documents/organization/120385.pdf>.

75. Anastasia Hendrix, "Post-9/11 Delays Hurt Refugees," The San Francisco Chronicle, Nov. 30, 2003.

76. U.S. Department of State, Bureau of Population, Refugees, and Migration, "Refugee Admissions and Resettlement," March 6, 2009, <http://www.state.gov/documents/organization/120385.pdf>.

77. Richard Shears, "World's First Climate Change Refugees to Leave Island Due to Rising Sea Levels," *Mail Online*, December 18, 2007, <http://www.dailymail.co.uk/news/article-503228/The-worlds-climate-change-refugees-leave-island-rising-sea-levels.html>.

78. "The developing international human rights and refugee norms provide a basis for extending protection to women asylum-seekers. The UNHCR has provided guidance in cases of women asylum-seekers, and immigration authorities in Canada, the United States, and Australia have all issued guidelines for adjudicators. However, notwithstanding these developments, the claims of women asylum-seekers continue to meet denials due to erroneous interpretations of the refugee definition by decision makers, as well as a fundamental lack of understanding of the applicable human rights norms and the relevant country conditions," Karen Musalo, Director of the Center for Gender and Refugee Studies (CGRS), "Gender Asylum Facts: Background on Gender and Asylum," <http://cgrs.uchastings.edu/about/facts.php>.

79. "Release of the Annual Trafficking in Persons Report," U.S. Department of State Briefing, Washington, DC, April 3, 2009, <http://www.state.gov/g/tip/rls/fs/2009/121359.htm>; UNODC, "Global Report on Trafficking in Persons," February 12, 2009, <http://www.unodc.org/unodc/en/frontpage/unodc-report-on-human-trafficking-exposes-modern-form-of-slavery-.html>.

80. Maryann Cusimano, "Operation Restore Hope: The Bush Administration's Decision to Intervene in Somalia," Pew case study published by the Institute for the Study of Diplomacy, Georgetown University, 1995, <www.guisd.org>.

CHAPTER NINE

Defending Cyberspace

Richard A. Love

"It's the great irony of our Information Age—the very technologies that empower us to create and to build also empower those who would disrupt and destroy. And this paradox—seen and unseen—is something that we experience every day."

—President Barak Obama[1]

"We strongly urge Muslim internet professionals to spread and disseminate news and information about the jihad through e-mail lists, discussion groups and their own websites. If you fail to do this, and our site closes down before you have done this, we may hold you to account before Allah on the Day of Judgment . . . We expect our website to be opened and closed continuously. Therefore, we urgently recommend any Muslims that are interested in our material to copy all the articles from our site and disseminate them through their own websites, discussion boards and e-mail lists. This is something that any Muslim can participate in, easily, including sisters. This way, even if our sites are closed down, the material will live on with the Grace of Allah."

—Al Qaeda[2]

The Baltic state of Estonia was subject to a massive denial-of-service attack that ultimately rendered the country offline and shut out from services dependent on Internet connectivity during a three-week period in the spring of 2007. Estonia's Internet infrastructure, including everything from online banking and mobile phone networks to government services and access to health care information, were disabled for a time.[3] The tech-dependent state was crippled and there was a good deal of concern over the nature and intent of the attack. Was this merely cyberhooliganism or was this a national security threat? Was this prolonged cyberattack a prelude to an armed attack, or something else? Was the attack carried out by terrorists, teenagers, or a state, or some combination of the three? Estonia joined NATO in 2004, therefore NATO carefully monitored its member state's response to the attack and worried both about escalation and the possibility of cascading effects beyond Estonia's borders to other NATO members. The scope of the attack was unprecedented; starting on April 27, 2007, about 1 million computers worldwide were reportedly used to conduct denial-of-service attacks.[4] The cyberattack corresponded to an Estonian–Russian dispute over the removal of a bronze statue depicting a World War II-era Soviet soldier from the center of the capital, Tallinn. The scale and impact of the attacks prompted Estonian Defense Ministry spokesperson Madis Mikko to compare the cyberattack to missile assaults on banks or airports, which would clearly be seen as an act of war.[5]

In the midst of the armed conflict with Russia, Georgia likewise was subjected to sustained and coordinated attacks on its electronic infrastructure in August 2008. Georgia complained that Russia engaged in cyberattacks timed with its military incursion into the South Ossetia region. At one point, a Georgia spokesman noted that "All Georgia websites have been blocked" due to widespread denial of service attacks.[6]

In both of these cases, circumstantial evidence points to coordinated Russian attacks, but attribution of the attacks is difficult; though both Estonia and Georgia point the finger at Moscow, proof establishing legal culpability is lacking. Legal culpability requires some proof of intent, and that is quite hard to establish in the faceless anonymity of cyberspace. Moreover, the attacks hit both government and private sector targets and certainly were aimed at inconveniencing individual citizens. In the Estonia case, Sergei Markov, a Russian State Duma Deputy, commented, "About the cyberattack on Estonia . . . don't worry, that attack was carried out by my assistant. I won't tell you his name, because then he might not be able to get visas." Markov reportedly added, "and, incidentally, such things will happen more and more."[7]

The cyberattacks on Estonia did produce an unexpected result. In 2008, directly as a result of the attacks, NATO opened a new center of excellence on cyberdefense to conduct research and training on cyber warfare in Tallinn.[8]

Cyberthreats appear in various forms and their impacts span the range from inconvenience to nuisance to crime to national security threat. Law enforcement officials have long known that terrorist organizations used communications technology to further their objectives. Sheik Ahmed Yassin, founder of Hamas, once stated, "We will use whatever tools we can—e-mails, the Internet—to facilitate jihad against the (Israeli) occupiers and their supporters."[9] Osama bin Laden and the al Qaeda network, Hezbollah, and Hamas use Web-to-mobile phone applications, computerized files, e-mail, and encryption to facilitate terrorist activities. These organizations make use of the Internet's distributive nature to organize, plan, and conduct their operations, thereby engaging in an "e-jihad," or holy war online. Captured al Qaeda computers revealed the group had been planning to destroy physical critical infrastructure such as dams and electric power grids by attacking the computer systems that control them. In June 2003, e-jihadists, spotted by IDefense, a cyber security firm, unsuccessfully attempted to take down the Bank of Israel's Web site.[10]

Some effects may be unintentional, like those created by malware, but pose a real and immediate security risk. For example, on January 25, 2003, the Slammer worm began infecting Microsoft's database software worldwide, causing cash machines to stop issuing money, taking most of South Korea offline, and slowing down the Internet. The virus, one of the fastest spreading worms in history, spread to most of the vulnerable hosts that could be found within 10 minutes.[11] One of the vulnerable hosts it penetrated was a private computer network at Ohio's Davis-Besse nuclear power plant. The Slammer infected the plant's computer system and disabled a safety monitoring system for nearly 5 hours, despite a belief by plant personnel that the network was protected by a firewall.[12] The plant was offline at the time of the attack, but the ability to tamper with a nuclear plant's monitoring system could have had disastrous effects if the plant had been operating.

Computer hackers in St. Petersburg, Russia, broke into Citibank's electronic money transfer system and attempted to steal more than $10 million by making wire transfers to accounts throughout the world.[13] Citibank later recovered all except $500,000 of the funds.[14] The leader, Vladimir Levin, was not subject to extradition to the United States because wire and computer fraud and abuse was not a violation of Russian law. However, when Levin left the safety of Russia 2 years later, Scotland Yard and the FBI arrested him at an airport outside London and extradited him to the United States. He pled guilty to transferring $3.7 million from Citibank customer accounts to accounts he controlled, and in 1998 a U.S. court sentenced him to a 3-year prison term and ordered him to make $240,015 restitution to Citibank.[15]

The ILoveYou computer virus first appeared in an e-mail attachment named Love-Letter-For-You that, when activated, produced an e-mail worm that overwrote files on hard drives and then mailed itself to every e-mail address contained in an infected Microsoft Outlook address book.[16] The virus spread its damage internationally, but when U.S. law enforcement officials located the suspected hacker in the Philippines, he could not be prosecuted. No antihacking law was yet in place in the Philippines.

Following the incident, the Philippines moved quickly to pass legislation and now has an antihacking law.

Computer operators at the Lawrence Livermore National Laboratory in California (operated by the University of California at Berkeley) discovered that unknown attackers were infiltrating their computer systems. Law enforcement authorities determined that because nothing of value seemed to have been stolen, no violations of law had occurred. The officials shelved the investigation. Cliff Stoll, a graduate student in astronomy, was not satisfied and conducted his own investigation. His research over 2 years concluded that the intruders had obtained sensitive information, including weapons and munitions data, from the laboratory's computers. Authorities later learned that the hackers sold this information to the KGB. Stoll's investigation eventually led to Hanover, Germany, where a German court tried and convicted 3 hackers of espionage, later placing all 3 on probation.[17]

As California suffered through a power crisis that included rolling blackouts, a hacker conducted a computer attack against a server under development at the California Independent System Operator electricity exchange. The attacker, who was apparently attempting to gain control of the server, went undetected for 17 days. The hacker was not able to access key operational systems, but if he had managed to gain control, the power crisis could have been significantly worse. The California Independent System Operator electricity exchange discovered the hacking and reported the intrusion to authorities, but local law enforcement officials treated the incident as an isolated event. The FBI, however, recognized the potential for catastrophic and cascading damage to already strained infrastructure and began an investigation.[18]

These cases illustrate the wide cyberthreat continuum we face today. The Estonian and Georgian cases demonstrate the opportunities for cyberattacks to be used as a tool of war; countries find it difficult to defend against or even identify their cyberattackers. The e-jihad example demonstrates the ability of adversaries to use asymmetric capabilities provided by information technology to attack opponents who otherwise could not be confronted conventionally. The Citibank case demonstrates the difficulty in coordinating law enforcement activities globally and the vulnerability of commercial entities to planned cyberattacks. The ILoveYou virus example represents the mutual vulnerabilities that users share in the interconnected environment.[19] The Lawrence Livermore National Laboratory case shows how difficult it is to quickly and correctly characterize the nature of an attack. Authorities first considered this attack a mere intrusion but were later convinced it was a concerted espionage conspiracy and a serious threat to national security. Finally, the California power case and the Ohio nuclear plant case illustrate the potential for catastrophic and widespread damage to infrastructure, industry, and ordinary lives. Each example also reveals, to some degree, the difficulty faced by commercial and government entities in understanding and defending against cyberthreats, and it demonstrates how those attacked—even after a close call—tend to dismiss the event as mere nuisance.

THREATS AND INTERDEPENDENCE

Computer threats are a reality in our private lives, corporate boardrooms, and government planning offices. Concern over the threat is well justified. As communications technologies converge and computer capabilities expand, it is as easy to manipulate the networks, systems, and computers that carry and compute data for good as for illegal purposes. This is true for several reasons.

Developers created the open architecture of the World Wide Web for efficiency, not security. Although the open nature of the Web allows for easy user access, it is difficult to control or exclude wrongdoers from committing illegal acts. The anonymity of the Internet allows both honest citizens and criminals the opportunity to act unnoticed. Both use the same infrastructure and enjoy protection of the same rights. Criminals can develop viruses, plan attacks, and organize complex fraud schemes in secret and in isolation and unleash their plans instantaneously or in stages if they choose, all at the touch of a few keystrokes. Criminals also have the ability to act globally, irrespective of territorial and jurisdictional boundaries that constrain state-based law enforcement. The absence of effectively trained law enforcement and substantial international coordination to combat cyberthreats is an invitation to criminals and adversaries. There is also an absence of cyber security specialists to manage the consequences of a cyberattack. In U.S. academic institutions alone, there are fewer than 250 active cybersecurity or cyberassurance specialists, many of whom lack either formal training or extensive professional experience in the field.[20]

Cyberattackers can choose the time and place of an attack, but those on the receiving end must respond reactively; except in the infrequent case of a tip, they rarely have the ability to proactively pursue their cyberattackers. In addition, attacks are not always limited to the intended targets. They are difficult to contain and often have unintended consequences that may lead to cascading failures among other systems. Finally, states, corporations, and individuals are mutually vulnerable. In many respects, the interconnected world is only as strong as the weakest states' capabilities, policies and laws, as well as the readiness and defense posture of private computer systems. Often states and corporations assumed to have adequate protection do not.

The growth of the World Wide Web also has greatly expanded the ability of individuals, states, and nonstate groups to commit crimes, challenge or undermine the national security of other states, and attack key infrastructures. Today's information technology is expanding the divide between our vulnerabilities and our ability to respond to threats. As individuals, corporations, states, and civil society are increasingly interconnected, the near future is likely to witness an increase in this divide. According to Forrester Research, electronic commerce generated sales worth $204 billion in 2008 and Forrester further forecasts that U.S. businesses will spend $953 million on Web analytics software alone by 2014, with an average compound annual growth rate of 17%.[21] The number of people using the Internet for business transactions is increasing. Maintaining security in the exponentially expanding wired environment presents a supreme challenge. More than 1.6 billion people are currently connected to the Internet, a number that is only growing.[22] How can policy makers modify or adjust the technology that propels the benefits of globalization (while at the same time exposing us to greater vulnerabilities) to minimize the unwanted costs?

The cyberthreat environment has prompted new thinking over how to craft solutions across the cyberthreat continuum. For example, critical infrastructures—those determined essential to the preservation of state interests—now include telecommunications networks, banking and finance operations, and access to resources in addition to traditional roads, ports, and rail lines. Private and governmental actors are working to forge partnerships to effectively combat cyberthreats, and they are organizing across borders to ease cross-jurisdictional challenges.

Since the events of September 11, 2001, security concerns over physical and cyber infrastructure have gained new emphasis as states struggle to develop plans and implementation regimes to enhance security. The terrorist attacks underline the fact that many threats today are regional, and global concerns that blur public–private distinctions may not be amenable to "go it alone" solutions. In the United States, 85 percent of critical infrastructure is privately owned, rendering government solutions without private cooperation hollow and likely to fail.[23] Foreign private ownership of domestic critical infrastructures increases the level of difficulty in crafting solutions.

Much of the critical information infrastructure in place today was developed with efficiency and cost concerns at the forefront of planning and development. With the current emphasis on security, is it time to rethink basic planning assumptions that focus on guaranteeing profits and efficiency? Many people are asking not only what can be done to patch the current system, but also whether the overwhelming need for enhancing security warrants a wholesale reevaluation and replacement of more vulnerable systems. Some of the most important players in the information technology industry now acknowledge the need for added security. Bill Gates has repeatedly made clear that he will make Microsoft's software less vulnerable to cyberthreats even if that means delaying the development of new applications.[24] When a private computer security expert discovered a dangerous design flaw in the Internet, experts from private companies met in secret at Microsoft headquarters to fix the problem before cybercriminals could exploit the "hole" in the Internet.[25] John Chambers of Cisco Systems has stated that he no longer regards security enhancements on Internet routers as extras but as necessities.[26] Governments have also recognized the need to protect against cyberthreats. In the United States, the National Strategy to Secure Cyberspace is constructed as an implementing component of the National Strategy for Homeland Security. The purpose of the strategy is "to engage and empower Americans to secure the portions of cyberspace that they own, operate, control, or with which they interact."[27] It gives direction to the federal government and agencies, state and local officials, private companies and organizations, and individual Americans on how to improve collective cybersecurity.

Decision makers in both industry and government face significant challenges in light of the variety of cyberthreats. Policy makers must balance the need for new laws and regulations to ensure security with the need to provide users access and privacy, all without putting unwarranted restraint on innovation and promising technology. Industry will not partner with government if security concerns are not balanced with maintaining open markets and allowing firms to remain globally competitive. The global nature of the technology and the fact that it spans public and private boundaries not only complicates the picture for leaders, but also offers potential opportunities if effective public–private relationships can be forged. Neither government nor industry alone has the means to solve the challenges posed by cyberthreats.

The comparative technological advantages once enjoyed by developed states are eroding as essential technology is developed not by government research labs but increasingly by the private sector and is available "off the shelf." As a consequence, new, state-of-the-art technology such as sophisticated encryption is available globally, enabling everyone including money launderers, rogue states, and terrorists to enjoy an asymmetric capability without the heavy research and development budgets of the past. States are interdependent, as are government and industry, and must rely on each other for an effective international response to cyberthreats.

CYBERTHREATS AND NATIONAL SECURITY

In 2000, a Japanese investigation revealed that the government was using software developed by computer companies affiliated with Aum Shinrikyo, the doomsday sect responsible for the sarin gas attack on the Tokyo subway system in 1995.[28] "The government found 100 types of software programs used by at least 10 Japanese government agencies, including the Defense Ministry, and more than 80 major Japanese companies, including Nippon Telegraph and Telephone."[29] Following the discovery, the Japanese government suspended use of Aum Shinrikyo–developed programs out of concern that Aum-related companies may have compromised security by breaching firewalls, gaining access to sensitive systems or information, allowing invasion by outsiders, planting viruses that could be set off later, or planting malicious code that could cripple computer systems and key data systems.[30]

From these facts, is it clear that the suspects were likely to attempt to overthrow the Japanese government? Had they engaged in espionage, criminal violations, or possible terrorism? Was this a threat to national security? Was Aum Shinrikyo conducting a legitimate commercial enterprise? Is it possible to tell? Clearly, considering the cult's history, the Japanese government proceeded under the assumption that this was a serious state-level threat. The example highlights the key challenges posed by cyberthreats: determining intent and determining the level and nature of the threat quickly and accurately.

Cyberthreats place enormous stress on security and criminal systems that rely on proving intent to secure a criminal conviction. Computer attacks can be instantaneous, time-delayed, or staged in waves. They can be anonymous or falsely attributed to unsuspecting users. It is difficult to identify with a high degree of certainty exactly who committed an act.[31] This is precisely why U.S. law enforcement solves only 2 percent of hacker cases, as compared to 80 to 90 percent of all homicides.[32] There is also no way to know for certain an attacker's exact motives or to quickly determine whether the attacker is part of a wider conspiracy. In a broader context, while authorities can identify individual hacks or intrusions, it is much more difficult to quickly judge whether individual attacks are part of a wider series of attacks. Even if a state recognizes that a concerted attack is underway, an attack is not likely to have purely military objectives. The military–civilian distinction breaks down, requiring government responders to alert and work with private infrastructure and systems owners to safeguard against the attack.

Both the security apparatus that developed to pursue Cold War security objectives and sovereign law enforcement organizations continue to struggle to adapt to new threats ushered in by globalization. Traditional responses to new security challenges such as cybercrime and cyberterrorism are failing to keep up with the methods and tactics that are available to state and nonstate actors alike.[33] In many respects, defense, that is the ability to effectively combat and mitigate the effects of an attack, lag far behind offense, the ability to conduct an illegal attack.

Because developed states, and most notably the United States, enjoy preeminent conventional and strategic military power, adversaries seek ways in which to inflict indirect or asymmetric harm on strong states and their interests abroad. Developed countries are reliant on information technology. Therefore, one area for exploitation by adversaries is attack on critical computer networks.[34]

A few examples illustrate the level to which developed states rely on computer networks and technology. The U.S. Department of Defense (DOD) infrastructure consists of more than 2.1 million computers, with 10,000 local area networks and 1,000 long-distance networks.[35] These figures do not even account for the millions of computer users who regularly do business with the DOD. In addition, GAO revealed that DOD computer users reported only a small fraction of systems attacks, and the number of annual attacks was much higher than reported.[36] A computer network attack has the potential for causing catastrophic injury to security and could have a strategic reach that would affect cultural sensibilities, including confidence in the government's ability to protect against threats and safeguard personal and commercial interests.[37]

Adversaries are developing the tools and doctrine necessary to conduct offensive cyberwarfare programs. A major challenge will be to find ways to defend infrastructure and protect commerce while maintaining an open society. Openness and ease of connectivity promote efficiency, but these attributes also make information infrastructures vulnerable to attack. Unlike the threats of the Cold War, which required state-sponsored infrastructures and installations, cyberthreats are strategically asymmetric, require no state sponsorship, and use commercially available equipment and facilities. A computer in a basement hardly qualifies as a weapons site. These threats can affect systems anywhere in the world, disguise origins and travel routes, and do it all instantaneously.[38]

Despite the potential magnitude of the harm and the strategic nature of the threat, many states—including the United States—continue to characterize cyberthreats as a law enforcement issue with possible national security consequences rather than as a frontline national security concern. As such, a foreign or domestic adversary that develops the ability to interrupt the flow of data will have the potential to weaken any entity that is incapable of responding. While there have been some noteworthy strides in developing law enforcement counter cyberattack capabilities, the potential scope and magnitude of harm that some attacks could cause warrant a national security rather than a law enforcement response.

The characterization of the cyberthreat—criminal versus national security threat—is important. The law enforcement community is fundamentally concerned with trials, convictions, and punishing wrongdoers who run afoul of criminal law. Thus, it is bound by statutory authority and concerned with evidentiary trails, burdens of proof, and expert testimony. However, democracies did not develop criminal law based on principles of efficiency. It was based on the understanding that law enforcement needed to afford certain principles, rights, and protections to the accused. Criminal law generally requires both criminal intent and a criminal act. Proving intent, however, is difficult in many computer-related crimes.

Issues that fall under national security, on the other hand, often focus solely on the act's illegality. Representing a threat to national security is sufficient for liability. An example may help illustrate this point. If a computer emergency response team detects a hacker, then the FBI may want the hacker to continue his or her activities in order to trace the hacker and develop an evidentiary trail. By following and monitoring the hacker's moves, his or her intent may become apparent. However, if such an intrusion were to occur against the Department of Defense's Central Command in Tampa, Florida, during a deployment (the command is responsible for U.S. military operations in the Middle East and South Asia), the military may wish to immediately terminate the hack and even strike back or "hack back" at the attacker.

But what if the attack is coming not from a single hacker but is being orchestrated by a state? Many countries are developing doctrines of computer attack and defense. The United States bases its information operations doctrine on its ability to attack an adversary's information and information systems while defending its own. The U.S. approach is to blind an adversary and keep it confused over the "ground truth" of the battlefield, thus interfering with the opposing senior leadership's ability to make sound decisions.

As seen during the events in Estonia and Georgia, the Russian Federation is also developing information warfare strategy and doctrine. The Russian concept of information warfare includes computer network attack and defense but is more expansive than the U.S. concept and includes the use of information to break down the ability of the human mind and body to function effectively. China is currently developing a unique information warfare strategy based on information weapons as unconventional warfare weapons and battlefield force multipliers.[39]

What state-sponsored information warfare operations have in common is the use of information technology to achieve strategic (national-level) or tactical (battlefield-level) effects in order to meet political or military objectives. Essentially, it is the conduct of warfare through the use of information technology. Specifically, the United States defines information operations as

> The integrated employment of the specified core capabilities of Electronic Warfare [EW], Computer Network Operations [CNO], PSYOP [psychological operations], Military Deception [MILDEC], and Operations Security [OPSEC], in concert with specified supporting and related capabilities, to influence, disrupt, corrupt, or usurp adversarial human and automated decision making, while protecting our own.[40]

If an incident appears to have the characteristics of a computer attack, then just what options are available to the government? Pursuant to the UN Charter specifically and the body of law known as the Law of Armed Conflict in general,[41] a state can use military force only when responding to an armed attack on its own territory. In addition, customary international law holds that a state must retaliate in self-defense and only to the extent necessary to terminate the initial attack and to prevent further intrusions.[42] Where does this leave a state after a cyberattack? The answer depends on the level and degree of damage caused by an attack. If a cyberattack causes physical damage or death to citizens by, for example, causing a dam to fail, then certainly a cyber-response would be warranted and probably some use of force would be justified. If, however, a hacker takes down a banking system, some would argue that regardless of the financial impact, since the rules governing use of force are based on casualties and personal harm, a state would then not be permitted the use of force, and a cyber-response might or might not be justified. In this case, considering the potential for unintended consequences that a response might cause, decision makers may want to find other alternatives. International practice recognizes that states may inflict great hardship on each other and their respective citizenry without such activity constituting the use of force or a violation of international law.[43] This is significant because information attacks will certainly create harm and hardship but may never constitute aggression or rise to the level of an armed attack. Law and policy have yet to evolve fully so that they can answer many of the questions posed by cyberthreats. The U.S. cyberspace policy should reserve the right to respond appropriately if the United States comes under computer attack, including the use of cyber weapons. However, a global consensus on how to effectively deal with cyberthreats still does not exist.

CYBERTERRORISM

Cyberterrorism, like terrorism itself, presents a definitional problem internationally. There is no recognized international definition for cyberterrorism. Each country has its own cyberterrorism rules. For example, the special legislation enacted by Japan to combat cyberterrorism defines it as the unauthorized entry into computer systems through communications networks such as the Internet and the damage caused to those systems as a result of the unauthorized access.[44] This expansive definition would constitute computer fraud and abuse in other states such as the United States, and such activities would not rise to the level of cyberterrorism. In the United States, the FBI defines cyberterrorism as a "premeditated, politically motivated attack against information, computer systems, computer programs, and data which results in violence against noncombatant targets by subnational groups or clandestine agents."[45]

Perhaps the best way to understand cyberterrorism is to view it as an extension of age-old terrorist principles adapted for use in the new high-tech environment. Using violence against noncombatants to cause fear, terrorists' activities are politically motivated and seek to coerce governments or civilians in furtherance of the terrorists' agenda. Cyberterrorists are thus politically motivated but make use of information technology and networks to further their agendas. Clearly, disrupting communications, airport, and utilities systems for the purpose of inflicting damage to achieve a political end are all cyberterrorist activities, capabilities al Qaeda is developing. In one example, a suspected terrorist group calling itself the Internet Black Tigers attacked Sri Lankan government computers with "suicide e-mail bombings" in an effort to overwhelm and disable government information systems, embarrass the Sri Lankan government, and draw attention to the cause of Tamil separatism in northern and eastern Sri Lanka.[46] Incidents such as this may become increasingly familiar as marginalized groups without political voices learn how to exploit Internet technology for their political ends.

Using the Internet to facilitate terrorist activities is another aspect of cyberterrorism. For example, Wadih el Hage, a prime suspect in the 1998 U.S. embassy bombings in Africa, sent encrypted e-mails under alias names to al Qaeda "associates." Ramzi Yousef, the planner of the 1993 attack on the World Trade Center, used encrypted files to hide details of a plot to destroy 11 U.S. jetliners. Philippine officials discovered Yousef's computer and sent it to the FBI for analysis. Two of the files took more than a year to decrypt.[47] U.S. officials also believe that alleged terrorist-sponsoring countries such as Iran and North Korea, and even Russia and China, have trained hackers in Internet warfare.[48]

For terrorists, cyber-based attacks have distinct advantages over physical attacks. They can be conducted remotely, anonymously, and relatively cheaply, and they do not require significant investments in weapons, explosives, and personnel. The effects can be widespread and profound. Incidents of cyberterrorism are likely to increase. They will be conducted through denial-of-service attacks that overload servers, worms and viruses, unauthorized intrusions, Web site defacements, attacks on network infrastructures, and other methods that are difficult to envision today. The former National Infrastructure Protection Center concluded that the potential for compound cyber and physical attacks, referred to as *swarming attacks*, is an increasing threat to the United States.[49]

So why does the vulnerability persist? Commercial off-the-shelf operating systems and applications are widely shared, and their vulnerabilities are widely known. In addition, because many technology developers and producers contract out work and services, often to overseas partners, there is opportunity for mischief whenever controls and quality-assurance procedures are not in place. The Internet is also a target-rich environment in which not all systems can be protected. Finally, cultural sensitivities, such as privacy rights, preclude intrusive security measures.

CYBERCRIME

A hacker used a U.S.-based Web site to gain unlimited access to multiple U.S. military, university, and private computer systems in 1995–1996. The FBI tracked the hacker to Argentina and notified a local telecommunications carrier, which in turn notified local law enforcement. An Argentinean investigating judge authorized a search of the hacker's apartment and the seizure of his computer. Argentinean officials investigated Julio Cesar Ardita for intrusions into an Argentinean telecommunications system, but Argentine law did not cover hacking systems in the United States, and the judge ruled that only the United States could prosecute him for these crimes. In the absence of an extradition treaty, Ardita agreed in May 1998 to come to the United States and plead guilty to felony charges of unlawfully intercepting communications and damaging DOD files and NASA computers. U.S. authorities fined Ardita $5,000 and sentenced him to 3 years probation.[50]

This example illustrates many of the challenges that law enforcement faces in overcoming cyber-related crimes. Authorities must address jurisdictional, substantive, and cultural issues. Information technologies pose a variety of challenges to criminal law and procedure. Many age-old crimes, such as fraud, theft, and money laundering, have qualitatively changed because of the new cybermedium. With the aid of computers and the Web, wrongdoers can perpetrate crimes with greater ease, speed, and anonymity. Individuals can easily copy and steal information, interfere with or co-opt commercial and public assets, and gain illegal access to private information. Other criminal activity, such as computer network attacks, virus disseminations, and hacking, likewise pose significant challenges because of the speed at which they take place and the magnitude of damage they can create.[51]

Cybercrime and cyberterrorism are not mutually exclusive because both are intent-based. For most crimes, a state prosecutor must prove that the suspect intended to commit the crime and indeed did so.

Cybercrime is the commission of illegal acts through the use of communications and information-based technology. Cybercrime includes fraudulent activities such as e-mail schemes, identity theft, and credit card fraud, as well as theft crimes such as electronic espionage, corporate espionage, and money laundering.[52] It also includes nuisance crimes, including transmission of viruses, system shutdowns, interference with network systems, denial-of-service attacks, and Web site defacements.

Cybercrime is also a tax because it increases the costs of doing business and passes those costs on to consumers.[53] In 2008, it is estimated that cybercriminals stole intellectual property from businesses worldwide worth up to $1 trillion.[54] The total dollar loss from cyber-related fraud in 2008 is estimated to be $264.6 million with a median dollar loss of $931.00 per complaint filed with the Internet Crime Complaint Center (IC3). This is up from $239.1 million in total reported losses in 2007.[55]

A FRAMEWORK FOR ADDRESSING THE PROBLEM

States, corporations, and industry are mutually vulnerable and interdependent with regard to cyberthreats. States and citizens must recognize that their own self-interests lie in multinational cooperation and the development of global information-related standards and practices. The challenges posed by cyberthreats cannot be overcome by the developed world acting alone. All states are stakeholders in combating cyberthreats. However, because of the informational advantages enjoyed by developed states and the costs associated with enhancing the information infrastructures of developing states, there is some reluctance to support open and multilateral solutions. For example, even though it is vulnerable to computer network attacks, the United States enjoys superiority if not dominance in the realm of information operations and information warfare. This dominance is perpetuated by U.S. attempts to limit the ability of other states to gain information capabilities via dual-use technology or antiencryption limitations.

A more robust understanding of the vulnerabilities and advantages posed by cyberthreats must be developed before a cogent strategy that aligns domestic and global policy will exist. The rise in the sheer numbers of online users as well as the numbers of cyberattacks warrants a more coordinated domestic and global response.[56] In analyses of how law and public policy can be used to combat cyberthreats, solutions often suffer from a lack of practicality and applicability to real-world circumstances. Therefore, in determining the proper policy course to pursue, states and private parties must first address whether there is a need for additional public–private cooperation or regulation. In other words, is the current system working? A state must then, in coordination with industry, consider whether the nature of the threat in light of the security requirements necessitates a coordinated international approach. Finally, if international harmonization is warranted, an international framework will have to be developed.

Though progress has been made, more needs to be done. Although better public–private cooperation is needed, should governments enact additional domestic laws to combat cyberthreats? The answer changes, depending on the state in question. In many developed states, comprehensive laws are on the books to punish wrongdoers; in others, no such prohibitions exist. Therefore, a case can be made for seeking international agreements on legal harmonization. The global community should pursue international agreements when a challenge has transboundary effects, represents an extraterritorial threat, and produces a failure in effective enforcement in response to a threat, or where there are highly divergent state practices and a need to harmonize law to increase effectiveness. Cyberthreats satisfy each criterion. So what are the options?

States and private-sector actors may rely on the ongoing development of international policy and law to combat cyberthreats. Although detractors term this the *muddle through* or *do-nothing* approach, it has the advantage of a more stable and arguably more gradual and balanced development because it builds on current structures. Another approach is to clarify legal ambiguities at the margin, modifying current policy while adapting it to evolving information technology and computer threats. This affords policy makers the chance to develop a strategy that fosters individual and specific critical information technology structures. These efforts may proceed through the United Nations or may concentrate on lower-level, bilateral, or multilateral agreements. This approach favors formalizing agreements where agreement can be found.

Additionally, in a more comprehensive fashion, global leaders could seek to harmonize domestic laws and expand criminal liability in a coordinated way for agreed-upon cyberthreats. This approach relies on promoting cooperation in investigations and prosecutions. Because of the inherent importance of information infrastructures globally, the international community could condemn certain actions and, considering today's environment, perhaps outlaw them as acts of terrorism or egregious cybercrimes.[57]

Policy makers should not construe the options above as either–or solutions but should consider them as appropriate responses to different challenges along the threat continuum. For example, cybercrime and anticyberterrorism laws may require a wider and more comprehensive approach, while criminal liability for fraud and hacking may better evolve at the margin.

In evaluating specific initiatives, global leaders should craft new international agreements to ensure that they are flexible enough to adapt to the changing technological environment, are tailored and scaled to the challenge, are reasonable and proportional to the threat they seek to overcome, and consider the unique values of the states involved (to use the U.S. example, consider the liberal democratic principles based on underlying constitutional rights).

While assessing the current global policy on cyberthreats, its successes and failures in the past, and the economic and structural importance of information infrastructures, policy makers should consider the option to clarify legal ambiguity at the margin highly attractive and able to generate consensus on key issues. It provides flexibility to respond to technological changes and takes advantage of existing laws. This is particularly true for cyberthreats, where the relative potential harm is great and the measures that could be used to combat the threat are so potentially sweeping.

The U.S. should lead the discussion on how best to develop a global framework, but should also lead by example. The first step in shoring up U.S. cyber defenses is to develop a coordinated, intergovernmental strategy that includes input and representation from state and local governments and industry. Industry owns the infrastructure, is leading the way in technological development, and is far more accustomed to working in today's global environment characterized by open economies, open societies and open technologies. And while we need a strategy that points to a strategic outcome, we also need a plan that provides practical guidance and direction that includes metrics and milestones against which to measure progress. Resources and manpower and the plans required to effectively marshal and use those resources and manpower need to be in place prior to attacks. Both strategy and plans need to account for the challenges that attacks through cyberspace pose, since they often overlap the divide between law enforcement issues and national security issues. For example, developing concepts that are geared in terms of countering cyber campaigns, not just single events, would go far in mitigating against the "single-incident" mindset of many responders.

A MULTILATERAL APPROACH

The effort by the Council of Europe to combat cybercrime provides an interesting case study in how to pursue cyber-related solutions. As an intergovernmental organization, the Council of Europe seeks to shape common European legislation for its member states. Among the council's stated purposes is to modernize and harmonize national legislation with a view to democracy, human rights, and the rule of law; to make justice more effective by proposing simpler, more flexible judicial procedures; to find shared solutions to the new legal and ethical problems which scientific and technological progress is causing for modern societies.[58]

In 1989, seeing the need for consistent computer-related legislation, the Council of Europe issued a recommendation on computer-related crime.[59] This was the first step in unifying European computer law. It proposed mandatory minimum standards and activities that member countries must criminalize, and another set of options that member states might wish to criminalize. Building on the success of its recommendations, the Council of Europe spent 4 years working on a Convention on Cybercrime, with help from the United States, Canada, Japan, and other non-members of the organization. The document opened up for signature to EU and non-EU members alike on November 23, 2001, and entered into force on July 1, 2004. Today 20 countries have ratified it including the United States and 26 more have signed the treaty.[60] The treaty establishes common definitions of computer-related offenses and content-related offenses.[61] It also names 4 types of cybercrime: confidentiality offenses, notably breaking into computers; fraud and forgery; content violations, such as child pornography and racism; and copyright offenses.[62] The convention has the full effect of a multilateral treaty with the force of law, but only among the ratifying countries.[63]

Among its provisions, the convention makes it a crime to create, download, or post on a Web site any computer program that is "designed or adapted" primarily to gain access to a computer system without permission. It also prohibits the development of software designed to interfere with the "functioning of a computer system" by deleting or altering data, and it allows authorities to order someone to reveal his or her passwords or phrases used in an encryption key.[64] The convention also requires Web sites and Internet providers to collect information about their users, a rule that would potentially limit anonymous remailers.

The Convention on Cybercrime raises many issues. For example, many in the United States accustomed to protection of privacy rights are concerned that the convention favors law enforcement capabilities over U.S. privacy rights. Privacy advocates worry that the convention may interfere with the ability of online users to speak anonymously and that anonymous remailers may be outlawed. The convention may also interfere with the ability of everyone from corporations to hackers to test the security of their own information infrastructures. Internet service providers claim the draft makes unfair demands on them by asking them to track Web users' online movements.

The Convention on Cybercrime illustrates how good ideas can become controversial when they move from the drawing board to implementation. As early as 1989, the Council of Europe recognized that domestic regulation alone was insufficient to overcome the cybercrime threat in Europe. There was widespread industry support and both the public and private sector recognized the need for legal harmonization. The threat posed by cybercrime is clearly an extraterritorial threat, effective enforcement is lacking, and there are highly divergent state laws and practices on cybercrime. So why is there controversy? New laws, particularly regional agreements, tend to establish legal norms for the largely unregulated realm of cyberspace. Regional agreements often become customary international law that may ultimately evolve into formalized treaties. In effect, Europe wrote the first international code of conduct and criminal code that a multilateral body accepted. By setting this benchmark, states and industries that did not have a voice in the process may find the European convention an attack on the unique values of other countries. Finally, and perhaps most significantly, the Council of Europe is a state-centric organization. Although industry applauded the council's efforts early on, the lack of transparency increased as the release date for the draft neared. The draft convention may be ratified by the member states, but industry has resisted it and will continue to resist. The lack of industry buy-in across the entire life cycle of the convention may render it a blunt and ineffective tool.

TOWARD CYBERTHREAT SOLUTIONS

Cyberthreats come in a variety of forms, including hacking, cybercrime, cyberterrorism, information warfare, and information operations. The cross-jurisdictional nature of these threats challenge sovereignty and pose a continuing challenge for an effective response. Information technology allows a wide range of actors to cause a wide range of damage and chaos across the cyberthreat continuum. To understand and overcome cyberthreats, policy makers must make two assumptions. First, states, industry, and individuals are mutually vulnerable and interdependent. Second, neither states nor industry alone has the authority or capability to solve the problems posed by cyberthreats. Much of the key technology and infrastructure lies in the private sector, while the authority to create and enforce laws and the legitimacy to enter into international agreements resides with states. Recognizing these two key assumptions and embedding them in planning and policy will go a long way toward developing cyberthreat solutions.

ENDNOTES

1. The White House, Remarks by the President on Securing Our Nation's Cyber Infrastructure, May 29, 2009.

2. Gabriel Weimann, "Al-Qa`ida's Extensive Use of the Internet," *CTC Sentinel* 1(2) (January 2008): 6

3. Robert Coalson, "Behind the Estonia Cyberattacks", RadioFreeEurope RadioLiberty, March 06, 2009.

4. Jack M. Germain, "The Art of Cyber Warfare, Part 1: The Digital Battlefield," TechNewsWorld, April 29, 2008.

5. Ibid.

6. Tom Espiner, "Georgia Accuses Russia of Coordinated Cyberattack", CNET News, August 11, 2008, <http://news.cnet.com/8301-1009_3-10014150-83.html>.

7. Robert Coalson, "Behind the Estonia Cyberattacks," RadioFreeEurope RadioLiberty, March 06, 2009.

8. NATO Fact Sheet, "NATO Opens New Centre of Excellence on Cyber Defence," May 14, 2008, <http://www.nato.int/docu/update/2008/05-may/e0514a.html>.

9. Barton Gellman, "Cyber-Attacks by Al Qaeda Feared: Terrorists at Threshold of Using Internet as Tool of Bloodshed, Experts Say," *The Washington Post* (June 27, 2002): A1; Jack Kelley, "Terrorist Instructions Hidden Online," *USA Today* (April 14, 2001). Operational details of future targets are hidden in plain view. As Kelley writes, "We recognize that cyber tools offer them new, low-cost, easily hidden means to inflict damage. Terrorists and extremists already use the Internet to communicate, to raise funds, recruit, and gather intelligence. They may even launch attacks remotely from countries where their actions are not illegal or with whom we have no extradition agreements."

10. <www.forbes.com/business/forbes/2004/0920/070sidebar.html>.

11. <www.caida.org/analysis/security/sapphire/>.

12. <www.securityfocus.com/news/6767>.

13. The accounts were global indeed and included Finland, Russia, Germany, the Netherlands, the United States, Israel, and Switzerland.

14. <http://news.com.com/2009-12-956901.html>.

15. Dorothy Denning, *Information Warfare and Security* (New York: ACM Press, 1999), 55.

16. A description of the ILoveYou virus can be found at <http://getvirushelp.com/iloveyou/>.

17. Denning, *Information Warfare and Security*, 206–207.

18. Charles Bickers, "Combat on the Web," *Far Eastern Economic Review* (August 16, 2001).

19. Referred to as *cyberplagues* by Dorothy Denning. See *Information Warfare and Security*, 269–281.

20. President's Information Technology Advisory Committee, "Cyber Security: A Crisis of Prioritization," Report to the President, February 2005, <http://www.nitrd.gov/pitac/reports/20050301_cybersecurity/cybersecurity.pdf>, 4.

21. John Lovett, US Web Analytics Forecast, 2008 to 2014, *Forrester*, May 27, 2009.

22. Internet World Usage Stats, May 2009, <http://www.internetworldstats.com/stats>.

23. <www.dhs.gov/dhspublic/interapp/press_release/press_release_0350.xml>.

24. Ariana Eunjung Cha, "Cybersecurity a Top Priority: White House Adviser Presses Computer Industry to Do More," *The Washington Post* (February 8, 2002): E1. Also see <http://www.microsoft.com/industry/government/csisiti.mspx> from 2003.

25. Joshua Cooper Ramo, *The Age of the Unthinkable* (New York: Little, Brown & Co., 2009).

26. Cha (see note 24 earlier), The White House, Remarks by the President on Securing Our Nation's Cyber Infrastructure, May 29, 2009.

27. <http://www.whitehouse.gov/pcipb/cyberspace_strategy.pdf>, 8.

28. Maryann Cusimano Love, *Public–Private Partnerships and Global Problems: Y2K and Cybercrime.* Paper presented at the International Studies Association, Hong Kong, July 2001.

29. Ibid. Cusimano Love adds, "The Japanese defense ministry used Aum-developed communications programs at 20 ground bases across Japan to gain more rapid access to the Internet. Aum programs were also used for airline route management and mainframe computer operations. The software companies earned the business through indirect subcontracting relationships, underbidding competitors by 30 to 40% because their employees, all Aum members, worked for virtually no pay."

30. Calvin Sims, "Japan Software Suppliers Linked to Sect," *The New York Times* (March 2, 2000): A6.

31. This is true even if the specific terminal from which the attack originated can be identified, because it may be difficult to say exactly who was at the terminal when the attack was planned and executed.

32. <www.microsoft.com/industry/government/csisiti.mspx>.

33. Virtually every benefit of the global era in some way poses a challenge to security. For example, the cheap cost of technology facilitates the rise of computer-related crime and cyberterrorism. The rapid transit of goods and people now challenges the ability of states to secure their borders. The free flow of data, people, and ideas makes it difficult to conduct intelligence gathering without running afoul of First Amendment guarantees. The growth of world markets and international investment aids in financing terrorism and engaging in money laundering.

34. But are the most technologically advanced states also the most vulnerable? According to Bangladeshi Deputy Prime Minister Datuk Seri Abdullah Ahmad Badawi, "Technologically superior states can also cripple the defenses and economies of victim states at will, again placing developing states at a disadvantage. . . . It would cost the average Bangladeshi more than 8 years' income to buy a computer, whereas it would cost the average American just 1 month's wage. And what would this repository of information, in which more than 80% of the content is in English, mean to 90% of the people worldwide who do not speak it?" See "Internet Widening Gap Between Haves, Have Nots," *New Straits Times Press* (June 5, 2000).

35. Scott Peterson, "Old Weapons, New Terror Worries: Russian and US Experts Meet this Month to Assess Terror Tactics, from Hacking into Systems to Seizing a Weapon," *The Christian Science Monitor*, April 15, 2004, <www.csmonitor.com/2004/0415/p06s02-woeu.html?s=widep>.

36. <http://www.gcn.com/16_32/news/32050-1.html>.

37. A comprehensive list of potential computer network attacks is beyond the scope of this paper, but a few to mention are using computers to reroute trains, corrupt databases, impose information blockades in or out of computers, alter traffic control systems, interfere with law enforcement emergency response systems, and corrupt key utilities. See Roger C. Molander, Andrew S. Riddile, and Peter A. Wilson, *Strategic Information Warfare: A New Face of War* (New York: Rand Corp., 1996); and the President's Commission on Critical Infrastructure Protection, *Critical Foundations: Protecting America's Infrastructures* (Washington, DC: U.S. Government Printing Office, October 1997).

38. John C. Gannon, "Intelligence Challenges through 2015." Remarks to Columbus Council on World Affairs, April 27, 2000, <www.cia.gov/cia/public_affairs/speeches/archives/2000/gannon_speech_05022000.html>. Gannon is chairman of the National Intelligence Council.

39. James Mulvenon, China and Cyberwar. Presentation to "Information Warfare Post Y2K: A National Security Perspective," Jane's Conference, Washington, DC, May 12, 2000.

40. <www.prwatch.org/node/4040>.

41. The Law of Armed Conflict (LOAC) is a body of international law that attempts to regulate conduct during armed hostilities in a manner that minimizes savagery but does not impede the ability of states and factions to enter into and carry out conflict. The rules and general principles of the LOAC are applicable to all conflicts, including those conducted in cyberspace.

42. Humanitarian law limits how much a state may punish an enemy. The most significant principles—to protect citizens and noncombatants—require a state to weigh the prospect of gain through military attack against harm. This principle, derived from customary law, essentially establishes that a response must be appropriate to a grievance and must be considered in light of objectives and possible casualties. See Martens Clause, 1899 Hague Peace Conference (attacks will be judged by effects rather than by methods).

43. Examples include boycotts and withholding medical aid or other needed resources.

44. "Government Drafts Plan to Combat Cyberterrorism," *Yomiuri Shimbun* (November 30, 2000).

45. <www.crime-research.org/articles/Cyber_Terrorism_new_kind_Terrorism>.

46. Jim Wolf, "Cyber Terrorism," *Scotsman* (May 13, 1998): 3.

47. Jack Kelley, "Terror Groups Hide Behind Web Encryption," *USA Today* (April 13, 2001).

48. <www.forbes.com/global/2004/0920/104_2.html>.

49. "'Chinese' Virus Targets Microsoft Security Hole," CNN, July 20, 2001; available at <www.cnn.com/2001/BUSINESS/asia/07/20/hk.codered/>. Update: <www.gao.gov/htext/d03715t.html> from 2003.

50. <www.gao.gov/htext/d03715t.html>.

51. In many respects, the realm of cyberspace represents the ultimate potential of economic liberalism: private self-regulation of human interaction, unfettered and instantaneous free flows of capital, and trade in a new, borderless space unconstrained by sovereign institutions.

52. Money laundering facilitates much illegal activity worldwide. However, it can also be seen as a theft crime that deprives the legitimate owners of resources the benefit of their property.

53. Anthony Lake, *Six Nightmares: Real Threats in a Dangerous World and How America Can Meet Them* (New York: Little, Brown, 2000), 46.

54. The White House, Remarks by the President on Securing Our Nation's Cyber Infrastructure, May 29, 2009.

55. International Crime Complaint Center, "2008 International Crime Report," Bureau of Justice Assistance, U.S. Department of Justice, 2008, p. 1.

56. Attacks on computers are on the rise. Notable cyberattacks and viruses include the attack on the CIA on September 19, 1996; the attack on the U.S. Department of Justice in August 1996; the attack on *The New York Times* in September 1998; the Melissa virus in 1999; the Naked Wife virus on March 7, 2001; and the Matcher virus on April 19, 2001.

57. Perhaps hijacking agreements could serve as a useful and instructive model.

58. Information obtained from the Council of Europe Web site, <www.coe.int/portalT.asp>.

59. Council of Europe, "Computer-Related Crime," Recommendation No. R (89) 9; <http://europa.eu.int/ISPO/eif/InternetPoliciesSite/Crime/crime1.html1>.

60. The U.S. Senate ratified the Convention on August 3, 2006. See, Council of Europe, Convention on Cybercrime, CETS No.: 185, Status as of: April 6, 2009, <http://conventions.coe.int/Treaty/Commun/ChercheSig.asp?NT=185&CM=&DF=&CL=ENG>.

61. For a discussion of the history of the Convention on Cybercrime, see Goldstone and Shave, "International Dimensions of Crimes in Cyberspace," 1945.
62. <http://www.cbsnews.com/stories/2004/09/16/tech/main643897.shtml>.
63. These efforts involve only developed countries; multilateral efforts in the developing world lag. It's not easy to persuade countries where Internet use is not yet pervasive to see cybercrime as an urgent problem. But an attack can be launched as easily from the Third World as from Europe or the United States, and the network will only be as strong as its weakest links.
64. Only Singapore and Malaysia have enacted such a requirement into law. This requirement may pose a substantial problem for the United States because it runs counter to the constitutional protection against self-incrimination.

CHAPTER TEN

Ecological Interdependence and the Spread of Infectious Disease

Dennis Pirages and Paul Runci

The swine flu outbreak began in Veracruz and neighboring Oaxaca states in Mexico, in late March and early April 2009. The virus quickly spread to all countries, causing the World Health Organization (WHO) to raise the international pandemic emergency alert level which prompted countries to activate their emergency response plans, stockpile vaccine, and survey and work to contain the spread of the virus. Swine flu H1N1 influenza virus is common in pigs and can spread to humans, but usually few cases are reported a year. When clusters of human cases appeared in 2009, Mexico reported the information to the WHO, due to International Health Regulations requiring countries to report within 24 hours any disease outbreak (public health emergency of international concern) that is serious, unusual, at risk of spreading internationally, or potentially disruptive of travel and trade. These regulations went into force in 2007, in response to lessons learned from the SARS (severe acute respiratory syndrome) pandemic of 2003.[1]

The SARS outbreak began in a remote region of Guangdong Province in China sometime in the autumn of 2002, when a previously unknown virus jumped from either horseshoe bats or masked palm civet cats to people. The virus quickly spread throughout the region, but news about the new disease outbreak was kept under wraps by the Chinese government, which classified the matter as "top secret." By February 2003 the disease had made its way to Hong Kong, carried by a physician from Guangdong province who had been treating patients exposed to this mysterious disease. From there the virus quickly spread to much of the rest of Asia, and eventually to 30 countries. The most affected Asian economies lost tens of billions of dollars as trade dropped off, tourists shunned the region, air traffic was dramatically curtailed, and hotel rooms remained empty. By the time this disease outbreak was brought under control, nearly 8,000 people had been sickened and more than 900 had died.

Mutating viruses are difficult to plan for, as they may not be responsive to existing medicines. This is why the world health community is now anxiously scanning for a potentially much more serious and lethal disease threat. Periodic outbreaks of avian flu (H5N1) among both wild and domesticated fowl are being scrutinized by experts who fear that this virus might mutate into a form that could be passed from birds to people more easily, or even from one person to another. Human deaths from this virus have been limited so far because the current form spreads from fowl to humans only on very rare occasions. But a modified form of this virus could spread around the world with flocks of migrating birds, or even traveling people, leaving millions of human fatalities in its wake.

Viruses, bacteria, and other pathogens have never respected borders. Throughout history microbes have moved across frontiers, carried by wind, water, explorers, migrants, merchants, and mercenaries. Most of the time, these unauthorized crossings have had little impact, but occasionally whole societies have been reshaped because of them. Deepening globalization is now causing growing concern over the potential development and spread of new and resurgent diseases across increasingly porous state borders.

Over the course of history, human beings have coevolved with millions of other animal and plant species as well as a host of pathogens. Only during the last century did technological innovation give *Homo sapiens* a clear, but perhaps temporary, edge in this evolutionary competition. But there is now growing evidence that pathogens are making a comeback in an increasingly interdependent and urbanized global system. Various plant and animal species, having been introduced into new environments through increased trade and transportation, are wreaking significant damage in many countries. The changes associated with increasingly open societies, open economies, and deployment of new technologies—growing economic integration, gradual disappearance of national borders, more rapid movement of people and goods among regions, weakening of the authority of the state, and changing patterns of human settlements and behavior—are combining to make the resurgence of pathogenic microorganisms, as well as the worldwide spread of various kinds of other potentially destructive species, an important threat to human security and well-being.[2]

The first modern humans lived some 100,000 years ago and inhabited areas that spanned eastern Africa and the Middle East. From there, a series of expansions and migrations moved people outward until most of the habitable world had been at least loosely settled 15,000 years ago.[3] Since then, there has been a slow but accelerating reintegration of these previously scattered and mostly isolated human populations into larger units. Thus, the Roman Empire, the Mongol empires, and European colonialism all represent ways in which previously isolated human populations have been absorbed into much larger administrative units. This long-term reintegration process could well culminate in the emergence of an immense global city over the next few decades. But each step in this reintegration of human populations has had significant ecological, political, and socioeconomic consequences, not the least of which has been the insecurity associated with the more rapid spread of infectious disease.

INTEGRATION AND DISEASE IN HISTORY

Homo sapiens is one species among millions that occupy the global ecosystem. Like most other species, *Homo sapiens* lives in and identifies with basic biological units called *populations*. Populations of any species are "dynamic systems of interacting individuals . . . that are potentially capable of interbreeding with each other."[4] The boundaries of human populations, which social scientists call *societies* or *ethnic groups*, could theoretically be located by mapping genetic differences that result from generations of in-group reproduction. But it is much easier to identify the boundaries of societies through marked gaps in communication efficiency. These communication gaps and inefficiencies both help to maintain and are maintained by so-called ethnic differences that are reflected in languages, behavior, values, and beliefs.[5] The great outward dispersals of the earth's early human populations resulted in a world inhabited by thousands of mostly isolated societies that were administered as clans, tribes, and kingdoms. These societies coevolved with other species and microorganisms within the constraints of shared local ecosystems. It was only with the creation of larger administrative units, such as empires, that the large-scale mingling of previously isolated peoples and the microorganisms they carried began.

The integration of previously small and isolated societies into empires and cities was accompanied both by bloodshed and a tragic death toll from infectious disease. William McNeill has observed that the growing Roman Empire was repeatedly wracked by the scourge of strange diseases. There were at least 11 microbial disasters in republican times. A major epidemic struck the densely packed city of Rome in 65 A.D., but that paled in comparison with a more widespread pandemic that began to sweep the empire in 165 A.D. Casualties from this latter plague were much higher: Approximately, one-quarter to one-third of those exposed to the disease died.[6]

In more recent history, the expansion of European commerce with settlements in the rest of the world has had similar disease ramifications. By the year 1350, the kingdoms of Western Europe had become large and densely populated enough to press against the carrying capacities of their land. These pressures resulted in local European famines in most years between 1290 and 1350 A.D.[7] At the same time, contacts and commerce between West and East were increasing, manifest in the growth of travel over lengthy trade routes between Europe and China. The intensification of caravan traffic across Asia and contact among previously separated peoples surged under the Mongol empires. At the height of Mongol power, the empires embraced nearly all of China and Russia as well as Central Asia, Iran, and Iraq.[8]

During this period of increasing European growth and expanded commerce, messengers, merchants, and mercenaries, among others, increased their travels and came into contact with new peoples. This increased contact inevitably resulted in an enhanced exchange of pathogens between Europe and Asia. From the European point of view the most infamous was *Yersinia pestis*, the cause of the "Black Death." The arrival of the plague in Europe in 1346 began a lengthy pruning process during which successive waves of disease trimmed the region's population by nearly 40 percent, the highest mortality rates being among those who lived in urban areas.[9]

Contact among previously separated peoples took another leap forward during the following age of European exploration and colonization. The ships of Christopher Columbus, which arrived in the Caribbean in 1492, were the first of a wave of European vessels that eventually brought the Europeans into contact with numerous indigenous peoples. This contact not only eventually resulted in the absorption of this territory into Spanish, Portuguese, British, and French empires, but also was responsible for pathogens that accompanied the conquerors wiping out a significant portion of these indigenous peoples. The military history of the period is replete with tales of miraculous conquests of huge numbers of indigenous peoples by mere hand-fuls of European troops. But, in reality, there were few bona fide miracles. Diseases spread by the invaders, particularly smallpox, killed approximately two-thirds of the indigenous populations, leaving them in disarray and un-able to muster a decent defense of their territories. As William McNeill has put it, "From the Amerindian point of view, stunned acquiescence to Span-ish superiority was the only possible response.... Native authority structures crumbled; the old gods seemed to have abdicated. The situation was ripe for the mass conversions recorded so proudly by Christian missionaries."[10] The spread of smallpox was followed by measles and eventually by typhus, with diseases from Africa such as malaria and yellow fever being transplanted into the American tropics. By the time these transplanted diseases had run their course, only an estimated 1 in 20 Amerindians in the affected areas had sur-vived.[11] Indeed, as the European colonial networks expanded to embrace much of the world, an unequal exchange of diseases took place, with the bulk of the disease casualties being among the conquered.

More recently, another spurt of disease accompanied the large-scale movement of military personnel during World War I. While the eyes of the world were focused on battlefield casualties, a deadly influenza pan-demic spread quickly around the world, often moving with the troops. By the time the casualties began to taper off, this unexpected spin-off from the war resulted in the greatest pandemic in world history. Estimates of the magnitude of this catastrophe vary, but somewhere between 30 and 50 million people died, many times the number of battlefield casualties.[12]

AN EVOLUTIONARY PERSPECTIVE

Since World War II there has been a tremendous acceleration in the pace of globalization and urbanization. The historical record indicates that such periods of growing interactions among previously separated peoples are often punctuated by serious outbreaks of disease. The last 50 years has wit-nessed the spread of exotic and lethal diseases in tropical areas of the world, several deadly influenza epidemics, and an HIV/AIDS pandemic that con-tinues to spread inexorably around the world. There is heightened fear that contemporary environmental change, more frequent international travel, growing bacterial resistance to antibiotics, and changing human behavior and settlement patterns are leading to outbreaks of previously unknown deadly diseases and a resurgence of others.[13] In spite of the development of a broad spectrum of antibiotics and new medical technologies, the world remains a biologically dangerous place. "At the root of the resurgence of old infectious diseases is an evolutionary paradox: The more vigorously we have assailed the world of microorganisms, the more varied the repertoire of bacterial and viral strains thrown up against us."[14]

The key to comprehending why there are so many new challenges to human microsecurity is to understand the nature of ecological interdependence. Populations of *Homo sapiens* have coevolved with a variety of other species within ever-changing physical environments. *Ecological interdependence* refers to the growth and maintenance of a delicate network of relationships among these organisms and between them and the sustaining physical environments. Rapid changes in any of these relationships can rebound to the detriment of human beings, other creatures, microorganisms, and even the ecosystem itself. Thus, a mutation in a potentially pathogenic microorganism, a rapid increase in populations of voracious pests, or even a change in rainfall can destabilize an ecosystem often with unfortunate results.

Over most of history, this coevolution has occurred within local and mostly isolated ecosystems. Because of mutual adaptation processes that involve the human immune system, localized bouts of nonfatal diseases have been common. But as previously separated societies are now being brought into more frequent contact by the pressures of globalization, there are complex and unforeseen disease consequences. The complicated local interdependence between human populations, other species, and various microorganisms now is moving to the global level.

The human immune system, which protects the body against diseases, is the product of countless generations of interactions between people and disease organisms. Natural-selection processes, which shape these immune systems, represent learning by experience. People born with weak immune systems usually succumb to deadly diseases and do not live to reproduce. People with stronger immune systems are more likely to survive, have children, and to pass on their genes to future generations.

Epidemics or serious disease outbreaks can develop when people come into contact with new pathogens. Therefore, people who move into new environments are at substantial risk of contracting new illnesses. This is why traveling business persons or scholars attending international conferences often come down with various illnesses upon their return, or why people who move from one geographical region to another are frequently ill during their first year of residence. Similarly, people or animals moving into new environments can bring new pathogens with them, thus exposing others to new diseases. And many diseases, such as HIV/AIDS and SARS jump from animals to people. Social and cultural practices can often accelerate the spread of disease. For example, among certain African tribes, marrying and supporting a widow becomes the responsibility of a dead husband's brother. Because many African males have recently died of HIV/AIDS, this custom has accelerated the spread of the virus from widows of HIV/AIDS victims to the dead man's extended family.[15]

Problems can also arise when changes take place in pathogens, sometimes making them more lethal to human beings. For various reasons, including environmental changes, exposure to chemicals or radiation, widespread use of antibiotics and antivirals, or interactions with other microorganisms, dangerous changes can occur in pathogens, potentially confronting immune systems with additional challenges.

Pathogens can also be liberated by people moving into previously unpopulated forests. Rapid population growth in tropical areas of the world is leading people to clear land for settlements at the edges of rain forests, thereby liberating various kinds of microorganisms resident in animals there. Thus, the human immunodeficiency virus (HIV, the proximate cause of AIDS) and Ebola, Marburg, and yellow fever viruses were probably first resident in monkeys; Rift Valley fever in cattle, sheep, and mosquitoes; and Hantaan virus in rodents. "These pathogens probably lurked relatively undisturbed in their animal hosts in the tropics, jumping to humans only on rare occasions. They had little opportunity to adapt to humans, who usually were 'dead end' host species, because the viruses would fizzle out once they rapidly swept through a small population at the edge of the forest."[16] But these and other pathogens now can make successful leaps from animals to larger and denser human populations, thus putting deadly new diseases in motion. In late 1997 and early 1998, for example, viruses made leaps from monkeys to humans in Congo (monkeypox) and from chickens to humans in Hong Kong. And in recent years scientists carefully scrutinize outbreaks of avian flu among birds in Asia and elsewhere, fearing that the virus would change into a deadly form that could pass readily among people.

Similarly, plant and animal species also can wreak havoc when they jump from their ecosystems of origin to ecosystems that have had no previous contact with them. Historically, plants and animals native to Europe had both positive and negative effects as they moved around the world with colonists.[17] In the contemporary world, it is often the unintended movement of plants and animals, largely as a result of expanded trade and travel, that can have devastating effects. In the United States, for example, species ranging from the blue water hyacinths from South America that now clog Florida's waterways to the Africanized honeybee, an aggressive stinger that was brought to Brazil in 1959 and then escaped North, are now having significant economic and environmental impacts.[18]

In summary, the major disease outbreaks and epidemics that historically often have transformed the nature of societies have occurred when human immune systems have encountered pathogenic microorganisms with which they have had little experience. When the Black Death arrived in Europe from Asia, nearly half the population was wiped out in many areas, thus leading to major sociopolitical transformations. Similarly, the "conquest" of the Americas by Europeans was aided and abetted by pathogens transplanted into biologically naive indigenous populations. This is why there are now concerns about weakening borders, state failures, civil wars, large-scale migrations, and the rapid integration of previously separated peoples into an emerging global city. Rapid movement of people, produce, animals, and microorganisms around the world creates worries about the resurgence of old diseases, the appearance of new ones, and the economic and environmental damage that can be done by hitchhiking creatures great and small.

ECOLOGICAL INTERDEPENDENCE: SOME EVIDENCE

Governments have been slow to react to the challenges associated with rapidly growing ecological interdependence. The contemporary concern about nonhuman immigrants in the United States remains much the same as it was in the 1870s when Spencer Fullerton Baird of the U.S. Fish Commission attempted to improve his dining experiences by bringing a new, tasty species of Eurasian carp into the United States. His venture was a great economic success and the fish became the culinary craze of the nation. But ever since then, the carp have been reproducing prolifically in U.S. waters, destroying habitats and crowding out native fish. The legacy of these attempts to make nature more productive through the introduction of new species lingers on in U.S. regulations. There is rigorous screening to catch potentially dangerous agricultural pests, but much less attention is paid to imported species that do not directly threaten to ravage crops. For example, state governments can allow the import of exotic fish species from other countries without even consulting their neighboring states.[19]

Until recently, the potential for the spread of infectious diseases in the United States was similarly downplayed. The development and large-scale use of antibiotics and other pharmaceuticals fostered complacency in the face of growing disease challenges. In 1969, for example, the U.S. surgeon general declared that infectious diseases had been conquered and that the time had come to focus on chronic diseases such as cancer and heart disease.[20] But things have been changing, and in 1995 the World Health Organization (WHO) felt it necessary to reemphasize that infectious

diseases are still the world's leading cause of death.[21] The Clinton administration went so far as to declare HIV/AIDS a threat to U.S. national security
in April 2000. And the technological optimism of an earlier era has begun to
fade in the face of the seemingly incurable HIV/AIDS virus and the resurgence of several diseases in antibiotic-resistant form. More than one-tenth
of the new cases of tuberculosis (TB) worldwide are now resistant to at least
one of the drugs commonly used to treat the disease. And between 1 percent
and 2 percent of all new cases are resistant to multiple drugs. In addition,
other serious diseases are also developing drug resistance.[22]

There is now ample evidence of the increasing threat of infectious diseases, but changes over time in the personal and economic impacts of various
diseases are difficult to quantify for several reasons. First, it is not necessary
for people to die from an infectious disease for the disease to deeply affect
their quality of life. Various debilitating diseases can disable large numbers
of people for considerable periods of time without actually making them
mortality statistics. Second, infectious-disease statistics are often deliberately
manipulated downward by some countries as a matter of national pride or
economics. Tourists prefer not to travel to countries known to be experi-
encing plagues! Finally, there is little reliable historical data to use as a baseline for assessing the extent to which disease has increased or decreased in
many areas of the world, particularly in the most poverty-stricken countries
where infectious diseases are likely to be most prevalent.

Given these caveats, in recent years about 15 million people have died
annually from communicable diseases. Respiratory infection—mostly influenza and pneumonia—have accounted for about 4 million of these deaths,
HIV/AIDS for nearly 3 million deaths, and diarrhea, tuberculosis, and
malaria, taken together, have accounted for another 5 million deaths.[23]
Approximately 33 million people now live with HIV/AIDS worldwide,
some 2.7 million are newly infected each year, and about 2 million die from
AIDS annually. In sub-Saharan Africa over 22 million people are now stricken
with HIV/AIDS; 75% of AIDS deaths occur in sub-Saharan Africa.[24]

Fifty years ago, many of these diseases surely afflicted human beings.
But it is unclear how much globalization and urbanization have affected
their geographic scope and prevalence. What is clear is that these diseases
now move much more rapidly along with the large flow of travelers and
agricultural commodities in the contemporary world. There is thus growing worry about a potential worldwide spread of killer viruses. In the
1990s, outbreaks of pneumonic plague, which is spread through the air,
killed hundreds of people in India and disrupted air travel in the region.[25]
Airports as far away as Kennedy in New York City were screening dozens

of flights daily for potential carriers. Also in the late 1990s, an outbreak of bird flu in Hong Kong caused a major drop-off in tourism and led to the culling of 1.5 million chickens and other birds in an attempt to stop the spread of the virus. In 2002–2003 an outbreak of SARS, a previously unknown virus, sickened more than 8,000 people and killed more than 900 as it rapidly moved from Southern China into 30 countries. And since 2005 the avian flu has periodically flared up in Asia and also moved into neighboring regions. As a result, hundreds of millions of chickens and ducks have been slaughtered and as of April 2009, 257 people have died when they contracted the disease from contact with infected fowl. The 2009 swine flu outbreak damaged the airline, tourism, and pork industries (even though the disease is not spread from eating pork).[26]

Although the many exotic species of flora and fauna that now travel around the world rarely kill people, they often do extensive economic damage. In the United States, it is estimated that more than 4,000 exotic species of flora and fauna have become naturalized (able to survive without human help) over the past century. But just 79 of those species cost the nation an estimated $97 billion between 1906 and 1991 in damage to agriculture, ecosystems, industry, and health. Most of the species brought into the United States unintentionally have been the inadvertent by-products of commerce, tourism, or travel.[27] It is difficult to estimate the toll from invasive species on the global level, but one estimate of the damage to crops from nonindigenous pests put the figure somewhere between $55 billion and $247 billion per year.[28]

Many new species make their way into the United States and other countries along with other imported commodities. Agricultural products, nursery stock, cut flowers, and timber often harbor insects, plant diseases, and snails, while bulk commodities such as gravel, sand, and wool often contain hidden seeds. Ballast water on commercial ships, taken on to provide stability at sea and often dumped when ships load at different ports, also has been a major transport medium for spreading nonindigenous species around the world.

ECOLOGICAL SECURITY: CONTEMPORARY CHALLENGES

Deepening globalization represents a growing challenge to human health as well as ecological stability. Although ecological interdependence grew at a gradual pace for some time, it is only recently that a confluence of rapid technological innovation and a worldwide diffusion of liberal economic ideology has created a historically unique climate that has accelerated these

change processes.[29] As globalization proceeds in tandem with human dis-
turbances of remote ecosystems where many previously unknown pathogens reside, the likelihood of new disease outbreaks grows. Pathogens that
have previously been restricted to isolated geographic locations have spread
rapidly and with relative ease to other areas as the world's transportation
networks have expanded.[30]

Diseases are currently being spread more rapidly and widely in two
ways: by increased travel and contact among people and by integration
of the world's food markets. More frequent contacts are now occurring
in densely populated cities and among human populations across political boundaries that once served as relatively impermeable barriers. Spatial separation is no longer a significant hindrance to human interaction as
technological advances have accelerated and expanded the possibilities for
transnational flows of information, money, goods, and people.

Professional journals and the mass media now carry accounts of
globalization-related public health incidents with alarming regularity as
pathogens old and new move worldwide along with the rising volume of
trade and travel. More than 2 million people now cross an international
border each day, up from only 69,000 in 1950. Since 1950, the number of passenger kilometers flown internationally has increased by nearly 100 fold.[31]

A second set of health risk factors emerges from the growth and deeper
integration of the world food market. Like other economic sectors, agriculture and food production have become increasingly globalized. Between
1997 and 2007, food imports into the United States more than doubled,
and only about 1 percent of these imports were inspected.[32] The growing
cross-border traffic in food and agricultural products increases the risks to
human health by creating more opportunities for pathogens to migrate
from their native environments in food shipments and cause disease outbreaks among people in other countries. This traffic also increases the likelihood of plant and animal diseases moving from one part of the world to
another. In 2001, for example, a strain of hoof-and-mouth disease that was
discovered in India in 1990 made its way to England and eventually to the
European continent, resulting in the slaughter of hundreds of thousands of
animals to prevent the further spread of the disease.

Part of the emerging food-safety problem results from trade liberalization. Although tariff and trade barriers in the agricultural sector have been
reduced and better transportation means that food products move more
rapidly from farm to market, health and food-safety standards and practices in many exporting countries remain poor. Thus, the risk of exposure

to food-borne disease is rising as more countries pursue export-oriented agricultural production under various worldwide and regional free trade regimes.[33] Moreover, the tension between food safety and free trade grows more acute when it becomes a matter of international economic diplomacy. This occurs, for instance, when more stringent food safety standards in importing countries are attacked as nontariff barriers to trade. Such conflicts highlight the challenges that increased economic interdependence poses to state sovereignty. Trade disagreements are increasingly likely to be settled by the dispute resolution bodies of free trade regimes such as the WTO or NAFTA, rather than by the actions of governments. Consequently, the limitations that such trading regimes place on state sovereignty conceivably make it more difficult for countries to deal effectively with growing risks to public health.

MIGRATION, URBANIZATION, AND DISEASE

While there is currently much greater contact among the various neighborhoods of the nascent global city, the neighborhoods themselves are becoming more densely packed and prone to the spread of disease. People are migrating much more freely among and within countries, often carrying pathogens with them. The United Nations has estimated that by the year 2015 there will be 33 high populated urban areas called megacities, having 8 million inhabitants or more. Twenty-seven of these will be in less-industrialized countries. The fact that the most rapid urban growth is occurring in the cities of the poor and politically unstable less-industrialized world raises additional health concerns given the limited resources, shaky health infrastructures, and inadequate institutional arrangements available to governments in these countries.[34]

Several forces are driving this urbanization trend. Environmental decline in rural areas of poorer countries is a major contributor to this growing migration. Degradation of the agricultural resource base is driven by a complex interplay of population pressures, desertification, deforestation, droughts, and salinization of soils linked to irrigation. These problems have contributed directly to increases in the number of migrating rural poor in many regions of Africa, Asia, and Latin America, as well as to declining agricultural productivity, particularly in marginal areas. Compounding matters, throughout the developing world population growth rates in rural areas are particularly high and numbers often exceed the sustaining capabilities of local ecosystems. The lure of urban areas, where economic opportunities often are perceived to be growing, becomes almost irresistible to many in the countryside for whom living conditions have grown increasingly difficult. Thus, the migration of marginalized rural residents to urban centers is propelled by a complex set of ecological and economic push and pull factors.[35]

The prevalence of unemployment, poverty, pollution from municipal and industrial wastes, poor nutrition, and an inadequate public health infrastructure (particularly sanitation and sewers) in urban areas means that the urban poor of these growing megacities in less-industrialized countries frequently encounter and carry a host of pathogens. They experience both the problems characteristic of poverty (deaths from infectious disease and higher infant mortality rates) and those characteristic of wealthier countries (higher rates of death from heart disease, cancer, and accidents). Nonetheless, many migrants in the developing world still regard themselves as better off in cities than in the countryside, where economic circumstances are often worse.[36]

This urbanization trend is now especially troubling for human health because of the rising incidence of infectious waterborne diseases (such as cholera, typhoid, and hepatitis A and E) and vector-borne diseases such as malaria that thrive around stagnant water, particularly in cities of the less-industrialized world. The ever-increasing numbers and densities of the urban poor also help to create conditions for the occurrence of serious disease outbreaks as well as for the persistence of endemic infectious disease.

Health threats associated with megacities are not limited to the less-industrialized world. Increases in diseases in New York illustrate the emerging threats that infectious diseases pose to all urban populations. New York witnessed a rebirth of TB in the 1990s as a result of the convergence of at least three trends: the spread of HIV/AIDS, the economic recession of the late 1980s, and budgetary reductions in public health programs. In the early 1970s, when TB appeared to be under control, programs in the United States aimed at detecting and controlling the disease were downsized and phased out. But then HIV/AIDS began its spread into segments of the urban population in the 1980s, creating weakened immune systems within which TB could make a comeback. When the economic recession of the late 1980s hit, it left poorer, TB-infected HIV/AIDS victims in New York (and elsewhere) unable to gain access to adequate medical care. As a result, many of the urban poor with active TB cases did not complete the suggested 6-month regimen of antibiotics, thereby helping the surviving bacteria become more drug-resistant.[37]

POLICY RESPONSES TO EMERGING HEALTH RISKS

These emerging health threats are symptomatic of the new security challenges raised by deepening globalization and increasing urbanization, and dealing with them requires comprehensive, sustained policy responses at both the national and international levels. But governments have been slow to respond to the challenges of infectious disease, and sovereignty issues have impeded development of effective international institutions with the power to deal with disease outbreaks. Until the SARS outbreak in 2003 illustrated how rapidly a deadly virus can spread in the contemporary world and how economically damaging such an outbreak can be, there was only modest concern about this kind of threat to human security. But the persisting threat that avian flu could change into a deadly form easily passed from person to person coupled with the specter of bioterrorism now have increased public concern about infectious diseases and have spurred greater international cooperation in attempting to contain them.

Surveillance, diagnosis, and response capability are the 3 key elements in preventing disease outbreaks and epidemics. The global revolution in telecommunications has greatly increased surveillance capabilities. The growth of the Internet has facilitated the development of 2 global surveillance and diagnosis operations. The first, the Program for Monitoring Infectious Diseases (Pro MED-Mail), now links more than 40,000 subscribers in 185 countries. It uses the Internet to circulate information about outbreaks of human, animal, and plant diseases from correspondents around the world. The World Health Organization uses the Internet to support communications within its Global Outbreak Alert and Response Network (GOARN). This network links laboratories around the world in an effort to identify pathogens likely to cause disease outbreaks and ensures the rapid arrival of technical assistance when outbreaks do take place. But the WHO has a limited budget and must tap into a network of other organizations to provide personnel and resources to fight disease. Private companies, such as Veratect, also provide disease surveillance information as paid subscription services.

There are many other governmental and nongovernmental organizations that are frequently mobilized in attempts to stem disease outbreaks. Among the most important of these is the Centers for Disease Control and Prevention (CDC) in the United States, which has several hundred personnel focusing on international health issues. Doctors Without Borders (Medecins Sans Frontiers) is an important private-sector organization that provides medical assistance and disaster relief to those in greatest need. In a typical year its volunteer staff embarks on nearly 3,500 aid missions.

And the Bill and Melinda Gates foundation has been very active in disease prevention in the less-industrialized world, including a major HIV/AIDS prevention effort in India.

These efforts, however, operate with significant limitations. Successful surveillance requires transparency (openness) in order to detect disease outbreaks, but politicians in affected countries often prefer less candor. Disease outbreaks can exact a significant economic toll from lost revenue due to cutbacks in tourism and trade. Furthermore, telecommunications and medical research capabilities are rudimentary in remote parts of poorer countries, where new diseases are likely to emerge. Even in the United States reporting of diseases to the CDC is somewhat haphazard and, due to inadequate funding, some state public health infrastructures have deteriorated to the extent that detection of diseases cannot be assured.[38]

But it is of little use to report on disease outbreaks if adequate in-country or international response capabilities do not exist. In the absence of such capabilities, local doctors, scientists, and public health officials have little reason to participate in reporting networks. The CDC and other organizations do deploy teams of epidemiologists to various parts of the world to assist communities where outbreaks occur, but they must be invited by the affected countries. Sufficient international response demands the creation of a more powerful and centralized agency with access to state-of-the-art laboratories, world-class staff, sufficient funding, and a political mandate to take the lead in responding to the threat of emerging or reemerging diseases. The WHO would appear to be the logical choice, given its established role as the coordinator of international health programs. Yet the WHO now lacks many of the necessary elements—authority, mandate, funding, staff, and facilities—sufficient for the task at hand.

This lack of a robust global program for responding to disease threats highlights important political dilemmas that are characteristic of global ecopolitics. For example, the Bush Administration's disposition to minimize involvement in international organizations flew in the face of a growing need for leadership and assistance in dealing with many undesirable side effects of globalization. Moreover, the greatest threats to world health frequently originate in poor countries and failing states, which have limited capabilities for managing them. And countries with the resources necessary to address such problems often lack the political will to use them in the absence of an imminent crisis. From the perspective of U.S. policy makers, for example, there has been little apparent political gain and perhaps potential damage associated with sponsoring costly new international programs designed to combat disease threats that are not yet perceived to be serious security concerns by the American public.

There are additional issues involved in attempting to curtail the potential spread of infectious diseases. For instance, some governments are reluctant to report on disease outbreaks for fear of serious economic fallout. Thus, when India experienced outbreaks of pneumonic plague in the 1990s, the government at first failed to provide information to the international medical community, anticipating de facto quarantines and declines in trade and tourism. Similarly, the outbreak of bird flu in Hong Kong not only resulted in economic damage from a loss of tourism, but also damaged the political fortunes of a new government. And initially China tried to cover up the extent of the SARS outbreak, understandable since the disease outbreak eventually cost China tens of billions of dollars in lost tourism and trade. If reporting is perceived as unlikely to muster adequate assistance in combating disease outbreaks but highly likely to result in economic losses of various kind, then denial rules and there is no advantage to reporting.

Finally, the dilemmas associated with international policy responses to emerging disease threats are indicative of some of the broader tensions incumbent in the process of globalization. In an increasingly integrated, interdependent, and technologically advanced world, the power of the sovereign state to control its own affairs is becoming more ambiguous. A revolution in telecommunications and information technologies, for example, has given more power to the international medical community by facilitating much more effective global surveillance of infectious diseases. While governments may attempt to resist this growing transparency, they are fighting a losing battle.

In effect, technology is now enhancing the ability of nonstate actors to play a key role in areas where governance is now lacking. The augmented power of international professional networks might, on the one hand, be viewed as enhancing the authority and legitimacy of government by helping to fill significant vacuums in government functions, particularly in poor countries. But, on the other hand, this power might as easily be viewed as weakening conventional governmental authority by expropriating some of the traditional responsibilities of government in the public health arena. The nascent responses to emerging disease threats, like the threats themselves, raise questions about the future of state sovereignty in an increasingly global system.

Thus, infectious diseases, many of which have played a major role in shaping societies throughout history, continue to have a strong impact on the welfare of people and governments. The complex interactions of technological advances in medicine and the growing levels of interdependence among the regions of the world are creating both new pathways for the transmission of disease and new weapons in the struggle against them. In the long run, however, one of the casualties of growing ecological interdependence might well be globalization itself as the increasingly rapid worldwide spread of human, animal, and plant diseases could create conditions that would provoke a strong reaction against globalization, possibly slowing, or even reversing, the process.

ENDNOTES

1. World Health Organization, "Swine Influenza," <http://www.who.int/mediacentre/news/statements/2009/h1n1_20090429/en/index.html> and "Frequently Asked Questions about the International Health Regulations," <http://www.who.int/csr/ihr/howtheywork/faq/en/index.html#faq05>.
2. See Dennis Pirages, "Microsecurity: Disease Organisms and Human Well-Being," *Washington Quarterly* (Autumn 1995).
3. Luigi Cavalli-Sforza and Francesco Cavalli-Sforza, *The Great Human Diasporas* (Reading, MA: Addison-Wesley, 1995), 157–159.
4. Kenneth Watt, *Principles of Environmental Science* (New York: McGraw-Hill, 1973), 1.
5. Karl Deutsch, *Nationalism and Social Communication* (Cambridge: MIT Press, 1964), 100.
6. William McNeill, *Plagues and Peoples* (Garden City, NY: Anchor Press, 1976), 115–117.
7. Henry Hobhouse, *Forces of Change: An Unorthodox View of History* (New York: Arcade, 1990).
8. See McNeill, *Plagues and Peoples*, Ch. 4.
9. Hobhouse, *Forces of Change*, 11–23.
10. McNeill, *Plagues and Peoples*, 208.
11. Ibid., 215 and references cited therein.
12. See Alfred Crosby, *America's Forgotten Pandemic: The Influenza Epidemic of 1918* (Cambridge, UK: Cambridge University Press, 1990).
13. See Laurie Garrett, *The Coming Plague: Newly Emerging Diseases in a World Out of Balance* (New York: Farrar, Straus & Giroux, 1994); Stephen S. Morse (Ed.), *Emerging Viruses* (New York: Oxford University Press, 1993); Tony McMichael, *Human Frontiers, Environments and Disease* (Cambridge, UK: Cambridge University Press, 2001).
14. Marc Lappe, *Evolutionary Medicine: Rethinking the Origins of Disease* (San Francisco: Sierra Club Books, 1994), 8.
15. See Stephen Buckley, "Wife Inheritance Spurs AIDS Rise in Kenya," *Washington Post* (November 8, 1997).
16. Ann Gibbons, "Where Are 'New' Diseases Born?" *Science* (August 6, 1993): 680.
17. See Alfred W. Crosby, *Ecological Imperialism: The Biological Expansion of Europe, 900–1900* (Cambridge, UK: Cambridge University Press, 1986).
18. See Elizabeth Culotta, "Biological Immigrants under Fire," *Science* (December 6, 1991): 1444–1447.
19. Ibid., 1444.
20. Cited in David P. Fidler, "Return of the Fourth Horseman: Emerging Infectious Diseases and International Law," *Minnesota Law Review* (April 1997): 773.
21. World Health Organization (WHO), *The World Health Report 1995* (Geneva: WHO, 1995).

22. David Brown, "One in Ten TB Cases Worldwide Resist Common Treatment, Survey Shows," *Washington Post* (Oct. 23, 1997); WHO, "The Big Guns of Resistance," Ch. 4 in *Overcoming Antimicrobial Resistance* (Geneva: WHO, 2000), <www.who.int/infectious-disease-report/2000/>.

23. Data from World Health Organization, The World Health Report 2004 (Geneva: WHO, 2004), Annex Table 2; World Health Organization, The World Health Report 2001 (Geneva: WHO, 2001), Annex Table 2.

24. UNAIDS and World Health Organization, *2008 Report on the Global AIDS Epidemic*, <http://data.unaids.org/pub/GlobalReport/2008/jc1510_2008_global_report_pp29_62_en.pdf>.

25. See Laurie Garrett, *Betrayal of Trust: The Collapse of Global Public Health* (New York: Hyperion, 2000), Ch. 1.

26. See Anthony Faiola, "Outbreak Threatens global Recovery," *Washington Post* (April 28, 2009), Donald G. McNeil Jr., "Avian Flu Cases in Egypt Raise Alarms," *The New York Times* (April 20, 2009), David Brown, "World Responds Swiftly to Track 'Bird Flu' Spread," *Washington Post* (Jan. 11, 1998); David P. Fidler, *SARS, Governance and the Globalization of Disease* (New York: Palgrave, 2004); Guy Chazan, "Threat of Bird Flu Spreads to Europe," *Wall Street Journal* (Aug. 18, 2005); <www.who.int/csr/disease/avian_influenza/country/cases_table_2009_04_-0/en/print.html>.

27. See U.S. Congress, Office of Technology Assessment, Harmful Non-Indigenous Species in the United States (publication no. OTA-F-565) (Washington, DC: U.S. Government Printing Office, September 1993), 69, 92; available at <www.wws.princeton.edu/~ota/disk1/1993/9325_n.html>.

28. Chris Bright, *Life Out of Bounds: Bioinvasion in a Borderless World* (New York: W. W. Norton, 1998), 176.

29. See James N. Rosenau, "The Complexities and Contradictions of Globalization," *Current History* (November 1997): 360–364.

30. See Stephen S. Morse, "Regulating Viral Traffic," *Issues in Science and Technology* (Fall 1990): 81–82.

31. Hilary French, *Vanishing Borders: Protecting the Planet in an Age of Globalization* (New York: W. W. Norton, 2000), Table 1-1.

32. The Associated Press, U.S. food imports rarely inspected: FDA lacks resources to assure safety of fish and other products, April 16, 2007.

33. Gerth and Weiner, "U.S. Food Safety System Swamped."

34. United Nations Centre for Human Settlements, *An Urbanizing World: Global Report on Human Settlements 1996* (New York: Oxford University Press, 1996), 6.

35. World Commission on Environment and Development, *Our Common Future* (Oxford, UK: Oxford University Press, 1987), 95–102.

36. World Bank, *Urban Policy and Economic Development: An Agenda for the 1990s* (Washington, DC: World Bank, 1991), 51; Mike Parnwell, *Population Movements in the Third World* (London: Routledge, 1993), 18–24.

37. Clark Merrill and Dennis Pirages, "Ecological Security: Micro-Threats to Human Well-Being," *Futures Research Quarterly* (Spring 1997): 49–50; Richard M. Krause, "The Origin of Plagues: Old and New," *Science* (August 21, 1992): 1074.

38. See Merrill and Pirages, "Ecological Security," 59–60; and Garrett, *Betrayal of Trust*, Ch. 4.

CHAPTER ELEVEN

Countering Weapons of Mass Destruction Proliferation

Richard A. Love*

"Today, the Cold War has disappeared but thousands of those weapons have not. In a strange turn of history, the threat of global nuclear war has gone down, but the risk of a nuclear attack has gone up. More nations have acquired these weapons. Testing has continued. Black markets trade in nuclear secrets and materials. The technology to build a bomb has spread. Terrorists are determined to buy, build or steal one. Our efforts to contain these dangers are centered in a global nonproliferation regime, but as more people and nations break the rules, we could reach the point when the center cannot hold."

—President Barak Obama (2009)[1]

"The Commission believes that unless the world community acts decisively and with great urgency, it is more likely than not that a weapon of mass destruction will be used in a terrorist attack somewhere in the world by the end of 2013."

—WMD Terrorism Commission[2]

On September 6, 2007, 7 Israeli F-15s violated the sovereign airspace of Syria and launched 22 rockets at the 3 objects inside a military facility in al-Kibar, Syria. Uncharacteristically, Syria did not label the strike an act of war or terror, no demands were made for retaliation and retribution, and there were no calls for the United Nations to condemn or even investigate the attack. In fact, both sides played down the event. Syria acknowledged simply that an air attack damaged an unused military building near the Euphrates. Israel, unlike their unrestrained outpouring of pride and joy following the 1981 strike on Iraq's Osirak reactor, refused to comment. More curiously, satellite photos appeared to show that immediately following the

*This chapter builds on research the author conducts at the Center for the Study of Weapons of Mass Destruction at National Defense University. The author can be contacted via e-mail at LoveR@ndu.edu.

attack, Syria quickly and systematically cleared the site of any traces of the building that was hit, virtually removing anything that would indicate a building there.

A baffled world started to piece together the parts of the puzzle. In 2007, Syria announced a desire to pursue nuclear energy as an alternative to oil as a hedge against a 10 percent annual increase in electricity use. Additionally, reports indicated that A. Q. Khan, the father of the Pakistani nuclear program and the head of a global nuclear proliferation network, visited Syria on several occasions, and had met with senior Syrian officials in Iran. One of Khan's best clients, the reclusive cash-strapped state of North Korea, was also believed to be active in Syria. Some noted that the Syrian building that was attacked was roughly the same size and had very similar dimensions to North Korea's Yongbyon nuclear reactor. But there was little conclusive evidence. Then, the video was released. On April 25, 2008, the United States released a video that included pictures of what appeared to be a gas cooled graphite moderated nuclear reactor in development. The size and configuration were nearly identical to the Yongbyon reactor and since no other state had built such a reactor in over 35 years, the Syria and North Korea link was largely proven to the satisfaction of most. The video also showed North Korean personnel inside the Syrian site.

The al-Kibar site controversy brings together many current proliferation trends. First, in an environment characterized by technology diffusion, global markets and open borders, the efforts and ambitions of one rogue state or even one lone individual can make a difference. Second, this case is a traditional horizontal proliferation problem—a state without a nuclear capability seeks to develop one and become a new nuclear capable player. Treaties and other nonproliferation regimes are designed specifically to eliminate the very type of threat al-Kibar represents, but they failed to do so. It raises the question of what other surprises are possible and how well resourced and capable are we to work against this type of surprise. And finally, "secondary proliferation" remains largely outside the reach and capacity of existing international control mechanisms, as demonstrated with actors like A. Q. Khan and the financial and transshipment networks that make the transactions possible and nuclear ambitions a potential reality. To some extent this is a problem that the states—parties that created the Nuclear Nonproliferation Treaty (NPT) and associated agreements—simply never anticipated. In many respects, international control mechanisms remain mired in a Cold War mentality and lack the flexibility to adapt to the emergent threat environment.

THE WMD THREAT ENVIRONMENT

The WMD threat environment is dynamic, driven by increasingly available technology and evolving quickly in ways that are difficult to predict. To confront that threat, innovative policy and flexible operational concepts that meet today's challenges and anticipate those over-the-horizon threats need to be pursued and implemented. But what are weapons of mass destruction? Is the definition based on the specific characteristics of a weapon, the immediate effects a weapon can produce, the catastrophic nature of the long-term effect, or is it convenient shorthand for policy makers? Before addressing strategies and tools to counter the proliferation of WMD, a few thoughts on WMD are in order. The tendency is to lump nuclear, radiological, chemical, and biological weapons together under the term *weapons of mass destruction*. While convenient, it is misleading since each weapon represents vastly different underlying technologies for development, weaponization, and delivery. Different concepts of operation apply to each, and countermeasures and consequence management procedures are implemented differently depending on the weapon used. With this in mind, a short review of the current status of nuclear, radiological, biological, and chemical weapons is required.

Nuclear Weapons

Nuclear weapons are, in a sense, the only "true" mass-destructive weapons. Motivations for developing nuclear weapons are varied, ranging from their unique destructive power and perceived deterrence value to their utility as instruments of coercion or blackmail, or as a means of advancing regional or geopolitical objectives, international prestige, or perhaps for domestic political motivations. Potential proliferators benefit from the fact that most of the basic research, as well as the basics of weapons design, are completed and widely disseminated via the Internet and other sources. This does not mean that the process is easy. Would-be nuclear powers were traditionally constrained by financial considerations or the time-consuming, labor-intensive nature of the development process. The key hurdle in developing nuclear weapons is the acquisition of fissile material—plutonium or highly enriched uranium (HEU)—for use in a weapon. While states traditionally sought to reprocess plutonium or produce HEU themselves, the potential for black market procurement as a cost-efficient alternative is highly attractive.

The A. Q. Khan network demonstrates that nuclear weapons technology and knowledge are spreading. With regard to state-based proliferation, there are 5 declared nuclear weapons states under the NPT (the primary international nonproliferation agreement): Russia, the United States, China, France, and the United Kingdom. India and Pakistan are not declared states under the NPT, but both countries—India in 1974 and 1998 and Pakistan in 1998—tested nuclear weapons. Israel has never admitted to having nuclear weapons but is presumed to have between 98 and 172 nuclear weapons.[3] North Korea announced that it had successfully conducted underground nuclear tests on May 25, 2009 and October 9, 2006, though intelligence estimates assess the yield as very low due to technical problems.[4] Finally, Iran is widely suspected of having clandestine nuclear weapons programs and is clearly interested in obtaining nuclear technology. It is estimated that the total number of nuclear warheads globally is 27,600.[5]

Nonstate actors are also interested in acquiring nuclear capabilities. Indeed, al Qaeda leader Osama bin Laden asserted in 2001 that he had acquired nuclear weapons, although he declined to indicate where they came from and has not since then provided any proof that al Qaeda has the weapons though the declaration is clearly proof of an intent and desire to acquire them.[6]

As denial and deception capabilities become more sophisticated, the potential exists for a new or different model of nuclear proliferation: one in which the amount of fissile material required for entry-level weapon designs is significantly reduced, and the facilities and activities required to produce such material are correspondingly smaller and less observable. Under these conditions, it may be possible for many countries to possess a latent capability to produce some number of nuclear weapons over time. Increasingly, "latent proliferation" may fit many states' needs to have access to strategic capabilities without the burdens associated with maintaining large industrial infrastructures or deploying large operational stockpiles. For example, Japan has a robust nuclear energy infrastructure and a world-class technology sector and though a global leader in disarmament, is widely recognized as having a latent nuclear weapons capability. In other words, should Japan perceive a threat to its survival, it could constitute a nuclear weapon in short order.

Response times will vary in this latent proliferation model, as countries position themselves relative to their technical capacity and their unique perceived threats. But whether a state seeks to preserve the capability to produce a few weapons very quickly or many weapons over a longer period (or something in between), the spread of relevant technologies is likely to reduce the amount of time required to acquire fissile material and the observable science and engineering of the activity.

This model of future nuclear proliferation is of great concern, since it could lead to rapid, competitive, nuclear proliferation in volatile regions or in response to geopolitical events. It also poses challenges for intelligence and for traditional approaches to nonproliferation that focus on limiting, controlling, or monitoring fissile material and its production. If the amount of fissile material required to create a credible nuclear device is reduced, a strategy premised on fissile material control becomes less credible. A better understanding of these issues is needed. How might this model of proliferation take shape, what choices will nuclear aspirants face, and how can the WMD community understand the technology and political dynamics in key regions?

Radiological Dispersal Devices

Another method for using radiation as a weapon is by means of a radiological dispersal device (RDD), which is "designed to disperse radioactive material to cause destruction, contamination, and injury from the radiation produced by the material."[7] An RDD is not a nuclear weapon, and it does not have the destructive potential of such weapons. For this reason, some refer to RDDs as *weapons of mass disruption* rather than as weapons of mass destruction and others refer to them as *mass contamination devices* since an RDD is designed to spread a radioactive contaminant over a large area. There are several types of RDDs, each using a different means of dispersing radioactive elements.[8] Explosive RDDs, popularly known as "dirty bombs," use conventional explosives to scatter radioactive material over a wide area, potentially causing contamination and casualties through radiation sickness. Passive RDDs involve simply placing an unshielded radiation source in a location where large numbers of people will be exposed. Atmospheric RDDs convert radioactive materials into a form that is conducive to transportation on air currents.

Although RDDs are not considered militarily effective battlefield weapons, the availability of radiological material through laboratories or even medical facilities makes such devices a relatively simple and straightforward way for nonstate actors to conduct a terror attack. The most noteworthy RDD incident occurred in 1995 when Chechen rebels planted an RDD in Moscow's Izmailovo Park. The RDD contained caesium-137 and dynamite; the caesium was likely removed from cancer treatment equipment. After reporters were notified about its location, the RDD was defused and did not detonate.

Unlike nuclear weapons, which require uranium or plutonium, RDDs can use a wide variety of radioactive materials, such as caesium-137 as noted earlier.[9] These materials are widely used in hospitals, educational and research facilities, industrial and construction sites, and laboratories—places with fewer nuclear controls and security, and more individuals with access, than military complexes.[10] RDDs do not necessarily cause a great deal of blast damage, but they do raise issues regarding potential long-term contamination of targeted sites. Depending on the type of radioactive material used in the device, cleanup and decontamination of target areas could be costly and time-consuming. Such weapons are unlikely to kill large numbers of people, but the presence of radioactive materials is likely to cause panic and apprehension among the population of a targeted area. These devices received considerable media attention post-9/11 with the arrest of that suspected al-Qaeda operative who was charged with plotting an RDD attack.[11]

Biological Weapons

The least-understood element of WMD remains the biological weapons threat. For older, better-understood traditional agents such as anthrax, there still remain important gaps in knowledge such as the ability to accurately model a release within an acceptable margin of error. Increasingly, scientists are developing genetic engineering techniques that eventually will be within the capability of scientists everywhere. This process is fueled by the growing diffusion of advanced biological techniques pursued in a wide variety of settings from pharmaceutical labs to universities to corporate development labs. Indeed, the "biotechnology industrial complex" becomes more global everyday as states make substantial investment to create what in their view is a strategically important industry. These technologies will allow the creation of infrastructures that can support bioweapons programs as well as advance legitimate scientific pursuits such as the development of vaccines and other pharmaceuticals. The net result, however, will likely be increased global access to biotechnology by terrorists determined to exploit the expertise and materials needed to execute biological attacks.

Biological weapons (BW) use microorganisms or toxins derived from organisms to cause disease in humans, plants, or animals. They come in many different forms, ranging from viruses to bacteria to rickettsiae to toxins. While there are many uncertainties with biological weapons, they are not new. In the Middle Ages, corpses with plague were catapulted over walls to break sieges, and in the Second World War, the notorious Japanese Unit 731 dropped bombs filled with plague-infected fleas over cities in Manchuria. With effects ranging from lower to higher lethality, they may also pose the risk of contagion. They can be genetically modified to make effects more severe and more difficult to diagnose and treat, as genetically modified pathogens are not found in nature and hence would not have a medical track record or treatment protocol. They may be employed as weapons of terror, or even against agricultural targets to poison food supplies, with potentially devastating economic or psychological effect. Many pathogens are endemic in certain regions of the world and therefore are relatively easy to acquire and their use is difficult to attribute.

As living organisms, many biological agents are affected by variances in environmental conditions, including the heat caused by an explosion, ultraviolet radiation, and changes in atmospheric conditions such as temperature. Thus the performance of a potential dissemination mechanism must be within certain tolerance levels in order to be effective. The challenge lies in finding a means of dispersal that does not kill the organism while spreading it in a form and in sufficient quantity that will increase the likelihood of infection.

Adversaries may find biological weapons attractive for several reasons. First, they may allow an attack with a low likelihood of discovery, since attribution is difficult. For example, the anthrax attacks that occurred in the United States in the fall of 2001 were not attributed to an attacker by the FBI until 2008. In that case, a series of anthrax-tainted letters were mailed to several media and government targets. At least 4 anthrax-filled envelopes were sent and 22 people were infected with pulmonary or cutaneous anthrax. Five died of pulmonary anthrax. It is estimated that hundreds were exposed and tens of thousands were put on the preventative antibiotics ciprofloxacin (Cipro) and doxycycline (Doxy) in Washington DC, New York, Florida, and Connecticut. Contamination efforts cost millions, not including the loss in productivity. And while microbiologist Bruce Edwards Ivins was identified by the FBI as the lone anthrax attacker, the investigation alone took more than 7 years and due to Ivins's suicide, the motivation for the attack may never be clear. Beyond attribution, the nature of many biological agents also makes it difficult to determine whether or not an attack has occurred, let alone who might be culpable. For example, if the agent used is one that is endemic to an area, an attack may be mistaken for a natural outbreak.

Second, the equipment, technology, and materials needed to produce biological weapons are in many cases quite similar to those used in the production of pharmaceuticals and other commercial products. As a result, the building blocks of a biological warfare program are widely available through global commerce and relatively easy to obtain. Because of the general availability of many necessary materials, the development of particular biological weapons may represent a relatively low-cost option (compared to nuclear weapons) for states or sub-state groups. Given the dual-use nature of much of the equipment and the precursor agents used in the production of biological weapons, concealment of a clandestine development program is possible. As the Soviet Union's Biopreparat organization demonstrated, it is even possible to hide such a program in "plain sight," collocating BW development facilities with legitimate sites such as pharmaceutical plants.

Third, the expertise needed to produce biological weapons is widespread, and the knowledge base is growing due to scientific advances in biotechnology and genetic engineering. This presents the concern that state-based programs and possibly terrorist groups could use these techniques to improve characteristics of existing biological agents or to combine genetic features of several agents to create "designer" pathogens. However, many advanced biotechnologies and techniques are beyond the current capabilities of terrorist groups, and in some cases would provide few advantages over existing "traditional" microbiology techniques. Some recently developed or emerging microbiology techniques require state support and funding of research and development. This, however, may not always be the case. The availability of literature on biological warfare and the growth of "communities of interest" focused on sharing BW information suggest that realistic opportunities for exploitation of new biotechnologies are growing.

Finally, biological weapons have a wide range of effects and can be used against a wide range of targets. This versatility can make it difficult for states to craft an appropriate response. For example, an anti-crop weapon, while potentially causing a great deal of economic damage, may not necessarily result in the loss of any human life. Similarly, an adversary may opt to use an antipersonnel biological agent that has mass-casualty but not mass-fatality characteristics. The lack of human fatalities (or the absence of massive numbers of fatalities) in such cases could complicate retaliatory efforts by the targeted country—especially if the attacker's identity is uncertain. An attacker could also employ multiple agents simultaneously to cause a range of effects, hampering identification and treatment efforts.

The Intelligence Community assesses that "perhaps" a dozen states today are actively pursuing offensive BW programs.[12] Although the Russian offensive BW program Biopreparat was ended by presidential decree in 1992, the restrictive nature of the Russian scientific culture and community raises lingering concerns that prohibited activities may continue. Furthermore, many Russian civilian facilities possess pathogen and toxin collections that lack adequate security or accounting measures. As with nuclear and chemical weapons, there is also the possibility that Russian scientists and technicians with BW knowledge could seek to improve their personal economic status by accepting employment in countries of proliferation concern.

Several other countries are suspected of pursuing offensive BW research, development, and possibly weaponization, including North Korea, China, and Iran.[13] Countries that have the potential to develop offensive biological weapons and that may possibly be conducting limited efforts include Pakistan, Cuba, Israel, India, and Syria.[14] Still other states retain a latent capacity to rapidly mobilize resources in support of BW programs. Most of these countries are parties to or signatories of the Biological Weapons Convention,[15] which provides that "Each State Party to this Convention undertakes never in any circumstances to develop, produce, stockpile or otherwise acquire or retain: (1) Microbial or other biological agents, or toxins whatever their origin or method of production, of types and in quantities that have no justification for prophylactic, protective or other peaceful purposes; (2) Weapons, equipment or means of delivery designed to use such agents or toxins for hostile purposes or in armed conflict."[16] Therefore, any offensive programs undertaken would violate their obligations under that treaty.

As biotechnology creates more opportunities and a greater array of options for proliferators, what traditionally has been a difficult intelligence target will become even more so, especially if intelligence assessments in the period ahead reflect a greater degree of caution. It will become more challenging to detect and monitor activities that could support proliferation, and almost impossible to predict the full range of options available to groups pursuing BW capability. Even if the West takes significant steps to improve intelligence capabilities in this area, a high degree of uncertainty seems unavoidable, and any future use of biological weapons almost certainly will come as a surprise. Developing countermeasures under these conditions is a major challenge.

Chemical Weapons

Chemical weapons (CW) make use of the toxic properties of various chemical compounds to kill, injure, or incapacitate. These weapons saw extensive use during World War I and were responsible for thousands of injuries and deaths. More recently, chemical weapons were used in the 1980s-era Iran–Iraq war, by the Iraqi government against its Kurdish citizens, and in a 1995 terrorist attack by Aum Shinrikyo on Tokyo subway commuters. Groups have long sought chemical agents for a number of reasons. First, they have been viewed as force multipliers on the battlefield or, more recently, as instruments of terror in urban areas. Second, the wide range of dispersal methods available, from very crude methods (such as that employed by Aum Shinrikyo in Japan) to crop dusters and other aerosol sprayers to sophisticated military munitions, leads to a range of different attack options. Third, some chemical weapons—especially "first-generation" weapons such as chlorine or phosgene—are relatively inexpensive, compared to nuclear weapons. Virtually any country with a reasonably sized industrial base (particularly in the chemical, petroleum, or pesticide industries) has the necessary infrastructure to produce at least first-generation chemical agents. Finally, the dual-use nature of much of the materials and equipment needed for the production of chemical weapons, including chemical precursors, allows for easy concealment of a development program.

The Chemical Weapons Convention (CWC) builds on and expands the Geneva Protocol of 1925 for chemical weapons and includes extensive verification measures such as on-site inspections.[17] The Convention is administered by the Organisation for the Prohibition of Chemical Weapons (OPCW), and is charged with conducting inspections of suspect facilities of the member states. According to Article 1 of the Convention, States Parties are obligated never under any circumstances:

(a) To develop, produce, otherwise acquire, stockpile or retain chemical weapons, or transfer, directly or indirectly, chemical weapons to anyone;

(b) To use chemical weapons;

(c) To engage in any military preparations to use chemical weapons;

(d) To assist, encourage or induce, in any way, anyone to engage in any activity prohibited to a State Party under this Convention.

Some states, however, retain active chemical weapons programs.[18] Russia, for example, maintains the largest CW stockpile in the world (approximately 40,000 metric tons), but is in the process of destroying its publicly reported stocks of agents. Many experts have lingering concerns that Russia has not declared its entire stockpile, as required under the CWC, and are concerned that its program has not been terminated.[19] Iran and Syria are believed to hold stockpiles of munitions and are pursuing development of advanced agents with foreign assistance.[20]

Libya's efforts in the chemical weapons arena attracted significant attention in the 1980s, especially with the construction of allegedly CW-related facilities at Rabta and Tarhuna. With the lifting of sanctions in 1999, Libya reportedly began renewing contacts with foreign suppliers to revive its CW efforts.[21] However, in December 2003, Libya publicly renounced its chemical weapons program along with its other WMD programs and has been working with U.S. and international representatives to dismantle its production capabilities.[22] India, as an original signatory to the CWC, declared its CW capabilities, opened related facilities to international inspection, and destroyed its stockpile of agents. China, North Korea, and the Sudan are suspected of having CW programs, with the former two believed to possess moderate to sizeable stockpiles.[23] Pakistan is assessed to have clear potential to develop chemical weapons, although it remains uncertain whether it is pursuing offensive development efforts.[24] Nonstate actors are also suspected of pursuing activities in chemical weapons, although the available evidence is sketchy and sometimes of indeterminate credibility.[25] A videotape was uncovered in Afghanistan that apparently shows dogs exposed to vapors from a "white liquid." Some experts speculate that the gas could be a nerve agent such as sarin.[26] Additionally, Ahmed Ressum, convicted for a millennium bomb plot on the Los Angeles airport, testified that he received instruction from al Qaeda on how to place toxins on doorknobs and that he was part of experiments which injected animals with a mixture containing cyanide and sulphuric acid.

Iraq had an active and advanced chemical weapons program prior to its 1991 defeat at the hands of the U.S.-led coalition. Even after the war, however, Iraq retained a latent capability and possibly hidden munitions stocks. UNSCOM, the UN Special Commission charged with implementing the non-nuclear provisions in Iraq following the first Gulf War, was unable to verify the destruction of several thousand chemical-filled munitions.[27] The U.S.-led coalition began inspections of Iraq's chemical-related facilities after its victory in 2003. The United States uncovered evidence that Iraq examined the possibility of resuming production of chemical agents in the 2001–2002 period, and evidence indicated that some proscribed CW-related research could have been conducted by Iraqi scientists.[28] However, no stockpiles of chemical munitions were discovered, and in January 2004, David Kay, the head of the Iraq Survey Group that investigated Iraqi's WMD programs, testified to the U.S. Senate Armed Services Committee that "We simply have no evidence" that Iraq maintained stockpiles of chemical weapons.[29]

EMERGING WMD-LIKE TECHNOLOGIES

Over the next 20 years, a number of advances in science and technology have the potential to transform major aspects of how people live—extending human life, reshaping the global economy—and how the world wages war. Devastating new weapons are possible through the application of these scientific and technological advances that rival the lethality of existing weapons of mass destruction. Indeed, the definition of what constitutes a weapon of mass destruction increasingly will be open to revision as these applications, which have the potential to fill large volumes of space with devastating lethal effect, take shape. Two technology areas have the greatest potential to yield new kinds of WMD: biotechnology and nanotechnology.

A new generation of biological weapons based on genomic research has the potential to create new capabilities not envisioned or restricted by existing arms control treaties. Examples include the following:

❏ Genetic weapons that target specific groups based on their genetic characteristics may be possible as an offshoot of ongoing research into assessing human health by reading metabolic signatures in human respiration. Preliminary results suggest that this technology could lead to ways of identifying race and ethnicity.

❏ Aptamers are strands of nucleic acid that act in a manner similar to antibodies. They bind and block cell receptors responsible for a variety of life-sustaining biological functions.

❏ Molecular poisons are nano-sized, microscopic particles whose size is one-billionth of a meter, capable of working at the subcellular level and engineered to create specialized effects that could cross the blood-brain barrier, disrupt genetic material, or trigger counterproductive immune system responses.

Nanotechnology can be both an enabler of highly lethal effects (e.g., the aforementioned molecular poisons) as well as a discrete form of mass destruction/mass disruption warfare. Current research in nanotechnology includes the development of explosive microdust, an ultra-high-explosive/ultra-incendiary material several times more potent than an equivalent mass of TNT. Visionaries in the field theorize about destructive nanites or "nanobots" programmed to carry out antimateriel or antipersonnel missions. Experiments in the United States demonstrated that nano-sized carbon particles can introduce respiratory distress or death in mammals.[30] Respected scientific associations in Europe also warned of the potentially toxic effect of existing nano-particle contamination of the biological environment.

WMD TERRORISM

If any one concept has taken hold in the past few years, it may be the "nexus of WMD and terrorism." Experts recognize that jihadist terrorists are seeking such weapons, will not be deterred from using them, and have the potential to wreak catastrophic damage. This truly is the nightmare scenario—one that concentrates the mind on better understanding the nature of this threat. Among decision makers today, there appears to be a working assumption that, with respect to terrorists and WMD, "possession = use," meaning if terrorist groups develop or acquire WMD, they will use them and not merely retain WMD for deterrence purposes. This is undoubtedly a prudent assumption, though as decision makers think more about the terrorist threat the United States faces and as they learn more about al Qaeda in particular, there is an opportunity to refine thinking about the specific dimensions of the "nexus" that defines so many of the worst fears.

Several incidents raised fears that terrorist organizations or other non-state groups could obtain and use WMD. One of the first of these incidents was the 1995 Tokyo subway sarin attack carried out by the Aum Shinrikyo cult and the subsequent police investigations that uncovered the extent of the group's WMD aspirations. The infamous Tokyo subway attack was only one of many attempts by Aum Shinrikyo to use WMD. One other attack at Motsomoto killed 2 and Aum also attempted to purchase a nuclear weapon and develop anthrax and spread it over Tokyo. More recent were the October 2001 anthrax attacks in the United States, which resulted in 5 deaths and 17 other infections,[31] the discovery of ricin, a deadly BW agent, in a January 2003 antiterrorist operation in London, and the finding of a ricin-tainted letter in the office of Senator Bill Frist in February 2004. Ricin was also found in Roger Von Bergendorff's Extended Stay Las Vegas hotel room on February 26, 2008 after he complained of difficulty breathing. Von Bergendorff was subsequently charged in a three count federal complaint, one of which was for possessing an illegal biological toxin. Finally, Osama bin Laden declared that the acquisition of WMD is a religious duty, and intelligence collected in Afghanistan revealed that al Qaeda was working to acquire nuclear, biological, and chemical weapons as well as a radiological dispersal device.[32] Two Pakistani scientists allegedly shared WMD information with al Qaeda sometime in or prior to 2001 and commented on the viability of a radiological bomb.[33]

Terrorist (and other sub-state groups) interested in WMD may be facing a shift in their motives and goals. For example, religious motivations are complementing or even superseding the political motivations that once drove terrorists. Combined with this motivating force is another perceived shift away from the previously held tenet that terrorists want more people watching an event than they want killed by that event. Indeed, mass-casualty events are becoming more common and the object of some jihadist terrorist: globalization broadcasts the psychological shock value of large numbers of fatalities to a wider audience, and allows mass casualties to be inflicted abroad, not undermining local audiences' sympathies for terrorist causes. However, there is a great deal of debate over the extent to which terrorist organizations may possess the necessary technical and financial resources to acquire effective WMD capabilities.[34] In practice, it is not as easy to do as it sounds. Even Aum Shinrikyo, skeptics frequently note, with almost a billion dollars in assets and highly trained and educated scientists, was unable to develop biological weapons or a truly effective chemical weapons dissemination capability. At the same time, that group's partial success and their ability to conduct an attack in roughly 3 days, coupled with known interest in acquisition and continuing advances in technology, suggest that sub-state actors may become increasingly WMD capable.

Indeed, there is a growing prospect that terrorist organizations will acquire WMD, either on their own or with the help of another, be it a country or a smuggling entrepreneur. The intent to acquire these capabilities is clear, the requisite materials and information are readily available, advances in technology will make this job easier over time, and use is likely if these weapons are acquired. Moreover, many proliferators such as Iran, Syria, and North Korea are known or suspected state-sponsors of terrorism, raising the possibility that such states could provide weapons or material/technical assistance to terrorist groups. However, the specific form of WMD-related assistance a state-sponsor would provide to a terrorist organization, and the circumstances under which that assistance would be provided, remain unclear. In addition to support and assistance from a state sponsor, another avenue for sub-state acquisition of WMD lies at the intersection of failing (or failed) states and WMD capabilities. In theory, a terrorist or sub-national group could take advantage of the collapse of a WMD-capable state to seize control over a portion of that state's WMD arsenal. This has been the ongoing concern over the safety of WMD arsenals, materials, and research labs in the successor states to the FSU. That such a situation might occur was a concern with Pakistan in late 2001, when there were serious concerns over the stability of the government and the security of Pakistan's nuclear stockpile.[35] These concerns arose again following two attempts to assassinate the former Pakistan president, Pervez Musharraf, in December 2003. In the spring of 2009, new concerns emerged over Pakistan's stability and the prospect of nuclear material leakage or direct acquisition of Pakistan's state program, as the Taliban competes for control over much of the Northwest Territory and Swat River Valley. In the words of the Commission on the Prevention of WMD Proliferation and Terrorism released in 2009, "Were one to map terrorism and weapons of mass destruction today, all roads would intersect in Pakistan. It has nuclear weapons and a history of unstable governments, and parts of its territory are currently a safe haven for al Qaeda and other terrorists."[36]

U.S. intelligence agencies have learned much since September 11, 2001, about al Qaeda's interest in and pursuit of nuclear, radiological, chemical, and biological weapons—so much so that it sheds a sobering light on how little the United States knew before then. Prior to September 11, intelligence agencies assessed that al Qaeda was focused primarily on simple chemical warfare agents, guided by an over-inflated sense of what these weapons could accomplish in achieving mass effects. The United States has since discovered that al Qaeda had in fact made a major investment in a range of chemical warfare capabilities, both simple and advanced. Analysis of an al Qaeda document recovered in Afghanistan in 2002 indicates the existence of crude procedures for producing mustard agent, sarin, and VX.[37] In his testimony before the Senate Select Committee on Intelligence in February 2004, former Director of Central Intelligence (DCI) George Tenet spoke of "a heightened risk of poison attacks" and the possibility of increasingly sophisticated delivery methods and tactics, including improvised chemical weapons that could create significant casualties in a crowded, enclosed area.[38] Indeed, the Commission on the Prevention of WMD Proliferation and Terrorism concluded that, "Al Qaeda had an active biological weapons program in the past, and it is unlikely that the group has lost interest in employing infectious disease as a weapon."[39]

Al Qaeda's biological weapons effort has been described by senior intelligence officials as sophisticated. In Afghanistan, the group was successful in acquiring the expertise and equipment needed to grow biological agents, including a dedicated laboratory near Kandahar.[40] Anthrax was an area of emphasis, and while U.S. intelligence agencies still lack a comprehensive understanding of this program, the Intelligence Community views this as one of the most immediate terrorist WMD threats the United States is likely to face.[41] It has come to light, for instance, that some of the September 11 hijackers made repeated inquiries regarding cropdusters and that state law enforcement authorities viewed this as sufficiently serious to twice ground cropdusters nationwide in the period after September 11 and to question more than 3,000 pilots and cropduster owners.

And the United States learned more in Afghanistan about al Qaeda's nuclear agenda, which is now described as ambitious in its pursuit of the materials and expertise required to construct a radiological dispersal device and possibly other kinds of nuclear devices. The Intelligence Community believes construction of a "dirty bomb" is well within al Qaeda's capabilities if it can obtain the radiological material, and terrorists likely understand how such a device could be used.[42]

Among terror groups pursuing chemical, biological, radiological, and/or nuclear materials, al Qaeda remains the most advanced and the principal concern. Still, it is vitally important to look beyond al Qaeda, as there are 2 to 3 dozen other terrorist organizations believed to be interested in acquiring WMD of some sort, particularly chemical weapons. And their interest may be driven in part not so much by an objective analysis of U.S. vulnerabilities as by the public and open discussions common in the United States about fears of WMD and the relative ease with which terrorists could mount devastating attacks. The al Qaeda leadership shows evidence of this. According to press accounts, an April 1999 memo apparently written by Dr. Ayman al-Zawahri comments on al Qaeda's decision to acquire chemical and biological weapons: "… despite their extreme danger, we only became aware of them when the enemy drew attention to them by repeatedly expressing concern that they can be produced simply."[43] As states move to improve their ability to defend against the classical forms of WMD attack, terrorists increasingly will look for novel and unconventional ways to use WMD to achieve strategic effects. Those charged with defending their borders can expect more numerous—and more sophisticated—threats and hoaxes that will command ever-greater response resources.

PROLIFERATION PREVENTION

Proliferation prevention is preventing the spread of weapons of mass destruction and their means of delivery. Traditionally, prevention mechanisms were seen in terms of horizontal and vertical proliferation. Horizontal proliferation seeks to prevent the spread of WMD weapons and technology to states that do not currently possess them. Vertical proliferation, on the other hand, seeks to prevent the increase in the number and destructiveness of weapons within a state already possessing them. In some ways, nonproliferation, the full range of political, economic, and diplomatic tools to prevent, constrain, or reverse the proliferation of NBC weapons and their associated delivery means, represents the concept of horizontal proliferation prevention focused on preventing acquisition. Nonproliferation has a long history and is the traditional focal point for the U.S. government's efforts. Such efforts include the Nuclear Suppliers Group, the NPT regime, export controls, and the Cooperative Test Ban Treaty, among others. Nonproliferation controls, such as the NPT, rely on state parties to control weapons and technology from spreading outside their borders. For example, the NPT requires the 5 declared nuclear weapons states to seek disarmament and to share peaceful nuclear technology with non-nuclear declared states. The non-nuclear weapons states in return promise not to seek nuclear technology for military or strategic application. Therefore, nonproliferation relies primarily on diplomacy and is based on the concept that sovereign states will adhere to their treaty commitments.

Counterproliferation is the full range of operational, primarily military preparations and activities to reduce and protect against the threat posed by WMD weapons and delivery means. Counterproliferation is a blend of vertical and horizontal prevention focused on preventing the use of WMD weapons. The concept of counterproliferation grew from a recognition in the early 1990s that nonproliferation geared to Cold War objectives ignored the growing concern over nonstate actors and also that there was the prospect that nonproliferation could fail (states might not live up to their treaty commitments). Thus, counterproliferation was envisioned as a tool to be used when diplomacy fails—when there is a threat of use or illicit proliferation.

As demonstrated by Libya and its attempt to develop a nuclear capability, the nuclear black market operated by the Pakistani engineer Abdul Qadeer Khan poses challenges to both nonproliferation (preventing WMD acquisition beforehand) and counterproliferation (stopping the spread of WMD in progress). This points to a larger lesson of the A. Q. Khan experience: that there will always be policy tradeoffs as the world seeks to contain proliferation in a complex and dangerous regional setting. The United States accepted official Pakistani assertions that there was no government involvement in Khan's activities, and did not challenge the pardon Khan received, which immunized him from criminal charges. For now, there seem to be more important imperatives in U.S.–Pakistan relations than nonproliferation. Indeed, with the installation of Asif Ali Zardari as the Pakistani president on September 6, 2008, official measures against A. Q. Khan were relaxed and he was released from house arrest in February 2009. The greatest private proliferator of nuclear weapons technology and components is now a free man.

Proliferation events are constantly shaping and reshaping the agenda for countering WMD. As decision makers confront a dynamic proliferation environment, policy must respond with agility and innovation. The Proliferation Security Initiative (PSI) is a good example of how a group of like-minded states is attempting to deal with the WMD proliferation threat in today's threat environment. Allies and international activities and institutions are indispensable, whether for strengthening the nonproliferation regime, deepening cooperation on interdiction, or pursuing rollback in specific countries.

STRENGTHENING PREVENTION—CHALLENGES OF INTERNATIONAL COOPERATION

Longstanding weakness in the international nonproliferation regime demands serious attention. In light of the A. Q. Khan revelations, continuing challenges from North Korea and Iran, and the likely consequences of WMD terrorism, gaps in the policy and legal framework for nonproliferation pose an unacceptable risk.

Strengthening the NPT Regime

The challenge posed by North Korea and Iran to the NPT regime, the pre-eminent global nonproliferation treaty, is a great concern to global peace. The NPT obligates the 5 acknowledged nuclear-weapon states (the United States, Russian Federation, United Kingdom, France, and China) not to transfer nuclear weapons, other nuclear explosive devices, or their technology to any non-nuclear-weapon state. Non-nuclear-weapon states agree in return not to undertake acquisition or production of nuclear weapons or nuclear explosive devices. Non-nuclear-weapon states are also required to accept safeguards that detect diversions from peaceful activities, such as power generation, to the production of nuclear weapons or other nuclear explosive devices and is done in accordance with an individual safeguards agreement. This agreement is negotiated and concluded between each non-nuclear-weapon State Party and the International Atomic Energy Agency (IAEA), the UN's nuclear watchdog agency. These agreements require that all nuclear materials be declared to the IAEA, whose inspectors have routine access to the facilities for periodic monitoring and inspections. If information from routine inspections is not sufficient to fulfill its responsibilities, the IAEA may consult with the state regarding special inspections within or outside declared facilities.

The actions of Iran and North Korea have created a crisis in the treaty regime. Some commentators have suggested that the NPT is now at a critical juncture and that the failure to deal effectively with Iran and North Korea may signal the beginning of the end for the NPT regime.

Without substantial progress in these two states, countries that have heretofore placed their faith in nonproliferation treaties may feel compelled to reconsider the wisdom of abjuring not just nuclear weapons, but possibly chemical and biological weapons as well. A cascade of WMD acquisition decisions resulting from further erosion of the NPT regime cannot be ruled out. In parallel, closing the "loopholes" in the NPT that have allowed countries like Iran to pursue a nuclear weapons capability under the cover of treaty compliance must be a priority for the United States and the international community. Better verification mechanisms and assurance procedures must be put in place to signal to the international community that a state party is in compliance and not seeking nuclear weapons covertly and under the cover of compliance.

With respect to the NPT, it is not an exaggeration to state that the treaty is at a historical juncture that requires a fresh look and decisive action. How hard the world and key players such as the United States, Russia, and China will push what amounts to an ambitious set of treaty reforms remains to be seen.[44] Other challenges face the NPT regime, including the concern by many non-nuclear states that the nuclear powers have shown no movement toward or interest in actually disarming nuclear stockpiles, a condition embedded in the NPT agreement. Indeed, the failure of the NPT review in the summer of 2005 stemmed in large measure from the inability of the NPT signatories to agree on an agenda. Countries such as the United States wanted to focus on preventing WMD terrorism and enhancing procedures to stem illicit WMD trafficking. The non-nuclear powers, led by countries such as Egypt, aggressively sought to put the issue of disarmament squarely on the agenda, seeking assurances and timeframes for the nuclear powers to disarm. The inability to resolve these differences ended the NPT review and may make the 2010 review conference contentious as well.

ADVANCING THE PROLIFERATION SECURITY INITIATIVE (PSI)

Today, a growing coalition of like-minded countries is planning, exercising, and executing interdiction operations aimed at disrupting the traffic in WMD- and missile-related materials and technologies. On May 31, 2003 in Krakow, Poland, then U.S. President Bush announced the Proliferation Security Initiative (PSI). The concept was largely developed as a result of the So San interdiction incident in 2002. In December 2002, U.S. intelligence assets tracked the unflagged vessel So San as it departed from North Korea with an unknown destination but was assumed to be bound for the Middle East. Acting on a request from the United States, Spanish special operations forces staged from the Spanish frigate Navarro intercepted and boarded So San. While searchers found a great deal of cement, the declared cargo, they also discovered nonmanifested Scud-B missiles, warheads, and fuel oxidizer. The Bush Administration, facing protests from North Korea and Yemen, conceded that the weapons and their components were the legally acquired property of the Yemeni government. Indeed, the Bush

Administration during this time complimented Yemen for being a staunch ally in the global war on terror. Subsequently, Spanish forces released the *So San* to deliver its cargo.[45] On December 11, 2002, just days after the United States relented to North Korea and Yemen and over *So San* and its cargo, the president unveiled the National Strategy for Combating Weapons of Mass Destruction, which identified aggressive counterproliferation as its principal element.[46]

Applying lessons learned from the embarrassing *So San* incident, the Administration developed and implemented PSI as a multilateral effort based on a statement of interdiction principles. These principles, created within the framework of existing international and state-based agreements and laws, enable partner states to disrupt and interdict the illegal proliferation of WMD. To be successful, PSI requires signatories to work domestically to strengthen laws and cooperatively to stop the trafficking of WMD-related material and technology to and from states and organizations that present a proliferation risk. PSI partner states commit to interdiction efforts using shared intelligence, timely communication, and multilateral action.[47]

This process was evident in the interception of the ship BBC *China*. The United States shared with Germany and Italy intelligence developed from its operations targeting the A. Q. Kahn network. This intelligence identified the likelihood that a Malaysian company was shipping nuclear technology to Libya via Dubai aboard a German-registered vessel.[48] Acting on that intelligence, and with operational assistance from the U.S. Navy, German and Italian officials coordinated the diversion of the ship to Italy. This operation represents the type of multilateral interdiction effort laid out in PSI. PSI advocates point to the fact that Qadhafi did not make any substantial public moves to initiate WMD rollback until after the interception of the BBC *China* and its cargo of centrifuge components.[49]

Today, the original 11 PSI partners have grown to a group of over 90 participating and supporting states. As PSI continues to expand its membership and its activities, it is not only complicating the efforts of proliferators, but also strengthening nonproliferation norms, providing a concrete means of security cooperation with allies and friends, and demonstrating that coordinated actions among like-minded states can be achieved without having to create new organizations or more formalized bureaucracies.

Progress along several fronts has been achieved in establishing the PSI global network of partnerships. Countries have committed to a statement of interdiction principles. Guidelines and processes are in place for the collection, analysis, and sharing of intelligence. New shipboarding agreements are extending available legal authorities.[50] Operational experts from participating states meet regularly to develop improved intelligence, military, and law enforcement capabilities to support interdiction activities. These capabilities are being refined in a robust exercise program.

The Obama administration is committed to building upon the success of the PSI framework and is developing ways to strengthen and institutionalizing the activity. The goal is to extend both the functional reach of the PSI framework and the breadth of international participation. In tandem with other elements of the global nonproliferation agenda, the solid diplomatic and operational foundation of the PSI provides a basis for making progress in strengthening prevention efforts. However, there are some concerns regarding the PSI approach to countering WMD.

ROLLBACKS

Rolling back a nuclear and other WMD programs remains a key component of the countering WMD vocabulary since the Indian nuclear test of 1974. While no longer a realistic policy choice in the near term on the Indian subcontinent, the rollback concept aptly captures what many seek to achieve in Libya, North Korea, and Iran.

Libya

Encouraging Libya to renounce both terrorism and WMD aspirations is a longstanding global and regional objective. As Colonel Muammar Qadhafi intensified his efforts to "come in from the cold," the West made clear the central importance of the WMD issue in any process of normalization. While Qadhafi may have believed he could achieve normalized relations and a lifting of U.S. sanctions while still maintaining clandestine WMD programs, this position became increasingly untenable as he witnessed the global reaction to the events of September 11, 2001. The campaigns in Afghanistan and Iraq demonstrated that the United States and allies were prepared to marshal significant force to eliminate terror and WMD threats posed by rogue states. This probably led him to conclude that he too could become a target of coalition military action. The seizure of the BBC *China* in October 2003 demonstrated that his nuclear program was no longer clandestine and that his procurement effort could be penetrated and shut down. According to some accounts provided by Libyan officials, the capture of Saddam Hussein in December 2003 underscored to Qadhafi the personal risks associated with rogue status. In considering these factors, one can see how the post-September 11 environment shaped Qadhafi's calculus of the benefits and risks in pursuing WMD and led him to openly renounce WMD and to accept comprehensive disarmament rather than attempt to maintain covert programs.

In this sense, WMD became a source of insecurity to Qadhafi and an impediment to his principal goal of reintegrating with the international community in order to address Libya's growing economic and social problems. By tying the removal of sanctions and the prospects for political and economic rehabilitation to Libya's WMD efforts, and by demonstrating a credible threat of military action, U.S. policy presented Qadhafi a powerful set of incentives to disarm. In this "carrot and stick" dynamic it is important to not underestimate the power of the carrot—that is, the promise of significant benefits. Economic sanctions by the United States and the United Nations beginning in the early 1990s hit Libya hard, and the regime's poor economic management compounded their effects. Libyan oil production during this time fell by more than half, with lost revenues estimated by the World Bank at $18 billion.[51] Plagued by outdated technology and mismanagement, the country's oil infrastructure suffered. The rising expectations of an increasingly young population created conditions that demanded a serious program of economic reform critically dependent on opening the Libyan economy to the outside world.

The circumstances of the Libyan case are unique, but the basic logic of rollback is evident: presented with the right mix of pressures and promised benefits, the motivations and behavior of even rogue regimes regarding WMD can change. It is this logic that informs current promotion of the "Libyan model" of disarmament to countries like North Korea and Iran. How viable is this model? Libya is certainly not the first country to give up its WMD program. Brazil, Argentina, South Africa, and 3 former states of the Soviet Union—Belarus, Kazakhstan, and Ukraine—all renounced and demilitarized their WMD programs. The larger question is how the Libya model fits into the broader context of WMD rollback and what lessons can be learned and applied to states of proliferation concern today.

North Korea

In principle, this same logic of rollback would appear to fit the North Korean case quite well. The basis for any agreement with North Korea is essentially the same—significant economic, political, and security benefits in exchange for comprehensive disarmament, (although in North Korea's case, focused acutely on their nuclear program). North Korea, in far more dire economic straits than Libya, would seem to have significant incentives to reach an agreement. But in reality, circumstances in Northeast Asia are far different. Unlike Libya, North Korea is nuclear weapon state and its tests of nuclear weapons on May 25, 2009 and October 9, 2006 demonstrated its capability. Moreover, there are indications that beyond its plutonium capability, North Korea is pursuing a clandestine uranium enrichment capability whose scope, maturity, and location are largely unknown. In this case, rollback is a far more ambitious and complex proposition, further complicated by the regime's hidden and unpredictable behavior coupled with significant gaps in intelligence of North Korean intentions and capabilities.

While Qadhafi's intentions ultimately became quite clear, no one knows whether Pyongyang is prepared to give up its entire nuclear weapons enterprise and submit to a process of complete, verifiable, and irreversible disarmament. The possibility cannot be ruled out that the regime's objective is to achieve normalized relations while retaining a covert stockpile or weapons production capacity. Certainly the regime has demonstrated through word and deed how powerful a lever they view the possession of nuclear weapons and weapons production potential to be, and Kim Jong Il may well see nuclear weapons as key to regime survival. And the intelligence challenges North Korea continues to pose for the West may lead him to believe that a clandestine nuclear program can in fact be maintained.

Testing North Korea's intentions is the objective of the continuing 6-party talks that seek to bring a halt to their nuclear program and ambitions and minimize the prospect of North Korean cheating. The idea of the 6-party talks is to engage North Korea in a multinational setting that includes regional powers Russia, Japan, China, and South Korea as well as the United States. By having more parties to the talks, it is hoped that North Korea will be more likely to honor its commitments. By engaging China directly in the negotiating process, the 6-party talks give Beijing a significant stake in a successful outcome and leverage China's longstanding relationship with (and knowledge of) Pyongyang.

Can this brand of diplomacy achieve rollback in North Korea? Realistically, there are few attractive alternatives, and policy options that would adopt a more confrontational approach toward North Korea are not likely to succeed without the active participation of the regional actors. While all parties to the talks undoubtedly are frustrated with North Korea's posture, it's highly unlikely that diplomacy will be exhausted any time soon. All parties have much at stake in a peaceful resolution and see the risks associated with confrontation as very high. To be sure, the payoffs for North Korea would be substantial, providing political legitimacy, enhanced security, and the means to revive an utterly failed economy. Viewed through the prism of cold rationality, these payoffs appear compelling. Nonetheless, there clearly are countervailing pressures. Given the value North Korea appears to place on nuclear capability and the leverage it buys, the progress they appear to have made, and their ability to conceal proscribed activities, an important practical question is whether the states to the 6-party talks may be compelled to consider outcomes short of "complete, verifiable, and irreversible disarmament" as the United States defines this goal. Put differently, what degree of ambiguity, if any, are the members to the talks willing to accept in North Korea's nuclear capabilities?[52]

Iran

The case of Iran is different still. Compared to Libya, Iran is much further along in assembling the infrastructure required to enrich uranium and re-process plutonium on a large scale. It appears committed to closing both these fuel cycles and achieving an independent capability to produce fissile material suitable for making weapons. It claims the right under the NPT to do so, and has made a huge investment over the last two decades to advance this effort. Compared to North Korea, Iran seems to take a less instrumental view of nuclear weapons; that is, they are not fundamentally treated as a bargaining chip but rather are central to the regime's ambitions for regional influence, the requirements of deterrence, safeguarding the Islamic revolution, and balancing Israel's perceived nuclear power. Moreover, while it faces significant economic challenges, Iran's economic vulnerability is far less acute than that of Libya or North Korea, given its indigenous energy resources and robust international trading relations. At the same time, the international community does not believe that Iran possesses nuclear weapons. Iran remains a member of the NPT and to date has worked within the IAEA framework to attempt to resolve compliance issues.

Given these conditions—a highly motivated, committed, and combative proliferator not facing dire economic circumstances—is there a credible rollback strategy premised on some achievable set of mutual benefits? The diplomatic track, while far from exhausted, has not yielded a satisfactory outcome to date. Led by France, Germany, and the United Kingdom, the EU Three effort has focused on getting Iran to suspend critical activities such as uranium enrichment in exchange for the supply of enriched uranium suitable to fuel power reactors and economic incentives. Tehran does not view this as a compelling trade. Is there a "grander" bargain to be made with Iran, one that gives them a sufficiently powerful incentive to reconsider the nuclear path? There appears to be little official thinking about this, and admittedly it is difficult to map the contours of such a grand bargain. What can Iran be offered that will be of commensurate strategic value to the possession of a nuclear capability? What combination of political, security, and economic benefits could induce them to forego the bomb?[53]

Policy is increasingly characterized in terms of a denial strategy aimed at slowing and disrupting the Iranian program. Through the IAEA and a variety of interdiction activities, the goal is to force Iran to bring more elements of its program under safeguards and prevent outside assistance from reaching the program while raising the costs associated with non-compliance.[54] If successful, such a strategy would complicate, make more costly, and delay Iran's acquisition of nuclear weapons capability. Conceivably, these problems could influence a decision by the Iranian leadership on whether to take the final steps to actually manufacture weapons. Conceivably, the delay imposed by a denial strategy could be long enough to allow a process of internal political change to alter the nature of the Iranian regime and its basic security outlook.

Behind the denial strategy is the threat of punitive action. Threats of military action may not compel Iran to give up the bomb, but they could create internal pressures to consider stopping short of manufacturing weapons and developing an operational stockpile. Keeping Iran at "threshold status" may not sound like victory and may not accommodate everyone's view of "rollback," but in the end—short of preventive war to keep Iran from going nuclear—it may turn out to be the least bad outcome.

THINKING ABOUT TERROR CAMPAIGNS

Terrorists think and act in terms of campaigns—an orchestrated series of violent acts intended to advance a strategic objective. It is hard to identify acts of terror that are not somehow part of a campaign, whether the time-span of that campaign is short or long. By contrast, crisis and consequence managers tend to think in terms of single events. Responding effectively to single events is daunting enough; responders have barely begun to think concretely about the challenges posed by multiple events. Yet this challenge must be faced in light of the risks and opportunities it presents.

The risks seem clear enough—a greater chance that policymakers and the responder community will make mistakes that exacerbate rather than ease fear and panic, impair response capability, or undermine the legitimacy of government at all levels. The opportunities presented by terror campaigns are principally to learn and adapt, gain the initiative, and exploit mistakes the terrorists might make. How these possibilities play out will be shaped by a number of factors, such as the speed and degree of simultaneity of attacks and the degree of clarity about the "who, what, when, where, and why" of the attacks. At early points when uncertainty on these questions is greatest, risks are likely to dominate. As terrorist capabilities and intentions become clearer, the prospects for an adaptive response should increase. And it is important they do so, because life under a prolonged state of emergency will undoubtedly create profound stresses to any society so affected.

If decision makers assume, prudently, that after an initial biological or chemical attack terrorists are "re-loading" for follow-on attacks, then it is equally prudent to expect the demands of dealing with the aftermath of an event to grow commensurately—perhaps "only" cumulatively at the local level, but probably exponentially at the country and international level as state leaders confront an overwhelming volume of "day after" demands.[55] At any level, the response to a biological terror campaign in particular will be resource-intensive in ways not fully understood today. Assistance from outside one's own borders almost certainly will be critical. How well a state can respond to an event and how well it can effectively communicate with its people in the face of a terror campaign will be far more challenging, and may lead to a lack of public confidence if not handled professionally and in a timely, accurate manner. All the keys to public information success will be more difficult to achieve when the threat is characterized by multiple events, perhaps with a variety of agents, and perhaps geographically dispersed.

What are the possible elements of a strategy directed at countering and preparing for a biological terror campaign? In the context of an extended terror campaign, states need to demonstrate their ability to adapt and steadily improve their response to multiple attacks, particularly with respect to public health, risk and strategic communication, and the maintenance of social order, including governance issues such as continuity of operations. Strengthening resilience is also an important, if less tangible, imperative here, to include the psychosocial factors relevant to coping with prolonged stress and the ability to respond to incidents both efficiently and compassionately. Just as important is to attack the adversary's ability to adapt—for instance, by denying him information, funding, training capacity, and strategic partners. This may be a more effective strategy against a terrorist organization than a true terrorist network, which is likely to command greater resources and exhibit greater resilience. Additionally, certain topics that generally have been taboo need to be discussed seriously. Confronting issues such as quarantine, triage, and martial law may not be avoidable, however uncomfortable these discussions may be.

CONCLUSION: PROLIFERATION CONTROL MUST GO BEYOND SOVEREIGNTY

The threat from the proliferation of weapons of mass destruction is global, networked, adaptable, and facilitated by private actors like A. Q. Khan who seek to benefit financially by exporting the world's most dangerous technology. Individual states cannot solve the WMD problem single-handedly, let alone hope to safeguard their own borders isolated from important global actors, be they public or private. Because of this, proliferation control regimes premised on state-to-state agreement are likely to fail since they ignore the growing threat posed by nonstate actors and the role the private sector plays in proliferation, wittingly or not. It is not enough to wish the NPT were "more verifiable" or to hope difficult states will cooperate more fully with the IAEA in the future. Indeed, the fundamental underpinnings of nonproliferation agreements are that states will fulfill their international commitments and that they have the capacity to do so, retaining the ability to control what goes on within their borders. But is this a viable reality? There are too many failing or failed states; too many opportunities for global networks, designed for speed, efficiency, and security in ways governments are not, to act globally.

To counter the proliferation of weapons of mass destruction, the cost to proliferators for engaging in this illicit activity must be raised exponentially. To do this, traditional nonproliferation activities must be expanded, but the key very well might be found in the private sector. It is on their networks—their ships, planes, and trucks—and through their financial institutions—investment banks, insurance, transshipping concerns—that illegal weapons and components are moved and paid for, and it is here that the process of proliferation, while arguably at its most automatic, may also be most vulnerable.

Certainly, states and corporations have different interests, motivations, and capabilities. But without engaging the private sector and finding mutual areas of interest to contain the spread of WMD, state-based initiatives alone are likely to be late and less likely to succeed given today's global threat environment.

ENDNOTES

1. The White House, Remarks by President Barack Obama, Prague, Czech Republic, April 5, 2009.
2. World at Risk, Report of the Commission on the Prevention of Weapons of Mass Destruction Proliferation and Terrorism, New York: Vintage Books, 2008.

3. Joseph Cirincione, Jon B. Wolfsthal, and Miriam Rajkumar, *Deadly Arsenals, Carnegie Endowment for International Peace* (Washington, DC: The Brookings Institution Press, 2005), 55.

4. Jeff Bliss, North Korea Nuclear Test Confirmed by U.S. Intelligence Agency, Bloomberg.com, October 16, 2006, <http://www.bloomberg.com/apps/news?pid=20601101&sid=aO7kW.RjqqaE&refer=japan accessed April 7, 2009>.

5. Joseph Cirincione, Jon B. Wolfsthal, and Miriam Rajkumar, *Deadly Arsenals, Carnegie Endowment for International Peace* (Washington, DC: The Brookings Institution Press, 2005), 55.

6. "Bin Laden 'has nuclear weapons,' " BBC, November 10, 2001, <http://news.bbc.co.uk/1/hi/world/south_asia/1648572.stm>.

7. Central Intelligence Agency, "Terrorist CBRN: Materials and Effects" (June 2003), 4.

8. Ibid; U.S. Nuclear Regulatory Commission, "Fact Sheet on Dirty Bombs," (March 2003).

9. RDDs could use Cesium-137, Strontium-90, or Cobalt-60, for example.

10. Central Intelligence Agency, "Terrorist CBRN: Materials and Effects" (June 2003), 4; U.S. Nuclear Regulatory Commission, "Fact Sheet on Dirty Bombs" (March 2003).

11. Dan Eggen and Susan Schmidt, " 'Dirty Bomb' Plot Uncovered, U.S. Says; Suspected Al Qaeda Operative Held as 'Enemy Combatant,' " *Washington Post* (June 11, 2002): A1.

12. Thomas R. Wilson, "Statement for the Record to the Senate Armed Services Committee on Global Threats and Challenges" (March 19, 2002), 18; Counterproliferation Program Review Committee, Report on Activities and Programs for Countering Proliferation (Washington, DC: Department of Defense, May 1995), 8; Barry Erlick, Testimony before the Permanent Subcommittee on Investigations of the Senate Committee on Governmental Affairs, in U.S. Senate, Global Spread of Chemical and Biological Weapons, S. Hrg. 101–744 (Washington, DC: U.S. Government Printing Office, 1990), 33.

13. Proliferation: Threat and Response; John R. Bolton, "Beyond the Axis of Evil," Remarks Made at the Heritage Foundation, May 6, 2002.

14. See, variously, Central Intelligence Agency, Unclassified Report to Congress on the Acquisition of Technology Related to Weapons of Mass Destruction and Advanced Chemical Munitions, 1 January through 30 June, 2001 (January 30, 2002); Proliferation: Threat and Response; John R. Bolton, "Beyond the Axis of Evil," Remarks Made at the Heritage Foundation, May 6, 2002.

15. The official title of the Biological Weapons Convention is "The Convention on the Prohibition of the Development, Production, and Stockpiling of Bacteriological (Biological) and Toxin Weapons and on Their Destruction." It entered into force on March 26, 1975.

16. Article I, Biological Weapons Convention, is the Convention on the Prohibition of the Development, Production and Stockpiling of Bacteriological (Biological) and Toxin Weapons and on their Destruction, 1975.

17. The official title of the Chemical Weapons Convention is "The Convention on the Prohibition of the Development, Production, Stockpiling and Use of Chemical Weapons and on Their Destruction." It entered into force on April 29, 1997.

18. Lowell E. Jacoby, Statement before the Senate Select Committee on Intelligence, February 11, 2003. In U.S. Congress Senate Select Committee on Intelligence, Current and Projected National Security Threats to the United States. 108th Congress, 1st session (Washington, DC: GPO, 2003), 7–8.

19. Proliferation: Threat and Response, 57.

20. Central Intelligence Agency, Unclassified Report to Congress on the Acquisition of Technology Related to Weapons of Mass Destruction and Advanced Chemical

Munitions, 1 January Through 30 June, 2001 (January 30, 2002); Proliferation: Threat and Response, 36, 45.

21. Central Intelligence Agency, Unclassified Report to Congress on the Acquisition of Technology Related to Weapons of Mass Destruction and Advanced Chemical Munitions, 1 January Through 30 June 2001 (January 30, 2002); Proliferation: Threat and Response, 47.

22. See, for example, Patrick E. Tyler, "American and British Weapons Experts Return to Libya," *The New York Times* (January 20, 2004): A3; Anton LaGuardia, "Western Experts Arrive to Begin Disarming Libya," *Daily Telegraph* (London), (January 20, 2004): 11; Stephen Fidler, "Libya to Admit Weapons Inspectors," *Financial Times* (London) (February 3, 2004): 11; and Stephen Fidler, "Libya Had Sizeable Chemical Weapons Programme," *Financial Times* (London), (February 7, 2004): 8.

23. Proliferation: Threat and Response, 11, 15.

24. Ibid., 28.

25. Nations in this category could include Egypt, Israel, and Vietnam, among others. For additional information, see, for example, Joseph Cirincione, Jon B. Wolfstahl, and Miriam Rajkumar, *Deadly Arsenals: Tracking Weapons of Mass Destruction* (Washington, DC: Carnegie Endowment for International Peace, 2002), 52; U.S. Congress, Office of Technology Assessment, *Proliferation of Weapons of Mass Destruction: Assessing the Risks*, OTA-ISC-559 (Washington, DC: U.S. Government Printing Office, August 1993), 65, 80–81.

26. Judith Miller, "Qaeda Videos Seem to Show Chemical Tests," *The New York Times* (August 19, 2002); "Al Qaeda video tapes obtained by CNN," CNN, August 19, 2002.

27. Blix, An Update on Inspection to the Security Council.

28. David Kay, Statement on the Interim Progress Report of the Iraq Survey Group, Before the House Permanent Select Committee on Intelligence, the House Appropriations Committee Subcommittee on Defense, and the Senate Select Committee on Intelligence, October 2, 2003, <http://www.cia.gov/cia/public_affairs/speeches/2003/david_kay_10022003.html>.

29. David Kay, Testimony on Iraqi Weapons of Mass Destruction Before the Senate Armed Services Committee, January 28, 2004.

30. "Nanomaterials Show Signs of Toxicity," *Science* 300 (April 11, 2003): 243, <www.ece.neu.edu/edsnu/mcgruer/nano/nanotoxicityscience0304.pdf>.

31. For more information, see Center for Counterproliferation Research, "Anthrax in America: A Chronology and Analysis of the Fall 2001 Attacks," November 2002.

32. See George Tenet, Testimony Before the Senate Select Intelligence Committee on Intelligence on the Worldwide Threat: Converging Dangers in a Post 9/11 World, February 6, 2002.

33. Peter Baker, "Pakistani Scientist Who Met Bin Laden Failed Polygraphs, Renewing Suspicions," *Washington Post* (March 3, 2002).

34. Center for Counterproliferation Research, *CBRN Terrorism: An Annotated Bibliography* (Washington, DC: National Defense University, November 2002), 4–5.

35. Douglas Frantz, "U.S. and Pakistan Discuss Nuclear Security," *The New York Times* (October 1, 2001): A3; John J. Fialka and Scott Neuman, "Will Pakistan's Warheads Stay Secure? If a War Topples Leader, Control Is Uncertain; Some Call Threat Slim," *Wall Street Journal* (October 4, 2001): A17; Paul Richter, "Pakistan's Nuclear Wild Card," *Los Angeles Times* (September 18, 2001): A2; Nigel Hawkes, "Pakistan Could Lose Control of its Arsenal," *Times* (London), September 20, 2001, n.p.

36. World at Risk, The Report of the Commission on the Prevention of WMD Proliferation and Terrorism (New York: Vintage Press, 2009), xxiii.

37. "Terrorist CBRN: Materials and Effects," Central Intelligence Agency, Directorate of Intelligence, May 2003, 1.

38. "The Worldwide Threat 2004: Challenges in a Changing Global Context." Testimony of Director of Central Intelligence George J. Tenet Before the Senate Select Committee on Intelligence, February 24, 2004 (as prepared for delivery), 4.

39. World at Risk, The Report of the Commission on the Prevention of WMD Proliferation and Terrorism (New York: Vintage Press, 2009), 11–12.

40. "The Worldwide Threat 2003: Evolving Dangers in a Complex World." Testimony of Director of Central Intelligence George J. Tenet Before the Senate Select Committee on Intelligence, February 11, 2003 (as prepared for delivery), 4.

41. Tenet, 2004, 4.

42. Ibid.

43. This memo was discovered in 2001 on a computer acquired by the *Wall Street Journal* that had been used by al Qaeda members in Afghanistan. Government officials are reported to have confirmed the authenticity of the files found on the computer's hard drive, which also contained a table of lethal doses for poisons according to body weight and a list of disease agents, including anthrax. See "Al-Qaeda: New Evidence of Chemical and Biological Weapons Pursuit," *Global Security Newswire* (January 2, 2002).

44. The president also proposed the following: creation of a special committee of the IAEA Board of Governors to focus intensively on safeguards and verification, and denying rotating membership on the board (and the special committee) to any state under investigation for proliferation violations.

45. David E. Sanger and Thom Shanker, "Reluctant U.S. Gives Assent for Missiles to Go to Yemen," *The New York Times* (December 12, 2002): A1.

46. Bush, Statement, December 11, 2002, <www.whitehouse.gov/news/releases/2002/12/20021211-8.html>.

47. Bush, Remarks to the People of Poland, May 31, 2003, <www.whitehouse.gov/news/releases/2003/05/20030531-3.html>.

48. Albright, op. cit.

49. John R. Bolton, Keynote Address at The American Enterprise Institute Panel: "The International Atomic Energy Agency: The World's Enforcer or Paper Tiger?" September 28, 2004, <www.aei.org/events/eventID.911,filter./transcript.asp>.

50. On February 11, 2004, the United States signed a shipboarding agreement with Liberia, a major flag of convenience state. This agreement provides authority on a bilateral basis to board vessels suspected of carrying WMD and delivery means materials. Similar agreements are being pursued with other flag of convenience states.

51. Libya claims losses of only $3 billion.

52. Undersecretary of State John R. Bolton spoke to this point in remarks in July 2004, particularly in reference to North Korea's clandestine uranium program and its insistence on maintaining a "peaceful" nuclear program: "We are interested in a lasting and meaningful solution to the threat posed by North Korea's nuclear weapons program … halting ongoing nuclear programs can only make sense when it is explicitly and credibly part of a clear plan leading to rapid dismantlement … North Korea's continued denial of its uranium enrichment program precludes a solution … [A]nd the United States knows that North Korea's nuclear programs are primarily intended to support its nuclear arms program. This is why we insist that the dismantlement of their programs must be complete, verifiable, and irreversible." "Lessons from Libya and North Korea's Strategic Choice." Remarks at Yonsei University, Seoul, South Korea, 21 July 2004.

53. According to British press accounts, in August 2004 Iran issued an extraordinary list of demands to its British, French, and German interlocutors. These demands include

access to advanced nuclear technology, provision of conventional weapons, and "security assurances" against nuclear attack (presumably from Israel). What concessions Iran would make on the nuclear issue was not clear. See Anton La Guardia, "Hand Over Nuclear Weapons and Know-How, Iran Tells Britain," August 11, 2004, <www.telegraph.co.uk>.

54. Speaking in August, National Security Adviser Dr. Condoleezza Rice said: "I do think that there are very active efforts underway … to undermine the ability of the Iranians under the cover of civilian nuclear cooperation to get the components that would help them for nuclear weapons developments." Meet the Press, August 8, 2004. In the context of the interview, this comment implied that Israel is engaged in such efforts.

55. The "re-load" phenomenon is discussed in Richard Danzig, "Catastrophic Bioterrorism—What Is To Be Done?" A report of the National Defense University Center for Technology and National Security Policy, August 2003. See pp. 1–2.

CHAPTER TWELVE

Globalization, Global Environmental Problems, and Transnational Advocacy Networks

Teng "Margaret" Fu

As people the world over watched the Olympic Games in China in 2008, they also learned about China's environmental problems which affect the whole planet. To provide for its huge population, China has engaged in rapid economic development such as building massive dam projects and factories. Chinese production for the global export trade has lifted China's economy, but harmed the environment. Water scarcity, desertification, acid rain, and air pollution are on the rise, affecting people beyond China's borders. China's carbon emissions now outstrip those of the United States and contribute to global climate change. But if global dynamics have facilitated environmental damage in China, can the tools of globalization also help protect the environment? Environmental activism is spurred by global telecommunications and networks elsewhere, but could these global tools help curb the actions of a totalitarian state?

The case of dams in China provides some interesting evidence. For hydroelectric power companies and local governments in Yunnan, southwest China, the proposal to build 13 large dams on the Nu/Salween River was expected to be approved without any complication, as the plan came at an opportune time. China's rapid development and its soaring demand for energy have brought a new wave of enthusiasm for the construction of hydroelectric power plants. Few places are better positioned for hydroelectric development than Yunnan, where rivers and waters have always been abundant, compared to the more populated and dry areas in East and North China. Necessary capital and technology for dam development should be easy to obtain, particularly with the central government's "Go West" development strategy in place, which aims to drive both Chinese and foreign investment for infrastructure projects into western areas of the country. China is keen on large dam construction, and boasts that it is among the world leaders in dam civil engineering, especially for undertaking the Three Gorges Dam project, the world's largest.

However, the surprise came when China's Premier Wen Jiabao did not approve the proposal; in May 2009 he called for more environmental assessment and evaluation, indefinitely postponing the project. It was the first time in Chinese history an organized public campaign successfully influenced the decision making on a major dam project, halting the project. The proposed Nu River dam projects have been scaled down from 13 to 4 eventually, if any are to be built. The suspension of the dam project and the scaling down of the project suggested a new era of anti-dam advocacy in China. Environmental journalist Wang Yongchen won the Conde Nast Traveler Environmental Award, a prize of $20,000, for her coordination of a massive campaign that has halted the construction of these 13 dams so far.[1]

The anti-dam campaign involves Chinese environmental organizations, such as Green Earth Volunteers and Green Watershed; Chinese research institutes, such as the Chinese Academy of Social Sciences; Chinese media; China State Environmental Protection Administration (SEPA); regional and international environmental and river protection NGOs and foundations, such as Thai and Burmese NGOs and affected people's organizations, Rivers Watch East and Southeast Asia and International Rivers Network; and UNESCO World Heritage Centre. These transnational actors spoke with one voice, used different channels of communication, and successfully influenced the Chinese government's decision making on the proposed 13 large dams on the Nu/Salween River.

The opposition based its advocacy on the norm of "sustainable development" that "meets the needs of the present without compromising the ability of future generations to meet their own needs."[2] Development is not merely an economic issue. Social and environmental dimensions should be integrated in the overall consideration of development. Nine of the thirteen dams proposed would be located in the Three Parallel Rivers World Heritage Site composed of Nu/Salween River, Jinsha (Upper Yangtze), and Lancang (Upper Mekong) Rivers. The site is regarded as one of the biologically richest temperate regions of the world, nurturing more than 6,000 plant species and supporting over 50 percent of China's animal species. Additionally, millions of people from at least 20 ethnic minority groups in Yunnan, China, and downstream riparian communities in Thailand and Myanmar have depended on the watershed for fishing and farming for generations. The 21.32-gigawatt 13-dam project (greater than the scale of the Three Gorges Dam with a capacity of 18.2 gigawatts) would trigger substantial environmental and social impacts, such as biodiversity loss and involuntary resettlement.

This case highlights 3 main themes that this chapter will explore. First, the causes, effects, and solutions of environmental problems increasingly are moving beyond state sovereignty. One state's behavior can influence the regional and global environment. States are more likely to face transsovereign environmental problems that one state, acting alone, is unable to mitigate. Second, the collision between economic development and environmental protection is real. Globalization exacerbates the conflict between quick development and environmental protection by spreading economic integration based on the principles of market liberation. Third, globalization, at the same time, alleviates global environmental problems by empowering transnational advocacy networks that represent the interests of traditionally weak actors. The emergence and rise of these transnational advocacy networks present hope for a more balanced and environmentally friendly globalization.

OVERVIEW OF GLOBAL ENVIRONMENTAL PROBLEMS

This section first offers a survey of some pressing global environmental problems, including global warming, hazardous wastes, and global biodiversity loss. It then discusses the difficulties involved in solving global environmental problems.

Environmental problems have drawn growing public attention over the last several decades. With the global trend of industrialization and the rise in population, the damaging impact of human activities on the natural environment is startling.

The world population reached 6.8 billion in 2009, up from 2.5 billion in 1950.[3] It is projected to exceed 9 billion by 2050 and most of the future population growth will be in developing countries. Feeding, housing, and supporting such a huge population will put enormous stress on land, water, energy, and other natural resources. Due to increasing demand for food and loss of arable land resulting from over-intensive cultivation, the need for agricultural land is expanding, which exerts the greatest threat to forests, wetlands, mountains, and biodiversity. Agriculture also dominates global water use. Nearly half of the world's people will experience water shortages by 2025, as water use increases with economic development, particularly for industrial and municipal use, in addition to agricultural irrigation. Water withdrawals and pollution further degrade natural ecosystems, as about half of all wetlands worldwide have been lost and more than 20 percent of the world's 10,000 known freshwater species are extinct, threatened, or endangered. Most of the increase in energy demand is still served by fossil fuels, although renewable energy usage is growing. As fossil fuel consumption and emissions of carbon dioxide, the major greenhouse gas, continue to rise, the result is a warming of the earth's surface at an unprecedented rate. The impact of climate change could have serious implications for food security, freshwater supplies, human health, and species survival.[4]

Global Climate Change

Global climate change is one of the most pressing and controversial environmental problems. The fourth assessment report (2007) of the Intergovernmental Panel on Climate Change (IPCC) concluded for the first time with near certainty—more than 90 percent confidence—that carbon dioxide and other greenhouse gases from human activities have been the main causes of global climate change since 1950.[5] IPCC, the leading international network of climate change scientists, was established by the World Meteorological Organization and the United Nations Environmental Program in 1988. It involves climate change experts from all relevant disciplines and in particular, representatives from governments. For their work on climate change, IPCC and Albert Arnold (Al) Gore, Jr. were awarded the Nobel Peace Prize in 2007. The fourth assessment report "essentially caps a half-century-long effort to discern whether humans ... could influence the earth's climate system in potentially momentous ways."[6] Observed changes in climate and their effects, according to the report, include:[7]

❏ Warming of the climate system is unequivocal, as is now evident from observations of increases in global average air and ocean temperatures, widespread melting of snow and ice, and rising global average sea level.

❏ Observational evidence from all continents and most oceans shows that many natural systems are being affected by regional climate changes, particularly temperature increases.

❏ There is medium confidence that other effects of regional climate change on natural and human environments are emerging, although many are difficult to discern due to adaptation and nonclimatic drivers.

Changes in climate could have major influences on ecosystems, hydrology, water resources, food production, coastal systems, and human health.[8] Global warming would change the rainfall and temperature patterns, increasing the intensity and frequency of severe weather events, such as droughts, hurricanes, and floods. Ecological systems and the mix of species that they contain would have difficulty adapting to the new environment. Such changes would affect soil characteristics and disturbance regimes (e.g., fires, pests, and diseases), favoring some species over others and changing the natural composition of ecosystems. Moreover, whereas periodic and chronic shortfalls of water caused by climate change could impose additional burden on countries located in arid and semi-arid regions, flooding and associated damages, such as dam and levee failures, are likely to become a larger problem in many temperate and humid regions. Furthermore, climate changes would influence the length of growing seasons and the timing of extreme or critical threshold events relative to crop development, impacting agriculture and food production. Potential detrimental changes in diseases, pests, and weeds are suspected as well, though their effects have not yet been quantified in most available studies. Coastal systems will be directly affected through sea-level rise and increase in storm-surge hazards. Currently, an estimated 46 million people live in areas that are at risk of flooding from storm surges. Climate changes will only exacerbate these problems, leading to disastrous impacts on ecosystems and human coastal infrastructure. Climate changes, in all, could affect human health through increases in heat-stress mortality, tropical vector-borne diseases, urban air pollution problems, and decreases in cold-related illnesses. Though it is unclear whether the intensity and frequency of hurricanes along the U.S. coast during the summer of 2005 were caused by climate changes,[9] the aftermath of powerful hurricanes such as Katrina and Rita can demonstrate the potential kinds of damage global climate change can cause, especially when these kinds of extreme weather events happen simultaneously on a larger scale.

Hazardous Wastes

Hazardous waste control is another important example of global environmental problems. With industrialization came record high levels of the production of toxic, explosive, flammable, and other types of hazardous wastes.

As environmental awareness rose in developed countries during the 1970s, domestic regulations regarding waste disposal became stringent, giving strong incentives for exporting hazardous wastes to developing countries with lower labor costs, less local opposition, and less-strict environmental laws that were often loosely enforced.

The North–South shipments of hazardous wastes drew public attention with several notorious incidents of illegal dumping.[10] In one case, the cargo ship *Khian Sea* spent almost 2 years at sea in search of a disposal site for 14,000 tons of incinerator ash containing lead and cadmium that had originated in Philadelphia, PA.. Eventually, the ship dumped 4,000 tons of ash on a beach in Haiti and the remaining 10,000 tons somewhere between the Suez Canal and Singapore.[11] Another example was the 1987 Koko, Nigeria case. Toxic industrial wastes from Italy were exported to Nigeria based on a deal struck between an Italian businessman and a Nigerian. The Nigerian resident was told the wastes were merely miscellaneous construction materials, and so he stored them in the backyard of his property. The scandal broke out when barrels of waste began leaking into the surrounding area, causing various health problems for residents and workers exposed to the highly toxic substances.[12]

Loss of Biodiversity

Yet another pressing area demanding environmental protection is species diversity. "In effect, we are currently responsible for the sixth major extinction event in the history of the Earth, and the greatest since the dinosaurs disappeared, 65 million years ago."[13]

More species are becoming threatened with extinction. The status of bird species shows a continuing deterioration across all biomes over the last 2 decades and preliminary findings for other major groups, such as amphibians and mammals, indicate that the situation is likely worse than for birds. Between 12% and 52% of species within well-studied higher taxa are threatened with extinction.[14]

According to the Living Planet Index (LPI), which measures overall trends in populations of wild species around the world, one-third of the world's biodiversity has been lost since 1970.[15] *Global Biodiversity Outlook 2* also concluded that "biodiversity is in decline at all levels and geographical scales," and called for targeted response options, including protected areas, resource management, pollution prevention programs, and so on, to reverse this trend for specific habitats or species.[16]

One of the richest, yet most threatened, sources of biodiversity is the forest, particularly rainforest ecosystems.[17] Rainforests exist mainly in the tropics of Latin America, Africa, and Asia. Besides being home to an incredible amount of biodiversity, including endangered species such as the orangutan, Sumatran tiger, and scarlet macaw parrot, rainforests play an important role in regulating climate, conserving soil, and storing and purifying water. Yet, human activities, such as logging, plantation development, cash crop cultivation, urbanization, and construction projects are destroying forests at an unprecedented rate. Every year, an area of rainforest the size of England is cut down.[18]

Another finding of scientists assessing the status of biological diversity is that inland waters are suffering most from human activities at present. "The two major documented extinction events in the twentieth century both took place in inland water ecosystems."[19] The Mobile Bay, Alabama, drainage in the United States was one of these events. The drainage basin used to be home for 9 families and around 120 species. However, after extensive dam construction, including 33 major hydroelectric dams and many smaller impoundments, as well as locks and flood control structures, at least 38 species are believed to have become extinct since the 1930s and 1940s. This kind of catastrophic impact on the diversity of freshwater snail fauna is likely to have been repeated at a smaller scale in many other, less well-documented, parts of the world.[20]

Challenges of Environmental Preservation

These international environmental trends are alarming, yet the transsovereign nature of the environmental problems complicates attempts to solve them. While part of the definition of sovereignty is a state's ability to control its land and other natural resources, increasingly natural resources may be degraded by global environmental trends that states are poorly positioned to control or respond to individually. The transboundary causes, effects, and potential solutions of such global problems present great challenges for global environmental protection.

First, global environmental problems are global commons problems. The old story of "the tragedy of the commons" took place in the historic commons, a centrally located pasture open to anyone for grazing livestock.[21] The "tragedy" occurred when each owner increased his or her herds to maximize benefits from the communal pasture. As the pasture was overgrazed, these herdsmen eventually destroyed the commons and their means of survival. Whereas the entire group would likely have benefited from limiting the number of grazing animals, with no institutional mechanism in place, none of the herdsmen had the incentive to limit their consumption of the common good when they were not sure if others would do the same. At the heart of this lack of motivation to cooperate in achieving common interests is the free-rider problem: If people know that they can enjoy benefits without contributing any effort, they choose not to contribute and thus free-ride on others' efforts.

Our natural environment is a global commons that transcends political borders. No single state can own or control air, water, or climate. States must thus share these "free" goods. The problem is that for the sake of development, the natural environment has been bearing the external cost that is not accounted for in the cost-benefit consideration of these economic activities. One country's reckless development may abuse and pollute critical common resources shared by many (as both raw materials and as sinks for pollution). Even worse, the resulting degradation may be disproportionably distributed, damaging other countries more seriously than the polluter state itself. The acid rain problem between Canada and the United States illustrates this point. Power plants in the Midwest region of the United States emitted pollution that traveled to Canada and caused acid rain damage on lakes and forests. Stricter restrictions on sulfur dioxide emissions in Canada could hardly protect the welfare of its citizens, because the major polluters were in the United States. The cost and benefit of U.S. power development was asymmetrically distributed between two sovereign states.[22]

Second, the structure of the international political system does not allow the use of third-party enforcement—Hobbes' classic solution to problems of collective action—to protect the global environment. While coercive enforcement can be used by a ruler to obtain taxes, labor, or other resources for the common good of the state, there is no supranational entity or world government with recognized authority to punish violators and maintain order in the global environmental policy area. The anarchic nature of the international system precludes the use of third-party enforcement as a solution to governing the global environment.

Third, the alternative solution of "stable institutions of self-government" is compromised by the uneven economic development of states. The gap between the rich and the poor countries of the world is enormous, and this North–South divide (developed countries versus developing countries) complicates the establishment and functioning of global environmental institutions.[23] Developing countries argue that the developed countries have exploited natural resources for their own purposes in the past and are responsible for most of the world's present pollution and resource depletion, including ozone depletion and climate change. Environmental protection is viewed as an effort by developed countries to forestall the economic growth of the South. While the North emphasizes environmental issues that threaten ecological stability, the South focuses on immediate needs for economic growth to survive and improve standards of living. The difference in the needs and policy agendas of the North and the South makes it difficult to reach consensus on international environmental policies.

Such was the major argument made by the G-77 and China during the international climate negotiations. The resulting principle of "common but differentiated responsibilities" acknowledges that while the protection of climate for present and future generations is an obligation for all members of the international community, industrialized and formerly communist countries with economies in transition have a responsibility to take the lead in addressing climate change.[24] The responsibility comes from their high historical emission of greenhouse gases and the assumption that they possess the financial and technological capabilities to control those emissions. The poor are hurt most by global climate, but have had the least responsibility for creating the problem, and have the fewest resources for adapting to it. Struggles of the Kyoto Protocol (whose targets expire in 2012) and current negotiations toward a post-Kyoto roadmap for greenhouse gas emissions reductions have revolved around such a North–South divide.

Fourth, environmental issues often involve scientific complexity and uncertainty that make reaching consensus on environmental protection policy difficult.[25] The lack of certainty on the scope, severity, and time frame of individual problems makes it difficult to infer causation, to attribute responsibility, and to design solutions. More certain economic and political interests often take advantage of this lesser certainty, dominating the policy-making arena. Climate change, biodiversity loss, and ocean fish stocks are examples of issues where scientific uncertainty obstructs progress in international negotiations.

GLOBALIZATION EXACERBATES GLOBAL ENVIRONMENTAL PROBLEMS

Globalization integrates capital and knowledge worldwide. With revolutions in communication and transportation technologies, information, capital, and values are able to travel more rapidly and easily throughout the world. The worldwide division of labor and specialization based on comparative advantage contribute to the increase in efficiency and growth in economies.[26]

These globalizing forces, based on liberal market principles, exacerbate global environmental problems. Market forces unleashed by globalization create various social and environmental concerns. Riding the globalization tide, market and landed private actors have assumed stronger roles in the decision-making process, often dominating social and political outcomes. Unfortunately, in this manner, the opportunities and rewards of globalization often are spread unequally, concentrating power and wealth in a select group of people and marginalizing others.[27] Moreover, to a large number of developing regions and countries, comparative advantages point to natural resources and raw materials. Engaging in global trade for survival and quick development relies on the utilization of these natural resources. As a result, environment and sustainability are put as lower priorities after economic development. Economic development is then expected to benefit the poor and the environment through the "trickle-down effect."

For example, by the 1970s, the dominant industrialization mindset of "first development, then environment" viewed large infrastructure constructions, including dam projects, as the means to achieving fast development. Development was perceived as man's conquest of nature. Dam construction, particularly, symbolized human progress from a life controlled by nature to the triumph of science over nature.

Dam advocates cross borders. They include transnational epistemic communities of engineers and scientists, multinational corporations, international development banks, and national bureaucrats, and economic globalization connects them. The International Commission on Large Dams (ICOLD) was established by a group of engineers, developers, and bureaucrats to collect information and coordinate the exchange of knowledge about big dam construction around the world in 1929. Multinational corporations such as Asea Brown Boveri, Siemens, GEC Alsthom, Kvaerner, Bechtel, and others grew rapidly during the 1950s and 1960s. The World Bank, Food and Agriculture Organization, United Nations Development Program, Inter-American and Asian development banks also played major roles in promoting the big dam industry. Bilateral aid agencies, such as the U.S. Agency for International Development and British Overseas Development Administration, were additional sources of funding and planning of these dam projects, in partnership with bureaucratic agencies in the development-oriented countries.[28]

Funding and technologies of large dam building were transferred through "open economies" and "open technologies" to developing countries in Latin America and Asia.[29] But the conventional wisdom of building large-scale dams to generate power and control floods has become suspect in the developed world during the last 30 years. Large dams, in particular, have been blamed for environmental destruction by environmentalists in the North (particularly in the United States, Sweden, and France)—the classic industrialization/modernization without any consideration for sustainability, economic equity, or justice. Therefore, as domestic environmental and social impact regulations in Western developed countries tightened, the large dam industry moved its attention to developing countries where rules were lax.

In this way, globalization potentially creates a "race toward the bottom" in setting environmental standards. Countries with lax environmental standards not only produce pollution and damage the global environment, but also put pressures on countries with high environmental standards in the global market competition.

Differences in the U.S. and Latin American levels of economic development and environmental standards are among the central concerns of critics of the North American Free Trade Agreement (NAFTA), Central American Free Trade Agreement (CAFTA), and the proposed Free Trade Area of the Americas (FTAA). With much lower environmental standards and looser enforcement mechanisms, Mexico may receive or "suck" U.S. pollution.[30] Even when local communities realize the environmental injustice and make efforts to reverse the negative impact, free trade requirements provide protection for multinational corporations. Metclad, a U.S. company, took full advantage of the NAFTA free trade agreement in its case against a Mexican municipality. After discovering the dumping site chosen by Metclad was a critical source of ground water that provided drinking water for the community, the Mexican municipality refused to grant a building permit to Metclad. However, the NAFTA Tribunal backed Metclad under a chapter of NAFTA and initially required compensation for violation of the agreement by the federal government of Mexico.[31] The loss of regulatory power of governments on events that have large social and environmental impact, in the face of free trade agreements, may well open the door for further global environmental abuse.

On the other hand, free trade rules also threaten countries with relatively high environmental standards. Embracing the market liberation principles for economic development, developing countries often view environmental regulations promulgated by environmentalists in developed countries as a new type of trade protectionism scheme, and use market liberation principles to get away with their bad environmental standards. In the 1991 "tuna/dolphin" case,[32] the U.S. Marine Mammal Protection Act required an embargo on Mexican tuna, because fishermen used tuna nets that killed dolphins. Yet, a GATT dispute resolution panel in Geneva declared the embargo illegal under the rules of international trade, which caused environmentalists to condemn the cruelty of trade liberation principles.

GLOBALIZATION ALLEVIATES GLOBAL ENVIRONMENTAL PROBLEMS

Market liberalizing forces spread by economic globalization contribute to a power imbalance between private interests and public interests, and between short-term interests and long-term interests. The state, which used to be considered a vehicle for protection of public interests, is losing both economic and political control, facing the rising power of private-sector and business organizations. The future restoration of the power balance seems to lie in the emergence and growth of transnational advocacy networks that are empowered by globalization as well.

Transnational advocacy networks usually involve international and domestic nongovernmental organizations, regional and international intergovernmental organizations, parts of the governments, media, and intellectuals that are bound together by "shared values, a common discourse, and dense exchanges of information and services."[33] These transnational advocacy networks make joint efforts in persuading, socializing, and pressuring states and international organizations to change their norms and behaviors with respect to issues beyond sovereignty, such as the environment. They blur the boundaries between sovereign states by building new links among domestic, regional, and international actors through pursuit of common issues and values. Margaret Keck and Kathryn Sikkink outline a few tactics these networks use:

> (1) *Information politics*, or the ability to quickly and credibly generate politically usable information and move it to where it will have the most impact; (2) *Symbolic politics*, or the ability to call upon symbols, actions, or stories that make sense of a situation for an audience that is frequently far away; (3) *Leverage politics*, or the ability to call upon powerful actors to affect a situation where weaker members of a network are unlikely to have influence; and (4) *Accountability politics*, or the effort to hold powerful actors to their previously stated policies or principles.[34]

So far, such networks have been successful in bringing about discursive and procedural changes by sharing resources and multiplying channels of access to international and domestic systems. They have played an indispensable role in promoting the norm of "sustainable development" and monitoring the implementation of principles and procedures such as environmental impact assessment.

The 1972 and 1992 United Nations Conferences heralded a change in the norm of development. The classic industrialization mindset of "first development, then environment" was gradually replaced by the norm of "sustainable development." Sustainable development was first regularized and institutionalized, at the international level, through the creation of the United Nations Environment Program, the first environmental unit at the World Bank—which eventually became the Office of Environmental and Scientific Affairs (OESA)—and an environmental wing of ICOLD after the 1972 United Nations Conference on the Human Environment in Stockholm, Sweden. It was further affirmed through the formation of the United Nations Commission on Sustainable Development, a Vice-Presidency for Environmentally Sustainable Development at the World Bank, and the Global Environmental Facility after the 1992 United Nations Conference on Environment and Development in Rio de Janeiro, Brazil.[35]

At the national level, the global normative framework of sustainable development was applied through the establishment of national environmental bureaucracies and the institutionalization of procedures such as environmental impact assessment.[36] Not a single national environmental bureaucracy existed before the 1972 U.N. Conference. But environmental agencies and ministries were established at a rapid rate thereafter, with about 60 by 1988, another 40 around 1992, and more than 100 by 1995. Procedures such as environmental impact assessments have spread along with the formal establishment of these bureaucratic agencies, prompting the inclusion of environmental evaluation as an essential part of the planning and implementation of development projects.

First, transnational advocacy networks contribute to the diffusion of these norms and practices by disseminating ideas and information, and soliciting and transferring needed resources across borders through the same technological and economic instruments globalization offers. The "debt for nature swaps" practice exemplifies innovative efforts of transnational environmental networks facilitated by open economies and technologies.[37] The negotiations of the practice usually involve, at a minimum, a sovereign state (the debtor country), a donor organization headquartered in another country, and a private creditor agency. Part of the developing country's debt is redeemed by nongovernmental conservation organizations in return for that country using funds to protect the rainforest or other conservation work. The first case was Conservation International from the United States trading Bolivian debt for the expansion and long-term management of the Beni Biosphere Reserve. Though the redemption is usually less than the face value of the debt, private banks are still willing to sell it because of the need to satisfy stockholders and preserve the bank's credit rating. In this way, a win–win situation emerges, as the debtor country is more than willing to shed part of the debt burden and the transnational environmental group is happy to make constructive moves toward the preservation of nature.[38]

Second, transnational environmental networks empowered by globalization challenge international capital markets face to face. Multilateral development banks increasingly claim to address environmental protection objectives in their loans and have eliminated environmental high-risk projects in the project evaluation stage. Aside from the adoption of the discourse on sustainable development, considerable procedural changes have also been implemented. Environmental impact assessments are practiced more seriously at all multilateral banks now.

For example, the transnational anti-dam network has focused on multilateral bank campaigns in pushing forward ideas of environmental protection, social justice, and human rights. A series of anti-dam struggles during the 1980s and 1990s against the World Bank signaled the start of efforts in reforming bank practices in project finances. Campaigns against World Bank-funded dam projects from Nam Choan in Thailand to the Xingu River in Brazil to the Sardar Sarovar Project in India's Narmada Valley played a leading role in restricting the Bank's involvement in large dam projects and adopting new policies regarding resettlement, environmental assessment, effects on indigenous people, and information disclosure.[39] The World Bank had scaled down its support for big dam building until the Nam Theun 2 dam project in Laos in 2005, which was the first major new dam project the Bank has supported in a decade.

These policies formed the basis for the Equator Principles, a voluntary initiative launched in 2003. The initiative stipulates environmental and social guidelines for private banks in project financing.[40] A growing number of international banks, including Citigroup, HSBC, and ABN Amro, have agreed to follow these principles, developing guidelines that prevent them from providing loans to projects that cause environmental damage and harm to local people.

Currently, the transnational anti-dam network strives to apply the Equator Principles to indirect financing, including bond issuance.[41] International Rivers Network and Friends of the Earth alerted the public that, by coordinating and underwriting bonds for the China Export-Import Bank, global banks, including Merrill Lynch/Bank of America, HSBC, Citigroup, BNP Paribas, and Goldman Sachs, helped finance socially and environmentally destructive projects in Sudan and Burma that they could not directly finance under their own environmental policies. When private banks have already made progress in reducing negative impacts of development projects by committing to the Equator Principles in direct loan practices, the challenge from transnational network groups in bond issues demonstrates the continuing efforts of these groups in promoting the norm of sustainable development.

Under such circumstances, the China Export-Import Bank adopted an environmental policy, followed by a more comprehensive "Guidance for the Environmental and Social Impact Assessment of China Export and Import Bank's Loan Project" in August 2008, requiring offshore project developers to complete social and environmental impact assessments before the Bank will approve a loan.[42] Although there are still difficulties implementing these new laws and regulations, they provide an unprecedented political framework that activists and citizens can use to hold dam builders accountable for their actions.

Third, transnational advocacy networks are more likely to influence states' decisions and to discourage behaviors that are potentially destructive to the global environment. The coming-together of domestic, regional, and international groups expands the space of activism and multiplies channels of access to both domestic and international systems. Domestic groups are empowered by the global sharing of information and resources. Meanwhile, international groups, with the linkage to local actors, are able to legitimize their activities and gain better insights on transsovereign issues. With the global spread and institutionalization of such norms as sustainable development, transnational advocacy networks seize and exploit modest political opportunities with enough other resources (strong social networks and powerful symbols). The modest opportunity is widened for more social and environmental changes, when the government makes initial tactical or genuine concessions. Eventually, serious discursive and procedural changes will take place.

The Nu/Salween River case at the beginning of this chapter may display the first transnational advocacy network that successfully affected China's decision making on matters of internal development. Indeed, during the anti-Three Gorges Dam campaign, international environmental groups were vocally involved. However, there was little cooperation or coordination on the level of a transnational advocacy network. International advocacy groups did successfully dissuade some international banks and associated corporations from joining the construction. Yet, the Chinese government proceeded without significant international investment. Thus, a closer review of the Nu/Salween case offers an important example for understanding how globalization assists the efforts of transnational networks in global environmental protection, especially considering the facts that

China is the world's fastest developing state, and economic development has been the paramount priority of the government.

The public campaign to protect the Nu River was arguably initiated by SEPA, a Chinese central government institution. On the Nu River project, poignant disagreement exists between SEPA and the National Development and Reform Commission (NDRC). NDRC approved the proposed project as early as August 2003, while officials from SEPA strongly opposed it. According to Wang Yongchen, the award-winning environmental reporter with the Central People's Radio Station and head of the Chinese environmental group called the Green Earth Volunteers, it was an official with SEPA that called her and requested assistance from more scientists who were familiar with the Nu River. The official hoped to build a strong alliance to reinforce SEPA's battle against NDRC.[43] Reportedly, Mu Guangfeng, vice director of the Environmental Impact Assessment Office and director of SEPA's Supervision Department sought assistance of Wang Yongchen, and his opposition "almost singlehandedly halted the momentum fashioned by Huadian and delayed the processes indefinitely."[44] Indeed, a strong anti-dam alliance was built—one that transcended state boundaries.

In addition to public forums, study tours, photo exhibits, petition letters, and other awareness-raising activities through Web sites and e-mails domestically,[45] Chinese environmental groups, journalists, and scientists built up their connection with downstream anti-dam groups at the Rivers for Life Second International Meeting of Dam-Affected People and Their Allies in Rasi Salai, Thailand, in late November and early December 2003.[46] The meeting was organized by Assembly of the Poor (Thailand), International Rivers Network (USA), and Southeast Asia Rivers Network (Thailand). It was funded by a group of international NGOs and foundations, including Action Aid Asia, the Ford Foundation, Novib, Oxfam America, Siemenpuu Foundation, and the Swedish Society for Nature Conservation. More than 300 activists and dam-affected people from over 62 countries attended the meeting, exchanging ideas and strategies and sharing experiences. It was at this meeting that Chinese activists made the initial contacts with downstream and international anti-dam activist groups, and coordinated future campaigns.

Chinese environmental groups joined the Rivers Watch East and Southeast Asia, a network of NGOs from the region, supported by their international allies, working to stop destructive river development projects in East and Southeast Asia and to restore rivers to the communities that depend on them.[47] Yu Xiaogang, of Green Watershed,[48] is the network facilitator for China. During the anti-dam campaign on the Nu/Salween River, the network collected and disseminated updated news on the status of the planned dam project on the Internet and through e-mails. It exchanged information regarding campaign tactics and coordinated concerted anti-dam efforts. The forum enabled Chinese groups to learn previous anti-dam experiences and international dam-building standards in other countries and regions.

Moreover, over 80 people's groups in Thailand and Myanmar, coordinated by the Southeast Asia Rivers Network, wrote a petition to the Ambassador of the Chinese Embassy in Thailand in December 2003, saying that the dams would bring devastating effects for people downstream.[49] Another letter of concern to the President of China, Hu Jintao, was signed by over 76 organizations from 33 countries in March 2004.[50] The letter emphasized that dam projects in the area "risk drastic impacts to all of these (environmental) resources" and that consultations with downstream riparian residents and affected communities need to be conducted according to international standards before any decisions are made.

Meanwhile, the International Rivers Network warned UNESCO of the possible impacts of the planned 13 dams on the Three Parallel Rivers World Heritage Site. Francesco Bandarin, Director of the UNESCO World Heritage Centre, sent letters of concern to both Tian Xiaogang, Secretary-General, Chinese National Commission for UNESCO, and Zhang Xinsheng, Chairperson of the World Heritage Committee c/o National Commission of the People's Republic of China for UNESCO in February and March 2004, respectively. The letters expressed serious concern about the potential threats such development projects could pose to the World Heritage Site and emphasized the necessity to carry out the environmental impact assessment on such hydropower projects. They also urged the Chinese government to provide information regarding the environmental impact assessment report for review by the World Conservation Union (IUCN), the advisory body to the World Heritage Committee on natural heritage. In addition, the letters brought attention to China's obligations under the World Heritage Convention and requested further information concerning the current policy regarding this World Heritage Site.[51]

The transnational campaign continued when Premier Wen made the decision to postpone the proposed project, an unprecedented major success of the public campaign against Nu River dams. Conservation International's China Office organized a symposium on Southwest Dams and Biodiversity Conservation in June, 2004, gathering 43 representatives from 23 NGOs and research institutes from across China. After the symposium, a letter was drafted and signed by the participants, including Green Watershed, Green Earth

Volunteers, scientists from Yunnan University, Sichuan Provincial Academy of Social Science, Chinese Academy of Social Science, and village representatives from Nu River Prefecture and Manwan, Yunnan. The joint letter was sent to the 28th session of the World Heritage Committee and the UNESCO World Heritage Centre, calling on them to act on the Nu River dam plan.[52]

At the 28th session of the World Heritage Committee in July 2004, IUCN's report raised concerns about the potential direct or indirect environmental and social impacts of dam construction in or around the Three Parallel Rivers site. The World Heritage Committee, in turn, expressed its grave concerns and invited the Chinese authorities to respond to the appeals by academics, scientists, and conservationists in China. Since that session, IUCN and UNESCO continued to express serious concerns, seek clarification on the 13-dam hydropower development proposal, and emphasize that the environmental impact assessment should be comprehensive and open to wide participation.[53]

During the anti-dam campaign, the media has also played a significant role in advancing the cause of the campaign. The debates on dam projects and the latest development of the Nu/Salween River project have received considerable coverage from "Green Net" of the *China Youth Daily*, *South China Morning Post*, *China Electricity Power Newspaper*, China Central TV, Hong Kong Phoenix TV station, *China National Geography Magazine*, *International Herald Tribune*, *The New York Times*, and other media.[54] Such media reports and broadcasts, while increasing the public awareness of the campaign, also effectively channeled social grievances to the Chinese leadership, influencing the decision-making process. The close monitoring of the media facilitates the efforts to hold traditionally powerful actors, such as power companies and government officials, accountable to international standards on sustainable development.

CONCLUSION: A MORE BALANCED GLOBALIZATION?

The transnational anti-dam campaign on the proposed 13 dam projects on the Nu/Salween River was successful in postponing the dam constructions. No project has been officially approved in the area, significantly delaying and perhaps stopping the earlier proposal of building dams on the Nu River. The prospect of outright cancelation of the project is high, although plans of scaling down 13 to 4 dams have been suggested. Either outcome demonstrates the success and effectiveness of the transnational anti-dam advocacy. Environmental activists remain active in calling for the public disclosure of the project's environmental impact assessment and further opening up China's dam development policy-making process for public participation. With open economies, technologies, and societies, the network has been successful in mobilizing and sustaining the anti-dam campaign over many years.

Global environmental issues are transsovereign problems by nature. Globalization, with its opening of economies, technologies, and societies, can aggregate the inherent difficulties in solving such transsovereign problems. Unrestrained human activities are the root causes of many environmental problems. Globalization allows the classic dilemma between development and environment to be staged on a larger scale, from national to regional and global.

Fortunately, globalization also empowers traditionally weak actors by connecting them to the world more quickly and easily. The emergence and rise of transnational advocacy networks, such as "debt for nature swaps" and anti-dam coalitions, signal the potential for a more balanced globalization. The capacity of these nonstate actors working together on issues beyond sovereignty is built on, and will further contribute to, the global spread and institutionalization of norms such as sustainable development.

ENDNOTES

1. Shi Jiangtao, "Wen Calls Halt to Yunnan Dam Plan: Premier Orders Further Environmental Checks," *South China Morning Post*, May 21, 2009, <http://www.scmp.com/portal/site/SCMP/menuitem.2c913216495213d5df646910cba0a0a0/?vgnextoid=04b52d76ede51210VgnVCM100000360a0a0aRCRD&vgnextfmt=teaser&s=news>; Woodrow Wilson International Center for Scholars, "Environmental Journalist Stops Plans to Dam China's Last Untamed River," October 12, 2004, <www.wilsoncenter.org/index.cfm?fuseaction=events.event_summary&event_id=96093>, accessed on September 20, 2005.
2. United Nations Department of Economic and Social Affairs, Division of Sustainable Development, "About Us," <www.un.org/esa/sustdev/about_us/aboutus.htm>, accessed on August 20, 2005.
3. UN Population Division/DESA, "World Population to Exceed 9 Billion by 2050," Press Release, March 11, 2009, <http://www.un.org/esa/population/publications/wpp2008/pressrelease.pdf>, accessed on March 26, 2009; United Nations Department of Economic and Social Affairs, "Global Challenge, Global Opportunity: Trends in Sustainable Development," Publication for the Johannesburg Summit 2002.
4. Michele M. Betsill, "Global Climate Change Policy: Making Progress or Spinning Wheels?" in Regina S. Axelrod, David Leonard Downie, and Norman J. Vig, (Eds.), *The Global Environment: Institutions, Law, and Policy* (Washington, DC: CQ Press, 2005), 103–124.
5. Elisabeth Rosenthal and Andrew C. Revkin, "Panel Issues Bleak Report on Climate Change," *New York Times*, February 2, 2007, <http://www.nytimes.com/2007/02/02/science/earth/02cnd-climate.html?pagewanted=1, accessed on March 27, 2009>.
6. Ibid.

7. An Assessment of the Intergovernmental Panel on Climate Change, *Climate Change 2007: Synthesis Report (Summary for Policymakers)*, November 2007, <http://www.ipcc.ch/pdf/assessment-report/ar4/syr/ar4_syr_spm.pdf, accessed on March 27, 2009>.

8. Robert Watson, Marufu C. Zinyowera and Richard H. Moss, IPCC Special Report on The Regional Impacts of Climate Change: An Assessment of Vulnerability, <www.grida.no/climate/ipcc/regional/503.htm#overview>, accessed September 24, 2005.

9. The evidence is mixed; while the frequency of hurricanes appears average, more of those hurricanes are higher intensity category 4 and 5 storms than ever before.

10. David Downie, Jonathan Krueger, and Henrik Selin, "Global Policy for Hazardous Chemicals," in Regina S. Axelrod, David Leonard Downie, and Norman J. Vig (Eds.), *The Global Environment: Institutions, Law, and Policy* (Washington, DC: CQ Press, 2005), 128–129.

11. "A Slow Burn," *Philadelphia Inquirer* (April 6, 1998): A14; James Ridgeway and Gaelle Drevet, "Dumping on Haiti: How Thousands of Tons of Philadelphia's Toxic Waste Ended Up on a Haitian Beach, and What the City of New York Is Doing About It," *The Village Voice* (January 13, 1998).

12. "Hazardous Waste Trade, North and South: The Case of Italy and Koko, Nigeria," Pew Case Studies, Georgetown University Institute for the Study of Diplomacy, <www.guisd.org>.

13. *Global Biodiversity Outlook 2* (Montreal, Canada: Secretariat of the Convention on Biological Diversity, 2006), <http://www.cbd.int/doc/gbo/gbo2/cbd-gbo2-en.pdf>, 10, accessed on March 29, 2009.

14. Ibid, 3.

15. World Wide Fund for Nature, Living Planet Report 2004 (Gland, Switzerland: World Wide Fund For Nature, 2004), <www.panda.org/downloads/general/lpr2004.pdf>, accessed on September 24, 2005.

16. *Global Biodiversity Outlook 2*, <http://www.cbd.int/doc/gbo/gbo2/cbd-gbo2-en.pdf>, 5, accessed on March 29, 2009.

17. Friends of the Earth, "Biodiversity: Disappearing Forests," <www.foe.co.uk/campaigns/biodiversity/issues/disappearing_forests/>, accessed on September 26, 2005.

18. World Resources Institute, "Global Forest Watch," <http://forests.wri.org/globalforestwatch-project-58.html>; Rainforest Action Network, "Rates of Rainforest Loss," <www.ran.org/info_center/factsheets/04b.html>.

19. *Global Biodiversity Outlook*.

20. Ibid. The other one is "Lake Victoria, shared by Kenya, Tanzania and Uganda, was until recently the home of a species flock of around 300 halpochromine cichlid fishes, of exceptional scientific interest, as well as of a number of other fish species. Following introduction of the Nile Perch *Lates niloticus*, and possibly also as a result of a range of other factors, at least half and up to two-thirds of the native species are now believed extinct or nearly so, with virtually no chance of recovery."

21. Garrett Hardin, "The Tragedy of the Commons," *Science* (December 13, 1968): 1243–1248.

22. Dr. Vicki Golich, "United States–Canadian Negotiations for Acid Rain Controls," Pew Case 452, Georgetown University Institute for the Study of Diplomacy, available online at <www.guisd.org>.

23. Norman J. Vig, "Introduction: Governing the International Environment," in Regina S. Axelrod, David Leonard Downie, and Norman J. Vig (Eds.), *The Global Environment: Institutions, Law, and Policy* (Washington, DC: CQ Press, 2005), 5.

24. Michele M. Betsill, "Global Climate Change Policy: Making Progress or Spinning Wheels?" in Regina S. Axelrod, David Leonard Downie, and Norman J. Vig (Eds.),

The Global Environment: Institutions, Law, and Policy (Washington, DC: CQ Press, 2005), 108–109.

25. David Leonard Downie, "Global Environmental Policy: Governance through Regimes," in Regina S. Axelrod, David Leonard Downie, and Norman J. Vig (Eds.), *The Global Environment*, 74.

26. Maryann Cusimano Love, "Globalization: A Virtue or a Vice?" in Siamack Shojai (Ed.), *Globalization: A Virtue or A Vice?* (New York: Praeger Publishers, 2000).

27. U.N. Development Program, Human Development Report 1999 (New York: Oxford University Press, 1999), 1–8; Ignacio Ramonet, "Dueling Globalization: Let Them Eat Big Macs," *Foreign Policy* (Fall 1999): 126.

28. Patrick McCully, *Silenced Rivers: The Ecology and Politics of Large Dams* (London: Zed Books, 1996).

29. For a detailed description of the changing dynamics of dam buildings in these countries, see Sanjeev Khagram, *Dams, Democracy, and Development: Transnational Struggles for Power and Water*, Ph.D. dissertation, Stanford University (August 1999), 3.

30. Ross Perot, *Save Your Job, Save Our Country: Why NAFTA Must Be Stopped—Now!* (New York: Hyperion, 1993).

31. Maryann Cusimano Love and Richard Love, "Multinational Corporations: Power and Responsibility," Chapter 5 in *Beyond Sovereignty* (Belmont, CA: Wadsworth/Thomas Learning, 2006).

32. Daniel C. Esty, *Greening the GATT: Trade, Environment, and the Future* (Washington, DC: Institute for International Economics, 1994), 34.

33. Margaret Keck and Kathryn Sikkink, *Activists Beyond Borders: Advocacy Networks in International Politics* (Ithaca, NY: Cornell University Press, 1998).

34. Ibid.

35. Sanjeev Khagram, *Dams, Democracy, and Development: Transnational Struggles for Power and Water*, 25.

36. Ibid.

37. Vicki Golich, "The Nature of the Nature Problem: Environmental Interdependencies," in Maryann Cusimano Love (Ed.), *Beyond Sovereignty: Issues for a Global Agenda* (Belmont, CA: Wadsworth/Thomson Learning, 2003), 288–289.

38. Ibid.

39. Sanjeev Khagram, *Dams, Democracy, and Development: Transnational Struggles for Power and Water*, 275; Robert Wade, "Greening the Bank: The Struggle over the Environment, 1970–1995," in Davesh Kapur, John P. Lewis, and Richard Webb (Eds.), *The World Bank: Its First Half Century*, vol. 2 (Washington DC: The Brookings Institution, 1997).

40. Megan Rowling, "Bond Issue Sounds Ethical Alarm," BBC, August 9, 2005.

41. Ibid.

42. Nicole Brewer, *The New Great Walls: A Guide to China's Overseas Dam Industry*, International Rivers (July 2008), 12.

43. Deng Jin, "Huanbao Xinliliang Dengtai de Taiqian Muhou" (Background of the Emergence of New Environmental Protection Force), *Nanfang Weekend* (January 27, 2005), <www.nanfangdaily.com.cn/zm/20050127/jj/jjxw/200501270033.asp>.

44. Andrew C. Mertha, *China's Water Warriors* (Ithaca: Cornell University Press, 2008), 122.

45. Yang Guobin, "Is There an Environmental Movement in China? Beware of the 'River of Anger,'" "Active Society in Formation: Environmentalism, Labor, and the Underworld in China, Woodrow Wilson International Center for Scholars Asia Program Special Report (September 2004), 4.

46. Aviva Imhof, Campaigns Director, International Rivers Network, phone interview, August 18, 2005.

47. Rivers Watch East and Southeast Asia, <http://www.rwesa.org/>.

48. Green Watershed is a Yunnan-based NGO involved in promoting sustainable development policies in river management and development. It also aims to build and expand local communities' capacity in the participation of decision making in river development projects.

49. Southeast Asia Rivers Network, "Petition to China from 83 Organizations from Thailand/ Burma on Upper Salween Dam," <www.searin.org/Th/SWD/SWDletE2.htm>.

50. Doris Shen, "Letter to President Hu Jintao," International Rivers Network, March 4, 2004, <www.irn.org/programs/nujiang/nu_hujintao_letter.pdf>.

51. Paragraph 56 of the Operational Guidelines for the Implementation of the World Heritage Convention states, "The World Heritage Committee invites the States Parties to inform the Committee, through the UNESCO Secretariat, of their intention to undertake or to authorize in an area protected under the Convention, major restorations or new constructions which may affect the World Heritage value of the property. Notice should be given as soon as possible (for instance, before drafting basic documents for specific projects) and before making any decisions that would be difficult to reverse, so that the World Heritage Committee may assist in seeking appropriate solutions to ensure that the World Heritage value of the site is fully preserved." Letters on file with author.

52. "23 Chinese Groups Write to World Heritage Committee over Nu River Dam Plan," e-mail communication on file with author.

53. IUCN Letter to Kevin Yuk-shing Li, February 25, 2005.

54. Wang Luxiang, "Da Jiangtang: Nujiang Shuidian Kaifa de Weixie" (Threats from the Nu River Hydropower Construction), Phoenix TV, June 28, 2004, <http://210.51.8.60/ home/zhuanti/fhxd/sjdjt/200406/28/282671.html>; Jim Yardley, "Beijing Suspends Plan for Large Dam," *The New York Times* (April 8, 2004), <www.irn.org/programs/ nujiang/index.php?id=041304_ihtnyt.html>; Jim Yardley, "Dam Building Threatens China's Grand Canyon," *The New York Times* (March 10, 2004), <www.irn.org/ programs/nujiang/index.php?id=041304_nyt.html>.

CHAPTER THIRTEEN

Mind the Gaps

Global Problems Outpace Institutions

Maryann Cusimano Love

"The human family is a dysfunctional family. What is needed is a network of structures, institutions, principles and elements of law to help manage in the best possible way the world's common good, which cannot be protected only by individual governments."[1]

—Archbishop Diarmuid Martin, Archbishop of Dublin and Former Vatican Representative to the United Nations and Specialized Agencies in Geneva

"It is extraordinary to me that you can find $700 billion to save Wall Street and the entire G8 can't find $25 billion to save 25,000 children who die every day of preventable treatable disease and hunger. That's mad, that is mad. Bankruptcy is a serious business and we all know people who have lost their jobs. But this is moral bankruptcy."

—Bono

"A world connected by trade and technology must be bound by common values."[2]

—Mary Robinson, Executive Director, Realizing Rights: The Ethical Globalization Initiative; UN High Commissioner for Human Rights, 1997–2002; President of Ireland, 1992–1997

Every year, 7 million children under 5 die of preventable causes—diarrhea, malaria, malnutrition—primarily in poor countries—approximately one Holocaust each year.[3] Two million people die from AIDS and 1.6 million die from tuberculosis each year, primarily because they are too poor to afford life-saving and life-prolonging medicines. In one hospital in Malawi, a trickle of patients with money come in one end of the building, pay $1 a day, and receive the life-saving triple cocktail medication that manages their HIV and AIDS. The other end of the hospital corridor is where most of Malawi's AIDS patients go. Too poor to afford the $1 treatment, they are brought to the hospital not for medicine or care but to die. They are ware-housed 4 to a bed, 2 head to foot on the mattress, and 2 on the floor below. Families gather to say goodbye, and the hospital waits for the disease to run its deadly course as other patients are treated just steps away.

This scenario is repeated every day throughout sub-Saharan Africa and developing countries in a life-and-death example of institutional gaps. The public health and government institutions of these regions do not have the capacity to save their citizens. Other countries have public health in-stitutions with greater capacity, but Malawi's problems are beyond their jurisdiction.

Because of sovereign jurisdictions, other governments do not regard it as their responsibility to help the dying. International response has saved millions of lives, but governments have promised more funds to the Global Fund to Treat AIDS, tuberculosis, and malaria than they have delivered.[4] Until the Doha meeting, World Trade Organization (WTO) rules pro-tected the profits of pharmaceutical companies more forcefully than they protected the lives of the sick and poor—and denied affordable generic drugs because of WTO rules that protected pharmaceutical patents.[5] Today, more lenient WTO rules allow governments to license generic pro-duction of essential medicines to fight public health emergencies. But this does little to aid the sick in Malawi, where the average life expectancy is 43 years and more than 53 percent of the population lives below the pov-erty line.[6] Malawi is too poor to produce generic drugs locally. Although a few multinational corporations (MNCs) have pledged to sell their medica-tions at reduced prices, these prices are still beyond the purchasing power of the poor in Malawi. Millennium Development Goal 6 aims to combat HIV/AIDS, to stop the spread of HIV/AIDS by 2015 and begin reversing it, but according to the WHO, developing countries are not on track to meet these targets. Seventy percent of those needing antiretroviral drugs in developing countries receive no treatment.[7] While great progress has been made in distributing antiretroviral drugs to the poor, much work remains; in many sub-Saharan African countries, fewer than 10 percent of those needing HIV/AIDS drugs receive treatment.[8]

As a heavily indebted, poor country, Malawi has implemented struc-tural adjustment programs required by the international financial institu-tions (IFIs) since the 1980s, cutting public spending internally (including on health care and education needed for HIV and AIDS treatment) in or-der to increase external debt repayment.[9] Such actions have led to legiti-macy gaps as the poor of the world question whether the WTO and other IFIs rightly represent their interests. It is also evidence of an ethical or values gap, as the market values pursued by pharmaceutical companies, governments, and IFIs are at odds with the important societal value of saving human life. A review by Doctors Without Borders found that only 21 out of 1,556 new drugs put on the market between 1975 and 2004 were for diseases endemic to developing countries.[10] At the same time, many more drugs were created for developed markets for non-life-threatening afflictions such as acne. The disparity results from market assessments of who can pay rather than from medical assessments of pressing human needs. Efficiently functioning markets can still allow millions to die. Markets create profits. They do not solve all human problems.

INSTITUTIONAL GAPS

Global economic and technological change is fast, while government, legal, and intergovernmental responses are slow. This creates institutional gaps between the problems of globalization and attempts to manage them.[11] These institutional gaps are growing. As on September 11, governments are often surprised by these gaps. For example, when the governments of the Philippines, Britain, and Japan wanted to combat problems of cyberthreats, they found they had neither the organizational nor the legal tools to do so.[12] They had to create new institutions.

Institutions range from "formal organizations, which have explicit rules and forms of administration and enforcement, to any stabilized pattern of human relationships and actions."[13] Generally agreed-upon societal norms and specific treaties or organizations with a routine way of doing business may be referred to as *institutions*. The institutions considered here, however, are a much narrower group: the organizations (whether unilateral or multilateral) that carry out foreign policy. By taking a narrower focus, we can examine theories of bureaucratic organizations as well as institutions writ large. Unlike the broader definition of institution (which can incorporate ideas, behavioral patterns, roles, and even ceremonies such as marriage), the institutions addressed in this chapter are specific in time and space. They have addresses. They are organizations that are generally arranged bureaucratically and hierarchically.

Existing states and international regimes are having difficulties coping with the challenges globalization brings because globalization creates and exacerbates institutional gaps. These institutional gaps fall into several categories: capacity, jurisdictional, participation, legitimacy, and ethical value. Capacity gaps are shortfalls in organizations or organizational strength, resources, personnel, competence, or standard operating procedures that hinder a state's ability to effectively respond to problems of globalization. Jurisdiction gaps are found when the writ of the problem extends farther than the authority of the institutions charged with responding to the problem. Participation gaps exist when people affected by globalization are excluded from partaking in the decision processes of managing or guiding globalization, earlier described as "democracy deficits." Legitimacy gaps are found when the institutions that manage or regulate globalization are not perceived by society as rightfully representing them. Ethical or values gaps arise when globalization is perceived either to have no ethical base or to promulgate values that are at odds with societal values or the common good.

All of the preceding chapters discussed capacity gaps, ways in which global problems challenge institutions' abilities to effectively respond. From containing terrorism to containing disease, capacity gaps vex state, multilateral, and private-sector institutions. Besides the problem of speed (institutions moving slower than global problems), there are other reasons why governments alone cannot effectively respond to globalization's problems. Many regimes have only shaky control over their respective territories. The last decade has seen an increase in the number of failed states and states destabilized by democratic and market transitions and internal conflict. Lack of institutional capacity and resources hamstrings many governments' abilities to respond to global problems.

Comparatively speaking, developed democracies are better equipped to meet the challenges of globalization because they have adaptive and well-resourced political and economic institutions that are capable of responding to the dislocations, disruptions, and unintended consequences that globalization brings. States with adequate educational and public health systems and access to technology, coupled with stable governance, allow people access, an on-ramp to the globalization highway. But for many developing and newly democratizing states, rule of law and political and economic institutions are weak; they lack the capacity and resources to respond to globalization's challenges. Even strong states may lack capacity, as growth in the private sector (legal and illegal) has outpaced growth in the public sector by design. Weak and strong states both have capacity gaps, as evidenced by the September 11 attacks. They are more severe for developing states, collapsing states, and states undergoing transitions.

Yet even strong states cannot manage global problems alone because the issues cross jurisdictional and territorial boundaries. Jurisdiction gaps are described throughout this book, arising when problems cross borders but governments are still constrained by borders in their abilities to respond. Cybercriminals and international terrorists attack from a distance. Bringing them to justice is complicated by these jurisdictional gaps. In addition, the private sector often has better information and technology for containing global problems, while public-sector capabilities lag behind. For example, the transportation and financial infrastructures exploited by the September 11 terrorists were all privately owned and operated, further complicating government's jurisdictional reach. Terrorism crosses international and public–private jurisdictions, making governmental responses necessary but insufficient to successfully manage these problems. As democratization and growing capitalism spread liberal political and economic systems globally, more states find themselves constitutionally limited in what interventions they may undertake in the private sphere. Even when states may wish to intervene, such as in the face of the global economic recession or grave public health threats, they may not have effective tools to do so. IGOs are also increasing in number, resources, functions, and power, but IGOs and states alone cannot solve globalization problems because many of the factors that constrain individual states also constrain collections of states. This again creates gaps between what institutions can do and what they are needed to do.

Institutional gaps also exist between rich and poor. Generally, the wealthy have institutions with more capabilities to act on their behalf; the poor often do not.[14] The rural poor have less opportunity to access globalization's benefits. Poor countries and peoples face institutional gaps that fuel the increasing backlash against globalization. Lacking resources, the institutions of poor countries are disadvantaged when bargaining with more powerful countries' institutions over the rules and regimes that govern globalization. For example, although most of the planet's populations are poor people living in developing countries, multilateral institutions such as the WTO and WIPO often favor the intellectual property rights and profits of MNCs at the expense of the poor (through TRIPS and TRIMS).[15] In what developing countries refer to as *biopiracy*, local farmers are being told they cannot continue practices of creating seed banks or certain traditional medicines without paying fees to MNCs who now own the intellectual property, patents, and copyrights for these. Although multinational pharmaceutical companies use the populations of developing countries for human testing of potential medicines in the research and development phases, these poor people and countries often do not share in the benefits of these medicines once they are approved because the poor cannot afford the cure.

Poor peoples and countries do not have adequate participation in the decision-making processes that channel globalization, from corporate boardrooms to annual World Economic Forum summits to the Group of Eight meetings. The 30 poorest member states of the WTO cannot afford to send delegations to represent and negotiate on their own behalf in Geneva. The participation gaps, capacity gaps, and asymmetric distribution of costs and benefits intensify dissatisfaction and backlash against globalization. Institutions that do not adequately protect developing countries and those that exclude them from decision-making processes are increasingly seen as illegitimate by those who are excluded. These various institutional gaps are self-reinforcing. Institutions must be perceived as legitimate to be effective, and participation gaps exacerbate legitimacy gaps, which in turn intensify capacity gaps.

The participation and legitimacy gaps also further the ethical and values gap. Many observers believe that corporations rule the world[16] and that globalization puts profits ahead of people. Although powerful multinational corporations seek profits, states seek wealth and development in globalization. Many decry the degree to which rich states, particularly the United States, drive globalization, putting market values ahead of other values. Most of the world's poor are not citizens of the developed states, leaving rich states with no jurisdictional or perceived ethical obligations to the world's dispossessed. Thus, whether driven by powerful companies or powerful states, many observers decry the ethical basis of globalization, believing globalization is driven by an ethic of crass materialism and consumption or Western (especially U.S.) cultural imperialism.[17] To the extent that this ethos pervades globalization, many people suggest that the violence and backlash against globalization will increase, producing a world in which the benefits of globalization reach too few people and countries, making the dynamics of globalization politically unsustainable.[18]

The ethical gaps are large and growing. Today, more than half of the world's citizens are not receiving the benefits of globalization, either because they are not plugged into the global economy or because they do not have institutions that can advance or protect their interests as participants in the global economy. Human life is lost, human development unfulfilled, and creation destroyed. This disparity between those who benefit from globalization and those who are left behind or vulnerable to its challenges is increasing. The world's poorest populations are growing, while the populations of developed countries are stable or slightly declining with the graying of the baby boomers. For example, world population is expected to grow from its current 6.8 billion to 9 billion in the next 15 years. Ninety-seven percent of that population growth will occur in developing countries and in already stressed urban areas—megacities such as Lagos and Mexico City.[19] Therefore, globalization's moral and ethical problems will only intensify. The values gap is exacerbated by the legitimacy, jurisdictional, and participation gaps. As Benjamin Barber notes, we must combat a malevolent interdependence (of terrorists and human smugglers, etc.) with a benevolent "democratic architecture of interdependence."[20]

POLITICAL SCIENCE AND OBSTACLES TO ORGANIZATIONAL CHANGE

How can we build institutions that better address global problems and better protect and promote peace and prosperity for more people on the planet? How can we change institutions to address the institutional gaps exacerbated by globalization? Political scientists have many theories about institutional change, but most of them tend to be pessimistic, emphasizing the obstacles to changing institutions. This chapter will consider 5 approaches in the political science literature on institutional change, those of rationalists, reflectivists, institutionalists, bureaucratic and organizational theorists, and political psychologists.[21]

Rationalists

Rationalists stress that institutions are rational reactions to the environments that states face. States create institutions because it is in their interest to do so. They expect that benefits will flow to them from the institutional arrangements that will be worth the cost.[22] Institutions reflect the power, resources, and interests of states at the time of their creation (which is why Germany and Japan, defeated powers when the UN Security Council was created, do not have veto power or status as permanent members of the Security Council). States create institutions, and thus states can change institutions whenever they want, which usually occurs when the distribution of power or resources has changed.

Sunk costs are an obstacle to institutional change, however. States are attentive to how much time, attention, and resources they have already poured into an institution, and thus they are not likely to change institutions quickly or lightly. The other permanent members of the Security Council have few incentives to change the institution to now include Germany and Japan.

Reflectivists

Reflectivists emphasize that institutions are constructed based on ideas, norms, values, culture, and history.[23] For example, although the structure of the United Nations represented the interests of the World War II victors, it also reflected the lessons learned from the failure of the League of Nations. The structure of NATO represented not only the interest of containing the USSR's power, but also ideas about promoting democracy in Western

Europe and cooperation among democratic states. States are not billiard balls moved only by power dynamics, and institutions are not mere puppets of states. An institution can assume a life of its own. Actors often do not know exactly what outcomes they want in advance, and value-based institutions help shape and create their interests. Ideas and norms change, and so institutions can change. But existing institutions will affect and constrain change.[24]

Institutionalists

Institutionalists stress the importance of history, path dependency, and chance. Actors never have the entire universe of possible organizational varieties from which to choose. They must choose from the options that are available to them; earlier selections narrow the options.[25] Even if another choice later appears more efficient, changeover costs may wipe out any gains. Gatekeeping and self-censorship are also obstacles to change. Dominant forms may actively work to keep out alternative forms, or alternatives may try to make themselves resemble the dominant form so they will be accepted into the system. People conceive of the world and themselves within current institutional frameworks (vertical linkages), and existing organizations have many standardized ways of doing business with other organizations (horizontal linkages). Vertical and horizontal linkages (concepts and relations with others) allow institutional structures to persist even after the circumstances created to deal with them have changed and institutions have become inefficient or outmoded. These links create formidable obstacles to institutional change.[26]

Change happens in fits and starts (punctuated equilibrium) and is constrained by the weight of existing organizational structures. Rapid change can occur unexpectedly if "a stable structure is stressed beyond its buffering capacity to resist and absorb [change],"[27] but such examples are rare because institutions actively influence the environment to promote their own survival. More often, old institutions are retrofitted to do new tasks. Even though these structures may not be the most efficient or logical way to tackle a new problem, the existing structure has the advantage of being available: "Credit cards can be used to open doors."[28] UN peacekeeping troops may be used to fight famine in Somalia; commercial airlines may be used as weapons. Having the tool often leads to its use.

Bureaucratic and Organizational Theorists

The bureaucratic and organizational approach stresses the role and effect of domestic and internal politics on institutional structures. Many theorists of this approach are "in-and-outers" in government service, so they focus on characteristics that policy makers and practitioners believe are important.[29] They describe bureaucratic organizations as semifeudal agencies, each fighting to protect its turf and to guard its missions, budgets, functions, personnel, resources, and autonomy. Internal conflicts may exist in organizations between bureaucratic chiefs and followers, but in general personnel are socialized (through training, standard operating procedures, and advancement incentives) into certain shared organizational viewpoints (vertical linkages).[30] Bureaucratic organizations may engage in strategic bargains with others. Agencies may give up subsidiary functions in order to protect primary ones. They may bow out of fights with more powerful agencies if they believe they cannot win and want to survive and preserve resources. But regardless of the specific strategy, organizations will seek to promote their own survival—and change will come slowly, in an incremental fashion, and when viewed as necessary to organizational survival. Change that is seen as threatening to the organization's missions, functions, budgets, autonomy, or personnel will be resisted.

Much of what is perceived as bureaucratic waste and inefficiency is actually the result of conflicting purposes given to public-sector organizations. Different expectations exist for public and private organizations. As Milton Friedman put it, "the moral responsibility of business is to make a profit."[31] Government organizations raise different expectations. We care about what they produce as well as how they produce it. In some cases, what is produced is so nebulous (national security, for example) and hard to measure that greater emphasis and constraints are placed on the process (which can be seen and measured). We may not be entirely sure what we want the military to do or how it may best produce national security, but we know a lot about how we expect the military to operate. For example, the U.S. military was under strict orders to integrate the armed services decades before the rest of American society integrated. We expect the marketplace to offer better treatment to those who can pay more. We expect the government to treat all citizens equally.

Because government bureaucracies face greater operational constraints than private bureaucracies, it is unrealistic to expect them to operate as efficiently as their private counterparts, but many organizational reform proposals are based entirely on this flawed premise. Proposals for UN and IMF reform often focus on the size of the organization rather than what it is needed to do; by definition, downsizing, defunding, and privatizing the existing machine for budgetary purposes are good (less is more, according to this view). Although cost savings, organizational efficiency, and simplified chains of command are all laudable goals, these reforms are not aimed at making the organization better able to manage global issues. Focusing exclusively on cutting budgets and bodies may actually hamper the United Nations' capacities to respond to global problems. Scholar James Q. Wilson is skeptical of trying to change organizations through additional regulations or external reorganization plans without parallel changes in internal incentives. If executives favor change, if they change the incentive structure (through training and promotion opportunities) to reward innovation and encourage the rank and file to innovate, then organizations may change—but such change will not be quick or easy.

Institutions are inherently political animals. Every organizational structure was created as a result of political negotiation enacted into law. Thus, every organization is based on the political coalitions that won out or the compromise that was reached in order to create an institutional structure. Powerful actors rarely get what they want because institutional structures represent compromise and bargaining among groups. In addition, institutions are not particularly adaptive or efficient in response to changes in the external environment:

> The choices about structure that are made in the first period, when the agency is designed and empowered with a mandate, are normally far more enduring and consequential than those that will be made later. . . . Most of the pushing and hauling in subsequent years is likely to produce only incremental change. This, obviously, is very much on everyone's minds in the first period.[32]

Structures may be quite ill-suited to organizational goals by design. In democracies, organizational structures were created by groups who wanted to address particular needs, curry favor with political constituents, or wrest power or functions from existing organizations. Controlling mechanisms were foisted on organizations by opponents who either did not want particular issue areas addressed or did not want the new organization to succeed or become too powerful, or sometimes by proponents of the original organization who, fearful that political opponents would control the organization at some future point, wanted to limit the damage the opponents could do. Changing institutions is therefore not about making more efficient structures, but about changing political balances. There are no easy answers—if they existed, they would have been implemented long ago:

> It would be nice to say that there is an easy way out of all this, that the nation can have an effective public bureaucracy if only it wants one. But this is probably not so. A bureaucracy that is structurally unsuited

for effective action is precisely the kind of bureaucracy that interest groups and politicians routinely and deliberately create ... [B]ecause they are forced to design bureaucracy through a democratic process, their structural choices turn out to be very different indeed from those intended to promote effective organization.[33]

Moe expects bureaucratic structures to be "grotesque" and "bizarre," not efficient or easily adapted. Ironically, this point is lost on many think tanks that produce many ideas of how to reform specific foreign policy organizations for greater efficiency and effectiveness without attention to changing the underlying political coalitions. Without the political support to bring them to fruition, these ideas often die on the vine.

Political Psychologists

Another helpful academic approach to understanding institutional change has been undertaken by political psychologists. These authors also stress the difficulty of changing conceptual or belief systems, and the ways in which outmoded beliefs can persist despite changes in external circumstances. Individual decision makers and small decision-making groups are important in international politics. People make policy, and people create and lead institutions, so people can bring about change. Conceptual change is necessary for institutions to change, but it does not come easily or precipitously, because change in beliefs is "gradual and ragged."[34]

For example, Deborah Larson studied the origins of Cold War ideas and institutions. For an extended period, policy makers themselves did not know what course of action to pursue and what to think about Soviet behavior and the nature of the new postwar world. They did not develop new beliefs in the abstract, but they were forced by circumstances to deal with the changed environment. They improvised and developed ad hoc policy responses, tinkering with a variety of sometimes contradictory approaches. Policy makers often knew their old ideas were inadequate, but they did not discard them quickly because they had no replacement theory. Decision makers were forced to act, and out of those actions they gradually developed new ideas, which they then used to justify their past and subsequent actions and to create new organizations. "Forged in the fires" of action and crisis, "ideology leads to the development of policy doctrines that become institutionalized through the creation of bureaucracies. In particular, the Cold War ideology underlay a vast expansion of the power and resources of the executive branch of the U.S. government."[35] Changing ideas made organizational change possible. Larson's account parallels our current period of institutional tinkering.

The literature agrees that change is difficult. It will be resisted by bureaucracies that see change as threatening to their missions, functions, budgets, personnel, autonomy, or standard operating procedures. Peripheral tasks will be easier to change than core tasks. In democratic systems, change can be initiated by legislators, prime ministers or presidents, interest groups, and voters, but even externally imposed changes need some degree of internal support if the proposed changes are to be carried out in accordance with the spirit of the law and not just its letter. Ideas may need to change before organizations can change, and they may change only through hands-on experience in grappling with a changed environment. Leadership, concepts, and coalitions are needed for change.

MACHIAVELLI WAS RIGHT: CHANGE IS THE ONLY CONSTANT

What is often overlooked in the literature's emphasis on the obstacles to organizational change are the facts that (1) change does occur, and (2) sometimes the same characteristics of bureaucratic and organizational behavior that are cited as obstacles to change can be marshaled to promote institutional change. It seems, after all these years, that Machiavelli is still right. Change is the only constant in politics. Perhaps the only thing organizations fear and resist more than change is their own obsolescence or threats to their survival. If organizations are seen as ineffective, outdated anachronisms, then they may have powerful incentives for reinventing themselves to survive with the changing times. It is not merely a matter of cosmetics. Organizations do not want to put their personnel or resources at risk. If older standard operating procedures are seen as no longer being able to protect personnel or resources, then organizations will have powerful incentives to change the way they do business. After September 11, there was little argument that institutions must change to better contain the threats of terrorism. After the global economic meltdown there was little argument that financial institutions must change to produce greater market stability and prevent fraud and cascading financial crises. The only debates have been over how best to do so.

Organizations do not want to appear outdated—and not just because they want to convince political decision makers of their validity, necessity, and fiscal worth. Although some bureaucrats may be concerned only with maintaining their paychecks, many others want to use their organizations to effectively perform tasks. Most bureaucrats consider themselves members of some profession, and their professional ethics prompt them to want to pursue effective action in their field. Thus, there will always be advocates for change within any institution: people who see better ways to do their jobs or who want to improve their institutions' abilities in a changing world.

Once these agents for change begin interacting with the environment, the results may be unpredictable. Gorbachev did not set out to dismantle the USSR. He tried to improve worker productivity and cut down on alcohol abuse on the job in an attempt to improve the performance of Soviet institutions. But the changes he unleashed had the unintended but eventual consequence of ending the Soviet empire.

As people engage in the process of changing institutions, the process may change the people as well. Perhaps you can't always get what you want in institutional structure. But if Larson is correct about how people revise their belief systems, then we may not know what we want until we engage in the process and begin to learn from experience. Thus, although action for change may come from individuals or political coalitions in alliance with reformers within institutions, the process may change as the institutions interact with the agents for change and vice versa.

Institutional change is occurring in fits and starts. As we experience the institutional gaps posed by globalization, new concepts for change, leaders, and coalitions are emerging to address globalization's gaps with the aid of reformers within organizations. Governments, multilateral institutions, and private institutions are hard at work, especially in addressing capacity gaps.

Governments of developed countries address capacity gaps by creating new bureaucratic organizations or changing old ones, changing laws and policies that direct these institutions, and adding resources. Poor countries have fewer resources to address their governments' capacity gaps, so IGOs and NGOs also work to bridge them. Multilateral organizations and NGOs address capacity gaps of state institutions in developing countries by offering technological assistance or training, for example, to bridge the digital divide. Although some businesses exploit low capacity in developing governments, most MNCs desire greater capacity in developing countries' institutions in order to have a stable and predictable business environment governed by rule of law. But poorer countries will always have fewer resources to fund their institutions, and in an effort to attract foreign direct investment may even forgo further tax revenues, further exacerbating capacity gaps.

State and multilateral institutions are increasingly trying to borrow or buy capacity from the private sector. Whether in deterring cyberthreats or terrorism, protection of critical infrastructure (largely privately owned and operated) requires the cooperation of the private sector. Governments and IGOs increasingly contract out to the private sector to provide key capacities. The Australian government, for example, hires a private company to run refugee camps. Private companies are de-mining Afghanistan and de-nuclearizing the arsenals of the former Soviet Union on behalf of the U.S. government. Through the voluntary Global Compact, the United Nations works to harness the capacity of businesses to fight environmental, human rights, and labor abuses. Working with the private sector has meant forming new collaborative networks to help monitor, report, and share information on problems; contribute to policy solutions; and implement policy to manage global problems. Across a variety of issue areas, diverse foreign policy institutions are widening their contacts and partnerships with the private sector.

Rather than creating entirely new state agencies to deal with global problems, existing institutions are developing new integrating and coordinating mechanisms that cross agency and public–private sector boundaries. For example, to avert Y2K-related problems globally, unprecedented public–private partnerships shared information about problems and best practices for solutions. Governments had neither the resources nor the know-how to tackle the problem, and most of the infrastructure to be protected was in the private sector. The private sector had selected sets of information but no forum by which to share that information across organizations and internationally. The costs of Y2K-related repairs were estimated at between $300 billion and $500 billion internationally. Problems still occurred. Some Italian prisoners had a century added to or subtracted from their jail sentences. France lost satellite communications with its troops in Bosnia. Four thousand U.S. small businesses failed to download Y2K-compliant credit-card billing software and lost business while banks reversed erroneous double and triple credit-card charges to more than 40,000 customers who made purchases in the first days after the date changed to 2000. But Russian nuclear missiles were not accidentally fired, air traffic control systems generally worked, and many other Y2K-related concerns were averted.[36]

Borrowing ideas from the private sector and from computer technology about connectivity, institutions are generally not trying to create large, new, hierarchical federal bureaucracies that attempt to control activities and impose policy solutions from the top down (as was done after World War II). Instead, state institutions are trying to serve as better facilitators, coordinators, and integrators of information and action across a wide variety of actors and issues. Networking may be difficult for government organizations because they are organized as hierarchical bureaucracies, whereas NGOs and other nonstate actors may not be. State institutions' roles, missions, functions, procedures, authority, accountability, and chains of command are often more clearly demarcated than those of nonstate actors. NGOs often have flatter and looser organizations, and bureaucratic government organizations may find it difficult to determine who's in charge. When a bureaucratically organized institution attempts to coordinate and integrate information and action with a less hierarchically organized institution, they may "talk past each other." The bureaucratic organization wonders how anyone can function in such fluid chaos without standardized ways of doing business. The nonbureaucratic organization wonders why the bureaucracy cannot be more flexible to the nuances of the emerging situation. Differences in communication, culture, and organization make networking difficult but not impossible, as when international bankers in the IFIs try to reach out more systematically to the NGO community.

To create new institutions or adapt existing institutions to better leverage the resources of the private sector, institutions must increasingly go not just beyond sovereignty but also beyond bureaucracy. Called postbureaucratic organizations, these organizational forms stress integrative and interactive networks that are based on ideas drawn from successful entrepreneurs and technologies.[37] Often when government reformers talk of moving beyond bureaucracy and "reinventing government," what they really mean is cleaning up bureaucracy and making government more like a business.[38] Despite the grandiose language of a "paradigm shift,"[39] these reforms really do not demolish bureaucracy but streamline and downsize overgrown and inefficient bureaucracy. Although it has some advantages, this approach is limited in how far it can go given the differences discussed earlier between businesses and governments. But some of the current reforms break down or circumvent bureaucracy's formal, rule-bound structures based on clear demarcations of hierarchy and office.

These postbureaucratic organizational forms are flatter and more adaptive, based not on hierarchical chains of command but on interdependent webs of actors.[40] The benefits of this type of structure are increased flexibility, increased information sharing regardless of rank or organizational affiliation, a greater emphasis on the job to be done than on bureaucratic rules or routines, and more fluid boundaries. These trends are facilitated by career patterns that no longer assume people will spend entire careers in one organization, and information technologies that allow the building of temporary networks of people who work together virtually on specific problems and may never meet face-to-face.[41] The problems are challenges in coordination, greater complexity, and questions of transparency and accountability.

These changes in organizational forms may help combat global problems. When the models of organization from business were large, cookie-cutter bureaucracies such as IBM, and when the external threat was a stable, monolithic, universal, hegemonic Cold War adversary, foreign policy organizations responded with large, bureaucratic, and hierarchical structures that heavily emphasized stable routines, rules, and standard operating procedures. Change makes sense now that external threats come from diffuse and decentralized networks such as cascading financial crises, terrorism, and international crime. Institutions need to be organized as networks to better fight networks. Yet sustained leadership, fresh concepts, and new political coalitions are necessary to make these changes.

MIND THE GAPS: BRIDGING INSTITUTIONAL GAPS

Globalization is intensifying institutional gaps, and there are many obstacles to institutional change. Yet change is occurring. To address capacity gaps, states and nonstate actors are partnering in new ways and using new, more networked institutional forms. To address jurisdiction gaps, governments harmonize laws and develop new or strengthen existing international regimes to better manage problems that go beyond state borders and jurisdictions. To address participation gaps, IGOs try to include NGOs in some manner in their activities. To address ethical gaps, some IGOs, NGOs, and MNCs adopt voluntary codes of conduct. To address legitimacy gaps, IGOs are increasing transparency, primarily by posting information about their activities on Web sites. But Web sites and ad hoc codes of conduct and NGO forums are not enough to bridge these gaps. Powerful political coalitions continue to obstruct efforts to better address participation, legitimacy, and ethical gaps. NGOs often work to build new political coalitions to bridge these gaps through organizing grassroots support and direct-media campaigns that pressure democratic governments internally and externally, as well as applying direct pressure on MNCs to better address pressing global issues. Governments and IGOs are more concerned with capacity and jurisdiction gaps than legitimacy, participation, and ethical gaps, but IGOs cannot be effective or sustainable if these other gaps are not addressed. Powerful governments and IGOs will be increasingly targeted for sometimes violent protests as long as these gaps worsen or go unaddressed.

In Lewis Carroll's classic story *Alice in Wonderland*, the white queen chastises Alice for an insufficient imagination and tells her that expanding her imagination requires daily practice. "My dear, sometimes I think six impossible thoughts before breakfast."

Perhaps during the stability of the nearly 50-year Cold War period, our imaginations atrophied. We did not give our imaginations much practice, as indicated by an exchange in 1986 between then-director of the CIA Richard Gates and Senator Daniel Patrick Moynihan. The senator, a former academic, had noticed that all economic indicators from the Soviet Union seemed to be pointing to an end to the Soviet empire. No one in Washington agreed with Moynihan's analysis because the Reagan administration and Congress were involved in unprecedented peacetime defense spending levels in order to combat the "evil empire" of the Soviet threat. In a Senate Intelligence Committee hearing, Moynihan asked Gates what plans the agency was making for how to deal with a post-Soviet world.[42] Gates responded, "[M]y resources do not permit me the luxury of sort of just idly speculating on what a different kind of Soviet Union might look like."[43] He did not see the point of making plans for the impossible.

Today we find that the impossible has occurred. The Soviet empire collapsed, a small band of nonstate actors brought thousands of deaths and billions in damages to the world's most powerful state, and unregulated markets did not spontaneously save us but failed us. Our thoughts have not caught up with the impossible. Like Alice, we have not figured out how to think about the strange new world into which we have unexpectedly fallen.

Markets and global problems are moving faster than institutional and conceptual responses to the challenges of globalization. Of all the obstacles to organizational change, the biggest one appears to be ourselves and our limited ways of thinking about our changed world. Too often the debates over globalization are portrayed as a choice between a globalization that puts profits over people versus no globalization at all. In reality, there are more choices than that. We do not have to choose between the current form of globalization, with its mix of benefits along with its excesses and problems, or a return to a more closed, isolated, and less interdependent world. Instead of debating over false choices, we can build institutions that better represent important values; better distribute the benefits of globalization; better mitigate the problems of open economies, open societies, and open technologies; and better protect and promote the common good, building a global infrastructure that advances more authentic human development.

Change is not easy, direct, or logical, and institutions created by democracies will not be efficient in the narrow economic sense. But these observations about the obstacles to change should not obscure the fact that change is occurring, even if it is hard-fought, long in coming, constrained by political parameters, and occurring unevenly in fits and starts. Institutions are minding globalization's capacity and jurisdictional gaps, though much work remains, especially with gaps in legitimacy, participation, ethics and values. If we learn by doing and we change our ideas about the world as a result of our actions in the world (not before our actions), then we will see greater change as a result of our experiences in the changed international environment. Attention to global issues can bring increased leadership, awareness, urgency, and changed concepts and coalitions toward the problem of institutional gaps, bringing more communication, cooperation, and coordination among a wide variety of public and private actors.

ENDNOTES

1. Archbishop Diarmuid Martin, speech to the "Humanizing the Global Economy" conference of the Catholic bishops of Latin America, Canada, and the United States, Catholic University, Washington, DC, January 28, 2002.
2. Mary Robinson, "The Ethical Globalization Initiative: Realizing Rights," <www.realizingrights.org/>; <www.eginitiative.org/>.
3. Jeffrey Sachs, *The End of Poverty* (New York: Penguin Press, 2005); Sachs, speech to the "Humanizing the Global Economy" conference of the Catholic bishops of Latin America, Canada, and the United States, Catholic University, Washington, DC, January 31, 2002.
4. Donald McNeil, "Health Fund Falls Well Short of Pledge Goal," *The New York Times*, September 28, 2007; The Global Fund to Fight AIDS, Malaria, and Tuberculosis, "Funding Gap," <www.theglobalfund.org/en/funds_raised/funding_gap/>.
5. World Trade Organization (WTO), Declaration on the Trips Agreement and Public Health, November 14, 2001 (Doha), <http://docsonline.wto.org/> (search for "Declaration on the Trips Agreement and Public Health").
6. Central Intelligence Agency, "The World Factbook 2009," <www.odci.gov/cia/publications/factbook> (check under Malawi).
7. United Nations, "Millennium Development Goals Report 2008," September 11, 2008, 30, <http://mdgs.un.org/unsd/mdg/Resources/Static/Products/Progress2008/MDG_Report_2008_En.pdf>.
8. Ibid.
9. WTO, "Trade Policy Reviews: Summaries and Conclusions," <www.wto.org/english/tratop_e/tpr_e/tp_rep_e.htm#malawi2002>.
10. Robert Weissman, *Daily Times of Malawi*, May 7, 2008.
11. Maryann Cusimano Love, "Globalization and Religion," International Studies Association annual meeting, Chicago, February 24, 2001; Maryann Cusimano Love, "Bridging the Gap: Globalization and Religion, and the Institutions of the U.S. Catholic Church," American Academy of Religions annual conference, Denver, CO, November 20, 2001; Maryann Cusimano Love, "Globalization and Religion," *Journal of Social Thought*.
12. Maryann Cusimano *Love, Public–Private Partnerships and Global Problems: Y2K and Cybercrime.* Paper delivered to the International Studies Association, Hong Kong meeting, July 2001.
13. Jack Knight, *Institutions and Social Conflict* (Cambridge, UK: Cambridge University Press, 1996), 2.
14. World Bank, "World Development Report 2006: Equity and Development," <http://wdsbeta.worldbank.org/external/default/WDSContentServer/IW3P/IB/2005/09/20/000112742_20050920110826/additional/841401968_200508263002017.pdf>.
15. WIPO is the World Intellectual Property Organization. TRIPS are Trade-Related Intellectual Property Rights, and TRIMS are Trade-Related Investment Measures.

16. David C. Korten, *When Corporations Rule the World* (West Hartford, CT: Kumarian Press, 1995); Richard Falk, *Predatory Globalization: A Critique* (Malden, MA: Blackwell, 1999); John Gray, *False Dawn: The Delusions of Global Capitalism* (New York: New Press, 1998).

17. Joseph E. Stiglitz, *Globalization and Its Discontents* (New York: W. W. Norton, 2003); Ignacio Ramonet, "Dueling Globalizations: Let Them Eat Big Macs," *Foreign Policy* (Fall 1999): 116–121, 125–127; Thierry Linard de Gueterchin, S. J., "A Christmas Present for the Ford Workers in the ABC of Sao Paulo," Centro Cultural de Brasilia: Global Economies and Culture Project, in conjunction with the Woodstock Theological Center, Georgetown University, Washington, DC, April 6, 1999; Dani Rodrik, *Has Globalization Gone Too Far?* (Washington, DC: Institute for International Economics, 1997).

18. Amy Chua, *World on Fire: How Exporting Free Market Democracy Breeds Ethnic Hatred and Global Instability* (New York: Anchor, 2004); James Mittelman, *The Globalization Syndrome: Transformation and Resistance* (Princeton, NJ: Princeton University Press, 2000); Mark Juergensmeyer, "The Worldwide Rise of Religious Nationalism," *Journal of International Affairs* 50(1); Benjamin R. Barber, *Jihad vs. McWorld: How Globalism and Tribalism Are Reshaping the World* (New York: Ballantine, 1995); Samuel Huntington, "Clash of Civilizations," *Foreign Affairs* 72(3), 22–28.

19. Population Reference Bureau, "2009 World Population Data," August 12, 2009, <http://www.prb.org/Publications/Datasheets/2009/2009wpds.aspx>.

20. Benjamin Barber, "Mutual Aid Society on a Grand Scale," *Los Angeles Times*, (November 17, 2002), <www.democracycollaborative.org/publications/books/barber_111702.html>.

21. Robert Keohane, "International Institutions: Two Approaches," *International Studies Quarterly* (1988): 379–396; Steven Weber, "Institutions and Change," in Michael W. Doyle and G. John Ikenberry (Eds.), *New Thinking in International Relations Theory* (Boulder, CO: Westview Press, 1997), 229–265; Stephen Krasner, "Sovereignty: An Institutional Perspective," *Comparative Political Studies* (April 1988): 66–94; Graham Allison and Philip Zelikow, *The Essence of Decision: Explaining the Cuban Missile Crisis*, 2nd ed. (Reading, MA: Longman, 1999); I. M. Destler, *Presidents, Bureaucrats, and Foreign Policy* (Princeton, NJ: Princeton University Press, 1972); Francis Rourke, *Bureaucracy and Foreign Policy* (Baltimore: Johns Hopkins University Press, 1974); Morton Halperin, *Bureaucratic Politics and Foreign Policy* (Washington, DC: Brookings Institution, 1974); Terry Moe, "The Politics of Bureaucratic Structure," in John E. Chubb and Paul E. Peterson (Eds.), *Can the Government Govern?* (Washington, DC: Brookings Institution, 1989); Deborah Larson, *The Origins of Containment: A Psychological Explanation* (Princeton, NJ: Princeton University Press, 1985).

22. Keohane, "International Institutions: Two Approaches," 386–387.

23. Weber, "Institutions and Change," 235; Michael Barnett and Martha Finnemore, *Rules for the World: International Organizations in Global Politics*. (Ithaca, NY: Cornell University Press, 2004); Martha Finnemore, *National Interests in International Society* (Ithaca, NY: Cornell University Press, 1996).

24. Finnemore, *National Interests in International Society*.

25. Krasner, "Sovereignty: An Institutional Perspective," 83.

26. Ibid., 66.

27. Ibid., 79.

28. Ibid., 80.

29. Allison and Zelikow, *The Essence of Decision*; I. M. Destler, *Presidents, Bureaucrats, and Foreign Policy* (Princeton, NJ: Princeton University Press, 1972); Rourke, *Bureaucracy and Foreign Policy*; Halperin, *Bureaucratic Politics and Foreign Policy*; Terry Moe, "The Politics of Bureaucratic Structure," in Chubb and Peterson, *Can the Government Govern?*

30. This is the most critiqued part of bureaucratic theory: the idea that "where you stand (on an issue) depends on where you sit (in which organization)." A cottage industry has developed to critique this aspect of bureaucratic theory. As convincing as these studies are that issue positions are not determined by organizational membership alone, it is important to note that Allison never said this was the only determinant of an actor's position; it is one factor among many. Also, many of these studies mistakenly conclude that bureaucratic and organizational dynamics were not involved when no conflict is seen among bureaucratic actors. If agencies often pursue strategic alliances, and especially if actors seek to reduce uncertainty and to be sure in advance of a meeting that they will not be blindsided, then a lack of conflict along agency lines at key meetings might not be evidence that bureaucratic politics theory has been disproved, but the phenomenon might actually be explicable according to the theory. Thus, the problem for Allison's theory is not that it has been proved wrong by numerous critical studies, but that it is too poorly specified to be proved wrong or right. Both evidence of conflict and evidence of its absence among agencies can be interpreted in light of the theory.

31. Charles Heckscher, "Defining the Post-Bureaucratic Type," in Charles Heckscher and Anne Donnellon (Eds.), *The Post-Bureaucratic Organization: New Perspectives on Organizational Change* (Thousand Oaks, CA: Sage, 1994), 27.

32. Moe, "The Politics of Bureaucratic Structure," in Chubb and Peterson, *Can the Government Govern?* 285.

33. Ibid., 329.

34. Larson, *The Origins of Containment*, 341.

35. Ibid., 349.

36. Love, *Public–Private Partnerships and Global Problems*.

37. Heckscher and Donnellon, The Post-Bureaucratic Organization. Also, a growing literature is developing in sociology on diffuse networks; see Stephen P. Borgatti, Ajay Mehra, Daniel J. Brass, Giuseppe Labianca, "Network Analysis in the Social Sciences," Science (February 13, 2009), 323(5916), 892–895; Mary Durfee and Paul Lopes (Eds.), "Networks of Novelty: The Diffusion of Ideas and Things," The Annals of the American Academy of Political and Social Sciences (Philadelphia: AAPSS, November 1999).

38. Al Gore, *Common Sense Government: Works Better and Costs Less* (New York: Random House, 1995); Al Gore, "Report on the National Performance Review," White House press releases on July 14, September 14, October 13, and December 5, 1994, and January 26, 1995; also see White House Documents, Office of the Press Secretary, "Gore Announces Initial Restructuring of Foreign Affairs Agencies," January 27, 1995; Donald F. Kettl, *Reinventing Government? Appraising the National Performance Review* (Washington, DC: Brookings Institution, 1994); Donald F. Kettl and John J. DiIulio, Jr., *Cutting Government* (Washington, DC: Brookings Institution, 1995); Ronald C. Moe, "The 'Reinventing Government' Exercise: Misinterpreting the Problem, Misjudging the Consequences," *Public Administration Review* (March–April 1994): 111–122; Gerald E. Caiden, "Administrative Reform American Style," *Public Administration Review* (March–April 1994): 123–128.

39. James P. Pinkerton, *What Comes Next: The End of Big Government and the New Paradigm Ahead* (New York: Hyperion, 1995).

40. Heckscher, "Defining the Post-Bureaucratic Type," 25.

41. Ibid., 27.

42. Daniel Patrick Moynihan, "Our Stupid but Permanent CIA: What Are We Going to Do about Reforming the Agency? Nothing," *Washington Post* (July 24, 1994): C3.

43. Richard Gates, as quoted in David M. Kennedy, *Sunshine and Shadow: The CIA and the Soviet Economy* (Cambridge, MA: Harvard University, 1991), 18.

CHAPTER FOURTEEN

Sovereignty: Who Cares?

The Future, and Why Sovereignty Is Not Enough

Maryann Cusimano Love

"The major threats we face in the 21st century—whether it's global recession or violent extremism; the spread of nuclear weapons or pandemic disease—these things do not discriminate. They do not recognize borders … Moreover, no one person, or religion, or nation can meet these challenges alone. Our very survival has never required greater cooperation and greater understanding among all people from all places than at this moment in history. Unfortunately, finding that common ground—recognizing that our fates are tied up, as Dr. King said, in a "single garment of destiny"—is not easy."

—President Barack Obama, May 17, 2009

"Where once nations depended on sovereignty alone to secure their destinies, today they depend on one another. In a world where the poverty of some imperils the wealth of others, where none are safer than the least safe, multilateralism is not a stratagem of idealists but a realistic necessity. The lesson of 9/11 was not that rogue states could be unilaterally preempted and vanquished by a sovereign United States, but that sovereignty was a chimera—that HIV and global warming and international trade and nuclear proliferation and transnational crime and predatory capital had already stolen from America the substance of its cherished sovereignty well before the terrorists displayed their murderous contempt for it on that fateful morning."[1]

—Benjamin Barber

"Partnerships among all stakeholders in society are increasingly a "must" in a world filled with complex global challenges."[2]

—President William J. Clinton, United Nations Special Envoy for Haiti and President of the United States of America (1993–2001)

Sovereignty—who cares? Why write a book about it, much less 4 books on the topic? For the more than 2 billion people, nearly one-third of the world's population, living in failed or failing states, sovereignty matters.[3]

They would like to see more sovereignty, in the form of law and order, good governance, basic capacity, effectiveness and fairness of the public sector—what academics call internal sovereignty, positive sovereignty, or domestic sovereignty. Nigerians traveling to the West are awed by the simple things: the fact that people obey traffic rules, that cars move in predictable patterns, that there are regular, routine, and transparent procedures for obtaining a driver's license in the Department of Motor Vehicles, and that money or connections will not excuse you from these procedures. They know a world in which blind men can obtain driver's licenses for the right fee, in which cars and trucks jump median strips and head the wrong way down highways in a high stakes game of "chicken" if it will get drivers around traffic tie-ups.

For the families of the 6 million people killed in the Congo, 2.5 million killed in Darfur, and 1 million killed in Iraq in the deadliest wars over the past 10 years,[4] sovereignty matters. Many are fighting for control over the sovereign state; others are fighting for self-rule, to break away and form their own sovereign state. Some are fighting for democratic sovereignty, to have the institutions of the state accountable to the people. For people of the Democratic Republic of Congo, Sudan, Palestine, and East Timor, democratic sovereignty matters.

For the 2.3 billion people (34 percent of the world's population) living in repressive states, and the 1.4 billion people (20 percent of the world's population) living in only partly free countries, sovereignty matters. It matters when the police throw your loved one in prison for criticizing the government, or for some unnamed or fabricated offense.[5] The 170 million killed at the hands of their own government leaders over the past century[6] knew the evils of sovereignty intimately. All these people daily experience predatory sovereignty, personal sovereignty (law is whatever the leader says it is, without democratic process or constraints), and criminal sovereignty (the co-optation of the state by criminal elements). What academics call negative sovereignty or the right of noninterference in states' internal affairs is what Kofi Annan decries when he says that "The sovereignty of States must no longer be used as a shield for gross violations of human rights."[7]

For the millions of immigrants out of 192 million migrants killed, imprisoned, or deported due to failure to obtain proper legal entry permission, and for the 15.4 million refugees in the world today,[8] and 27 million victims of human trafficking, pushed out of one country's borders but unable to begin life anew in another country, sovereignty matters, as the sovereign effectively denies access to jobs, food, shelter, health care, education, travel—opportunities that glimmer out of reach across the border.

Yet for those of us lucky enough to live in functioning, developed, democratic states, with positive sovereignty and democratic sovereignty,

sovereignty is not enough. It is better than living in failed states, predatory states, and nondemocratic states, to be sure, but sovereignty isn't all it is cracked up to be. For the nearly 3,000 families who lost loved ones on September 11, the unquestioned sovereignty of the United States could not protect or save them from marauders in the sky armed with box cutters. For the 33 million people around the world infected with HIV or AIDS, sovereignty cannot save them from traveling, devastating pathogens.

As people everywhere move beyond sovereignty, they do so for different reasons. People in failed and failing states, and people in predatory and criminal states look beyond sovereignty to networks of IGOs, NGOs, and even MNCs to help save them from their crumbling or abusive sovereign structures. For people in developed, democratic states, we look beyond sovereignty because even generally fair and functioning states cannot save us from pressing global problems that go beyond borders.

Sovereignty is not extinct; it persists, but in new forms and functions. We reinvent it in practice each day in our struggles to manage global issues.

GLOBALIZATION'S UNINTENDED CONSEQUENCES

Much of this book has been about globalization's unintended consequences. States, IGOs, and MNCs worked to build international markets and to create the political, economic, and technological infrastructure that made the global marketplace possible. States courted foreign direct investment and technological advancement. Through a variety of economic and political liberalization policies, states deliberately worked to increase the size of the private sector while curtailing public-sector expenditures so the private sector would not be "crowded out." They pursued these policies to increase economic development and prosperity, believing that wealthy states are strong states.

Western states sought to promote open societies, believing that democratic states are more stable trade partners and are less likely to go to war with other democracies. States did not intend, however, to create the infrastructure for global problems to thrive. State governments did not realize that the new actors and dynamics created by globalization would also drain autonomy, choice, and freedom of action away from states. Sovereignty is based on territory, yet the new economy and new actors' prosperity do not derive from territory, making them less beholden to states. How can these new dynamics and actors be managed within a system of sovereign states? How can states maintain law and order, justice and peace against licit and illicit private-sector actors who are increasingly powerful?

POLICY PRESCRIPTIONS

Policy prescriptions for managing globalization and the global problems created by open societies, economies, and technologies fall into 3 main categories: state-centric (public-sector) approaches, nonstate-centric (private-sector) responses, and mixed (public–private) responses.

The State-Centric Approach

The state-centric approach to global problems suggests that states strengthen their capacity to fight global problems, enhancing law and order institutions, control over borders, markets, multilateral cooperation among states, and interagency cooperation within states to increase states' efficacy of response.[9] In essence, this approach argues that the same forces that facilitate global problems and undermine sovereignty (open technologies, economies, and societies) can be harnessed or managed to fight global problems. States need to better use the same new technologies and market forces that are being used against them in global problems. If we could just make states smarter and get them to work together better, then states would be able to meet these challenges more effectively. If states were equipped with better technologies, with enhanced state capacity, then cooperating and sharing information and implementation would be possible and more effective across and within governments. After all, terrorists and drug traffickers are using the most advanced emerging technologies and are developing strategic relations with other criminal cartels. Why can't states do the same in their efforts to stop these illicit activities? State-centric responses can be unilateral, focusing on building the capacity of states internally. They can also be multilateral, focusing either on increasing IGO capacity or on federal, functional cooperation among government agencies (as when police or judges share information and cooperate across borders).

Anne-Marie Slaughter argues that government agencies and officials at all levels are working together across borders in unprecedented government networks to manage global problems. These connecting, harmonization, enforcement, and information networks help address capacity and jurisdiction gaps. And to the degree that government actors are democratically elected, these government-to-government networks are more legitimate, democratic, and accountable than partnerships with unelected actors such as MNCs, and NGOs. Horizontal networks coordinate action and information across governments, while vertical networks allow international coercion through state-to-IGO delegation. The result is a "New World Order" of "disaggregated sovereignty." Sovereign units respond to global problems, but they do so through new government networks.[10]

State-centric responses are seen most often in the efforts to fight the global problems of terrorism, drug smuggling, cyberthreats, transnational crime, and WMD proliferation. This is not surprising: These issues touch most closely to the security sectors where state identity and activities are strongest and where states have always been active. Interdiction, improved intelligence and law enforcement capabilities, interagency and IGO efforts to improve information sharing, cooperation, and enforcement are all examples of state-centric responses to global problems. The Proliferation Security Initiative is an example of a state-centric approach to improve countries' abilities to interdict WMD weapons and materials. Even progressive and creative programs that are fully in the cooperative security rubric—such as the Cooperative Threat Reduction programs to stem proliferation from the former Soviet Union (FSU)—fit into this category. Attempts to increase nuclear material protection, control, and accountability (MPC&A) by increasing security at FSU nuclear labs and facilities by installing security cameras, detection devices, modern accounting and storage procedures, and so on are oriented at strengthening the capacity of states.

The Nonstate-Centric Approach

The nonstate-centric policy approach emphasizes the importance of the private sector in responding to global problems. It also emphasizes the limitations of trying to work through the state for help in curtailing activities that largely fall in the social and economic sectors where the reach of liberal, capitalist states is the shortest. If state capacity is (or should be) weakening, then why ask the state to solve global problems? Why not go directly to the private sector, where the resources exist to attack the problem?

This approach emphasizes developing new responses and infrastructure that utilize nonstate actors such as NGOs and MNCs. Corporate codes of conduct to improve international environmental and labor standards, shareholder and consumer activism to change MNC policies, efforts to get pharmaceutical companies to voluntarily reduce prices and increase access to essential medicines for poor countries and people, market solutions to overcoming poverty problems through FDI, increased trade, and microbusiness (for example, Nakornthon Bank) are nonstate-centric policy prescriptions. Direct action campaigns by NGOs to change corporate or consumer behavior (for example, convincing the tuna industry to adopt dolphin-safe fishing techniques) effect change regardless of governmental participation. Efforts to fight global problems of refugee flows, disease, and environmental degradation tend to focus more readily on nonstate-centric approaches. NGO activities have traditionally been strongest in these areas. The efforts of the Gates Foundation to immunize children and fight HIV/AIDs in Africa, and the efforts of ProMED (the Program for Monitoring Emerging Diseases), a global electronic mail network that facilitates reporting on and discussion of disease outbreaks around the world, are also nonstate-centric responses.

Mixed or Public–Private Approaches

Finally, there is a third way. If public- and private-sector responses alone cannot effectively manage global issues, then why not combine the two? Public–private partnerships can reap the benefits of each separate approach while minimizing some of the problems of one approach alone. By combining the benefits of state legitimacy and enforceability with the flexibility and resources of the private sector, more traction can be brought to bear on difficult global issues.

The state still has important levers that can be used to fight global problems. David Victor of the Council on Foreign Relations invokes a Star Wars analogy. The dark side of enthusiasm about using private-sector responses is that you still need the force of the state. A state can provide threats or force, serve as negotiator or facilitator of private-sector interactions, and back-stop private-sector initiatives with a safety net baseline of law that provides more universally implementable and enforceable norms. States provide not only the sticks but also the carrots of incentives, and they can focus direction. The state has the added advantage of being familiar and available. But neither the state nor the private sector can do it alone. The choices are not between multilateralism and unilateralism, integration and fragmentation, federal government and local government, and public sector and private sector. To manage global problems, we must use all of the networks at our disposal. Choice of the institutional instrument will be based on who has the established network assets in a sector. He or she who has the network becomes the partner with the foreign policy organizations.

For example, Stephen Flynn argues that greater cooperation between the government and private-sector transportation, critical infrastructure, and shipping firms through information sharing, transparency, and in-creased security measures at the point of origin would greatly reduce trafficking in refugees, persons, drugs, and weapons, and improve responses to climate change and natural disasters as well as terrorism. The private sector wins with faster, more assured transit that boosts brand identity and leads to less money lost to stolen shipments, less time lost to backups at the border, and fewer invasive border inspections. The government wins allies in trying to manage global problems and gains information with which to better target government security and border control resources.[11] Debt-for-nature swaps, the World Commission on Dams, the United Nations Global

Compact, the Roll Back Malaria Initiative—all of these are public–private partnerships.

Thorsten Benner and Jan Martin Witte note, "Governance has gone global—and so have questions of legitimacy and accountability. The old 'club model' of international politics as a closed shop involving just governments is defunct. International organisations, nongovernmental organisations (NGOs), transnational companies—all play vital roles alongside national officials in global policymaking. Why bother with partnerships? A more appropriate question should be: What other useful mechanisms are available?"[12]

Benner and Witte argue that problems of transparency, accountability, and legitimacy can be addressed by building checks and balances into the partnerships, not with a single mechanism but through "pluralistic systems of accountability." These can include leveraging reputational accountability, peer accountability, financial accountability, process accountability, transparency about sources and uses of funding, and performance accountability.[13]

If states alone cannot adequately respond to global problems, then why is it important that they be part of the multipronged approach? The most important advantage states have is that they exist. They do not have to be built from scratch. They are familiar, with addresses and known processes that are understood and available for interaction, allowing the opportunity for transparency and accountability. States may not have the ability to command or compel resolution of a global problem, but they are uniquely positioned to coordinate, communicate, facilitate, and cajole action from a variety of other actors who look to the state to fill that conduit function. States are a focal point for citizen imagination and demands. Whether or not states can solve global problems alone, the question is still raised by the public and the media, "What is the state doing about it?"

In addition, governments are often perceived to have the political legitimacy to act on behalf of the populace in foreign affairs. Although foreign policy bureaucracies in democracies are generally not staffed by elected officials, they are created and funded by elected officials, and they can be held responsible to elected officials. Thus, state institutions must have some degree of political support to exist at all; on the other hand, it is not clear whom MNCs and NGOs represent, to whom they are accountable or how they can be held accountable, or how much political legitimacy and support they command. Why not use the institutional advantages states have of being available as a forum?

Underlying these differences over how to best respond to global problems are different assumptions about the future of the sovereign state. Is the sovereign state retreating, its power becoming more diffuse in a globalized economy? Susan Strange argues that power is moving from states to markets as states either abdicate more functions to nonstate actors or vacate certain functions altogether.[14] There is some evidence from the preceding chapters in favor of this view. Nonstate actors are increasingly taking on functions that were traditionally performed by states, even in the security sector. The example of debt-for-nature swaps supports Rosecrance's idea of the declining importance of territory relative to the rising importance of market forces.[15] If states are losing power to nonstate actors and market dynamics, then responses to global problems should be aimed at nonstate actors and market forces.

Others argue that the sovereign state is still the fundamental unit in the international system. Sovereignty took centuries to develop and will not disappear in a few decades, and there are no well-developed alternative organizing units ready to replace sovereign states.[16] The preceding chapters offer some evidence to support this view. Terrorism highlights that the state is still important enough to be worth fighting for. If this is the case and state actors still reign supreme, then efforts to fight global problems should still be aimed at states and strengthening state institutions or perhaps at developing more cooperative ventures among states.

There is a third way. If sovereignty is changing but not dead, then fighting global problems may require a combined approach in which a wide spectrum of policy responses are undertaken and coordinated, aimed at both state and nonstate sectors. If we are in a period of transition or turbulence[17]—in which a changed economic system has created new actors and dissipated the power of states in crucial economic, public health, and social sectors, but in which state actors are still important in the law enforcement and security sectors—then a combined approach is necessary. Just as new interstate highways are often built alongside existing two-lane highways, new networks using new actors must be built while the old state actors are still functioning.

For all of the advantages of pursuing public–private partnerships, there are also obstacles. Many were discussed in Chapter 13, but there are also the problems of working with many different actors and integrating a wide variety of responses. More actors require greater coordination, communication, cooperation, prioritization, transparency, and accountability, which increases the level of difficulty. Pursuing a combined approach also necessitates vigilance for threshold effects and unintended consequences. For example, policy responses may need a certain level of funding for a protracted period of time before a program may yield results. But if policy responses are split over a variety of state and nonstate venues, then resources may be diluted or a plan of attack may be pursued for too short a period, never reaching the threshold necessary for effective action. Unintended consequences apply to every approach. Because action must be coordinated among a wider variety of players, it may be more difficult to anticipate the full ramifications of a wider array of actions in public–private partnerships. For example, funneling attention and funding to nonstate actors and sectors could further undermine state sectors and actors. As new highways are built, sometimes the old roadways fall into disuse.

Continued monitoring and attention to coordination, prioritization, and accountability are necessary. Yet none of these critiques is unique to public–private approaches, though they may be more intense with them. State-centric and nonstate-centric prescriptions also share these obstacles. For example, government bureaucrats are not elected, and government bureaucracies are not necessarily transparent, accountable, democratic, or legitimate. Combating terrorism, organized crime, or drug trafficking in one sector or region may merely drive it into another area. All approaches require building political support, coordination, communication, prioritization, transparency, and accountability—and all may encounter resistance to change by existing organizations, threshold effects, and unintended consequences.

DOES SOVEREIGNTY STILL REIGN?

If state-centric responses are still necessary along with other approaches in dealing with global problems, then does this mean that Krasner and Spruyt are right? Is there no competitor to the sovereign state out there right now, so sovereignty still reigns by default? Not exactly, because sovereignty is changing in significant ways. Vertical and horizontal linkages may still anchor sovereignty in place, but they are breaking down. The anchor is becoming dislodged.

It is instructive to remember Hendrik Spruyt's story of how fundamental change came about the last time and ushered in the sovereign state: The economy changed. New elites were created who benefited from the new economic system and needed a new form of political organization to better accommodate them and their economic practices. Ideas changed, new organizational forms emerged and competed, and, after centuries of flux, the sovereign state eventually won out.[18]

There are many parallels today. The economy has changed. The new economic system is increasingly based on information, technology, and services, which are less dependent on the control of territory. The means of production, capital, and labor are mobile, not fixed. Players who make use of modern information, communication, transportation, and financial technologies reap the benefits of increasingly open borders and economies.

Political systems that make room for the new economic system reap profits in foreign direct investment, and so regime types as distinct as the

Chinese communist system, the Mexican emerging democracy, and the Iranian theocracy are all simultaneously undertaking reforms to make themselves more attractive to investors' capital and technology flows.

New elites are emerging who profit from the new economic system. Typified by George Soros, Bill Gates, Carlos Slim, Warren Buffet, and Ted Turner, these "new imperialists"[19] increasingly follow no flag. They are passionate about expanding technologies and markets, and they are frustrated by what they see as anachronistic state barriers to investment and trade flows. The international business classes attend the same schools, fly the same airlines, vacation at the same resorts, eat at the same restaurants, and watch the same movies and television shows. Independent of national identities, these elites mobilize to try to make states facilitate market dynamics. Some call it the "Davos culture" after the Swiss luxury resort where the annual World Economic Summit met.[20] Sociologist Peter Berger calls it the "yuppie internationale," a culture typified by the scene in a Buddhist temple in Hong Kong of "a middle-aged man wearing a dark business suit over stocking feet. He was burning incense and at the same time talking on his cellular phone." Berger believes these cultural ties have made peace talks in South Africa and Northern Ireland go more smoothly: "It may be that commonalities in taste make it easier to find common ground politically."[21] Can it be that leaders who all shop at the Gap and eat at McDonald's find political antagonisms quaint and unnecessary? In what he dubs the "Golden Arches Theory of Conflict Prevention," and the "Dell Theory," Thomas Friedman argues that "no two countries that are both part of a major global supply chain, like Dell's [computers], will ever fight a war against each other as long as they are both part of the same global supply chain," and no two countries with McDonald's restaurants have ever gone to war with one another.[22] Even though clearly there are many economically underprivileged people around the world who do not partake in this lifestyle, the values of this new elite percolate into the rest of society as people mimic the behavior of the elites and strive to better their economic situations to one day rise into the wealthier classes.

Ideas are changing (including ideas of authority, identity, and organization), facilitated by the new information technologies and changes in the economy. Never before in human history have we been able to spread ideas so quickly and widely. Modern communication technologies allow an ever-wider swath of the planet to be tuned in to the same advertisements, the same Web sites and social networking sites, the same entertainment shows, and, thereby, to some of the same ideas about consumerism and personal freedoms. Identity is becoming less tied to territory. If identity and authority do not stem from geography, then what is our new church, our new religion? In the European Middle Ages, identity came from Christendom, the Church, while authority stemmed from spiritual connections. In the modern era, identity was tied up with the nation state; authority corresponded with geography. Now authority and identity are increasingly contested. Strange believes we now have Pinocchio's problem: The strings of state control, authority, and identity have been cut, but no new strings have been fastened.[23] States no longer are the supreme recipient of individual loyalties, especially because they no longer fulfill basic services and functions and other actors have stepped into the gap. Firms, professions, families, religions, and social movements have all significantly challenged the state's territorial and security-based claim to individual loyalty. We are left to choose among competing sources of allegiance, authority, and identity, with no strings to bind us like puppets to one source of authority, and with more freedom to let our conscience be our guide.

Certainly the new economy would like identity to be formed around consumer products—you are what you wear, what you consume. Advertisers spend billions to imprint brand loyalty at an early age, and all the advertising of Apple/iPod, Nike's swoosh, I'd-like-to-buy-the-world-a-Coke, and Microsoft's One World Internet Explorer icon share a common theme: that identity stems not from national borders but from consumer products. Identity is therefore just as mobile as the economy. You are not born with it. You can buy it. Alternatively, some see identity as increasingly flowing from professions and firms: You are what you do, and your commitment is to your profession rather than to a specific state. As Rosecrance describes it, "Today and for the foreseeable future, the only international civilization worthy of the name is the governing economic culture of the world market."[24] Benjamin Barber refers to this popular, consumer market culture as *McWorld*.[25] As market values permeate various cultures, certain ideas emerge as prized: the value of change, mobility, flexibility, adaptability, speed, and information. As capitalism becomes our creed, with technology as our guide, distinct national and religious cultures are becoming permeated with common market values.

There are alternatives to market values, however. Religious organizations and NGOs promulgate alternative ethics to materialism, a globalization in which we are not merely consumers or a governance problem but human beings, each with irreducible sacred dignity. This vision of globalization prescribes putting people before profits, and ethical values before market values. These organizations use the tools of globalization to promote their views of humanizing globalization. For example, the Internet is a popular tool for organizing and proselytizing by many faith groups, including traditional Islam. Pope Benedict XVI uses Facebook, YouTube, Twitter, e-mail, Web sites, and iPhones and iPods to communicate and proselytize.[26]

Ideas of organization are also changing and are based on models from the marketplace and technology: computers, the Internet, and the market are diffuse, decentralized, loosely connected networks with a few central organizing parameters but strong ties to the activities of individual entrepreneurs. Foreign policy organizations are, in some instances, going beyond bureaucracy, creating flexible, innovative, coordinating networks.

Creative public–private partnerships are the wave of the future in solving global problems. Rather than trying to become draconian, big brother states (which would conflict with the goals of open societies, open economies, and open technologies), it makes sense for governments to look toward civil society for help in managing global problems. But states must be aware of the costs of contracting out. In privatizing, not only do governments lose some control over policy, but also private entities may present obstacles to the government's agenda as profit or other motives conflict with important public policy goals.[27] Although privatization and "moving beyond bureaucracy" are popular buzzwords and phrases in today's budget-conscious political climate, changes in state architecture have consequences for how we think about political authority, identity, and organization.

Ideas drawn from experience of the new economic system are helping to shape new ideas of political organization. A resurgence of IGOs simultaneous with increased attention to local governance may not seem at all strange to a civilization used to surfing the Internet and using a system that is simultaneously globally connected and only as good as the local link.

Rosenau believes that as individuals become more analytically skillful, the nature of authority shifts. People no longer uncritically accept traditional criteria of state authority based on historical, legal, or customary claims of legitimacy. Instead, authority and legitimacy are increasingly based on how well government authorities perform.[28] Love's description of the numbers of refugees and migrants voting with their feet seems to support this claim. Thus, while scholars disagree about the sources of identity and authority in the emerging era, they agree that these ideas are changing.

Finally, new forms of political organization are beginning to emerge, as evidenced by the European Union and the increasing roles and profile of IGOs. Thus, even if, as Spruyt maintains, the sovereign state is still supreme, 3 out of 4 of his indicators of fundamental change are already here: Changes in economy, elites, and ideas are in evidence, and even though no new form of political organization has unseated the sovereign state, new forms are beginning to emerge around the sovereign state that are chipping away at functions previously performed by it and changing its role.

GOING GLOBAL VERSUS GOING LOCAL: THE STATE CONTRACTS OUT

Are new forms of political organization emerging to accompany these changes? Many commentators have noted the irony that globalizing forces are spreading and deepening at the same time that virulent forms of nationalism or tribalism are evident in internal wars.[29] There are several reasons why this is not surprising. First of all, scholars on nationalism note that ties to ethnic or national groups increase under threat.[30] Therefore, it makes sense that at precisely the time when globalizing forces threaten local identities, there is resurgent attention to local ways of life.

Threat is only one piece of the puzzle, however. Transitions to liberal economic and political forms are destabilizing. Virulent nationalisms can be resuscitated as a means of finding a scapegoat for tough times. The fact that there once was a violent form of nationalism does not mean, however, that future conflicts will break out along national or ethnic lines. Many of the most highly developed states today once endured bloody civil wars—the United Kingdom, the United States, and France.

Previous conflict by itself is neither an indicator nor an explanation for later conflict. For example, most journalists and pundits described the cause of conflict in the Balkans as "ancient ethnic hatreds."[31] But this no more explains the conflict than does noting that the sun rose before the fighting took place, and because A came before B, A therefore caused B. Poland and Czechoslovakia also experienced "ancient ethnic hostilities," yet violent nationalism did not plunge these societies into internal war as occurred in the former Yugoslavia. Economics was a pivotal trigger in bringing violent nationalism to Yugoslavia, while Poland and Czechoslovakia had gentler transitions from communism. As the economic situation deteriorated in Yugoslavia, politicians sought to protect their own national groups. Leaders exploited nationalist tensions to explain away economic woes and distance themselves from their communist pasts, often using the media as their megaphones of hate.[32] Michael Brown notes that bad leaders, bad neighbors, bad internal problems, and bad neighborhoods can also fire nationalism into internal conflict.[33] Paul Collier notes that countries dependent on natural resource economies, with high unemployment and stagnating economies are particularly vulnerable to "the conflict trap," as money is available to continue the conflict and without other attractive economic engines there are high incentives to control the public purse. There is no straight causal line between violent nationalism in the past and violent nationalism in the future. However, states undergoing difficult transitions are more vulnerable to such violent forms.

Going global and going local are connected in another way as well. A study of 12 states over the past 20 years showed a correlation between indicators of open societies, open economies, and open technologies and government decentralization. States that increased in openness over the time period also increased in government decentralization (the amount of money and decision-making power that went to the local government level as opposed to the central government). States that stayed closed in the same time period did not experience government decentralization. Correlation is not causation, and so the forces of open economy, open technology, and open society and government decentralization might be caused by some third factor (the IMF, for example, as international investors pressure states both to decentralize governments and to privatize markets). But initial evidence does show that there are "simultaneous trends in globalization and decentralization."[34] Decentralization and open society, open market, and open technology forces go together.

By this view it is not an accident that the highly centralized states of the communist Soviet Union and Eastern Europe, the apartheid state of South Africa, the military regimes in Argentina, and the social-welfare states of the United Kingdom and the United States are undergoing decentralization simultaneously. Big government has been downsized all over the planet; when leaders and populations have wanted to increase government activity in response to the economic recession, it has been difficult to do;[35] power increasingly moves to local governments in federated systems and to nonstate actors. Sometimes the central state government retains authority over certain functions but no longer performs the functions itself, as when Australia contracts refugee camps out to private companies or Britain debates hiring mercenary soldiers:

> Global changes occurring today are creating new, complex, and decentralized systems of networks that are radically different from the old centralized systems of governance which controlled the process of international activities and decision making.[36]

How can it be that local government is making a comeback all over the globe at the same time that IGOs are becoming more important? The state is contracting out functions to several actors simultaneously: IGOs, NGOs, MNCs, and local governments. Horizontal networking now trumps vertical hierarchy as an organizing principle. The strong, hierarchical central governments of the 20th century—the fascist states, the communist states, even the Rooseveltian social security state—are receding. In the 21st century, the sovereign state remains. But this is not the state that we drove into the last century.

THE SPEED OF CHANGE

If the sovereign state is changing and new forms of political organization are emerging, then will change take centuries this time around? When sovereignty emerged, competing political forms coexisted for centuries before feudalism receded and the sovereign state emerged as the standard. Skeptics believe that it will take a similarly long time before current changes in economic or social structures mount a fundamental challenge to the sovereign state system, in part because those who benefit from the existing state system will fight to keep it. But the end of feudalism and the rise of sovereignty took place in an era when the modes of transportation and communication were horseback and slow-moving ships. Might change occur more quickly now in an era of jet planes, the Internet, faxes, e-mail, personal computers, and cell phones?

The rate of change is different from what it used to be. As Susan Strange notes,

> What is new and unusual is that all (or nearly all) states should undergo substantial change of roughly the same kind within the same short period of twenty or thirty years. The last time that anything like this happened was in Europe when states based on a feudal system of agricultural production geared to local subsistence gave way to states based on a capitalist system of industrial production for the market. The process of change was spread over two or three centuries at the very least and in parts of eastern and southern Europe is only now taking shape. In the latter part of the twentieth century, the shift has not been confined to Europe and has taken place with bewildering rapidity.[37]

Ideas are spread instantaneously in an era of wireless, mobile satellite networks, as fast as an Internet connection. The "one world" advertising themes of Nike, Microsoft, and UPS may contain a grain of truth in highlighting the ramifications of a wired planet to which many of us are plugged in.

The idea of punctuated equilibrium draws the analogy that institutional change may occur rapidly over a limited period of time in unexpected ways. Rather than the Darwinian idea of change as slow, steady, continuous, and gradual, punctuated equilibrium stresses that change is "usually accomplished rapidly when a stable structure is stressed beyond its buffering capacity to resist and absorb. These evolutionary shifts can be quirky and unpredictable as the potentials for complexity are vast."[38]

Is the fast rate of change that open economy, society, and technology forces have unleashed comparable to the rate of change of sovereign states to keep up with new environmental circumstances? This is particularly important as more states become democratic, because democratic state institutions are often slow to act, with opportunities for gridlock and delay built into the state structure. Democracy was never organized to be effective or efficient. Shared powers and separate institutions with checks and balances among them is a hedge against tyranny, not a recipe for efficiency. By putting different parts of government at each other's throats, it was hoped that government might stay off the people's backs and that deliberation and perspective might result from democratic procedures. Tyranny has many faults, but it can act quickly. The government does what the ruler says, whether it is right, just, legal, or in the public interest. The Nazi government, for example, was chillingly systematic and efficient in its use of industrial technology to conduct the Holocaust. Government becomes much more slow and bothersome when those in charge have to consult others about what to do, and when they have to factor in civil rights, civil liberties, and accountability to the law. In an era of cell phones, high-speed internet, and laptop computers, where the economy and technology place great value on speed and efficiency, we forget that democratic institutions were not built for speed. As Alexis de Tocqueville noted, the miracle of the system is that it works at all.

If the rate of external change vastly exceeds the institution's ability to respond, then will sovereign institutions be stressed beyond their ability to evolve and adapt? Buffeted by external blows, sovereignty continues to limp along, pocked by capacity, jurisdiction, and other institutional gaps. But as the speed of technological change outpaces the sovereign state's ability to hobble and hotwire responses, the limp may become more pronounced and perhaps (though no time soon) eventually fell the sovereign state.

CONCLUSION: THE SHIP OF STATE

At what point do we have a new ship of state? Scholars agree that change is occurring. The sovereign state is not obsolete and will continue to play a role along with other actors on the international scene. But there is disagreement over sovereignty's future. We are in a period of transition. We do not know yet whether the state can be retrofitted to weather the storms of changes in economy, elites, and ideas, or whether these changes will someday bring about new forms of political organization.

The situation is analogous to a famous puzzle in the study of philosophy: the ship of Theseus. There are three different ways the ship of Theseus problem is discussed. The first stems from its origins in Greek mythology. Theseus was the son of Aegeus, the king of Athens. Theseus sailed away to fight a heroic battle, but after slaying the Minotaur he forgot to change the sails to indicate the victory to his father. Sailing in the same old sails unwittingly brought about tragedy, as his father did not realize the battle had been won because the changed situation was not immediately apparent by viewing his son's ship. In a fit of despair, Theseus's father committed suicide, throwing himself from a cliff into the sea.[39] The analogy here is to the discussion in Chapter 13 about institutions. Many of our foreign policy institutions were built to fight strong states, not weak states and global problems. We have not changed our institutional sails consistent with the new situation, and we flirt with disaster and unintended consequences by traveling with our old sails.

The more pressing analogy, however, concerns the other two ways in which the problem of the ship of Theseus is discussed, questioning the nature of change and identity. If the planks of a ship are removed one by one over intervals of time, and each time an old plank is removed it is replaced by a new plank, then is it a new vessel? At what point did it reach critical mass to call it something new?[40]

This is the question we now face in considering the sovereign state. In Chapter 1, we considered 10 functions of states that Susan Strange believed are either no longer being performed or are at least being shared with other, nonstate actors. Scholar William Zartman posts his own list. In discussing failed or weak states that are collapsing, he lists 5 basic roles states perform: as the decision-making center of government; as a symbol of identity; as controller of territory and guarantor of security; as an authoritative and legitimate political institution; and as a system of socioeconomic organization, the target of citizen demands for providing supplies or services.[41] Although Zartman offers this list as a litmus test for when weak states are failing because basic state functions are no longer being performed, many of these functions correspond with Strange's and other authors' observations of roles that all states (weak and strong) formerly undertook but no longer fulfill.

The chapters of this book show that states are no longer the sole decision-making centers. MNCs, IGOs, and NGOs increasingly make decisions about matters that were traditionally handled by states. Economic decisions increasingly take place in corporate boardrooms, on the floors of international stock exchanges, and in the conference rooms of the IMF, and states increasingly react to, rather than generate, these key decisions. States are being challenged as symbols of identity and as authoritative, legitimate political institutions, as citizens increasingly place their loyalties elsewhere. Even strong states can no longer unilaterally control territory or borders or secure territory from external threats.

Alternative institutions—from MNCs to NGOs and IGOs—are increasingly the targets of citizen demands for services that citizens do not believe the state can supply. If the sovereign state is no longer performing the basic functions associated with sovereign states, then at what point does sovereignty cease? If the primary innovation of the sovereign state was its connection of exclusive authority to territory, then what does it mean for sovereignty if the state's connection to territory is being severed and states derive less authority or power from territory, and if authority is becoming disaggregated and overlapping?[42] Rosenau argues that authority is no longer automatically conferred to the traditional sources on the basis of customary legitimacy claims, be they legal or geographic, but that people are instead judging legitimacy and authority on the basis of performance. If sovereignty is no longer about territory, then what is it about? If territory is at the heart of sovereignty and territory is removed, then is what's left still sovereignty? How many planks must be pulled for us to recognize it as something different?

The difference between the case of sovereignty and the changes that occurred to the ship of Theseus are these: The ship's planks were replaced exactly in the same manner and to fulfill the same functions. The planks were not altered to turn the ship into a rocket. In the case of sovereignty, however, materials are changing to slowly give the vessel a facelift. Such changes might be correlated to the changes in regime and administrative type from the authoritarian regimes and regimes with the strong central government functions typical of the 20th century to the decentralized, networked, capitalist, and democratic regimes of the 21st century.

However, the changes this volume discusses are not just changes in sovereignty's face or outward appearance; they are changes in its nature. Unlike the ship of Theseus, the ship of state is changing the very functions it performs and how it performs them. If sovereignty is as sovereignty does, and what sovereignty does is changing, is sovereignty itself changing?

The final analogy with the ship concerns the nature of change. Some philosophers argue for foundationalism—that sound principles need to be laid out first before new concepts can be built on them. But Otto Neurath argues that we seldom have the luxury of changing our ideas in a pristine vacuum and starting from scratch. Instead he argues that "we are like sailors who must rebuild their ship on the open sea, never able to dismantle it in dry dock and to reconstruct it there out of the best materials."[43]

Certainly this is analogous to the descriptions of change offered by political psychologists, as forged in experience. Humans learn by doing, and as we experiment with states contracting out, networking with various organizations including public–private partnerships, we learn new ways of thinking about human organizations. These experiences are changing how we exercise and think about sovereignty. The ship's wheel is being replaced while the ship is still in operation. New planks are added and old functions are jettisoned while we are under way. Nonstate actors are cropping up and assuming functions that states used to perform. New policies toward global problems are evolving, utilizing nonstate sectors at the same time that state responses are being fine-tuned. We are not dry-docked and awaiting the emergence of a new ship of political organization, but we must go forward while we are in the midst of major construction.

The problem with our ability to track changes in the sovereign state is that we are used to the system; we are not good even at contemplating what the alternatives to sovereignty might look like. We are truly conceptual prisoners. Ideas matter, and outdated ideas can kill. Changes can occur in unintended ways, and they can occur rapidly when threshold effects are reached. Even though Krasner concludes that the sovereign state "will not be dislodged easily, regardless of changed circumstances in the material environment" and that sovereignty is so entrenched that "[i]t is now difficult to even conceive of alternatives," he acknowledges that surprises are possible.[44]

The *Titanic* was a supposedly unsinkable ship that hit an iceberg in the dark and sank within hours, killing more than 1,500 passengers and crew members. Similarly, the sovereign state is hitting many unforeseen obstacles in the dark side of globalization. Gaps in our institutions are already painfully apparent. Because the seas of change are turbulent, we have a moral obligation to think about the unthinkable, build better institutions, and consider alternatives if the impossible were to occur and the ship of sovereignty turned out not to be unsinkable after all. Urgently needed are new thoughts on how we might better organize humans, as well as more specific ideas about the organizational shapes into which sovereignty might morph or that might rival or replace sovereignty at some time in the unknown future. These ideas are developing out of our experiences of economic and technological change as our ideas about organization are informed by the new organizational structures we use in the marketplace and on the Internet.

Sovereignty is not going away, but it is evolving, decentralizing, networking, and contracting out. States increasingly coordinate policy among a wider variety of public and private actors. Richard Neustadt describes a U.S. political system in which the president is more powerful than other political actors but rarely has the ability to command or compel. Instead, the president must persuade others to pursue his preferred outcomes.[45]

The state is entering a similar position. It may be more powerful than NGOs, IGOs, and MNCs, depending on the case and the situation, but it rarely has the power to command or compel outcomes on global problems. Instead, states have to assume new roles as coordinators, facilitators, initiators, and salesmen in order to persuade action on global problems. This places burdens on state institutions, requiring organizational changes and adding more functions for states to undertake though not necessarily control. Neustadt notes that an increase in duties does not equate to an increase in power or in the capacity to fulfill new duties, and that adding more duties without means is equivalent to being a glorified clerk, not a powerful entity. For the immediate future, sovereignty will be first among competing forms, but there will be a "return to history" in the sense of a return to cross-cutting, nonhierarchical, ad hoc, and relative forms of order and organization.

Yet integrating action among a wider variety of players also opens new opportunities for policy and offers greater possibilities for effectively managing global issues than old-style unilateral responses. NGOs and MNCs frequently "forum shop"—that is, move an issue across borders to a more hospitable institutional venue for a chance at better resolution. We are no longer stuck with sovereignty only; we can often choose from and move among a variety of institutions. We are engaged in an exciting period of organizational pluralism and experimentation. International political problems have gone beyond sovereignty. We must also go beyond sovereignty in theory and in practice, changing our ideas and our institutions to better respond to the life-and-death challenges of globalization's gaps.

ENDNOTES

1. Benjamin Barber, "Declare Our Interdependence!" September 13, 2003, <www.thinkingpeace.com/pages/Articles/Archive1/arts040.html>.
2. President Clinton, as quoted in the endorsements for Jan Martin Witte and Wolfgang Reinicke, UN Global Compact Office, "Business UN usual," 2005, <http://globalpublicpolicy.net/businessUNusual/>.
3. Foreign Policy and the Fund for Peace, "The Failed State Index," *Foreign Policy* (July/August 2005), <www.foreignpolicy.com/story/cms.php?story_id=3098>.
4. <http://unstats.un.org/unsd/mi/pdf/MDG%20Book.pdf>.
5. Freedom House, "Freedom in the World 2009," <http://www.freedomhouse.org/uploads/fiw09/FIW09_Tables&GraphsForWeb.pdf>, 18.
6. Greg Noone, "Genocide and Crimes Against Humanity," presentation 2004.
7. Kofi Annan, Nobel Prize Acceptance Speech, December 10, 2001.
8. These figures include the UNHCR numbers of 11.4 million refugees plus 4.6 million Palestinian refugees from UNRWA numbers. UNHCR, *2007 Statistical Yearbook* (December 2008), 23–25.
9. Francis Fukuyama, *State-Building: Governance and World Order in the 21st Century* (Ithaca, NY: Cornell University Press, 2004).
10. Anne-Marie Slaughter, "America's Edge: Power in the Networked Century," *Foreign Affairs* (January/February 2009); *A New World Order* (Princeton, NJ: Princeton University Press, 2004).
11. Stephen Flynn, "Homeland Insecurity," *The American Interest* (May/June 2009); *The Edge of Disaster: Building a Resilient Nation* (New York: Random House, 2007); Stephen Flynn, "America the Vulnerable," *Foreign Affairs* (January–February 2002).

12. Thorsten Benner and Jan Martin Witte, "Everybody's Business: Accountability, Partnerships, and the Future of Global Governance," in Susan Stern and Elisabeth Seligmann (Eds.), *The Partnership Principle: New Forms of Governance in the 21st Century* (London, Archetype Publishers, 2004); Mirjam Bult-Spiering and Geert Dewulf, *Strategic Issues in Public–Private Partnerships* (Blackwell 2007).

13. Ibid.

14. Susan Strange, *The Retreat of the State: The Diffusion of Power in the World Economy* (Cambridge, UK: Cambridge University Press, 1996), 189.

15. Richard Rosecrance, "The Rise of the Virtual State," *Foreign Affairs* (July–August 1996): 59–60.

16. Stephen D. Krasner, *Problematic Sovereignty: Contested Rules and Political Possibilities* (New York: Columbia University Press, 2001); Stephen D. Krasner, *Sovereignty: Organized Hypocrisy* (Princeton, NJ: Princeton University Press, 1999); Stephen D. Krasner, "Sovereignty: An Institutional Perspective," *Comparative Political Studies* 21 (April 1988): 74; Kenneth Waltz, "Globalization and Governance," *PS: Political Science & Politics* (December 1999): 693–700; William H. McNeill, "Territorial States Buried Too Soon," *Mershon International Studies Review* 41 (1997): 269.

17. James N. Rosenau, *Turbulence in World Politics* (Princeton, NJ: Princeton University Press, 1990).

18. Hendrik Spruyt, *The Sovereign State and Its Competitors* (Princeton, NJ: Princeton University Press, 1994), 62, 75.

19. Mark Leibovich, *The New Imperialists* (New York: Prentice Hall, 2002).

20. Samuel Huntington, *The Clash of Civilizations and the Remaking of World Order* (New York: Simon & Schuster, 1996).

21. Peter L. Berger, "Four Faces of Global Culture," *The National Interest* (Fall 1997): 24.

22. Thomas Friedman, *The World Is Flat: A Brief History of the Twenty-first Century* (New York: Farrar, Straus and Giroux, 2005), 421; Thomas L. Friedman, *The Lexus and the Olive Tree: Understanding Globalization* (New York: Farrar, Straus and Giroux, 1999), 195–196. Some question the "Golden Arches theory" after conflict between Russia and Georgia in August 2008, but the conflict never reached the level of a war or major armed conflict with over 1,000 deaths in battle, as 365 deaths were estimated by Human Rights Watch and government officials. Thomas Friedman, *Hot Flat and Crowded* (New York: Farrar, Straus and Giroux, 2008).

23. Strange, *The Retreat of the State*, 199.

24. Richard Rosecrance, *The Rise of the Virtual State: Wealth and Power in the Coming Century* (New York: Basic Books, 2000), 59–60.

25. Benjamin R. Barber, *Jihad vs. McWorld* (New York: Ballantine Books, 1996).

26. Reuters, "Pope Benedict Wants to Meet You on Facebook," May 22, 2009; Jon W. Anderson and Dale F. Eickelman (Eds.), *New Media in the Muslim World: The Emerging Public Sphere* (Bloomington: Indiana University Press, 1999).

27. Peter Passell, "U.S. Goals at Odds in a Plan to Sell Off Nuclear Operation," *The New York Times* (July 25, 1995): A1.

28. Maryann Cusimano, "James Rosenau and Monica Lewinsky," *PS: Political Science and Politics* (December 1999). Interestingly, Rosenau's thesis explains why President Clinton's approval ratings did not diminish and even improved during his impeachment hearings. The media and conservative thinkers have been at a loss to explain why the U.S. public was not more exercised about President Clinton's extramarital affair, its moral implications, and its effects on the dignity of the presidential office. But if the public judges legitimacy and authority by performance criteria, not by appeals to tradition or moral authority, then breaches of tradition and morality would not affect the

public's perception of Clinton's legitimacy or authority. If performance criteria are all that matters, then Clinton's poll ratings make sense given the low unemployment rate and strong performance of the U.S. economy during his administration, especially while European and Asian economic growth rates were simultaneously flat or declining. According to Rosenau, it would seem that political leaders can "get away with" quite a bit as long as it does not interfere with their record of concrete achievements.

29. Amy Chua, *World On Fire: How Exporting Free Market Democracy Breeds Ethnic Hatred and Global Instability* (New York: Anchor, 2004).

30. Ted Robert Gurr, "Minorities, Nationalists, and Ethnopolitical Conflict," in Chester Crocker, Fen Osler Hampson, and Pamela Aall (Eds.), *Managing Global Chaos* (Washington, DC: U.S. Institute of Peace, 1996), 53–78; David Little, "Religious Militancy," in Crocker et al., *Managing Global Chaos*, 79–92; Ernest Gellner, "Nations and Nationalism," in Richard Betts (Ed.), *Conflict after the Cold War: Arguments on the Causes of War and Peace* (New York: Macmillan, 1994), 280–292; Louis Kriesberg, "Regional Conflicts in the Post–Cold War Era: Causes, Dynamics, and Modes of Resolution," in Michael Klare and Daniel Thomas (Eds.), *World Security: Challenges for a New Century* (New York: St. Martin's Press, 1994), 155–174; Donald L. Horowitz, "Ethnic and Nationalist Conflict," in Klare and Thomas, *World Security*, 175–187.

31. Robert D. Kaplan, *The Coming Anarchy: Shattering the Dreams of the Post Cold War World* (New York: Vintage Books, 2001); Robert D. Kaplan, *Balkan Ghosts: A Journey Through History* (New York: Vintage Books, 1994).

32. Susan Woodward, *Balkan Tragedy* (Washington, DC: Brookings Institution, 1995).

33. Michael Brown, *The International Dimensions of Internal Conflict* (Cambridge: MIT Press, 1996), 579.

34. Jong S. Jun and Deil S. Wright, *Globalization and Decentralization: Institutional Contexts, Policy Issues, and Intergovernmental Relations in Japan and the United States* (Washington, DC: Georgetown University Press, 1996), 1.

35. President Clinton declared the era of big government dead, referring to the end of welfare as we knew it and reforms that downsized the federal government to the smallest it had been since the Kennedy administration. Similar downsizing efforts have been underway internationally as privatization and "e-government" spread. Structural adjustment policies trim government spending in developing countries.

36. Jun and Wright, *Globalization and Decentralization*, 3–4.

37. Strange, *The Retreat of the State*, 87.

38. Krasner, "Sovereignty: An Institutional Perspective," 79.

39. Robert E. Bell, *Dictionary of Classical Mythology: Symbols, Attributes and Associations* (Santa Barbara, CA: ABC-Clio, 1982), 207.

40. Rodrick M. Chisholm, *Person and Object: A Metaphysical Study* (LaSalle, IL: Open Court, 1976), 89–92.

41. I. William Zartman, *Collapsed States* (Boulder, CO: Lynne Rienner, 1995), 5.

42. Rosecrance, *The Rise of the Virtual State*.

43. Otto Neurath quoted in A. J. Ayer (Ed.), *Logical Positivism* (Glencoe, IL: The Free Press, 1959). This is sometimes referred to as *Neurath's ship*.

44. Krasner, "Sovereignty: An Institutional Perspective," 80.

45. Maryann Cusimano Love, "Filling the Gaps," *America* (August 3, 2009); Richard E. Neustadt, *Presidential Power and the Modern Presidents: The Politics of Leadership from Roosevelt to Reagan* (New York: The Free Press, 1990).